Imagery for Getting Well

Clinical Applications of Behavioral Medicine

Deirdre Davis Brigham

with
Adelaide Davis
and
Derry Cameron-Sampey

W. W. NORTON & COMPANY, INC. • NEW YORK • LONDON

First published as a Norton paperback 1996.

Printed in the United States of America

First Edition

Composition by Bytheway Typesetting Services, Inc. Manufacturing
by Haddon Craftsmen, Inc.

Book Design by Justine Burkat Trubey

Library of Congress Cataloging-in-Publication Data

Brigham, Deirdre Davis.
    Imagery for getting well : clinical applications of behavioral
medicine / Deirdre Davis Brigham ; with Adelaide Davis and Derry
Cameron-Sampey.
        p. cm.
    "A Norton professional book."
    Includes bibliographical references and index.
    ISBN 0-393-70225-1
    1. Medicine and psychology.   2. Medicine, Psychosomatic.
3. Imagery (Psychology)   4. Clinical health psychology.   I. Davis,
Adelaide.   II. Cameron-Sampey, Derry.   III. Title.
    [DNLM: 1. Imagination.   2. Mental Healing.   3. Behavior Therapy-
-methods.   BF 367 B855i 1994]
R726.5.B75   1994   616'.001'9—dc20   93-46069   CIP
DNLM/DLC   for Library of Congress

W. W. Norton & Company, Inc., 500 Fifth Avenue, New York, NY 10110
W. W. Norton & Company, Ltd., 10 Coptic Street, London WC1A 1PU

1 2 3 4 5 6 7 8 9 0

To my dearest Robby

Contents

Acknowledgments

My sister, Adelaide Eleanor Davis, inherited our mother's genes and genius for creating images with words. Seeing Adelaide's metamorphosis from lawyer-state's attorney into a powerful and beautiful therapist has been one of the joys of the CETTING WELL journey for me and for those whose lives she has touched so deeply.

My dear friend, Derry Cameron-Sampey, has made sure that my subjects and predicates match and that I not become so mired in my dense prose that no one understands me. She has adroitly thrown my sentences up in the air, juggled them, and allowed them to land with a new clarity, expressing what I *really* wish to say. Her droll and often outgrageous comments in the margins kept me laughing through what might have been an onerous task.

My daughter, Rosalind Craig Brigham, has protected me, kept me centered, and sustained GETTING WELL over the last year as I was writing this book. Her grace, generosity of spirit, and gift for dealing with people have become even more pronounced as she comes into her own as a person and a therapist.

My incredible father, Orville Rhoads Davis (who, at 93, has written five books for my one this year), has given me the legacy of translating a vision into a workable program and bringing seemingly disparate elements together into an integrative whole. His innovations in education over the past century have inspired me in my design of GETTING WELL — extracting the best and most beautiful that each person has to offer.

Carolyn Peterson, a loyal friend and staff member, made GW the focus of her graduate studies and has graciously allowed me to use a major portion of her thesis in this book. Gayla Bacon and other staff members have been splendid supporters and kept me from wearing too thin. And Geoffrey and Karen Brigham have been sources of comfort and inspiration during this project.

My husband, Robert Cyril Brigham, is the *sine qua non* of my writing this book, a glorious human, and the love of my life. He has shared with me the times of joy and has uplifted me through the valleys that inevitably come. His willingness to support me (and GETTING WELL) on his professor's salary for the last two years has made it all possible. He is the best!

My editor, Susan Barrows Munro, envisioned a book from a paper I wrote, saw the "song hidden in egg," and has abundantly contributed her wisdom, expertise, and enthusiasm to the creation of this volume.

Imagery
for
Getting
Well

SECTION I

The Dream and
Its Rationale

Be patient toward all that is unresolved in your heart and try to love the questions themselves like locked rooms and like books that are written in a very foreign language. Do not now seek the answers, which cannot be given to you because you would not be able to live then. And the point is to live everything, Live the questions now. Perhaps then gradually, without noticing it, live along some distant day into the answer. —*Ranier Maria Rilke*

The great thing about science is that the questions are so much more important than the answers. Theology tends to make the mistake of straining for answers, even answers that claim to be final. Science lives with the questions. The really great questions are never finished answering. —*George Wald, Nobel Laureate*

I learned at least this by my experiments. That if one advances confidently in the direction of his dreams, and endeavors to live the life he has imagined, he will meet with a success unexpected in common hours. He will put something behind and will pass an invisible boundary. —*Henry David Thoreau*

1

Multiple Personalities, Epiphanies, Agoraphobia, and the Birth of GETTING WELL

Sit down before fact like a little child, and be prepared to give up every preconceived notion. Follow humbly wherever and to whatever abyss nature leads, or you shall learn nothing. —*T.H. Huxley*

Multiple personality may shed new light on the nature of the mind and its elusive relation to body and brain function. —*Thomas J. Hurley, III*

The whole issue of mind-body plasticity seems about to undergo a major reformulation if what we are now beginning to learn from people with multiple personalities is developed fully in clinical and research terms. —*Ilya Prigogine*

We've all heard about the psychologist who had an exceedingly interesting pair of clients—a set of identical twin boys. These five-year-olds were absolutely identical in every respect except that one was a consummate optimist and the other an egregious pessimist. Being a good psychologist, he devised a clinical study to investigate this phenomenon. He set up one room that was full of everything a young boy could want—new games and toys, ice cream, cake, and candy—and left the little pessimist there for an hour. He set up another room for the little optimist, but this room he filled with manure.

At the end of the hour he went to check on the wee pessimist, and there he was in the middle of the floor crying his eyes out. "What's the matter, son?" he inquired. "You have just about everything that a boy could want in this room." The lad sobbed. "The toys will get old and break, the ice cream will melt, and the cake and candy will make me sick," he wailed. The psychologist then checked on the little optimist. There he was in his room full of offal, joyously digging away, and singing. "Son," he asked, "why are you so happy?" The child turned his brown-smeared, shining face toward the psychologist. "With this much manure," he said breathlessly, "there's got to be a pony in here somewhere!"

And that's what *Imagery for Getting Well* is all about: creating the image of meaning in despair, finding joy in crisis, and imaging hope in tragedy. In other words, it is about seeing the pony in the mire of a life-threatening or chronic condition.

Our personal images—our core beliefs about the world and ourselves, our quality of hope, our attitude toward life—have everything to do with how well we live, how we handle crises, and how our bodies function. For example, we've all known people who seem to be inundated constantly with what most of us would agree are tragic circumstances, yet who retain a sanguine view of their circumstances and a sense of joy about their lives. Then there are others who see life only as fear and catastrophe in the making, although the circumstances of their lives would seem benign to most of us.

What makes the difference in such people? I believe it shows clearly in their imagery and core beliefs. Our images and beliefs are the windows through which we see the world. If the panes of these windows are inappropriately rose-colored, we may tend to disregard items that could negatively affect our survival. For example, feeling a suspicious lump but dismissing it could result in getting medical help too late. On the other hand, if the panes in our imagery windows are distorted like those in a fun house mirror, ordinary events may take on a terrifying aura. Our bodies and psyches respond to the eidetic distortion, rather than to the event, and the stress chemicals begin to flow (usually distorting the physical and emotional impact even further). On the other hand, seeing events as basically neutral through clear panes of glass, perhaps judiciously tinged with the rose color of hope and trust in the universe, provides a nurturant ambiance for a high quality of life as well as for optimal functioning of our bodies.

The importance of one's outlook on the world was brought home to me as a fledgling therapist nearly twenty years ago with one of my first clients, who had multiple personality disorder (MPD). I conceptualize the condition as the creation of altered states of consciousness, altered ways of imaging, and an altered perception of the world when the individual's real world is totally unbearable and unsurvivable. Usually there is heinous physical and emotional abuse involved, so the child creates multiple personalities in order to survive.

At the time, MPD was a relatively rare diagnosis, so equipped with the testing skills of my recent degree in clinical psychology, I did a full battery of tests on each of the five principal personalities. The testing (WAIS and WISC-R, Draw a Person, MMPI Mini-Mult, Rotter Incomplete Sentences Blank, Bender Gestalt, and the Word Association Test) manifested in the subject five different ways of seeing the world and processing sensory data. The handwritings were also different, four being right-handed and one left-handed. There were different answers to questions of medium-to-hard difficulty on the verbal portions of the IQ tests, and approaches to the drawings were different.

If the IQ tests were examined separately, each personality scored in the normal to bright-normal range; however, if the results were overlaid, the full score was in the superior range. (There appeared to be some sharing of ability on the performance tasks of the IQ tests, and interestingly, each of the drawings had objects done in fives, such as the number of petals on a flower, birds in the sky, or branches on a tree.) Essentially, at least five different persons were functioning within the same body—each with a different set of core images about life, each with different cognitive abilities, and each with a different window on the world.

These different mind-sets (image-sets) manifested personalities with quite different qualities: abject fear and abandonment, burning hostility, cool intellectuality, flagrant sexuality, and total enjoyment of life. And these changes could occur as quickly and dramatically as flipping from channel to channel with a television remote control.

One morning Jill (when dealing with subjects, I have not used the real names of persons or personalities in this book) came for her session with a terrible case of the flu. She could hardly breathe, her chest was congested, her nose was running, and she had laryngitis. She was a wheezing mess! During the session, I asked to talk to Jane, another of the personalities. In the six or so seconds it took for the transition, Jane appeared—with none of the symptoms Jill was manifesting! There was no congestion, she was able to speak normally, and there was no coughing or runny nose. When I asked her about this, she said, "Oh, I'm not the one who is sick, Jill is. She's so stupid, she's always catching something."

In that six seconds, not only had a "world image" changed, but a body had also changed, significantly. My mind was already boggled by the implications of the personality changes in the same body, but seeing concrete evidence that the body was changing chemically with each change in the psyche was an incredible personal epiphany! Being caught up in the excitement of the new cognitive psychology, I could easily believe that changing thoughts, beliefs, or images could change one's emotional response to the world. Yet here was evidence that one's imagery could also change the functioning and chemistry of one's body. Carrying this a step further, I realized this amazing "ability," which emerged from a condition usually thought of as "pathological," was potentially available to anyone willing to change basic images or attitudes.

On another occasion, Jill arrived in terrible pain from having poked a pencil in her ear. Again, a shift in personalities occurred, and there was Carol, in no pain whatsoever, describing to me the circumstances that surrounded the incident with the pencil. Several years later, Jill actually had surgery for a compressed vertebra which was causing pain for her and one of the other personalities—but which had not caused pain for the remaining personalities.

It would take a volume to describe all the differences among the personalities, from food preferences to food allergies, from smokers (three) to nonsmokers (two), decided differences in accents and energy levels, and the distinct effects of alcohol and drugs in the different personalities. One personality occasionally drank and fully felt the effects of alcohol while the others responded from slightly to not at all. But I can tell you I was absolutely fascinated that a change in the way they imaged or perceived their worlds allowed what was at least five different physical and mental organisms to occupy the same body.

My naive observations foreshadowed the work that Nicholas Hall, Ph.D., and others have done with multiple personalities—documenting with blood samples the changes that occur in the six seconds it takes for a different "mind" to take over a body. One of the most interesting examples was his finding a full-blown diabetic personality among others who evinced perfectly normal blood sugar levels (Hall, 1992). A speech pathologist has found that the voice patterns of each personality are different, and a multiple of whom I have knowledge has tested alternately positive and negative on a number of HIV tests. Carrying this line of thought a bit further, one wonders whether it could it be possible for one personality to have cancer or HIV and the others not, and whether the nature of the personalities' images have an influence on the particular results of the blood work?

Multiples are well-known to heal quickly and some researchers have noted that they do not age as quickly as others. Thomas Hurley (1985) reports a multiple who attributed her fast healing and robust health to a couple of personalities who spent 24 hours a day imaging the body's health and well-being.

And perhaps one of the biggest questions: Is this a phenomenon only of this pathological condition and not something we can assume about a "normal" person? My own intuitive feeling that the so-called multiple personality is a magnifying glass revealing how the "normal" personality works was reinforced in a talk by James Fadiman, "Being in the Right Mind at the Right Time," at the 1991 Fourth World Conference on Imagery in Minneapolis. In this thought-provoking talk, he suggests that all the characteristics defining multiple personality disorder are indeed quite vividly present in the "normal" person. He asked the audience if anyone had ever argued with themselves ("Who was it you were arguing with?") or whether people in the audience had ever found themselves at a destination they had not intended when they started out ("Who drove you there?"). "Do you ever respond differently in different situations?" Fadiman continued. And, indeed, most of us had to admit virtually all the characteristics that define the classical diagnostic category of multiple personality disorder were quite vividly present in us "normal" persons.

With a little knowledge of hypnosis (which essentially deals with imagery), I had characterized the workings of the multiple personalities as a variety of hypnotic trances triggered by the demands put upon the primary personalities by the social situation or environment in which they found themselves. Thus a sexual situation or an intellectual situation would draw forth the very trance (or complex of images) defining a particular personality. This hypothesis led me to more extensive training in hypnosis with Theodore X. Barber, Ph.D., a brilliant man who helped hypnosis to become more "user friendly" not only to me but to an entire generation of professionals. Following Barber's lead, I began to see hypnosis as a heightened state of suggestion (or openness to a variety of images) rather than a unique state of consciousness needing a "trance" to evoke it. When I accepted his intimation that we could choose the direction our mind (or images) pursued and speak directly to our bodies, the whole world of the mind-body connection began to unfold more fully for me.

In my hypnosis training I observed long-term, severe pain disappear within minutes, saw destructive habits of years standing relegated to oblivion, and heard documented tales of women who were able to breast feed infants they had adopted. It appeared to me that by changing our images and mind-set, our bodies and lives could be changed. And if we could in some way get this mind-body connection under control, the entire face of medicine could be expanded incalculably.

At that time, of course, my interest lay more in how to reintegrate Jill's several personalities than in changing the face of medicine. However, an epiphany had occurred for me which totally changed my core beliefs about our human potential, an epiphany which opened new doors in my own life and which eventually would allow me to believe things I would never have thought possible.

In contemplating Jill's "condition," I saw it, too, was caused by major shifts in consciousness—that each personality was formed possibly as a result of an epiphany on her part. I saw that each new conglomerate of structuring her images was preceded by a subconscious "Aha," such as, "Aha, if I look at my world in this new way, it is not as painful or awful or scary." Like pattern changes with a turn of a kaleidoscope, Jill's pieces of perception and imagery fell into a totally new pattern with each new shift of consciousness.

Contemporary research on spontaneous remissions and miracles has been done by the Institute of Noetic Sciences (IONS). This group, founded by astronaut Edgar Mitchell as a result of his heightened experience on his journey to the moon, funds research into extending models of human potential. As a part of IONS' Remission Project, Brendon O'Regan and Caryle Hirschberg examined thousands of examples of "remarkable recoveries" chronicled in the literature and found that a shift of some sort frequently preceded them. Others, e.g., Patricia Norris and Nicholas Hall, have suggested that "miracles" tend to follow a shift of consciousness, or "epiphany," which might be in the form of a religious experience, of imaging oneself in a totally new way, or even of falling in love. Of course, an epiphany does not guarantee healing; however, it seems it does set the stage and may be a necessary condition for those events we call miracles.

The dictionary defines "epiphany" as "a spiritual event in which the essence of a given object of manifestation appears to the subject, as in a sudden flash of recognition" (a new image?). It is a right-brain synthesis of disparate perceptions and images into a new eidetic Gestalt—a holy moment, a "eureka" experience, a transcendent consciousness, or an uncovering of meaning. An epiphany is imaging the "pieces" of a puzzle in a fresh way that leads you to a dazzling "Aha"; it is catching the point of a joke, having the kaleidoscope of your images of the world fall into a totally new and beautiful pattern, or seeing someone you had regarded as an enemy in a new image as a human with the same needs and wants as you. It is re-imaging a disastrous, traumatic experience as one full of profound meaning, experiencing the divine in the commonplace, or changing your perception. In fact, I have heard a "miracle" defined as simply a shift in the way one sees things. Thus, in the child who develops a multiple personality disorder, the epiphany may simply be: "I know that I will die if I do not leave this situation in the only way I know how to."

At the time I was seeing Jill, in the mid-1970s, the word "imagery" was somewhat foreign to me, so I tended to use words like "perception," "biofeedback," "belief," "thought," "cognitive rehearsal," "covert sensitization," and "mental picture," words tinged by my cognitive behavioral training in clinical psychology. Through my work as a therapist at a large regional medical center, I had the delight of meeting Joseph Wolpe, M.D., the brilliant founder of the respondent conditioning branch of behavior therapy and author of one of my graduate school texts, *The Practice of Behavior Therapy*. The hospital's mental health center had arranged for him to train physicians and other professionals in the then-new field of "relaxation training." This is essentially a mental process in which one can affect one's own arousal of one's heart rate, respiration, and blood pressure. For example, reducing physiological arousal reduces the individual's perception or image of discomfort.

Dr. Wolpe drew on the board a picture of a cat which became aroused by a shock from the floor of its cage. The cat soon became so sensitized that just showing it the cage would elicit the same level of arousal as the electric shock. This is essentially how our own conditioned fears begin. To extirpate those fears, we must reverse the process.

Dr. Wolpe pointed out that the two branches of the autonomic nervous system, the sympathetic nervous system and the parasympathetic nervous system, could not work full force at the same time. When the sympathetic system (in charge of the "fight or flight" response) is activated, the parasympathetic system (in charge of digestion, sexual arousal, and relaxation) shuts down. Conversely, when the parasympathetic system is activated through deep muscle relaxation, the sympathetic response is toned down significantly. He called this process "reciprocal inhibition," whereby one pairs the state of relaxation with the thought of an anxiety situation — based on the premise that you cannot be both anxious in your mind and relaxed in your body at the same time. From this he developed a technique called systematic desensitization in which patients couple relaxation with increasingly fearful mental pictures. Pairing a relaxation response with the scary image diminishes the physiological arousal associated with that situation. As a result the anxiety's power is broken and the person has a much higher probability of experiencing the actual situation without the normally accompanying physiological arousal.

Although this may seem axiomatic now, in the medical and psychological community of nearly 20 years ago it was revolutionary. Indeed, I credit Joe Wolpe as being one of the giants of the behavioral medicine revolution. Certainly he brought the disparate pieces together for yet another major epiphany in my own life, and gave me the research reinforcement and intellectual impetus to put this mind-body philosophy into clinical psychotherapy practice long before it had a name. For the next 12 years, I voraciously read all the literature in this field, went to all the workshops that even remotely applied, and used all relevant practices I could in Orlando Regional Medical Center's mental health center.

I facilitated stress management groups which combined relaxation training, systematic desensitization, assertive communication (another of Dr. Wolpe's "children"), and cognitive restructuring, as well as nutrition and exercise. Internists began referring to us those patients whose anxiety or depression was interfering seriously with their physical problems, and the hospital referred patients whose panic or anxiety was interfering with necessary procedures such as surgery, anesthesia, or self-injection. All of our results reinforced my epiphanies (or perhaps my epiphanies, which changed core beliefs and their attendant images, helped create the outcomes). And as time passed, I began to see that physical outcomes were not nearly as important as the changes in quality of life our patients experienced and the sense of power that these techniques returned to them.

I particularly remember Janine, a diabetic who came into our stress management group with her blood sugars of approximately 500 under control by insulin. (With diabetes, hypertension, and other conditions kept in control by powerful medicines, it is particularly important to work closely with physicians because the mind-body relationship is so strong that an individual can easily "overdose," given some of the potent emotional/behavioral strategies we use.) Janine had significant retinopathy, and was moderately overweight and very discouraged about her life and marriage. During her ten weeks, she started an exercise program (imaging the exercise as making her insulin receptors very sensitive to even small amounts of insulin), changed the way she ate (seeing the protein and complex carbohydrates she was consuming as "treats" which met all of her physical and emotional needs), and changed her relationship to herself (experiencing herself and her needs as important and imaging herself as good and deserving and able to handle any situation that came along).

Before she completed the stress management group, she was off insulin entirely and went on to maintain a normal blood sugar level through several months of follow-up. Her retinopathy probably didn't change much, although she swore she was seeing better. *But her life changed.* She looked different, there was a joyful lilt to her voice, and she felt totally involved in each moment of living. She found her relationships with her husband and family evolving into satisfying parts of her life. And she felt at peace.

Also during this time, a number of individuals who fit the new diagnoses "agoraphobia" and "panic disorder" came into my caseload. These were interesting conditions that seemed to strike individuals who were unusually perfectionistic and/or needed to be in control of their feelings and lives. Typically an affected individual would have a physiological reaction (rush of adrenaline, racing or "pounding" heart, and/or hyperventilation) which might be almost random in origin and have nothing to do with his or her immediate situation. Because the body sends a message to the limbic system ("The body is experiencing an anxiety reaction, therefore there is something to be anxious about!"), patients typically feel as though they will "go crazy" or die within a few minutes. In any situation, this spontaneous reaction creates a sensitization to the image of the situation. This results in the avoidance of that particular place or situation (public bathrooms, malls, crowds) in the future and creates feelings of panic (and imminent death) even when only the image is present. Eventually, a conditioned complex of fears (agoraphobia) may come into play, causing the individual to avoid any possibility of encountering the feared arousal, and sometimes to become totally house-bound.

At that time, agoraphobia and panic disorder were viewed as emotional disorders by most professionals, thus the idea of changing cognitions and images to change one's emotional state was precocious but not outrageous. However, it appeared to me to be a clear-cut, mind-body challenge that involved changing body chemistry and not merely changing feelings or behaviors.

Many of those with panic disorders were extremely reluctant to take psychotropic medication (fearing side effects and loss of control), while others were so eager to get out of their emotional pain that they would have taken anything. I was lucky to have a couple of supportive psychiatrists doing medical supervision of the patients in the clinic; they let the patients choose whether or not they wanted medication and, either way, supported what I was doing in the group. Members who chose the medication and stress management group route tended to do less well in the long run than those who had only the group (according to self-report and our observations). The "medication group" showed better results in the beginning, but as they "gave credit" to the medication as empowering their more adventuresome behavior they seemed to have a less powerful image of themselves as agents and became somewhat emotionally dependent on the medication.

During the ten-year life of this panic disorder clinic, many of the seeds for the design of the GETTING WELL program were sown. Participants in this clinic had the most prodigious abilities as creative imagers. They could take the smallest piece of evidence and build it into the most incredible and terrifying possibilities for their future. As a result, we had no problem with patients being able to image; rather, the problem was to effect shifts in those images so they would not wreak havoc with the clients' bodies and lives!

The essence of this rather complex group was to change images, cognitions, and perceptions in order to change behavior, which in turn increased each individual's self-image and power. For example, after training in relaxation, we would have the participants choose several anxiety-provoking scenes, ranging from mild to extreme. Then, while still relaxed, they were asked to image their least anxiety-laden situation until they could do so and remain relaxed. As they progressed in this systematic desensitization, they remained relaxed as they introduced progressively more fearful mental pictures. Another such activity is Meichenbaum's stress inoculation, which involves first relaxing and then seeing oneself in an anxiety- or anger-provoking scene. In the next step, individuals image themselves saying reassuring words such as, "I can handle this. Just relax and take it one step at a time. Think how good I'll feel when it is over." As a result, the patient's body is reprogrammed so a frightening image does not disturb it, and the imagery is reprogrammed so the body no longer reacts so strongly to the mental picture. After the patients' images of the situations and their ability to handle the situation had altered, they began to tackle more complex steps toward achieving their behavioral goals, such as staying at a mall for 15 minutes or making a request of a partner.

One of my most effective interventions in the group had no fancy name. It occurred during the initial group session, after I had participants share their stories about trips to the emergency room during which they thought that death was imminent. At this point, I would pull out a "guarantee," and reassuring them that we had never lost a group member to psychosis or death by anxiety, offered an official-looking written document saying they "would not die or go crazy from anxiety or panic." Although there were some titters or expressions of disbelief, they always lined up to have me sign their personalized guarantee.

Just imagine a shift in imagery from the panicky feeling of impending death to a merely uncomfortable, but harmless, physical reaction. Not infrequently, the "guarantee" was all that was needed for such a major epiphany to take place, with the remaining sessions then used to expand the range of possibilities. Years later, participants would tell me that, whenever they felt the warning signs of a panic attack, they would think about the guarantee and hear my voice saying, "It's uncomfortable, but not dangerous."

The group strongly reinforced changes in behavior (both cognitive and physical), so that participants began trying new actions and new perceptions on for size. The boundaries of their perceived worlds and their abilities to deal with these worlds began to expand. At some point, all the small steps taken to change their images of themselves, their relationships, and their worlds came together, and an epiphany took place. There was a perceptual shift, and miraculously their whole lives changed.

For example, Jack had been a truck driver for years; then one day, as he said, "Something came over me that seemed like a heart attack." He went to the emergency room, where a battery of tests uncovered only a benign mitral valve prolapse. However, he was so sensitized to the experience that driving his truck became almost impossible, and he finally gave up trucking after a couple more "heart attacks" took him back to the emergency room. A few additional attacks caused him to give up nearly all driving, and he began to see physician after physician, only to be told there was nothing physically wrong with him. Many thousands of dollars later, on the brink of requesting exploratory surgery, he arrived at the panic clinic—a broken man with images of terror controlling his life.

It was not a simple process, but after several months of sorting what was mainly a spontaneous, harmless physiological reaction from the mental creations which precipitated a further, terrifying reaction, Jack began changing his images. He realized that he probably could expect to have those spontaneous rushes of catacholamines for the rest of his life, but allowed himself to image them as bursts of excitement or a "gift of energy" instead of the picture of terror they formerly created. He did go back to work (not as a truck driver), and it was a new man who drove back occasionally to see me and tell me how good life was. Once he even took from his wallet his guarantee, which was grey and creased from having been unfolded and refolded many times. "I don't have to pull it out anymore," he said, "I just know it's there and know that I'm not going to die from the feelings." He was particularly proud that, in any situation, he had become able to change his images and thus to change his life.

There were many "Janines" and "Jacks" and many more small and large epiphanies for me and for those precious few associates who believed in this crazy new way of approaching emotional and physical illness. We were taking the emphasis off the diagnosis and focusing instead on living fully — in which case the condition fades into the background. Although there were pockets of acceptance within the hospital, the medical model continued to prevail and physicians still viewed this new way of looking at disease and life rather suspiciously. I have personally never considered behavioral medicine to be an "alternative treatment." Rather, I have always seen it as adjunctive, as empowering "the human factor" and allowing a person the best shot at whatever treatment he and his physician have chosen. But I can understand the reservations held by the medical community, particularly those which surfaced when I jumped into a situation frought with political innuendos just because I had an epiphany. To look before I leaped was certainly only the first of the many lessons I had to learn!

In this book, I want not only to convey to you the techniques that patients have found useful and life-affirming, but also to share the lessons with which I have been confronted both politically and personally and the ways in which I have learned or not learned them. You, too, will be a pioneer, and the life of the pioneer is not lived in comfort zones. You, too, will have to "walk the talk" and "put your money where your mouth is," if you and your patients are going to grow and live fully.

An enormous breakthrough in my life occurred when I read Simonton, Matthews-Simonton, and Creighton's book, *Getting Well Again*. My experience had allowed me to embrace fully the mind-body connection with cardiovascular, endocrine, and other disorders. But, *cancer* — what exciting possibilities that held! And recalling my multiple personality patients who had demonstrated amazing healing powers in their image shifts from personality to personality, I intuitively saw the truth in what these authors were saying.

As things happen, cancer patients started showing up in my caseload, and the direction of my life began to shift once again. My understanding of imagery moved from just visualizations to the full sense of imagery as involving all the senses. One of my first cancer patients, Chris, was terrified about her lung cancer, with its prognosis of only a few months of survival. She just did not respond to the Simontons' wonderful visualization of the immune system fighting the cancer and of her chemotherapy working powerfully. After a couple of abortive attempts, she explained that she had spent a large part of her life as a jazz musician and was an "ear person." When I suggested that she record her own imagery tape, she seemed somewhat ambivalent. Nonetheless, she dusted off her baby grand, which had lain idle for years, and created the most extraordinary jazz depiction of the immune system-cancer battle, with the heroic chemotherapy coming through and the tumor growing smaller and smaller. Even better, she started playing her piano again and became involved with the jazz she loved so much. And, yes, Chris' tumor got smaller for many months, and she eventually tripled her prognosis. But, best of all, she really started living again.

For some time, I had tried without much success to have the hospital let me try a PNI program within the medical section. Although I had been allowed to design and implement a highly successful stress management/relaxation program for patients recovering from heart attacks and open heart surgery, the administration seemed to feel involvement with the oncology unit was just too premature. For my part, what I wanted to do simply could not be done properly in a once-a-week group or individual session in the outpatient mental health Center for Life Management. I was bursting with wonderful ideas and no place to properly implement them!

Then a phone call came from a colleague who had tried a number of times to lure me away from Orlando Regional. His family had been touched by cancer, and he gave me the challenge of designing exactly the program I wanted for cancer patients at Orlando General Hospital. Despite my fierce commitment to security and safety zones, I realized that I *couldn't not do it*, and I tentatively agreed, knowing it really meant risking everything. Several restless nights later, I came fully awake, to see the entire program before me in every detail. I felt a little like Mozart getting the image of the whole symphony in an epiphany, and then finishing the job by simply writing it down. Perhaps that is too exalted an image, but I do know it *was* all there before me. All I did was spend a few weeks putting the specifics of the components down on paper in correct order.

A 28-day program seemed appropriate both to follow behavioral learning principles and also to include all the essential components. I pulled together everything I felt was integral to a life joyfully, wholly, and peacefully lived, from being able to handle stress to being able to laugh and create and connect in some sort of "spiritual" way. The stress management and the spiritual/philosophical ("high-level awareness") elements were to be "lessons" each day. I started writing up the "lessons," not counting, just getting them written down as quickly as possible. When I felt I had finished, it turned out that I had 27 stress management lessons and 29 high-level awareness lessons, so I simply moved one I had considered borderline into the other pile. They also fell beautifully into each of the four-week sections, having essentially the same rhythm, though not the same lessons.

And thus GETTING WELL emerged from a birth canal filled with serpentine turns, lighted by dazzling epiphanies, and guided by an enchanting image of people, including me, changing their lives and living more profoundly, more peacefully, more healthily, and more joyously.

2

The Relationship of Imagery, Emotions, and Cognitions to Psychoneuroimmunology and Behavioral Medicine

For centuries, it was a given that emotions could affect our health; ancient philosophers, folklore, and even our grandmothers' maxims purported that recovering from an illness required more than a prescription. Why did they believe that intangibles like hope and joy and purpose could help heal the body? Today's scientific researchers are asking that question and many of them believe that what they are discovering may be leading us into a new future of medicine, one that draws from the best of both worlds: modern science and ancient wisdom. —*Bill Moyers*

All of the body's major systems—the autonomic, endocrine, immune, and neuropeptide systems—are communication channels whereby the person's thoughts and images activate the genetic material and cellular structures to reorganize according to new information to help a person toward healing. —*Barbara Dossey*

The study of extraordinary human attributes requires appropriate methods and theories. That's why I call for an integral empiricism—involving data from many disciplines that are subjected to rigorous critical scrutiny through the practice of an expanded, more open-ended science. —*Michael Murphy*

D r. Robert Ader, editor of the 1981 seminal volume in this field (*Psychoneuroimmunology*), not too surprisingly coined the word "psychoneuroimmunology," PNI for short. PNI is essentially the study of the connection between the mind/emotions, the central nervous system, the autonomic nervous system, and the immune system. Although Dr. Herbert Spector's term "neuroimmunomodulation" and Dr. Leonard Wisneski's mouthful, "psychoneuroimmunoendocrinology," mean essentially the same thing, I find those terms somewhat limiting; for surely I am involved in "psychoneurocardiology" when working with heart patients or in "psychoneuronephrology" when working with kidney patients. Perhaps a more apt term would be "psychoneurobiology" or, as Dr. Wisneski has suggested, "biopsychology." However, PNI seems to have gained a certain public acceptance, and we will continue to use that term principally, despite its limitations.

Dr. Patricia Norris (1988), Director of PNI at the Menninger Clinic, has remarked on the intensity of study in this field regarding the role of the autonomic nervous system, the limbic/hypothalamic/pituitary axis, and the neuropeptides and other neuromodulators in the self-regulation of the immune system. Pointing out that there is "hard-wired" communication between the brain and body (neurons) as well as "soft wiring" through the neuropeptides and other neurotransmitters, Norris notes that the chemicals in the brain which control our moods, actions, and perceptions are made not only by the brain but also by the immune system (as well as other systems of the body). This means that we have a clearly established cybernetic feedback loop between the central nervous system and the immune and other systems of the body. As a result, not only do psychological/emotional/eidetic states affect the systems of the body in this loop, but the systems of the body in turn influence psychological states.

Pat Norris' parents, Drs. Elmer and Alyce Green (with Walters, 1969), proposed a rationale for mind-body regulation. It was their suggestion that perception (or imagery) elicits mental and emotional responses which generate chemical responses in the limbic system, thus activating the pituitary and bringing about physiological responses. These physiological responses are then perceived and responded to, in turn, completing a cybernetic feedback loop.

To effect change in the system, it is possible to intervene anywhere inside of it. However, for us "psychological types," the easiest, and perhaps most obvious, intervention point is at the level of perceptions, emotions, cognitions, or images. I would like to suggest that for every change of the mind, emotion, body, and spirit, there is a preceding or concomitant image, whether on the conscious or the unconscious level. As a result, emotions, thoughts, behaviors, bodily reactions, and automatic physiologic functions are all accompanied and/or preceded by an image which is possibly, but definitely not necessarily, visual. This hypothesis, which has been tested in research and observation by many (including Norris and Dr. Robert Kunzendorf), is a *sine qua non* for clinical PNI.

Whether we use "PNI" or "biopsychology" or another term to describe this field, there is the implication of scientific research rather than just intuitive observation or practice. We speak of PNI as being a new field, yet its principles have been in practice since the beginning of medical history. The distinguishing mark of PNI is its attempt to observe and quantify and then to put this knowledge into some semblance of order. It is, in a certain sense, proving by the scientific method those things that *we have always intuitively known to be true!*

For millennia, imagery, intention, ritual, and other mental/emotional processes have been the tools of the shaman and other such healers. The entire history of man is replete with healing rituals and practices heavily involved with mental pictures, metaphor, and transpersonal images. Jeanne Achterberg has written a stunning and profound volume, *Imagery in Healing: Shamanism and Modern Medicine*, which articulates the history of imagery within the history of medicine before it was put asunder by the dualism of Descartes and as it is rising again under the rubric of behavioral medicine and psychoneuroimmunology.

In 1987, while a member of a scientific delegation to China whose mission was to exchange behavioral medicine knowledge with Chinese physicians, I was fascinated with Qi Gong, an ancient martial/healing art. We heard legends dating back several thousand years of Qi Gong masters stabbed in the chest by an enemy with spears which bounced off, leaving the masters unscathed. Further, there were tales of masters trampled by horses, picking themselves up, dusting themselves off, and continuing in the fray. Of course, Qi Gong is used in present-day China more as a healing art and protection from disease than protection from hordes invading the country. Using the power of breath (energy) and intention (image energy), Qi Gong makes changes in both the energy "within" an individual's body and the energy "outside" the body. I find in describing Qi Gong that it is difficult not to use terms of Western duality, rather than describing it in terms of the unity of the "Qi" (life, breath, energy).

The unity of the mind and the body was almost axiomatic, even in Western medicine, until several hundred years ago. Unfortunately, this close connection of the mind (soul) and body was seen to be hampering the direction of "modern medicine," since it was believed that in performing surgery one not only intruded into the body but also "played around" with the soul. Such action was, of course, unacceptable to the Catholic Church of that day.

Scientist-philosopher René Descartes came to the rescue, rationally and artfully severing the mind from the body. He posited that the two were absolutely separate, although parallel, entities with only miniscule communication through the pineal gland. Based on this thinking, physicians could do whatever they wished with the body without fear of damaging the soul! And, of course, the logical assumption then followed that whatever happens in the mind and soul could have no effect on the body.

The positive side of this shift in consciousness was that Western medicine was able to develop into the wondrous body of knowledge, procedures, medications, and interventions it has become today. On the negative side, however, this view effectively removed all responsibility from the individual for his/her own health and healing, and gave an outré cast to any interventions an individual might perform in his/her own behalf.

At the turn of the century, Sir William Osler, who not only was one of the fathers of modern medicine but also anticipated the field of psychosomatic medicine, stated that the care of tuberculosis depended more on what the patient had in his head than what he had in his chest. Unfortunately, although his thoughts contained the seeds for the field of psychoneurobiology, they lay buried in infertile soil for decades.

As medicine approached the mid-twentieth century, there was some general concession that a physical illness could possibly have some psychological impact on a person, yet to speak of the activities of one's mind having an impact on one's body remained almost heretical in most respected circles. As an undergraduate at Wellesley during this time, I was quite interested in the work of Walter Cannon and his idea that emotions and images (although perhaps not defined in those terms) could trigger the physiological "fight or flight" response. While I was in graduate school, the work done in the 1950s by Flanders Dunbar, Franz Alexander, and Hans Selye in the area of psychosomatic medicine was of particular interest to me, in that psychological factors were credited in the inception and support of certain physical conditions. This meant, for example, that the mind could influence the gastrointestinal and cardiovascular system and could even touch the "untouchable" autonomic nervous system. However, most scholarly reviews of this work at that time found incalculable flaws in the assumptions and work of Dunbar and her associates, and the status quo continued to prevail.

One of the giant stars in the PNI galaxy, Lawrence LeShan, began publishing articles in the 1950s suggesting that cancer had psychological correlates. Although there had been recognition in the literature that such medical problems as asthma, ulcers, and migraines (e.g., Dunbar, Selye, and Alexander) could have psychological correlates, it was a major step to suggest that an organic disease as devastating as cancer could have *any* psychosomatic basis. LeShan, a clinical and experimental psychologist, acknowledged the necessity of generating hypotheses that could be tested by the scientific method. However, he realized the problems inherent in arriving at cause-and-effect scientific proof in any area involving the human personality. Unlike medical researchers, LeShan could not use animal studies from which to extrapolate. And to this day, he has strong feelings about offering a putatively helpful psychological intervention to one group and not offering it to the control group (LeShan, 1992).

Daunting as rejections by hospitals and research centers of his pioneering work must have been, Larry LeShan has persevered for decades. In that time he has both written and inspired work that firmly establishes the link between emotions and catastrophic illness. Perhaps one of his greatest gifts to the field has been leading us beyond the idea of "cure" to the importance of truly living and "singing one's own song" until that last breath is drawn. A fine scientist and a gifted psychotherapist, LeShan laid the philosophical groundwork for clinical psychoneuroimmunology that underlay Norman Cousins' hypotheses, the Simontons' investigations, Jeanne Achterberg's work, and the work of many others, including my own in GETTING WELL.

Neal Miller, the father of biofeedback, is one of the titular heads of behavioral medicine and, as such, is deeply involved in the beginnings of PNI. Miller (1969) challenged the idea that the autonomic nervous system (ANS) was unresponsive to all but a classical conditioning paradigm (e.g., Pavlov's dog). He believed that operant or instrumental conditioning could be used to effect change in the ANS. From my graduate school days, I remember his studies using biofeedback/operant conditioning, in which a rat controlled the flow of blood to *one* of its ears. Based on his studies, Miller suggested that if we could be made aware of the responses of our autonomic nervous system, we could modify these responses. His work also brought forth some of the first mentions of imagery in recent literature. His favorite image was that of a lemon being cut and tasted, of seeing the knife go through the skin, smelling the lemon oils, and tasting the tartness of the lemon. Through the use of this and other such images, he pointed out that a whole system of the body previously thought unresponsive to mental processes (the ANS) was actually amenable to modification through mentation.

Although deep problems were encountered in the replication of Miller's original rat studies, his concepts eventually led to the development of biofeedback. And, though the early promise of biofeedback has not been realized, it has in many ways started to crack the mind-body nut. Harris Dienstfrey (1991) put it well when he said, "Miller's great achievement was to wrest the autonomic nervous system from the brute world of mechanical physiology to its proper place, in the body that has a mind — even if, to Miller, the mind is a brain." Although Neal Miller was unable to open his own research doors with his key, that very key may well have opened other doors which will take us far beyond the half-kept promise of biofeedback.

I have wondered if Miller's missing link might be in the area of the mind as imager, rather than the mind as brain. Bob Kunzendorf (1990) has followed a similar line of thought in suggesting that specific mental images are identical with particular neural events. If this is true, then vivid imagers should be better able to activate those neural events and better able to control whatever physiological responses are affected by those neural events.

Kunzendorf concludes that it makes more sense to reduce biofeedback and Pavlovian conditioning to special cases of vivid imaging, rather than the other way around. He cites Mowrer's theory (1977) that conditioned responses are really *un*conditioned responses to vivid anticipatory *images* of the unconditioned stimulus. Thus, only animals *with vivid anticipatory images* will respond to the conditioned stimulus; likewise, humans with vivid imagery are going to respond more strongly to biofeedback and other conditioning. Howard Hall (1983) and John Schneider and his associates (1990) have found that immune responsiveness was increased with images alone, without any conditioning. And, indeed, the intensity of the response corresponded to the intensity of the imagery.

Biochemist Candace Pert dramatically opened the doors separating body and mind with her identification of the neuropeptides. Dr. Pert was one of the first researchers to find that in order for opiates and other psychotropic drugs to work, there must be receptor sites in the brain. These receptor sites were also found to be scattered throughout the body, not just in the brain. Pert and her colleagues took a further step: "If the brain and the other parts of the body have a receptor for something taken from *outside* the body, it makes sense to suppose that something produced *inside* the body also fits the receptor. Otherwise, why would the receptor be there?" (Pert, 1986, p. 9). Hence, the fact that the brain is responsive to morphine and other opiates indicates that the body is able to produce its own morphine (the beta-endorphin neuropeptide).

In my early days in behavioral medicine, I was interested in the idea that the benzodiazepines (Valium, Xanax, etc.) bind to the opiate/benzodiazepine receptor sites. This suggested to me that the body also had the ability to produce its own anti-anxiety medication as potent as that obtained from the pharmacy—without side effects or the threat of dependency! This was particularly valuable in working with people affected by panic disorder who resisted psychotropic medication. It became reasonable to believe they could produce their own anti-anxiety chemicals (through exercise, laughter, and imagery), and thereby feel more in control of their lives.

Over the years, Pert and her associates have identified 50 to 60 neuropeptides, some of which are substances considered to be "hormones" produced by a specific gland. For example, it turns out that insulin is not just a hormone; it is a neuropeptide which is created, stored, and has a heavy concentration of receptor sites in the limbic system (the seat of emotions in the brain). Accordingly, the brain, as well as the pancreas, has the ability to produce insulin. Receptor sites for these chemical purveyors of emotions, the neuropeptides, have been found in virtually every system of the body, including the gut and the immune system. At the beginning of her work, Pert believed that the emotions were in the head or in the brain; however, she now believes that they are in the body as well—forming an incredible information/communication network.

The implications of Pert's findings for the field of PNI are enormous. In her talk at the Symposium on Consciousness and Survival, sponsored by the Institute of Noetic Sciences in October 1985, she stated, "I believe that neuropeptides and their receptors are a key to understanding how mind and body are interconnected and how emotions can be manifested throughout the body. Indeed, the more we know about neuropeptides, the harder it is to think in the traditional terms of a mind and a body. It makes more and more sense to speak of a single integrated entity, a 'bodymind.'" Hence, "gut feelings" may indeed reflect feelings emanating from our viscera, and depression in the head may parallel depression in the immune system.

Ernest Rossi, author of the thought-provoking book, *The Psychobiology of Mind-Body Healing* (1986), has incorporated Pert's important work and suggested that the neuropeptide and the communication system formed by the receptor sites is the psychobiological basis of therapeutic hypnosis and the whole area of mind-body healing. Rossi argues cogently that how we believe and how we project those beliefs in images affects our being, right down to the cellular level. Indeed, in more recent years he has hypothesized that the effects go even further—to the genetic level.

In a brilliant paper, "From Mind to Molecule" (1990), Rossi suggests that the concept of "information" is the common denominator that lets us bridge the mind-body gap. Molecules of the body modulate mental experience just as mental experience modulates molecules of the body. Therefore, in the mind-brain connection, the neural networks of the brain encode state-dependent memory and feeling-toned complexes of the mind's words, images, etc., from the information substances (hormones, neuropeptides) received from all cells of the body. The brain and the body connect through information substances via the hypothalamic-pituitary-endocrine axis. And finally, in the cell-gene connection, cells receive information substances from the brain to evoke gene information which completes the loop—communicating back to the brain. The idea that these information substances produced by the body (including estrogen and "male" steroids) form a powerful basis for the concept of state-dependent learning (SDL) and that this SDL underlies hypnosis/psychotherapy/imagery is a potent concept.

The revised edition of *Psychobiology of Mind-Body Healing* (1993) is a masterly compendium of research in this quickly evolving area. Rossi not only has generated a number of intriguing research hypotheses which have the potential for a world of exciting implications for PNI, but he also offers over a dozen finely honed teaching tutorials for clinical applications. My thinking owes a deep philosophical debt to Ernest Rossi, and I believe his work is essential and fundamental reading for any responsible clinician in the behavioral medicine field.

Carl Simonton, M.D., is another in the initial wave of pioneers in PNI who risked scorn and sometimes ostracism by his medical colleagues in order to publish the hypotheses he and his associates had generated from observations of "terminal" cancer patients. For a man who does not seek the limelight, this surely was a sacrifice of great magnitude.

In his practice as a radiation oncologist, Simonton noticed that patients with a positive attitude and mental set seemed to live longer than those without a positive outlook who received exactly the same medical treatment. He teased out these relevant psychological factors, among which were seeing the cancer as weak and confused, the treatment as eminently effective, and the immune system as powerful—essentially imaging a positive outcome not only for the disease but also for one's life. *Getting Well Again* (1978) is a classic volume, emphasizing the importance of psychological factors and imagery in the healing process. Simonton's later book with Hensen, *The Healing Journey* (1992), evinces the spiritual evolution of his thinking and presents an expanded approach to teaching those principles of healing to cancer survivors.

Drs. Jeanne Achterberg and Frank Lawlis (1980, 1984) have added immeasurably to the philosophy of and research on the mind-body connection. Their intense study of the relationship among imagery, beliefs, attitudes, and stress and the progression and remission of cancer and other life-threatening conditions has given us a body of literature which is statistically sound yet excites the imagination. Occasionally, on a discouraging day, I thumb through my copy of *Bridges of the Bodymind* (1980) to remind myself of the pure excitement of our field.

Achterberg and Lawlis have suggested that our culture's push for individuals to bottle up feelings such as anger, fear, and hostility may have an effect on the high incidence of cancer and other "lifestyle" illnesses in our society. They cite their pilot research with the criminally insane (who, indeed, *do* act out these feelings) as having found there was little if any cancer among them. Yet this is a population in which most people smoke and otherwise abuse their bodies. Achterberg and Lawlis have also speculated upon ways in which morbid fear (e.g., of a curse or a hex) itself has actually killed people, and have wondered whether diseases such as cancer, heart disease, and AIDS, whose diagnoses carry a great deal of fear, could have an element of voodoo death about them as a result of the fear they invoke in individuals.

A major contribution to the field was the development by Achterberg and Lawlis of several instruments to measure the impact of imagery on conditions such as diabetes, back pain, rheumatoid arthritis, and cancer. The Image-CA, perhaps the best known of these, allows a quantifiable "score" to be given to the image in relationship to the disease. Their excellent work has inspired a plethora of research and extended the possibilities of clinical applications immeasurably.

For over a decade Dr. Howard Hall (now at both Rainbow Babies and

Children's Hospital and Case Western Reserve in Cleveland) and his associates have looked at the question of whether a healthy individual can voluntarily alter immune functions by employing a relaxation/imagery technique. Hall was one of the first not only to examine the concept of voluntary immunomodulation but also to bring it under the close scrutiny of a fine scientific eye. In his first studies (1983), a small, but real, increase in numbers of lymphocytes as well as increased responsiveness of the immune system was observed. Further studies (1990a) have indicated that practice is an important variable in the effectiveness of immunomodulation. He is now looking at clinical populations and the effectiveness of immunomodulation on people who have an established condition.

Inspired by the work of Achterberg and Lawlis, Dr. John Schneider and his associates (1990) have reported successful studies using imagery to increase the adherence, or "stickiness," of neutrophils (an important immune component). Schneider and his team found that the specific functions of cells may be influenced by imagery if the person is aware of those functions. They also concluded that the intensity of the physical response reflected the vividness of the imagery *and* if one "worked too hard" it negatively affected the response.

Nicholas Hall, Ph.D., of the University of South Florida likes to begin his talks by reading a lascivious passage from *Lady Chatterley's Lover*. He then challenges his audience to doubt that images can cause powerful bodily change. Hall, one of the most prolific researchers in the field of PNI, is presently focusing much of his attention on HIV disease. He has been particularly active in the scientific examination of the power of the placebo effect, the imagery of hope, the effect of imagery on the immune system, selective disease in multiple personalities, and miraculous cures and spontaneous remissions, as well as of psychological factors in the disease process. One of his most intriguing recent projects is a study of how the immune components of professional actors vary as their roles change.

The 1980s produced excellent studies on the role of stress and emotions in the disease process (Jensen, 1987; Kiecolt-Glaser & Glaser, 1987; LeShan, 1989; Levy et al., 1990; Polonski et al., 1988). Locke and Colligan (1986) have an excellent review of psychological factors and the immune system in their volume, *The Healer Within*. Robert Ader and his associates have brough forth the second edition of *Psychoneuroimmunology* (1991), which deals with a number of aspects of the immune system and in particular takes a look at the interaction between the immune system and psychological factors.

In a provocative paper Roger Booth and Kevin Ashbridge (1993) have proposed that the immune system and the nervous system (the psyche) are a single integrated entity with a common goal of establishing and maintaining a self identity. The immune system's function of defending the body against invaders (determining what is "self" and "not-self") is analogous to the psyche's function of giving meaning to ourselves and our world, and establishing boundaries. For example, Booth and Ashbridge suggest that an allergy (an innocuous substance causing a physiological reaction) for the immune system is analogous to a phobia to the nervous system. These speculations are brilliant — but unproven and controversial in the scientific community. However, they unleash a host of delicious possibilities for clinical theory and intervention, the most compelling being that as one builds the integrity of the psyche, it may be reflected in the soundness of the soma.

Lydia Temoshok, a fine researcher, has carefully examined the links between psychosocial factors and disease outcomes in HIV disease and cancer. In *The Type C Connection* (1992), she and Henry Dreher give compelling evidence that psychological factors may predispose a person to disease status. She has proposed that cancer patients reveal a Type C "behavior pattern" (as opposed to "personality"). This behavior is marked by non-expression of anger, the tendency not even to be aware of or experience "negative emotions," compliance with external authority and lack of assertiveness in relationships, and an overconcern with meeting the needs of others and insufficient engagement in meeting one's own needs. She found that Type C individuals' repression of feelings and numbness to fear, anger, and sadness required biological changes. To create such numbness, the system may flood itself with morphine analogues, such as beta-endorphins, which may also may suppress the immune system.

Of particular interest is some of the work done by Gary Schwartz (1990) and his associates on the connection between the *repression* of emotion and the disease process. For example, Schwartz has cited abundant data linking subjective-physiological dissociation (inflexible repression) with compromised immune functioning and physical illness. He hypothesized from his clinical observations at the Yale Behavioral Medicine Clinic that the development of repression under certain circumstances is healthy. To reach this conclusion, he treated a number of highly intelligent, successful teenagers and adults whose biological, social, and psychological functioning was compromised as a consequence of pervasive repression. Although they had picked up some unhealed physical scars along the way (e.g., migraines, Crohn's disease, hypertension, ulcers, allergies), they had survived abuse and other serious problems at home. In dealing with these problems they had elected to suppress their needs for love and affection; to repress feelings of loneliness, depression, anger, and fear; and to become overachieving children and "successful," overachieving adults. Schwartz's clinical philosophy of praising the clients for using those defenses that allowed them to survive a difficult situation, yet allowing them to explore more flexible defenses that are kinder to the body, reflects the GETTING WELL approach. This similarity will be explored further in Section II on "Clinical Applications."

For a couple of decades, James Pennebaker (1990) has been studying the relationship between the ability to share one's feelings and the physical health of individuals who are able to do so. He finds that "confessional writing" can lead to salubrious changes in the immune system and better health in general. Pennebaker infers that the inhibition of thoughts, feelings, and images takes a considerable amount of physiological work, which puts a great deal of pressure on the autonomic nervous system and immune system. Apparently, it is beneficial to allow these repressed images to reconstitute themselves on paper, where, over the period of the writing, there seems to be a structuring and then a resolution of the pain and the harmful effects of those "hidden" feelings and images.

Jonathan Shedler, professor of clinical psychology at the Institute of Advanced Psychological Studies at Adelphi University, presented work at the 1992 meeting of the American Psychological Association suggesting that repressing psychological distress leads to an overreaction to stress and a higher risk of heart disease. And although overt emotional distress is not healthy, suppressing that distress is even worse physically for the individual.

The area of "psychoneurocardiology" has a distinguished history of bridging the mind-body gap. Friedman and Rossman's seminal work, *Type A Behavior and Your Heart* (1974), quickly translated into "mental behavior and your heart." Robert Eliot, M.D., further focused that mental behavior into cognitions and perceptions in his delightful book, *Is it Worth Dying For?* (Eliot & Breo, 1987). (I've found the answer to that question can turn into an epiphany very quickly!) Redford Williams, M.D., of Duke University Medical Center, has put the Type A hypothesis under the knife of scientific inquiry, refining the concept into a more heuristically viable one dealing with perceptions, images, and world view.

Dean Ornish, M.D., has been one of my heroes since the publication of *Stress, Diet & Your Heart* (1984). At last someone brought it all together: diet, exercise, and psychological intervention with a "spiritual" feel to it. In his landmark study done with heart disease patients (Ornish, Brown, & Scherwitz, 1990), intensive lifestyle changes (very low-fat diet, exercise, support, and meditation) measurably reversed coronary artery blockages without drugs or surgery in 82 percent of the 48 patients studied. The majority (55 percent) of heart patients in a comparison group which did not embrace such lifestyle changes became measurably more ill. This is exciting from a behavioral medicine point of view; it becomes even more stirring when one considers the probability that one's approach to life may underlie disease (*Dr. Dean Ornish's Program for Reversing Heart Disease*, 1990). Ornish states, for example, that the perception of being isolated is a fundamental cause of feeling stressed. As a consequence of this belief, he designed the Opening Your Heart program to focus on opening the heart to feelings, to inner peace, to others, and to a higher self—essentially opening the heart to connectedness and unity. These are decidedly unscientific concepts leading to scientific proof of healthier hearts!

David Spiegel, M.D., a physician well known for his work in hypnosis, was initially quite doubtful of the PNI claims that psychological elements may be a factor in the disease process. Accordingly, he and his associates (1989) examined a ten-year-old, controlled, prospective study to disprove this hypothesis. Using metastatic breast cancer patients (due to the similarity in their medical treatment), he randomly assigned the 86 women in his study to either treatment groups or control status. The intervention groups met once a week for a year, providing support and imagery, while the control group received only medical treatment. At the end of the ten years during which the women's progress was followed, Spiegel et al. found that members of the treatment group had lived twice as long as the controls, and that the several women still alive at the conclusion of the research were all from the intervention group. These results are particularly striking considering that the intervention was minimal. Although we cannot in good conscience project from these data, one wonders what the results would have been had the women in the intervention group received more intensive psychological intercession in addition to the standard treatment.

Although Speigel's data have begun to shift the perceptions of physicians who had doubts about the PNI movement, acceptance has been slow. At the 1991 meeting of the National Institute for the Clinical Application of Behavioral Medicine held in Orlando, Florida, Dr. Michael Lerner of Commonweal remarked on the substantial scientific support that the Speigel et al. study gave to mind-body claims. "Yet, had this been a new chemotherapy," he added, "do you want to guess how big the headlines would have been and how much National Cancer Institute money would have been poured into the replication of that study?"

Headlines report daily that we are losing the war on cancer; there is no truly effective medical treatment in sight for HIV disease; coronary arteries are generally reclogged within a year after bypass surgery; and there is no effective treatment for MS, lupus, or chronic fatigue syndrome. The truth is that, although modern medicine has created physical miracles within our lifetime, it may be approaching the limits of its effectiveness. PNI, however, is a field of treatment whose time has arrived. Indeed, it may be a major thrust of medicine in the 21st century. Rather than seeking new techniques or more powerful chemicals, traditional medicine may well begin looking to behavioral medicine, prevention, and PNI to extend the continuum of care.

The data of Ornish, Speigel, and their colleagues suggest that psychological interventions can extend life. Beyond this, I firmly believe that *every* condition has major psychological and emotional factors in its inception and maintenance. However, I also believe that we as mind-body practitioners will have lost immeasurably if we buy only into outcomes of extending life or "curing" a condition. Extending life *may* be a side effect of what we practice; however, we will have lost the meaning of the whole movement if "medical model" outcomes of "cure" or increasing length of life are allowed to lead us. "Healing" involves not only the body but also the mind, the emotions, and the spirit. Surely a portion of our focus must be on helping the person mobilize inner resources that will enable the fullest success with standard treatment. However, physical healing is only one element. The process of living, quality of life, values, human meaning, connectedness, and healing in the deepest sense—of minds, spirits and of our planet—must be our major concerns and objectives if we are to be true to ourselves.

During the last decade I have been greatly influenced by the journal *Advances* and the publication *Noetic Sciences Review*. I credit *Advances* (originally published by Eileen Rockefeller Growald's Association for the Advancement of Health, and now published by the Fetzer Institute) with carrying behavioral medicine far beyond purely lifestyle components while remaining scientifically robust. Pushing me toward new explorations and frontiers has been the task of the *Noetic Sciences Review*. Indeed, the Institute of Noetic Science (IONS) stays on the leading edge of science, philosophy, and psychology, and also funds scholarly, cogent research programs on emerging world views in science and society. Although my graduate degrees are in "scientific" areas (clinical psychology, public health, and exercise physiology/nutrition), perhaps my first love is my undergraduate major, philosophy. Those studies provided the conceptual core of GET-TING WELL, and I credit IONS with giving me scholarly, scientific backup as I began treading this wondrous, but uneasy path.

Ruth Buczynski, Ph.D., deserves special attention for founding the National Institute for the Clinical Application of Behavioral Mecicine (NICABM), establishing international conferences on the Psychology of Health, Immunity, and Disease, and supporting GETTING WELL early on. Her energy, determination, and grace have created these splendid meetings which have fostered the interconnection of pioneering clinicians in behavioral medicine and have stimulated and changed the whole field.

As an undergraduate, I was intrigued with the concept of the "philosopher king," the political ruler who guided his minions wisely in the way of ethics, personal meaning, Truth, and the Highest Good. In the field of

PNI, it appears we are dealing with a new breed of scholar—the "philosopher-scientist." This individual is an assiduous scientist who incorporates, but transcends, the scientific method and reaches hungrily into the realms of philosophy, spirit, values, and ultimate purpose.

Willis Harman (1991) of IONS speaks of the reconciliation of science and metaphysics, the healing of the mind and body, which Cartesian dualism put asunder. He suggests a "wholeness science," based on the assumption that we contact reality through both physical sense data, which form the basis of science as we know it, *and* a deep "inner knowing" in an intuitive, aesthetic, spiritual, noetic, and mystical sense. According to Harman, this assumption would allow the "evidence" of "inner explorers" of various cultures, stimulate research in the full spectrum of states of consciousness, and look at the realities "waiting to be discovered, at the highest reaches of the human consciousness by all people."

This transcendent thought process can be seen in the work of the new scientist-philosophers. Joan Borysenko (1990), a respected cancer-cell biologist from Harvard, now focuses on the spiritual/mystical and the importance of "remembering" the radiant, whole beings that we all are. Jeanne Achterberg, a fine scientist and astute researcher, looks into the healing power of the primordial images of our deepest humanity. Dean Ornish's personal encounter with illness and depression while a medical student carried him into spiritual areas with profound and continuing impact on his practice of medicine. Howard Hall, John Schneider, and Bob Kunzendorf are men who think deeply, whether they are designing research, discussing the transformative power of grief, or talking about the meaning of life.

Nicholas Hall, Ph.D., is quick to insist that one be extremely careful in using present resesearch to "prove" conceptual leaps that have very little to do with the research. However, with equal alacrity, he asserts the validity of some rather "miraculous" mind-body occurrences. "But, we can't say research proves it or even backs it up. Research, as we now know it, follows a Euclidian model, which allows us to study events only if they fall into categories such as straight lines or perfect circles," Hall (1993) explains. "Human events just don't do this. They don't fall into neat geometric categories." Continuing to be true to the scientific method, this personable adventurer into the mysteries of healing, himself, fully embraces life, reaches into recondite areas of the human experience, and emphasizes the process and meaning of life rather than its extension.

Joel Elkes, M.D., is a pioneer in bridging the gap between concept and practice. His Arts in Medicine program at the University of Louisville's College of Medicine has drawn together artist/scholars (such as Clifford Kuhn, M.D., Vija Lusebrink, Ph.D., Lounette Humphrey, M.D., Alice Cash, Ph.D., Marti Ising, and others) in the areas of art, music, drama, movement, and even comedy to broaden the boundaries of psychiatry and medicine. First-year medical students at the University of Louisville voluntarily arrive a week early for immersion in expanded lifestyle choices — meditation, art, movement, nutrition, noncompetitive play, supportive interactions, communication skills, and spiritual awareness. The designer of this innovative program, Leah Dickstein, M.D., a dean of the medical school, feels that budding physicians need to come from wholeness in their own lives, not only to survive the rigors of medical school but also to be able to heal others effectively.

Dr. Ronna Jevne (1991) and Dr. John Shaffer (1986), both of whom have divinity degrees in addition to being PNI clinician-researchers, are looking at both the meaning of hope and the transformation of images as potent implements in the healing process. Larry LeShan and Pat Norris assiduously adhere to the guidelines of scientific inquiry yet newly enrich our beings with the implications of their thought and touch our souls with the beauty of their writing.

Larry Dossey (1989) and Carl Simonton are respected physicians, but both break the tight cage of the medical model and move us into the mysteries and glories of "Era III Medicine" and transpersonal healing. Jon Kabat-Zinn (1990) and Ellen Langer (1989), fine research psychologists committed to hard scientific inquiry, have beautifully articulated the importance of "mindfulness" to the healing process. And, of course, Bernie Siegel (1989) has brought it all together, touching the heart and raising the consciousness of the layperson in a way no one else has.

Virtually all these scientists with whom I have had contact have experienced some major trauma in their lives that has allowed them to transcend the limits and parameters of scientific intellectualism and move into the world of philosophic spirituality. And while they are demanding and assiduous scientists when it comes to plying their craft, they do not see it as science for the sake of science. Instead, their science integrates into lives and minds in a way far more extensive than in clinical trials. Science becomes a springboard to the universal. One realizes while reading their works or talking with them over a cooling dinner that they are poets and philosophers in addition to being scientists. And it is indeed comforting to see this movement led by extraordinary humans with fine minds open to all possibilities — especially possibilities that cannot easily be confirmed by clinical trials.

Of all these, however, perhaps the "philosopher king" for me was Norman Cousins. Although not trained as a scientist, he had an excellent eye for good research and possessed the gift of vision for the future for PNI. He was particularly astute in projecting seeds of promising research or other "givens" into hypotheses for researchers to test. He was also brilliant in garnering research funds for testing those hypotheses. I particularly appreciate the support and kind words he had for GETTING WELL when we were struggling for a foothold in the PNI arena. Both the PNI community and I miss him, but we are ever grateful for his vision of the connection between science and meaning.

In mentally reviewing the history of philosophy, one realizes that the manner in which the culture interprets the nature of the physical world is a crucial determinant of the parameters and limits of thoughts. Thus, in many ways we must look to the field of physics for the structure our concepts about the nature of reality will take. I see the mind-body field as being profoundly indebted to Albert Einstein for redefining our universe, mind/energy/matter, time, and space. Barbara Brennan (1988), a physicist turned healer, says, "Our old world of solid objects and the deterministic laws of nature is now dissolved into a world of wave-like patterns of interconnections. What we used to call 'things' are really 'events' or paths that might become events" (p. 25).

Dr. David Bohm (1980), a protégé of Einstein's, has theorized that a hologram may be an accurate metaphor for the universe, suggesting that although primary physical laws cannot be discovered by attempting to break the universe into its parts, the whole universe is nevertheless reflected in the smallest of its quanta. Dr. Karl Pribram (1969), a well-known brain researcher, has accumulated evidence that the brain's structure is holographic and that intelligence, memory, and sensory information do not reside in a part of the brain; rather, they are spread throughout the entire system. Bohm's assertion that a subatomic particle can manifest itself as a particle or a wave (matter or energy) provides us with the context in which "paranormal" phenomena such as psychokinesis and "miracles" can be understood. Aerospace physicist Robert Jahn and psychologist Brenda Dunne (1987) have taken these ideas further and produced compelling experiments validating the effect of mind on matter. And certainly this review would not be complete without the seminal assumptions of the new physics, which has given us a world view, a flowing blueprint, within which to understand and expand the principles of PNI.

This chapter has been only a *selective* review of the "literature" and is not meant to be exhaustive in any way. And, indeed, this is a very *personal* review of the literature, reflecting the major influences in my own experience and those which I used in the design of GETTING WELL. There are many more philosopher-scientist-clinicians than are mentioned here or in future chapters of this book. As I meet and talk with clinicians and researchers throughout the country, I am impressed by their intelligence and scientific rigor, deeply touched by their warmth and humanity, and excited by their creativity and courage.

3

Imagery as a Foundation for a Multimodal Behavioral Medicine Program

The emotional brain and the visceral brain are the same. There's nothing the brain can say that the immune system can't hear. — *Patricia Norris*

The human mind is capable of whatever we assign to it.
— *Jeanne Achterberg*

Imagery is a dating service between people and themselves.
— *Martin Rossman*

We must learn imagery is everything, says Patricia Norris, Ph.D., and I agree. I take the same broad view of imagery, seeing it as the salient element of hope, goal-setting, hypnosis, cognitive activities, optimism, humor, emotions, perceptions, core beliefs, and epiphanies. I believe it is the crux of how we experience ourselves, our bodies, our environment, our relationships with others, and our spiritual life.

There is virtually nothing in our many avenues of experience that we do not image in some way. Every voluntary behavior is preceded by an image of what will occur, no matter how brief or elusive to our consciousness this image may be. The mere act of closing a door elicits an image of the behavior. If one images moving clumsily toward the door, that is likely what will happen. However, if one images smoothly and elegantly opening and closing the door, it is more likely such a sequence will follow. There are no guarantees that this eidetic blueprint will totally define the behavior, yet the probabilities are increased that the behavior will match the blueprint.

The field of sports psychology is built upon the premise that the body-mind does not know the difference between an actual event and an eidetic one. Gerald Epstein, M.D. (1989), an imagery specialist, suggests that during imagery one is creating memory for completed neurophysiological connections: A new model for behavior is being created. Anees Sheikh, Ph.D. (1978), has cited research evidence that mental practice has the same effect as actual practice. Watching the Olympics on television has made us aware that most world-class athletes use imagery. Sports commentators have observed that virtually every athlete goes through every aspect of his or her performance prior to the event. In addition, many athletes image self-confidence and seeing themselves accepting the gold medal. Imaging does not take the place of years of training and practice; however, imaging success gives those athletes who use it the leading edge. Similarly, for persons with life-challenging conditions, imagery and other PNI techniques are not a substitute for medical treatment or good nutrition, yet these strategies give those individuals the best shot and a higher probability of success in their treatment.

It is well accepted among experts that we all image constantly. (The most common imagery consists of negative, non-trusting, insecure, failure-oriented, worried ideation and usually produces behavior and lifestyles of the same nature.) Thus, our mission is not to teach imagery, but to change and transform existing images into ones that will form the basis for the life and health we wish. Because our minds do what they are programmed to do, like the sports psychologists we are helping individuals to rehearse imagery for the goals *they*, not someone else, desire for their minds, bodies, and spirits. Certainly, imagery is not a substitute for action, but it is a requirement as a model for what is to occur.

Our emotions are both preceded and accompanied by images. Our stress is created by perceptions and images. Our relationships are mightily affected by the images that accompany our core beliefs. The ways in which we relate to the world and to others are dictated by our images of ourselves and how we image our futures. Additionally, the science of PNI indicates that our images affect the operations of our immune system, as well as other systems of the human organism.

Dr. Karl Pribram (1969) was instrumental in conceptually releasing the mind/memory/intelligence from the confines of the brain through his interpretation of the findings of Karl Lashley's studies of specific memory sites in the brains of rats. Lashley (1950) trained rats to run a maze, then surgically removed various parts of their brains he felt were responsible for the memory and had them run the maze again. No matter what portion of each rat's brain he excised, the rat could still run the maze. Indeed, as more of the brain was removed, each rat's motor skills were affected, but its memory of the maze was still intact. Pribram found these data to be extraordinary because they suggested that memories were not contained in specific cells or engrams of the brain. It appeared, rather, that just as a fragment of holographic film contains all the information of the whole, each cell of not only the brain but the whole organism contains memory.

Pribram's hypotheses continue to be validated and expanded by research with recent studies which indicate that memory (at least in mice) may be mediated by certain genes (Medina, 1993).

In a talk at the National Institute for the Clinical Application of Behavioral Medicine conference (1991a), Deepak Chopra, M.D., pointed out that we replace all the atoms in the lining of our gut every five days, our skin every month, our liver every six weeks, our fat every three weeks, our DNA every five weeks, and our skeletons every three months. In fact, 98 percent of the atoms in our bodies are replaced every year. If there is a tumor in the liver, its atoms are also replaced every few weeks, and damaged arthritic joints are reconstituted every few months. If this is true, how is it that our bodies remain recognizable to ourselves and others over the months and years?

Chopra answers that our consciousness remains 95 percent the same from day to day, and it is our consciousness (or imagery) that is the blueprint for what happens to our body, mind, and spirit.

Most of us consider our consciousness as something that arises from the matter which is our body or brain—that consciousness is a by-product of the materialistic events of our biochemistry. Using the work and theories of Pert, Einstein, Bohm, and others as a basis, Chopra turns the model around and asserts that molecules do *not* produce thought; rather, thought produces molecules. Indeed, it may be more appropriate to say that consciousness creates our brains as opposed to the reverse. Thus, our consciousness (our imagery) provides the working blueprint for the body, as well as for its tumors or calcium deposits or atherosclerosis—reproducing the same phenomena over and over. Following this paradigm, we see that in order to change our bodies—and, more importantly, our lives—we must effect a change in our consciousness (which is 95 percent the same from day to day). Such a model would account for epiphanies being the common thread in "miracles"—with a major shift in consciousness preceding a change in physiology.

In designing the GETTING WELL program, I realized that a tumor or clogged artery was at some level a metaphor or manifestation of aspects of a life gone awry, a consciousness not flowing with the natural order or, as Larry LeShan put it, "a foiled creative fire." Obviously, reversing this process requires more than designing a clever imagery for the immune system and practicing it three times a day. It requires more than just making a person feel he or she has social support, more than doing family therapy, more than having a smiling face or a "good attitude." It requires providing an atmosphere in which people can safely examine the essence of their consciousness, explore the meaning of life and personal meaning, expand the limits of human potential, trust themselves and the universe, and be applauded for "singing their own songs." It means providing fertile soil for the seeds of hope and especially for the seeds of epiphanies—those wonderful flashes of insight, those holy moments when our kaleidoscope of consciousness shows itself to us in a totally new and meaningful pattern. It means tapping into all aspects of a person's life and imagery. And providing the fertile soil optimally requires that the person be immersed in new possibilities for thought, for life, and for consciousness.

Epiphanies do not happen in comfort zones. It seems to be the nature of the beast that if we are not pushed, we choose to see things in prescribed comfortable ways—and our consciousness continues to be 95 percent the same. Life-challenges create wonderful "teachable moments." Unfortunately, however, most people turn away from these extraordinary windows of opportunity. Instead, they want that tumor removed or that quadruple bypass completed so they can go back to "life just the way it was" before they got sick. On the other hand, those individuals seeking out the GETTING WELL program have had the initial epiphany of seeing their condition as the irritating piece of sand from which a pearl can grow.

I believe GETTING WELL's remarkable success in turning lives around is attributable to its selection by just such people—those who have the courage to get out of their comfort zones even when it means throwing themselves into scary, uncharted territory. Such people are aware that, although the potential rewards are great, the path is rough and thorny. Those who choose to make the journey at GETTING WELL are, indeed, what Bernie Siegel would call "exceptional patients."

Imagery, seen as parallel to what Chopra refers to as consciousness, underlies all aspects of GETTING WELL. We all image constantly, whether it is that small fraction of sensing of which we are aware or that vast base of the iceberg not immediately available to our awareness. Our particular culture is especially attached to the visual sense of imagery, yet visualizing is only one aspect. Imagery involves all sensory channels—sight, sound, touch, kinetics, taste, smell, and what Dr. Eugene Gendlin (1981) calls "the felt sense." As we proceed, we will find that imagery also involves extrasensory or transpersonal channels, and that perhaps our imagery and intention have power that extends far beyond our own mind and being.

As Jeanne Achterberg said in a talk at the Fourth World Conference on Imagery in 1991, we must take as solid fact that, in order for the mind and the systems of the body to initiate their dance, the consciousness must move into the intelligence and machinery of the cell and touch that machinery and intelligence—and the message from the mind to the cell must be so unique that it allows the cell's intelligence and machinery to move in an entirely new way. Achterberg speaks of four different kinds of shifts in consciousness (shifts in imagery) that seem to effect changes in the way the consciousness communicates with cellular structure.

Type I involves events, places, times, relationships, and actions in life associated with dramatic healings. Achterberg points out that, in fact, these functions are a by-product of the events themselves. For example, feeling joy or being passionately in love brings about a massive shift in immune and cardiovascular functioning. Sandra Levy and her associates (1988) found that women who defined their lives as joyful were *much* less likely to have a recurrence of breast cancer than those with a more negative view. The research also shows that events or relationships can negatively affect cellular function. Walking into an oncologist's waiting room precipitates an immediate drop in immune function. The most significant factor in heart attacks is the time of the week (Monday, at around 9:00 a.m.). Thus, the effect that time, events, and relationships have on our consciousness is a major element of the bodymind choreography.

The Type II bodymind dance with the DNA involves a major shift in personal mythology in the path one takes—a personality shift, according to Achterberg. Multiple personalities, in which each personality has immune responses of his or her own, are good examples. She also cites as examples those people who have shifted from being helpless victims to becoming "peaceful warriors" (those who work for a transcendent cause but who are capable of defending established boundaries).

Type III is the deliberate and conscious ritual of connecting with the cells of the body through consciousness, with the goal of changing one's physiology. This kind of imagery is powerful and makes physiological changes; however, it changes *only* the function that is the focus of consciousness, but does not change that which one is *not* actively imaging. Achterberg used two groups of students—one group imaging an increase in T-cells and the other focusing on increasing neutrophils. The T-cell group was successful in increasing T-cells, but there was no change in neuts, while the neutrophil group increased neutrophils but had no change in T-cells. Indeed, there is an isomorphic connection between what one images and a change in cells, yet even the most learned scientist does not know the full implication of these changes. To "have control of one's body through imagery" is extremely complex, and would involve the full-time attention of one's consciousness, even if it were possible.

Type IV consciousness shifts involve ritual, which is a self-generated formal act that carries one into sacred space. Achterberg defines as sacred that space where the intent of the healer and healee is to seek meaning and transcendence. She says that external accoutrements such as the availability of medical treatment, objects of comfort, or even sanitary conditions do not matter, and even the source of the healing is dubious—symbol, intent, image, the power of the imagination, and the ability of human beings to sustain themselves in the most unfortunate condition. The importance of ritual is an inextricable element in the stories of survival of prisoners of war, hostages, and those trapped in the wilderness with no hope of rescue. We also find that ritual is an integral part of transcending cancer or AIDS when no medical hope has been given.

GETTING WELL integrates all four types of imagery/consciousness that Jeanne Achterberg articulates. Each one is important in its way; however, the synergy generated by emphasizing all four creates the ambience in which miracles of all sorts occur—physical, emotional, and spiritual.

The GETTING WELL program, a not-for-profit, outpatient behavioral medicine program for people with life-challenging conditions, provides an in-depth, intensive, "awakening" experience. This 28-day program has translated the PNI literature into viable life techniques for people with cancer and other life-challenging conditions such as cardiovascular disease, multiple sclerosis, chronic pain, systemic lupus, HIV disease, rheumatoid arthritis, neurological dysfunctions, gastrointestinal disorders, and diabetes. Because of the profundity of the approach, we require a *minimum* of 14 days in the program, which is in operation daily from nine in the morning until late afternoon, seven days a week.

The program was originally designed for cancer patients only; however, people with other diagnoses soon requested admission—and did well. With very little adjustment we found we could deal effectively with a variety of conditions without sacrificing intensity or individuality.

People frequently ask how we can deal with such diverse diagnoses as immune deficiency diseases, autoimmune diseases, and heart disease. This question may reflect a certain misunderstanding about GETTING WELL. To many, the name GETTING WELL implies "getting well from the disease," rather than the actual meaning of *getting well in the deepest sense.* The program focuses not on the disease, but on the creative giftedness and wholeness that we all have within. Because there is so much more right about us than there is wrong with us, I like to concentrate on the overwhelming percentage that is *right,* rather than on the few cells or functions that have gone astray. I tend to think that when we focus on the "diagnosis" (or what is wrong), it expands and begins digging holes in our "wellness." I see the people coming into GETTING WELL as healthy individuals who may be having some problems with their heart or cancer cells or walking ability. When we focus on and qualitatively expand the image of health, it seems to overtake the system and relegate "the disease" to the place it deserves—the background.

Participants are frequently referred by nurses or physicians; however, more typically participants seek out the program themselves. If the person lives locally, we have him or her come in for an interview. This way, individuals are able to judge more clearly their readiness to make the commitment of time and energy to this consuming venture. With people from out of town, most of the interviewing is done by phone. We do not make promises or guarantees, of course, about *quantity* of life. We do, however, make it clear that this is an emotionally challenging program and that the *quality* of their lives and relationships may change deeply. I don't recall refusing anyone who really wanted the program; however, I have discouraged some who seemed desperate for a "miracle" yet lacked the energy levels to actively participate in the program.

Imagery is a pervasive thread through the six or seven daily sessions at GETTING WELL. Even the daily individual sessions focus on the participant's designing idiosyncratic imagery for the presenting problem — whether that be taming the immune system, confronting in imagery the perpetrator of early sexual abuse, or developing the image of meaning and worth in one's life.

A description of the program elements in a typical day at GETTING WELL follows, and Figure 1 presents a visual overview of the weekly schedule. Section II will examine each of these elements separately and convey the rhythm of each component over the 28 days of the program.

Initial Testing

Initial psychological testing (which was *de rigeur* when we were in a hospital setting) included not only standard tools such as the MMPI and Rotter Incomplete Sentences Blank, but also imagery-based instruments such as the Image-CA (Achterberg & Lawlis, 1984) and a modified House, Tree, Person (HTP).

The Image-CA involves a brief guided imagery: seeing the disease, imaging the immune system mounting an attack, and seeing treatment effectively dealing with the disease. The participant is then asked to draw his images of the condition, the treatment, and the immune system's or the body's healing work. These drawings can be scored for perceived strength of the body's response, the effectiveness of treatment, and the invasiveness of the disease process. At the Third World Conference on Imagery in Washington, DC, in 1989, John Schneider cited studies indicating that the Image-CA has a better predictive value than blood studies — that a perceived *positive* outcome will eventuate 93 percent of the time, while a perceived *negative* outcome is 100 percent likely to occur.

With apologies to Jeanne Achterberg and Frank Lawlis, I have developed for our participants the "Image-GW" a generic rendering of the Image-CA which can be used for all types of conditions — not just cancer. We use the resulting participant drawings to help generate guidelines for the individual for imagery training throughout the rest of the program.

Our modification of the HTP employs a formal evocation of images of a house, a tree, and a person before the participants are asked to draw them. The drawings generate a good metaphorical view of the person's feelings about him/herself, his/her family, strengths, and relationship with

Figure 1. Daily Schedule for GETTING WELL

	Monday	Tuesday	Wednesday	Thursday	Friday	Saturday	Sunday
			←EXERCISE ON YOUR OWN→				
9:00	Stress Management	Group Therapy	Stress Management	Stress Management	Group Therapy		
10:00	Group Therapy	Imagery Training	Graduate Group	Group Therapy	Stress Management	Stress Management	Stress Management
11:00	Imagery Training	Stress Management	Group Therapy	Therapeutic Touch	Imagery Training	Imagery Training	Imagery Training
12:00			←LUNCH→				
1:00	Expressive Therapy	Laughter and Play	Laughter and Play	Laughter and Play	High-Level Awareness	Expressive Therapies:	Laughter and Play
2:00	Expressive Therapy/L & P	High-Level Awareness	High-Level Awareness	High-Level Awareness	Laughter and Play	Music/Recreation	Right-Brain Workshop
3:00	High-Level Awareness	Expressive Therapy	Expressive Therapy	Expressive Therapy	Expressive Therapy		
4:00	Individual Tx. PRN		Bodywork Group	Individual Tx. PRN	Friday Seminar	*Scheduled video	*Scheduled video
5:00	→	Meditation Group	30-minute Massages (Optional)	→		→	→
6:00	Family Support Group	→					
Evening	*Sched. video	*Sched. video	Sched. video	Sched. video	Videotape (Gallagher)		

Evening | Watching videos, journaling, audio cassettes, reading from the rich resources therein. The video schedule appears near the video bookcase. We feel it is quite important to follow the schedule so that everyone experiences each video.

*Sched. Videos: We have scheduled videos so that you do not miss anything from the rich resources therein. The video schedule appears near the video bookcase. We feel it is quite important to follow the schedule so that everyone experiences each video.

the world, in addition to the traditional pathologic markers such as depression and anxiety. The HTP is an imagery window on some of the emotional conflicts that may be affecting quality of life as well as the healing process. Frequently, the HTP also reveals unrecognized strengths upon which the person can build.

Stress Management

Stress management usually starts the day. It is "left-brain" oriented and designed to seduce the typical products of our educational system into the concept that stress is how we perceive situations rather than what is actually happening "out there." This daily session makes heavy use of imagery in changing participants' perceptions of stress through cognitive/imagery restructuring. The result is a disturbing event's being imaged in a manner less stimulating to the sympathetic nervous system, which in turn reduces the secretion of cortisol and the catecholamines, which destroy the balance of the immune system. The concepts of stress inoculation (Meichenbaum, 1977) and systematic desensitization (Wolpe, 1969) are combined into strategies in which imagery is used to elicit a parasympathetic effect, graded images of a present or future stressor are conjured, and participants sees themselves as powerful, in charge, and successful at handling the situation.

Techniques from neurolinguistic programming (NLP) may be employed to distance the individual from a stressful situation. Such a technique might involve having an individual "watch" a movie of himself performing in a panic-filled situation. It might entail imaging one's *bête noire* in diapers, in a hamster ball, or in another situation that evokes feelings of powerlessness.

Similarly, assertiveness is reinforced by having the participant image himself accepting a personal right, and being aware of how he feels and appears physically, how he feels emotionally, how people are responding to him, etc. In other aspects of assertiveness training and communication skills, imagery rehearsal precedes behavioral rehearsal in sessions.

Goal-setting, an important dimension of stress management, relies heavily on imagery both in breaking down long-term goals into manageable short-term goals and in producing an "inner video" in which the participant sees himself successfully accomplishing the short-term goals and rejoicing as long-term goals are achieved.

Group Therapy

The daily "process group" at GETTING WELL focuses mainly on giving and receiving support, expressing feelings, instilling hope, and deepening self-esteem and relationship skills. When you think of the typical "imagery training" of children in our culture, you realize the enormous job of imagery restructuring and behavior reprogramming we have to do in group. For the "normal" person there are issues of trust, of worthiness as a person, and of feeling fear if you are a male or anger if you are a female. Our norms discourage expressing feelings and even caution against "hoping for the best" in a superstitious attempt to keep the worst from happening.

In group therapy we reinforce behavior, which in turn creates new images of speaking freely about feelings, of building hope, of "being okay just the way you are," and of feeling and receiving empathy. Perhaps one of the biggest lessons learned in group is seeing conflict between members as an opportunity to enhance communication rather than something to be avoided.

When we speak of instilling hope, it is not "hope" of the variety of "I hope I get a new Porsche," "I hope my tumor disappears," or "I hope my mother will treat me better." These are all "hopes" that have to do with the externals in our lives over which we ultimately have no control. Certainly, it may be helpful to keep an optimistic attitude toward these externals, but we cannot allow their outcomes to either make or destroy our lives. The hope that we try to instill has to do with inner power and meaning rather than with control of externals. It is hope in the sense that an individual learns: "Whatever happens, I can handle it, and I can find the gift of meaning in it."

Imagery Training

Imagery training is a daily staple of the GETTING WELL program. First, we explore where the person "is" in imagery (both through dialogue and the Image-CA). We are looking not only at imagery in reference to the illness or condition, but also at the basic way the participant's world is imaged and experienced. We usually start out with guided imagery, but move quickly into encouraging participants to develop creative, idiosyncratic imagery consistent with their values as well as with their conscious and unconscious core beliefs.

Basic relaxation and breathing are taught, a "special place" is incorporated, and anchors (sensory associations to desired images) are developed. The special place and the anchor are used together. For example, a person's special place in a piney woods forest where only deep and total relaxation exist may be paired with the sensory anchor of rubbing the thumb and middle finger together. An anchor can be used in the future not only to elicit the full image instantly but also to deepen the image.

A wide variety of imagery experiences (from a generalized "healing light" to specific immune system "wars" against the cancer cells) is offered to expand and develop the participant's individual imagery. An important aspect of the formalized imagery sessions is reframing treatment such as chemotherapy or radiation from uncomfortable, noxious images into "elixir of life" or "healing beams of light energy from a radiant star." The important connection between PNI and standard medical treatment is empowered during this session, which frequently allows the undesirable side effects of medical treatment simply to disappear. This session is also used to introduce and reinforce images and techniques for pain management. A variety of images is presented, and individual work may be done to hone the techniques. Participants are encouraged, actually empowered by input from the group, to craft their own creative imagery tapes.

Dr. John Shaffer's (1986) transformational fantasy techniques are closely interwoven into the imagery work and are particularly useful for getting to the unconscious image, bringing it to consciousness, and allowing the person to transform that image into a more healthy one for his or her life. Even though "cookbook" imagery exercises serve a purpose, the real work involves giving the participant the skills to tap into and change old, nonviable imagery into new blueprints for life. Shaffer is a genius, and we have brought him from St. Louis several times to train our staff and our participants. Unfortunately, although his is a quite straightforward and ultimately simple technique, it is not something one can read about and then accomplish effectively. Training with Shaffer is a mountaintop experience that no worker in this field should miss!

Nutrition and Exercise

In recent years, research has increasingly indicated that sound nutrition and regular exercise are significant factors in not only the prevention but also the treatment of cancer, cardiovascular disease, and other life-challenging conditions (e.g., Ornish, 1990; Sporn & Roberts, 1983). We find that imagery plays an important role in adherence and compliance as well as in enhancing the effects of good nutrition and aerobic exercise. In GETTING WELL didactic material is offered regarding the important roles of beta carotene, protective indoles, complementary complex carbohydrates, and fresh fruits and vegetables, along with other nutritional information. In addition, we present material on the importance of exercise in reducing loss of lean muscle mass, stimulating lymphatic circulation, increasing core body temperature, and increasing endorphin production.

Participants are encouraged to image these salubrious changes taking place (such as carrot juice being directed to a tumor and reducing its size, the tumor area being bombarded by oxygen from aerobic activity, or the weak cancer cells being destroyed by increased body temperature). Imaging an overall feeling of health and well-being while eating or exercising seems to actualize the body's becoming whole, healthy, beautiful, and powerful. At GETTING WELL, we appreciate Dr. Brugh Joy's (1979) statement: "I believe that if you put fine food into a body with a crummy mind, you get a crummy body; but if you put crummy food into a body with expanded awareness, you get a fine body." However, we carry this further and suggest that when one puts fine food into a body with expanded awareness, an extraordinary state of being can occur.

Exercise is a particularly difficult behavior to implement, yet it is critical for the cardiovascular, cancer, diabetes or other chronic disease patient to include in his or her lifestyle. It is important for the physical aspects of the disease, of course; further, exercise is wonderful for the management of pain, depression, and anxiety, and also builds feelings of inner power and self-control, which are crucial for psychological well-being.

Aerobic exercise, in addition, seems to enhance right-brain receptiveness and "creativity." Participants are encouraged to use aerobic exercise time to guide imagery and positive affirmations or to solve problems creatively. For example, seeing oneself as a magnificent jaguar exercising effortlessly frequently taps into ancient, atavistic memories of being the animal we were designed to be before we were fettered by the configurations of modern, chronic disease-producing "civilization."

Laughter and Noncompetitive Play

Laughter and noncompetitive play are so important physiologically and emotionally that they comprise a formal daily session at GETTING WELL. Physiologically, laughter promotes muscular relaxation as profoundly as relaxation training (Cogan, Cogan, Waltz, & McCue, 1987), and produces beta-endorphins which increase pain thresholds and enhance lymphocyte proliferation (Gilman, Schwartz, Milner, Bloom, & Feldman, 1982), reduce depression and anxiety, and increase feelings of well-being. Berk (1989) indicates that "mirthful laughter" enhances immune function. In his study looking at the effect of laughter on the immune system, those who watched a video of the comedian Gallagher had increased natural killer cell activity. Even the anticipation of seeing the video positively affected immune function.

At GETTING WELL, patients tell funny stories; learn to juggle; watch "Candid Camera," Gallagher, and other funny videos; and play childhood games noncompetitively. Learning to laugh and play is frequently the most difficult part of the program for people with life-challenging conditions, because many, with some reason, feel they have nothing to laugh about anymore. At the core of this belief is the reality that they have long since "put away childish things" and entered into the "consensus trance" image of the competitive, "good" adult in our culture. And although we may feel a real accomplishment at having "matured," unfortunately, our cultural expectations of the "adult" are not necessarily in the best interest of our bodies.

GW participants, frolicking with a multicolored parachute, blowing soap bubbles, or playing "Simon Says," experience the triggering of muscle memories and images of the happy child within — the child who is curious, playful, powerful, creative, and able to heal quickly and naturally. In addition, seeing the humorous, ridiculous side of a situation allows a person more options and a better perspective for handling it, and when people have an alternative way of viewing things, they are not helpless. To enhance their perspectives, participants may be encouraged to stage an impossible situation as a farce, with themselves as both audience and actors in the play — enjoying the outrageous and amusing aspects of their own human comedy. The point of all laughter and play therapy is, of course, to move from a morbid, unhealthy eidetic stance to an imagery stance of creativity, hope, fun, and fulfillment.

High-Level Awareness

High-level awareness is the philosophical and spiritual component of GETTING WELL which focuses on *thriving* as opposed to merely surviving. Frequently, work may be done on identifying and extirpating psychological "weeds" (such as guilt, depression, resentment, lack of forgiveness, helplessness, blame, codependency, and poor self-esteem) from the garden of a full, joyous, healthy life.

Although many of these weeds are identified in a rather analytical, left-brain process, the uprooting is usually effected with right-brain, guided or unguided imagery processes. For example, group members may be asked to identify that region of the body in which they feel guilt or anger. (This is, all too frequently, the site of the illness.) Participants are then asked to give the anger or other feeling a name, shape, texture, color, sound, movement, smell, and even a taste. They are then encouraged to uproot and remove the emotional blockage from their beings by whatever method they choose, releasing it "to the light" or "to the universe," after which we suggest they fill the remaining space with power, love, healing, light — whatever feels right.

As the weeds are removed, powerful new seeds are sown — seeds of forgiveness, unconditional love for oneself and for others, connecting with the flow of life or the waves of the universe, empowerment, nurturing the child within, a positive world view, joyfulness, and/or mindfulness. We prefer to see destructive behavior, attitudes, images, and even disease as having a positive (although perhaps unconscious) intention as far as having protected the individual in the past. Now the participant can "reframe"

(Bandler & Grinder, 1975) or reimagine himself, using healthier, more viable, and creative options to enable positive seeds to be realized in a physically and spiritually healthy manner.

The intent of high-level awareness is to expand the individual's human potential, to awaken him or her to new avenues of consciousness. We strive to help participants become the persons they were born to be, and in doing so to proudly "sing their own song."

Expressive Therapies

It is no accident that expressive therapies usually follow high-level aware-ness each day, since it is through expressive therapies that we carry our work to yet another level and tap into the unconscious process. Through the use of music/sound, movement, drama, poetry, mask-making, journal-ing, bibliotherapy (Block, Mott, Swanson, & Wallace, 1992), and drawing/painting/sculpture, various imagery channels are opened to participants for their exploitation.

A typical exercise, recreating one's healing imagery in an idiosyncratic medium, consistently yields incredibly meaningful and creative results, from paintings to collages to poetry to the tape created by the jazz pianist whom I mentioned earlier. Although many of the exercises are designed to elicit and reinforce the image of perfect, joyful functioning, others are designed to reveal metaphorically blockages to emotional and physical healing. For example, the exercise of "drawing one's family as anything but humans" is a particularly revealing activity with excellent therapeutic potential.

In expressive therapies, as with laughter and play, there is frequently a great deal of resistance from participants. "I can't write" or "I'm not an artist" is a familiar plaint and must be confronted with grace and under-standing, but also with firmness. In this safe atmosphere, it usually takes only a few days before the individual is participating fully and rejoicing in the forthcoming epiphanies.

Therapeutic Touch

Therapeutic Touch (TT) (Krieger, 1979) is a peace/healing offering in the program which is in some senses mechanical, yet deeply eidetic. TT in-volves the use of intensive directed imagery for the healing in the deepest sense of others as well as of oneself. It is based on the assumptions of Eastern medicine that illness or pain are merely blockages in the body's energy field, and when one intentionally "manipulates" the energy field, blocks can be dissipated. Therapeutic touch might be thought of as "laying on of hands" without religious overtones. The weekly workshop in TT crackles with the excitement of sharing with each other the individual and collective power of imagery and intention. (It is similar in feeling to sessions I have spent with Qi Gong masters in China.) Each session produces a few "miracles," from pain disappearing to a diabetic's feeling sensation in his foot for the first time in years. Frequently, however, the big "miracle" is the bonding of the participants to each other in the spirit of love and universality.

Believing, as do some physicists, that consciousness is the most powerful force in the universe, I see in TT the actualization of the *physical* power of imagery. This may be manifested in seeing oneself as being healthy, in touching another with the intention of healing and love, in praying for an enemy, in projecting a healing white light around a loved one, or in imaging world peace.

Individual Therapy

Individual therapy frequently focuses on exorcising the demons of earlier trauma/loss that interfere with the healing process in the broadest sense. We use a variety of imagery techniques, including neurolinguistic programming (Bandler & Grinder, 1975), transformational fantasy (Shaffer, 1986), eidetic psychotherapy (Sheikh, 1978), Gestalt therapy, and whatever else *works*. We have found that the program itself provides deep, intensive psychotherapy for its participants—most of whom would never have considered *therapy* for the emotional pain they have internalized. They are usually considered to be the "well-adjusted" individuals in our society, persons not needing psychological assistance. Yet we must remember that the emotional *Zeitgeist* of our culture is a prodigious producer of "the diseases of civilization," so that psychological "adjustment" often portends physical problems.

Family Therapy

I know of no life-challenging condition that is not a family illness—from chronic pain to cancer to cardiovascular disease to autoimmune diseases. As a result, I believe that family involvement is extremely important from many perspectives. Family members may be even more scared than the patient about the outcome of the illness, and may have an even deeper sense of helplessness than the person going through it (Sotile, 1992). Quite often, these family members hesitate to articulate these feelings to the patient. In addition, when the participant makes major changes as a result of the program, he or she may return to a system in which those salubrious changes are actually destructive.

GETTING WELL has a weekly group for family members and/or significant others only. In these sessions, family members can express and work through their fears, depression, feelings of hopelessness, and concerns about their loved ones. To accomplish these goals, we may use family sculpture, genograms, Gestalt, and other mind/body techniques complemented with traditional interactive therapies. Separate family sessions are available to participants at their request.

In addition, each GW participant is encouraged to have a family member attend the program with him or her. One participant chose to have her husband with her the first and last weeks of the program, her mother came the second week, and a dear aunt for the third week. Despite the frequent trips to the airport, it worked out well. In this manner, the partner is there not only to reinforce change in the participant's life, but also to make significant changes in his or her own life so as not to be left behind. It is exciting to see partners come initially to "help" their mates and then find themselves making astounding mindstyle changes — often seeing their relationship reach levels of satisfaction not previously imagined by either.

Follow-Up

Follow-up is important in order to maintain the gains made in the program. Weekly sessions for problem-solving and extending the imagery experience are available for those who live close by. We also try to put "graduates" in touch with counselors or support groups in their part of the country which are "in tune" with a responsible PNI philosophy. For example, there is a thriving group in Atlanta and others are emerging in other cities. In addition, telephone support by our volunteers and staff is always available.

Synergy of Program Elements

"The whole is greater than the sum of its parts" is certainly true of GET-TING WELL. Every element taps into a somewhat different aspect of each person's human potential. Enlightenment in one area creates ripples in other areas, resulting in exponential leaps in understanding and experiencing for most participants.

Exceptions to this process are rare; in fact, the only ones I can recall involved people who were in the program less than the minimum of 14 days. We have found that an "expected therapeutic crisis" takes place sometime between days eight and 12, a time during which "nothing makes any sense" and/or the person approaches a life issue he or she is fearful of pursuing. At that point, a participant often feels the program "isn't working" and becomes reluctant to continue. It is of the utmost importance that the participant continue through this crisis and not turn and run. To keep the person in the program the extra few days, our team is not above begging, bargaining, and performing other manipulations. And then the "magic" happens! (And it always happens.) When the synergy takes hold, wild horses cannot keep the participant from completing the full four-week program in some manner or form. I must admit that none of us feels bad upon hearing: "You really were right about my hanging in there; I can't believe what is happening with me now."

And with the synergy come the epiphanies—people imaging possibilities in their lives they never thought could exist. And that is what GETTING WELL is all about!

4

Caveats and Issues for the Behavioral Medicine Clinician

Primum non nocere. [First, do no harm.] — *Hippocratic oath*

The psychosocial aspects/interventions and cancer research have trod an unfortunate path by presenting life expectancy as the primary goal, devaluing any qualitative outcome. We would argue that increasing the length of life as a goal pales by comparison to living with grace, clarity, and meaning (however one defines these values).
— *Jeanne Achterberg and Frank Lawlis*

Many scientists argue that because supernormal abilities violate certain assumptions of physics and biology and because they can't be verified in controlled experiments, such things don't really exist. But I think it is short-sighted to reject such phenomena merely because they transcend . . . the tools we've designed to measure them . . . it's more reasonable to conclude . . . [they] belong to a new domain that requires special methods and tools to study them. — *Michael Murphy*

For many physicians tentative acceptance of the PNI movement came to a crashing halt in 1985, with the publication in the *New England Journal of Medicine* of a study by Cassileth and her colleagues indicating that emotional factors had no effect on survival of a group of patients with advanced malignant disease. In the same edition, an editorial by Dr. Marcia Angell suggested that many of the current mind-body beliefs were not only scientifically unjustified but also actually damaging to patients with serious diseases, since the beliefs promoted "false hope" and "guilt" in these patients. According to Angell, when a patient is led to believe he or she has control over a disease, that patient may become infused with false hope. This in turn leads to feelings of guilt in patients who do not progress, causing them to blame themselves. And if the patient's family members, physicians, etc., also hold the mind-body beliefs promoted by PNI, they may begin to blame the patient for lack of progress, too. Soon this "blame the victim" attitude may be evident in their behavior toward the patient; in worst case scenarios, it may even be verbalized to the patient, with unthinkable results.

Although Dr. Cassileth was disturbed by the interpretations the medical community gave her article and almost immediately restated the implications of her conclusions (Locke & Colligan, 1986), the damage was already done. The whole field of psychobiology fell under a shadow of doubt and suspicion in the minds of all but the most enlightened physicians.

Unfortunately, research funding in our field tends to follow the "medical model," with focus on extension of life rather than quality of life, even when researchers espouse quality of life in conversations and correspondence. Questions arise regarding the ethics of withholding from control groups interventions that will most likely improve the quality of life (in addition to extending the length of life), particularly in studies which replicate a "successful" study (e.g., the Speigel study which essentially replicated the Simonton study). Achterberg and Lawlis (1992) write:

> More vital than any theoretical or academic issues are the implications of the research on the participants. Depriving cancer patients from any treatment that meshes with their worldview or belief system and is probably helpful (at worst, benign) is unethical, inhumane, and unkind. We cannot conclude otherwise, having listened with gratitude and humility to the stories of the co-participants in our research who have responded to their diagnoses with courage and insight. The triumph of the human spirit continues to place our petty concerns about research design in perspective. (p. 4)

In 1988, I examined and rebutted the *NEJM* article and editorial (as well as a subsequent article in *Vogue* by Switzer in 1987) in one section of my thesis for a master's degree in exercise physiology and wellness. Cassileth et al.'s research study used questionable interpretations of the psychological testing and dealt with a population (those with end-stage pancreatic cancer) that had only an infinitessimal chance of improvement, giving their study essentially a "basement effect." Sadly, the only criterion of the research was length of life. Although all three articles were rife with overstatement, demonstrated a lack of understanding of some of the primary writers in the field, and displayed several problems with the idea of cause and effect, they *did* address various issues needing attention. Coming to this realization was a moment of growth for me. In my zeal, I had wanted to quash the "enemy," so it was gratifying to realize I could learn from my critics. Attending to their points is crucial in PNI practitioners' becoming credible to physicians as well as to the lay population.

In designing and implementing a responsible PNI program, one must consider legitimate potential hazards to the participant. Although I delight in the passion and fervor of "New Age" devotees, I recognize that all too frequently there are ends left untied and many implications left unattended. And damage *can* be done to the individual! Once, as a small child, I had a holy moment in which I realized that I could "have my cake and eat it too"; I believe behavioral medicine can likewise have its cake and eat it too. In other words, I am convinced that we can retain the passion yet incorporate responsibility, creating an even more powerful process.

Guilt about the Illness

The behavioral medicine movement of the last two decades has emphasized making personal decisions about lifestyles and mindstyles that affect one's health—with the emphasis on taking responsibility for one's life. This is a major shift from the traditional outer locus of control (physicians, surgery or a pill can do whatever needs to be done for the body) to an inner locus of control (I can make changes in my life that will positively affect my health). From the research it is fairly clear that how and what we image may have an effect on how successful medical treatment will be—affecting the quantity of life as well as the quality of life. Thus, for some it is an easy step from responsibility to guilt if they do not achieve the predicted physical outcomes—or do not achieve them quickly enough.

Lifestyle habits and behavioral patterns (smoking, alcohol consumption, lack of exercise, improper nutrition, etc.) are strongly implicated in the initiation and development of most illnesses. In addition, the evidence is quite clear that psychological stress plays a significant role in the development of conditions such as cancer, heart disease, and even injuries that lead to chronic pain. Although most people see taking responsibility for these variables as empowering, there are many who feel guilty for having smoked (or for continuing to smoke), for not handling stress well, or for not doing those things they "should" do.

I have known of physicians who discouraged patients from going into an effective PNI program because the guilt the patients might feel if they didn't get well could have been painful and destructive. Indeed, such guilt may well be a side effect of PNI strategies. Yet one does not give up effective treatment because of the side effects. In a letter written to me a few months before his death, Norman Cousins pointed out that physicians do not give up prescribing chemotherapy because patients suffer the side effects of nausea, hair loss, etc. Noting that radiation or chemotherapy treatments for cancer do not always work, he asked, "Should a person feel guilty because treatment worked in someone else and not in him?" This is an excellent point—yet, people *do* feel guilty.

As skilled mental health professionals, we must be able to deal with the side effect of guilt, remaining exquisitely sensitive to its presence rather than just dismissing it as unimportant or trivial. Bearing in mind that merely being in the field may make us especially attuned to "self-responsibility," we must not make light of patients' initial grappling with owning—much less empowering—an inner locus of control. "It's silly to feel guilty over *that*," may come to our minds or, *horribile dictu*, to our lips; however, this is a very real and complex struggle for the individual. Sensitivity to the issue of guilt is important. Often the participant may not express inchoate guilt feelings because of the desire to be a "good patient." In other words, the participant may end up feeling guilty for feeling guilty! As facilitators of the process, we must meet the challenge with sensitivity, creativity, and the full complexity it demands.

"We choose everything that happens to us." This is a thesis one encounters repeatedly in the writings of Louise Hay and other New Age authors. Although I generally consider it to be a useful and empowering hypothesis, to the beginning pilgrim on the healing journey this phrase can be extremely disconcerting and even destructive. Certainly a great deal of useless or destructive guilt can be generated if the hypothesis is glorified or forced by the therapist. For example, patients will reply: "I didn't choose to have lupus," "I certainly didn't voluntarily create my chronic fatigue," or "I didn't will the cancer on myself." Remembering that healing usually does not take place in comfort zones, I encourage these patients to try the hypothesis on for size from time to time and to take away whatever is useful from it. However, they must also be made aware that whatever is not useful needs to be let go for the moment, and perhaps tried on for size later. This shaping of perceptions seems to produce less guilt, while permitting the amount of "cognitive dissonance" needed for growth and resolution to continue.

Some people have read about the emotional factors in the development of diabetes, cancer, or heart disease, and categorically state: "Emotions cause cancer; I can control my emotions; therefore, I am guilty of causing my cancer." This is typical of the all-or-nothing thinking of Western culture. Our society tends to have very simplistic ideas of cause and effect: When we are faced with an effect, there *must* be a cause—a single cause. Even physicians, whose training should militate otherwise, tend to give credence to a single or only a few causal factors of a disease condition. Yet, there is an extremely complex web of causality for "lifestyle" diseases such as cardiovascular disease, cancer, and diabetes. The diagram for the causal web for heart disease takes up half a page of a textbook (Ross & Mico, 1980) and involves 25 to 50 factors, from heredity to nutrition to emotional style. I like to point out to participants that there are causal factors about which nothing can be done, such as heredity or age, but there are other factors upon which we *can* have an impact, factors such as nutrition, exercise, and emotional style. Taking responsibility for those lifestyle matters which are under our control may change only the *probabilities* for the outcome of the condition. However, when we take back the power, we can change the *quality* of our lives. Most importantly, we must take ourselves "off the guilt hook" concerning those things we did before we were aware of their impact upon our health. Awareness and intention are important aspects of responsibility; in all fairness, we cannot blame ourselves for earlier benighted decisions.

Frequently, we use the "guilt issue" to have participants examine their motives for entering GETTING WELL, especially when they have physical results clearly in mind. We remind them that being *too* focused on outcomes may actually deter the achievement of those outcomes. Al, one of the first patients in the program, is one such example. He entered GETTING WELL with a poor prognosis for colon cancer which had metastasized to his liver and lungs. Al had been success- or outcome-oriented his whole life, and he approached the GETTING WELL program in the same way: He wanted to get rid of the disease *entirely*. Actually, within several months there were no tumors left except for three or four in his lung which his physician had said were "inactive and not going anywhcre." Yet Al wasn't satisfied. As a result, he was not able to turn his attentions to living his life thoroughly and joyfully because, in his words, "I haven't done something right; I still have those tumors."

Although I was pleased to see Al live far longer than anyone expected, I wish I had known more at that time about dealing with guilt and about refocusing on quality of life. Nonetheless, I see my experience with dear Al as a turning point for the program, because I learned that outcomes are not nearly as important as creating peacc of mind and living fully until one dies—whether that be three months, three years, or thirty years. When we can lift the burden of the outcome, we can frequently lift the burden of the guilt.

As you may have noticed, I have been presenting left-brain, intellectual strategies for reasoning guilt away, and these strategies are quite appropriate interventions—but limited. Guilt is really a right-brain, emotional phenomenon that must be dealt with on its own terms. At the 1990 World Conference on Imagery in Minneapolis, Joan Borysenko, author of *Guilt is the Teacher, Love is the Lesson,* cited a research project that inextricably linked guilt with low self-esteem. The higher the individual tested on a self-esteem scale, the lower was his/her score on a guilt scale, and vice versa. This means that when we see guilt, we are also seeing self-esteem issues. When the individual begins to deal with those self-esteem issues, the pervasive guilt begins to dissolve. So we essentially use the guilt induced by the condition as a springboard to the issues—how participants see themselves and how they fit into the world.

Pam, a 30-year-old woman with chronic fatigue syndrome, was overwhelmed with guilt because of a history of drug use and other such acting-out as a teenager. She was sure she had "caused" her current condition by her behavior during that period of her life. Using her guilt as a springboard, we began looking at Pam's feelings of unworthiness and her lack of trust in herself, which had roots in her emotionally barren family system. The attention she had sought as a teenager by being "spectacularly perfect or imperfect" was examined, and through imagery techniques she began to uncover her "worthy, wonderful self." As Pam's lovable self emerged, her guilt began to fade. Toward the end of her program, she remarked, "The drugs made a certain sense to me at the time, but what's really important is *now* and how I choose to live my life from now on."

When the emotional aspect of guilt/self-esteem has been resolved, the individual's eyes open to the rational arguments. Frequently, however, the rational arguments are no longer necessary!

"Blame the Victim"

"Blame the victim" has much in common with the guilt issues; however, the perpetrator is usually someone other than the patient—perhaps a physician, friend, therapist, or relative. Our outer-locus-of-control society has an addiction to judgments, guilt, and blame as a means of maintaining leverage over people and situations. Having heard media-hyped ideas about the "mind curing illness if one wishes or tries hard enough," the pseudo-enlightened may ask such questions as "Why do you want your cancer to spread?" or "Why don't you want your lupus to improve?" or even "Why aren't you getting better; do you have a death wish?" All too frequently I have heard patients quote questions of this type as having come from a therapist or "friend." Frankly, I have to wonder about the ulterior motives or control issues involved in those questions, particularly when they are asked at a therapeutically inappropriate time. Their effect can be devastating, particularly if posed *before* the patient has dealt adequately with guilt issues.

Another twist to the blame issue occurs when the "victim" blames the "perpetrator." Jenny was quite aware of stress factors relating to her ovarian cancer. Her husband had been a major source of stress for her, so she argued, "My husband caused my cancer." To assist Jenny in confronting her problem, we did major work on "simplistic ideas of cause and effect" and "taking responsibility for one's stress." Their marriage is not out of the woods, but at least both Jenny and her husband have a firmer grasp of their roles and responsibilities in their situation.

Concerns such as guilt and blame for the disease pose a dilemma for the practitioner. There may be significant psychological issues blocking the healing process that need to be addressed. Such issues cannot in good conscience be suppressed, yet bringing them forth before a client is ready risks having the client put up defenses, insist that there are *no* emotional factors in his or her illness, and drop out before the healing process has taken place. Or worse, the client may feel destroyed by the guilt engendered, further burdening her when she needs all her strength to get well.

As therapists we may have hypotheses about psychological factors in a given participant's disease; it is important, however, to trust the process of providing fertile soil for enlightenment, subtly planting the seed, and letting the individual discover and harvest the epiphany. Allowing the individual the gift of self-discovery is a true gift of love. It is my opinion that the confrontive techniques of the recovery movement are counterproductive in a setting such as GETTING WELL; however, this does not diminish my strong philosophical stand concerning the emotional factors found in virtually all illness and the efficacy of imagery for healing the mind and the body.

Indeed, there will always be those who will "blame the victim." As therapists, however, we must be sure that we do not do so either overtly or implicitly, and that we facilitate the participant's moving quickly from the role of "guilty victim" to one of empowered director of his own life drama.

False Hope

Norman Cousins has stated, "There is no such thing as false hope. Hope is a desire for a positive outcome. There is no disease that has killed 100 percent of the people diagnosed with it." In other words, even when one is looking at "outcome-oriented" hope, the *possibility* of a positive outcome is always there.

Prognoses by physicians are based on statistics—"averages" of what would be expected, given a diverse population with the same diagnosis. However, statistics do not tease out what outcome is expected with a person of a given age or certain physical constitution or mind-set. In addition, the studies from which statistics are compiled frequently use people of lower socioeconomic status who get free treatment while in the study, and who tend overall to have poorer health prognoses for a variety of reasons (Achterberg, 1985).

Most "poor" prognoses indicate *only* a 30 percent or 20 percent or 10 percent chance that, say, the person will be alive at the end of two years. However, if the person is working with imagery and other mindstyle changes that shift the odds, there is a strong probability that the individual will have the leading edge for the "winner's circle." And even if there is a 99 percent chance of a negative outcome, why not go for that positive one percent? After all, there is nothing to lose and everything to gain, including a high quality of life, whatever the physical outcome.

Ronna Jevne's book, *It All Begins With Hope*, and Norman Cousins' work, *Head First: The Biology of Hope*, are replete with examples of the physical potency of hope. Although we cannot prove beyond the shadow of a doubt that a hopeful, powerful image of the future will extend life, Brendan O'Regan has suggested that "to argue for the *absence* of a mind-body connection could be viewed as offering the patient *false despair* in contrast to the much feared problems of offering false hope" (1989).

I have been impressed by a rat study (Rodin, 1986) done at Johns Hopkins. The breed of rat used was able to swim for 80 hours while out in the wild before it became fatigued and drowned. In the laboratory, however, the same type of rat, placed in a tank of water it saw as inescapable, would die within a few minutes. The researchers surmised that the rat died as a result of the effects of an overdose of catecholamines induced by fear and the image of hopelessness. If further proof is needed, studies (Solomon, 1985) have shown that the very diagnosis of AIDS causes compromising change in the immune system. And how many people have we known who internalized the image of "a year to live," and died almost to the predicted day? I wonder how many "premature" deaths have been caused by patients' accepting prognoses without question—when actually they could have "swum their 80 hours."

It goes without saying that to make promises or guarantees to patients about extending life or changing disease status through imagery or any other strategies would be unconscionable. However, I believe I can *almost* promise that their lives will be better, and that their conditions will take a less prominent place in their minds. And, although I do not always articulate this, I believe that even "hope" will take on a new meaning for them.

Most people come into GETTING WELL with a definition of hope that has to do with outcome, rather than with a state of being or an attitude. They learn, however, that a core philosophy of GETTING WELL is that an inner locus of control is a more powerful and ultimately more satisfying way of living life than is empowering our health, our relationships, or our material goods to give our lives meaning. If the fulfillment of hope depends on positive outcomes, disappointment will be frequent. GETTING WELL's philosophy concurs with Vaclav Havel's statement about hope, which he made three years before becoming president of Czechoslovakia. "Hope is definitely not the same thing as optimism," he said. "It is not the conviction that something will turn out well, but the certainty that something makes sense, regardless of how it turns out" (Symynkywicz, 1991). Considering these words, one realizes that there can be *no* false hope!

Denial

Often hope is seen as denial, and caregivers may come brandishing swords to extinguish it. And in dealing with addictions, perhaps denial is an evil that must be expunged at all costs. But ours is a different situation. It has been my experience that denial serves useful and protective purposes, and that the patient will let it go when it is no longer needed. Of course, denial can be a danger if it prevents the individual from receiving needed treatment; however, that is not often the case. Norman Cousins put it well when he said to accept the diagnosis but deny the prognosis. In other words, do what needs to be done medically, but don't become someone else's statistic.

In one of his audiotapes Carl Simonton spoke of a research study done with breast cancer patients in which they were divided into four groups according to their attitudes toward their disease and then their attitudes were compared with their outcomes. Those in the first group accepted their disease and actively worked with their physicians in treatment. The second group denied they had breast cancer. The third group stoically accepted the fact that they were *victims* of cancer and impassively went through treatment. The fourth group felt totally helpless, overwhelmed, and hopeless. Not surprisingly, members of the fourth group did the least well, while members of the first group had the most positive outcomes. Interestingly, the denial group did almost as well as the actively participating first group in outcomes. However, Simonton noted, if the denial were to have been precipitously pulled out from under them, they would immediately have become members of the "hopeless" group. So obviously denial is a very delicate process, which requires equally delicate handling.

As professionals, we sometimes feel the patient must be told "the truth." Unfortunately, however, as Ronna Jevne has pointed out, truth for medical personnel is frequently in the form of statistics. "If patients believe the odds to be the truth, they tend to comply by dying on time," she noted. "The word of anyone in authority is very powerful." She is right, of course. On the other hand, it is important for those patients to consider as "authorities" other patients who have survived cancer, heart disease, diabetes, HIV, or lupus.

Don was seriously ill, but definitely not ready to die, when his wife asked for a nurse to come in to relieve her. The nurse immediately went to work on what she saw as Don's denial and began pressuring him to face the reality that he was going to die soon. Although I feel certain that the scene was not quite this grim and contentious, Don began feeling deep resentment at her intrusion on his hope. When I saw his obituary in the paper several weeks later, I wondered if he had "faced reality" and simply given up.

Sara was a beautiful woman of 72 whose treatment for pancreatic cancer "hadn't worked," and her physician gave her three months to live. Family members were beside themselves and brought her to GETTING WELL two months before the doctor's prognosis date. Her husband and children were choked up with sadness and fear, but Sara sat quite serenely, wearing a soft smile. "I am a woman of great faith, and I believe there is nothing there; and if there is, my God will take care of it," she told us calmly. She had gone through treatment to placate her family, but her

X-rays clearly showed a tumor of significant size on her pancreas. She liked the concept of the program, but I think she was motivated to enter GETTING WELL to help her husband with his almost catatonic depression, which had been precipitated by her illness (he came into the hospital at the same time she did). She completed the program a few weeks before she was supposed to die, and had X-rays taken on the day she came to town for her third weekly follow-up group. She told the group that the X-rays would reveal nothing—no tumor. And the next week, when she returned to group, we found that was the case. In fact, the physician could not even find traces of where the tumor had been. Sara lived for over two years after that—years packed with travel with her transformed husband, years filled with joy in her new life.

In the face of such evidence, I truly believe that we must respect denial!

Replacing Standard Treatment

I want to make it absolutely clear that imagery and other behavioral medicine strategies are an *adjunct* to traditional medicine. They are powerful adjuncts, but they are *not* substitutes for medical treatment. Particularly when working with diabetics or hypertensives, we must work closely with the their physicians to avoid overmedication since patients may behaviorally or eidetically reduce their need for medication. Although Dean Ornish (1990), in his study on coronary artery disease, replaced surgical and drug intervention with diet, exercise, and meditation, the patients were monitored by sophisticated medical devices and were under the supervision of cardiologists.

It makes little sense to eschew the remarkable advances in medical technology when patients are faced with life-challenging conditions. In such cases, one must use all the modalities available, from medicine to behavioral tactics to psychosocial strategies to spiritual interventions. There should be no question about using every accessible path and stocking one's armamentarium with every available vehicle for healing.

Of course, the focus is somewhat different when medical treatment has failed, has reached its productive limit, or is only palliative—as is frequently the case in autoimmune disorders. Actually, some of the most dramatic changes have taken place in patients who were sent home by their physicians to "get their affairs in order" because there was nothing else *medically* that could be done. (Often, this is read by patients as "There's nothing more to do, so get ready to die," and they do.) However, for the exceptional patient such a statement is a challenge to move in new directions and, perhaps for the first time, to take responsibility for his or her own health. In the past, physicians have been in a bind when the standard options have not worked and the patient begs to know if there is "something more to be done." However, a number of physicians now use GETTING WELL as an option, rather than suggesting some "last resort" experimental treatment that may vastly impinge on quality of life while offering little possibility of success.

We have frequently encountered patients who were so fearful of surgery, chemotherapy, or other interventions that they wanted to just drop out of conventional treatment and do it themselves. After making it clear that we are biased toward medical intervention, we have accepted several such patients. While participating in our program, nearly all of them experienced shifts in their beliefs, attitudes, and images that enabled them to choose life-saving treatment.

In a slightly different vein, a number of patients feel such a loss of choice when diagnosed with a serious illness that they elect to refuse essential treatment in a misguided effort to return control to their lives. In a responsible PNI program, these patients learn myriad ways to restore power to their beings so they are "freed" to *choose* to accept the treatment they need.

Jack was a 29-year-old man whose two major fears in life were cancer and chemotherapy. When he was diagnosed with testicular cancer (which is eminently treatable with surgery and chemotherapy), he quickly had the surgery but panicked at the thought of chemo. When he entered GETTING WELL, Jack felt distraught and totally out of control of his life. The Image-CA reflected his seeing the chemo as a poison that would kill the cancer cells but would also kill the healthy cells—and him along with them. (Not a good way to go into chemotherapy!) As we worked with him on his imagery and on developing an inner locus of control, a new image evolved for Jack. He began to see his chemo as "the elixir of life" rather than a toxin. He reported feeling very powerful as he told his physician of his choice to have the treatment, which, of course, went smoothly with few side effects. Today, Jack credits his eventual recovery to a masterful blend of mind and medicine.

Focusing on the Physical Outcome
Rather Than on the Process

Medical science is outcome-oriented, and that is as it should be. When I go to my physician with a touch of pneumonia, I do not want to be told, "Dee, let's look at this pneumonia as a message that your life needs changing and that your imagery should be more vivid." Although it might be true, what I really need is a prescription for a course of antibiotics. In other words, I want medicine to be outcome-oriented!

On the other hand, applying that same outcome orientation to psycho-biology is, I believe, not only inappropriate but also destructive to the philosophy of living one's life to the fullest. When a "goal" is the object, whether it is winning a game, making a certain amount of money, or reducing atherosclerosis, we easily lose sight of enjoying the game and of being in the moment or fully embracing life. It is the "American way" to be goal-oriented and outcome-oriented, yet this style at best militates against quality of life, and at worst may indeed be a killer.

It certainly isn't "bad" to want to be rid of pain or to want X-rays to show improvement, yet if happiness or the quality of life is dependent upon outcomes the enjoyment of life becomes a very qualified experience, reliant upon factors that are ultimately out of our control. At GETTING WELL, the focus is on the journey rather than its destination, on peace of mind rather than remission. We believe that when one is deeply involved in the process of life, power is taken back from outcomes, and those outcomes are no longer the controlling factors in one's life and happiness.

Focusing on outcomes seems to lead to concentrating on the disease rather than paying attention to one's whole, healthy person. I believe that emphasis on the few cells that have gone astray but which represent only a small fraction of the total working of the body actually "expands" the disease in one's life. When that attention is focused instead on the process, on peace of mind or on health, it is the health rather than disease that tends to expand in one's life. I like to focus on the image of a person's healthy cells and healthy systems expanding and becoming so powerful that they take over the whole organism. When the process is seen that way, it's more likely to happen that way.

It continues to amaze me that when we let go of outcomes as the ruling factor in life, the outcomes themselves become more positive. Or perhaps we see those outcomes as teachers rather than goals, and the specific makeup of the outcome comes to matter less.

One very real danger of focusing on outcomes is seen in what I call "post-recovery existential crisis" (PREC) or "the happily-ever-after myth." PREC occurs when the physical outcomes are actually those which were desired, so that all the ingredients for "happiness" are present, yet a feeling of emptiness and meaninglessness results.

Nancy, a school teacher from Georgia, to all appearances had her dream come true. After a struggle with lung cancer, she was declared in remission by her physician nearly a year before she came to GETTING WELL. Yet the 45-year-old woman who sat in my office was drowning in fear, hopeless-ness, and helplessness. "Yes, I'm going to live," she said, "but life has no meaning for me. I see my life as being like the song, 'Is That All There Is?'" Although she was not actively suicidal, Nancy talked about wanting to go to sleep and just not awaken in the morning.

Nancy spent several weeks at GETTING WELL, fearlessly delving into some childhood emotional issues that were keeping her from seeing herself as a vital human being. She spent time reconnecting with her spirituality and reuniting with the wholeness and health within her. As she left for home, a new person, she said, "I'm not going to let my body lead me around by the nose again! I am the one who is creating powerful meaning in my life."

Nancy had been healed physically, but healing had not taken place on the emotional, psychological, and spiritual levels. Focusing solely on physical healing had diverted her attention from the other levels of healing, the ones that give life its true meaning and fullness.

Our focus on the process makes us aware that neither death nor exacerbation of the disease is a failure. The only failure is not living life's every moment to the fullest. In my own journey of the last few years, I have been coming to the realization that death may be the final healing—our true connectedness with the universe and the energies of nature. Of course, GETTING WELL people die, yet almost without exception the family describes it as "a beautiful death." And we frequently hear, "Thanks to GETTING WELL, our loved one lived until that final moment."

Indeed, the process is so much more important than the outcome!

Truth with a Capital "T"

Ours is a program that seeks to expand the intellectual, emotional, and spiritual horizons of participants. As therapists, we must respect the personal healing paths of individuals, while helping open as many doors as possible to stretch the consciousness. Sometimes, however, it is tempting to push our own "truth with a capital T." Adages such as "trusting the universe" or "I create my own reality" may have been *our* key to resolving a personal crisis, yet the very concept may be untenable, or even frightening, to someone newly embarking on a healing journey. In such cases, our arguing the validity of a belief could cause damage not only to our relationship with the individual but also to the individual's own progress toward "enlightenment."

In *Cancer as a Turning Point*, Larry LeShan puts forth the belief that our culture makes available to us a rack of ready-to-wear clothes, often not quite the right size, which we are required to fit ourselves into. I like to believe that at GETTING WELL we offer many racks of designer ideas in a variety of sizes, all of which participants may try on to their hearts' content.

When offering a new thought or belief, I have found it effective to ask a person to "try it on for size." How does it feel? What would be the consequences if the individual internalized and incorporated this belief into his or her imagery system? If it works for the person—wonderful! If it doesn't—that's all right, there are many others to sort through and choose from.

Part of our obligation as facilitators in the healing process is to help the individual who is confronting psychological blocks to healing. "Coming on like gangbusters" rarely accomplishes the goal and frequently sacrifices the therapeutic relationship. A very tentative approach is frequently successful. I might say, for example, "Something just occurred to me that may be totally off the wall, but possibly . . . " or "This probably doesn't apply to you in any way, but . . . " Since it's "off the wall," the individual doesn't feel obliged to take your "advice," and you haven't put yourself in a win/lose situation. Furthermore, you have planted the seed, which will germinate when the time is right.

Doris was a 38-year-old woman whose exacerbation of MS had left her nearly blind and partially paralyzed. Her condition had worsened after a contractor double-crossed her and her husband on the dream home they had planned for years. Her anger and bitterness held no bounds. After several days of listening to her recount her victimization, one of us threw out the possibility that being able to forgive and "let go" of the contractor might increase her power in the situation. "No way!" was her immediate response. Yet a week later Doris admitted, "You know, I'm letting that guy run my life. I'm almost trying to show him how rotten he is by making him responsible for my being sick. But he doesn't care, so I'm going to take my life back from him!" And indeed, she did, and as she did, her symptoms regressed. The seed was planted gently, and we did not dig it up daily for inspection, which points out both the need to make interventions and the need to respect the timing and direction of the individual's healing.

We as professionals must hold our opinions loosely; however, I do have one Truth which I never compromise. That Truth is: "We are born good, radiant, and luminous beings, full of power and potential. When we reach that 'true self' through the layers of cultural programming, we will find wholeness, goodness, beauty, and incredible power." I have yet to find a counter-example to this truth!

Expression vs. "Letting Go" of Feelings

At some point in the process of taking personal power back from situations, we may choose forgiveness over anger and bitterness—or, as A Course in Miracles suggests, choose love instead of fear. Indeed, these are powerful and enlightened choices; however, we as facilitators must be aware that this is not a magic, one-step process.

Frequently, the salient emotional blockage to the healing process is repression/denial of feelings. If the individual goes directly from denying feelings to forgiveness, one repressive defense may be inadvertently traded for another. Therefore, it is important to be sure the person recognizes and feels comfortable expressing those feelings before he or she is "released to the light" (or whatever).

Donna, a meek, 60-year-old woman with breast cancer that had metastasized to her lungs, had learned her lessons well as a child. She knew that "nice" girls never get angry, and certainly, one should not have (much less express) any "negative" feelings toward one's parents. Before she came to GETTING WELL, she had "forgiven" her parents, yet she still felt the old, familiar heaviness within.

At GW, Donna decided to retrace her steps and deal with some of her repressed anger. She worked assiduously for a couple of weeks on recognizing and expressing her deep anger and bitterness toward tyrannical parental figures through journaling, drawings, transformational fantasy, and other imagery techniques. A big step for Donna was becoming accustomed to saying, "I'm angry, and it's OK." Soon she moved to the point of being able to say, "It's all right for me to be angry, but I'd prefer to respond to this situation in a different way, with different feelings."

Through her progress in GETTING WELL, she was finally able to truly let go of decades-old issues, and it was a newly confident and glowing Donna who returned to her home in South Carolina. "I feel so light," she said with a smile, "It's as if I'm gliding and floating through life."

"Professionalism"

After establishing GETTING WELL, I found my role as a "professional" changing drastically. Somehow the emotional and even the physical distance touted as "professionally appropriate" in graduate school and expected from a therapist in a mental health center was no longer working. As we began to have more nurses, counselors, social workers, teachers, physicians, and other professionals participating in the program as clients, I realized this was a human-to-human situation, that the other therapists and I were as much participants in the process as we were facilitators for getting well. In other words, the participants in GETTING WELL were teaching lessons as important as the ones they were learning! Not taking on the role of "expert" does not mean, however, that we neglect professional responsibility around confidentiality or patient privacy. Certainly, that goes without saying.

My wise and lovely friend, Ronna Jevne, suggests this human-to-human orientation requires that we caregivers be aware of our limits and able to come to terms personally with helplessness and ego attachments. We must come to some resolution with our own issues, our own garbage, our own countertransference. We need to be aware of our own feelings about death, life, loss, and ourselves. We must be able to touch when appropriate, shed tears unashamedly, and love without conditions. In essence, we need to allow ourselves to be fully human and to share that human experience with another.

In Jevne's insightful book, *It All Begins With Hope*, she quotes an open letter from a patient to her caregivers:

> Just because you understand my disease, doesn't mean you understand me. To understand I am ill does not mean that you understand how I experience my illness. I am unique. I think and feel and behave in a combination that is unique to me. You do not understand me because you have a label for my disease or because some distant relative of yours dies of it. It is not my disease or treatment that you need to understand. It is me. This could happen to you.
>
> And don't tell me you understand. Even if you had the same disease, you could not fully understand. I am tired of being told to:
>
> - "Deal with your feelings" . . . by those who flee from any intimacy with me and cringe when I confront them.
> - "Get your life in order" . . . by those whose lives are obviously cluttered with the unimportant.
> - "Accept your pain and loss and even face death" . . . by those who avoid the very topic.
> - "Live with your limits" . . . by those who move about freely.
> - "Live life to the fullest in the time that you have" . . . by those who shield their reactions from any form of intensity.
> - "Accept dependence" . . . by those who have the resources to assert rigid safe ways of being.
>
> Don't tell me about hope:
>
> - until you have heard my pain.
> - until you are willing to be present for me.
> - until you can stop judging me. (pp. 162–163)

Another injunction could be: "Don't take credit for my healing or feel responsible for my exacerbations—that impinges on my personal power." Unfortunately, clinicians sometimes do feel a little grandiose when techniques work. Humility at being privy to such a wondrous process is certainly more appropriate.

Perhaps the most important lesson for us all, "professional" and participant alike, is the lesson of love. Loving does not mean not doing our job of confronting or pointing out blockages to healing that the participant is unlikely to see, but it does mean that we do so with respect for the person as an individual. Loving does not mean losing sight of our own limits and needs, but it does mean having love and respect for our own boundaries and recognizing our own emotional baggage.

Emmanuel's Book (Rodegast & Stanton, 1985) points out that love is easy when people and circumstances are the way we wish them to be. However, the true test comes when nothing is the way it "should" be, and when others are living up to none of *our* "expectations." When we can freely and totally accept and love under those conditions, when we're able to put aside our own "stuff" to see the shining light in another, we have learned the lesson of love.

SECTION II

Clinical Applications of Imagery for Getting Well

However interesting, plausible, and appealing a theory may be, it is techniques, not theories, that are actually used on people. — *P. London*

You are in charge of your state of being. You have learned to be exactly the way you are and you have the remarkable human capability to learn to be another way. Choosing ways of thinking, feeling, and doing which contribute to your health pleasures rather than your health problems is the nitty-gritty of being well. — *Ronald J. Pion*

The spacetime view of health and disease tells us that a vital part of the goal of every therapist is to help the sick person toward a reordering of his world view. We must help him realize he is a process in spacetime, and not an isolated entity in the world of the healthy and adrift in flowing time, moving slowly toward extermination. To the extent that we accomplish this task we are healers. — *Larry Dossey*

5

Stress Management I: Changing Perceptions

The happiness of your life depends upon the quality of your thoughts; therefore, guard accordingly. —*Marcus Antonius*

Perception can make whatever picture the mind desires to see. Remember this, in this lies either heaven or hell, as you elect. —*A Course in Miracles*

I saw that all things that I feared, and which feared me, had nothing good or bad in them save in so far as the mind was affected by them. —*Benedict de Spinoza*

There is considerable evidence from clinical and laboratory research that stress can influence susceptibility to cancer and other chronic diseases as well as the course of the disease itself, and that chemicals produced by the stress response (such as cortisol, adrenaline, and other catecholamines) have a profound effect on the systems of the body.

The immune, cardiovascular, endocrine, digestive, and neurological systems are designed to withstand *occasional* floods of these stress chemicals. However, when the "assaults" are frequent, daily occurrences, changes begin to happen within these systems that allow the organism to adapt to the chemicals. Those adaptations may take the form of raised blood pressure, lowered immunity, or increased blood-sugar levels, on a temporary basis. If this pressure continues, the adaptations move to chronic status, followed by the death of the organism. With this in mind, it is not surprising that life-challenging conditions are most likely to strike or exacerbate during a period in which a person is not handling stress well. Additionally, the very presence of a life-challenging situation in itself presents multiple stressors.

Whether or not a person's body experiences the ravages of stress depends upon that person's perception of the situation or the environment and how he or she interprets various circumstances. In other words, the way one perceives and handles stress critically affects whether or not the stressor has a physiological impact. The intensity of stress is determined

69

by the meaning that is assigned to it and the rules we hold about how we will cope with it.

At GETTING WELL, stress management is usually the first session of the day, and for good reason, when the personality of the typical participant is considered. One must remember that the profile of the person who chooses the GETTING WELL program includes descriptions such as "adult," "verbal," "normal" with regard to society's view, and "left-brained" as far as the thrust of his or her education. This individual is usually quite in tune with the doctrines of medicine and the scientific method—both left-brain, intellectual enterprises. As it is our philosophy to begin at each individual's particular emotional and psychological level, a stress management session is a good place to start. Usually the idea of "stress management" is nonthreatening, because being "stressed out" has a certain cachet in our culture and the elements of the stress response are almost mechanistic from a medical point of view. Stress management is essentially didactic, tapping into the comparative comfort of being in a "class" situation rather than a "therapy" setting. This session focuses on skills, strategies, and cognitive structuring, and is fundamentally the "knowledge" base of the program.

However, not infrequently we attract individuals (usually males for whatever reason) who unequivocally state that they have no stress in their lives. Frank, who grew up in a stoic European household, came into the program after surgery for a 17-pound cancerous tumor in his abdomen. His marriage was deeply flawed from a lack of communication, partly due to the long hours he spent at work. And his job position in middle management made him fodder for demands from both above and below. Yet on his first day in GETTING WELL, he stated, "I really have no stress in my life." My associate and I threw up our hands in despair. Indeed, Frank's stoicism and denial filtered the stressful events in his life directly into his tissues without even the whisper of cognitive involvement. After a few days, he admitted, "I had no idea how much wasn't right about my life, yet somehow it didn't seem right to acknowledge it. I guess it has something to do with my idea—no, my father's idea—of how a man should be."

Although most individuals are not as determined to deny stress and stressors as Frank was, most do need to spend time identifying stress and its sources in their lives. For this reason, stress management consists of 28 daily sessions, which focus on identifying stressors, building resources to deal with them, and/or learning to change one's perception of them—thereby reducing one's level of stress chemicals and increasing peace of bodymind.

One's perception of stress deeply involves one's image of the world, of oneself, and of others. Changing perceptions of "stressful" situations eventually involves a shift in which one takes "responsibility" for his or her stress—from the outside world to the place of one's innermost being.

How Images Affect the
Physiological Stress Response

We believe it is important for participants to have a good theoretical image of what happens physiologically when one approaches a stressful situation. To this end, I have made a poster, an enlarged version of Figure 2. In the position labeled "Environmental Stressors," I place a picture of the head of a roaring saber-toothed tiger gleaned from a long-ago *National Geographic*, and I tell this story *con brio*:

> The door opens, and poised in the doorway is a ferocious feline, yellowish-orange fur with deep brownish-orange stripes covering its supple body. It begins to move toward me, and I notice the sinuous muscles rippling, the white claws glinting as the fearsome animal draws stealthily and dangerously nearer. I am mesmerized by its amber eyes "burning bright in the forest of the night." As the tiger approaches my space, it eyes me hungrily, sits back on its massive haunches, and opens its steel-trap jaws to roar . . . and I notice two sabre-like teeth protruding from each side of its jaw . . . and I know that my arm or maybe even more of me is going to be breakfast for this creature . . . and I am out of here! I prepare to flee from the building and into the street, where I most assuredly will be run down by the traffic . . . but even that is better than meeting a terrible fate with this monster. But _____ suddenly stops me, crying, "Dee, wait! wait!" I trust this person so I do wait in front of those powerful jaws which are poised to bite . . . and I hear . . . "Meow," and a little orange-striped kitty cat rubs against my leg and purrs.

Then I pull out the picture of a cat and indicate that the tiger really was just a cuddly, harmless, friendly kitty. I explain that in my attempt to flee this situation, I was actually putting myself into far worse danger than I would have experienced in dealing with a cat (even if I were allergic). All the facts were correct (except, perhaps, for size, genus, and species); yet, because I *perceived* the cat as a tiger, my body responded to the life-threatening, saber-toothed tiger. At this point, we go through the physical reaction my body experienced because of my perception: racing heart, sweating, increased blood pressure, panting, etc.

This is a wonderful jumping-off place to explain the eidetic and cognitive judgment processes and how they are crucial in the response our bodies make to what are essentially neutral events in the environment. Using the poster, we look at the sensory input (sight, sound, taste, smell, textures, kinesis, etc.)—that is, the process by which the "environment" enters our being. When the sensory image has been received, an evaluation process takes place. The decision-making/judgment area of the brain asks, "Is this a threat to my survival?" The judgment is colored by everything in the past that has happened to the organism as well as, I believe, intuitive-genetic-instinctive factors. A decision is made at perhaps an unconscious level that the object of the sensory input is harmful, neutral, or

Figure 2. The Stress Response

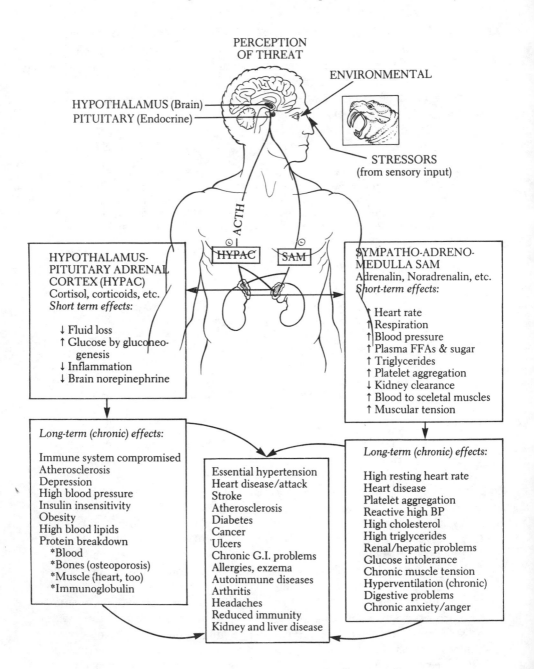

PERCEPTION
OF THREAT

ENVIRONMENTAL

HYPOTHALAMUS (Brain)
PITUITARY (Endocrine)

STRESSORS
(from sensory input)

ACTH

HYPAC   SAM

HYPOTHALAMUS-
PITUITARY ADRENAL
CORTEX (HYPAC)
Cortisol, corticoids, etc.
Short term effects:

↓ Fluid loss
↑ Glucose by gluconeo-
    genesis
↓ Inflammation
↓ Brain norepinephrine

SYMPATHO-ADRENO-
MEDULLA SAM
Adrenalin, Noradrenalin, etc.
Short-term effects:

↑ Heart rate
↑ Respiration
↑ Blood pressure
↑ Plasma FFAs & sugar
↑ Triglycerides
↑ Platelet aggregation
↓ Kidney clearance
↑ Blood to sceletal muscles
↑ Muscular tension

Long-term (chronic) effects:

Immune system compromised
Atherosclerosis
Depression
High blood pressure
Insulin insensitivity
Obesity
High blood lipids
Protein breakdown
  *Blood
  *Bones (osteoporosis)
  *Muscle (heart, too)
  *Immunoglobulin

Essential hypertension
Heart disease/attack
Stroke
Atherosclerosis
Diabetes
Cancer
Ulcers
Chronic G.I. problems
Allergies, exzema
Autoimmune diseases
Arthritis
Headaches
Reduced immunity
Kidney and liver disease

Long-term (chronic) effects:

High resting heart rate
Heart disease
Platelet aggregation
Reactive high BP
High cholesterol
High triglycerides
Renal/hepatic problems
Glucose intolerance
Chronic muscle tension
Hyperventilation (chronic)
Digestive problems
Chronic anxiety/anger

beneficial. We must remember that the area which evaluates sensory input is the only window the body has on what is happening "out there." When a decision has been made by our unconscious Supreme Court that the situation is a threat to survival, the message is conveyed to the hypothalamus (considered a part of the "brain"), which chemically communicates with the pineal or pituitary gland (generally considered the master control center for the "body").

The pituitary begins mobilizing the body for what it understands to be a threat to its survival, releasing adrenocorticotropic hormone (ACTII) as well as activating hormones for the adrenal medulla. The adrenal medulla pumps adrenaline, noradrenaline, and other catecholamines into the bloodstream, increasing heart rate and blood pressure as well as shifting blood flow from the smooth muscles of the digestive system to the skeletal muscles (to enable fight or flight). Plasma glucose, triglycerides, and free fatty acids increase, so they may be used by the body as fuel; platelet aggregation increases (aiding blood clotting); and kidney clearance is reduced.

With the activation of the adrenal cortex by ACTH, cortisol is poured into the bloodstream. Cholesterol production is increased for its fuel value and cortisol causes the pouring of glucose into the bloodstream, starting the process of gluconeogenesis, which is the creation of glucose for energy fuel to be used after the stores in the liver have been exhausted. Most frequently, glucose is created by breaking down the body's protein (muscle tissue, bones, and organs), which causes floods of insulin to allow the muscles to use the glucose. This, in turn, desensitizes the insulin receptors on the cells so that more and more insulin is required for the body to effectively use sugar fuel.

Cortisol also protects the body from loss of fluids by causing the kidneys to shut down, thus preventing loss of water, and the blood to thicken, enabling it to clot more easily and to minimize its loss from possible wounds. In addition, inflammation is cut drastically. Although this sounds like a positive feature, it actually means that the immune system stops its work during the time of threat, preventing the body from fighting microbes or cancer at the same time it is dealing with tigers!

Certainly, these changes in response to my "saber-toothed tiger" are not life-threatening; they would indeed be beneficial if a tiger were actually threatening me. Our bodies were developed hundreds of thousands of years ago, when these stress responses were necessary to give us the ability to run or fight. The main threats then may have been tigers or even other cave men, and those situations probably did not present themselves terribly frequently. Hence, there was probably plenty of time for the stress chemicals to recede or for those involved to work or run off their effect, leaving no long-term damage.

Today, however, those once-useful chemical reactions can turn toxic. Although our society has very few real tigers ready to attack us, we do encounter multiple "kitty cats" daily, which we interpret to be life-threatening tigers—and our bodies don't know any better than to respond to that image. As a result, our bodies remain in an almost constant state of physiological arousal—particularly during times of high stress. For example, when Kiecolt-Glaser and Glaser (1987) took blood samples from medical students studying for finals, they found levels of cortisol consistently higher than would be expected in people with Cushing's syndrome—a condition in which excessive cortisol levels cause diabetes, heart disease, low immunity, obesity, and osteoporosis!

As kitty cats and the stress reaction become a way of life, more permanent changes take place in the body. Blood lipids such as cholesterol and triglycerides may be continuously elevated, blood sugar may be chronically higher than normal, and the blood may thicken and clot within the vessels more easily. Resting heart rate and blood pressure are elevated, and digestive, renal, and hepatic problems become chronic. The immune system is compromised, becoming either underactive or selectively overactive (as in autoimmune disorders). The several hundred cancer cells the body normally produces in a day may go unnoticed by the immune system, giving them the opportunity to begin developing into a tumor. Atherosclerosis, chronic muscular tension, depression, anxiety, insulin insensitivity, and even obesity may result from the increased blood cortisol levels. And as the body chronically breaks down proteins to gain glucose, immunoglobulins, bones, muscle mass (the heart, too!), and other blood constituents may suffer.

As the months and years go by, this method of physiologically adapting to the environment begins to harden into specific diseases such as heart disease, stroke, diabetes, cancer, atherosclerosis, depression, panic disorder, ulcers, chronic gastro-intestinal problems, allergies, eczema, arthritis, headaches, kidney and liver disease, essential hypertension, and autoimmune diseases. It may even determine whether HIV turns into full-blown AIDS.

We are not saying these diseases are caused by stress; nevertheless, the way one perceives stress is a major factor in whether that person's genetic/environmental propensity toward a given disease is realized.

Victoria, an elegant *grande dame*, had been hospitalized for chest pains and a possible heart attack. She listened pensively as I told my saber-toothed tiger story. Finally, her eyes lit up and she related the circumstances leading to her hospitalization. She had been out on the freeway, where a "very rude chap" cut her off. She spent the next few minutes trying to exact fair retribution, made a few of her own points, and he apparently made a few points in return. Almost immediately Victoria experienced severe chest pain, and drove to the hospital. "That man cutting in front of me was a 'kitty cat,' wasn't he?" she mused. "And I nearly killed myself by reacting as though he was a saber-toothed tiger!" In many ways, Victoria was lucky to be alive to experience that epiphany. We all know of people dying of heart attacks triggered by an over-reaction to a "kitty"; however, who knows how many other people have been put at extreme risk because of a lifetime of these misinterpretations? Of course, the good news is that we *can* change those distorted images, and cause our minds and bodies to turn in healthier directions.

Modifying Images to Change the Stress Response

This section includes discussion of several techniques I have found helpful over the years in empowering people (including myself) either to change perceptions of stressful situations or train a stressor to trigger a more relaxed physiological response than it did in the past.

Systematic desensitization (SD) is a technique developed a number of years ago by Joseph Wolpe (1969) in his relaxation clinic at Temple University. SD invokes the principle of reciprocal inhibition, which simply means that one cannot be both relaxed and anxious at the same time. Wolpe believes that the things we fear in reality we also fear in imagination — thus things we no longer fear in imagination can no longer disturb us in the real situation.

In a group setting, this exercise, which takes at least an hour to complete, is best done after an introduction to the concept of subjective units of discomfort (SUDs). SUDs involves rating a variety of anxiety-producing situations from 1 to 10, with 1 indicating very deep relaxation and 10 showing a state of veritable panic.

We ask participants to choose a situation in the 6–7 range to work on. They further break the situation down into a series of successive approximations. For example, a woman is anxious about telling her husband some of her needs she feels he is not meeting. She may first see herself writing what she wants to say in a notebook; then she may see herself saying what she wants to say into the mirror. A further step might be seeing herself practicing with a friend, and then finally imaging herself telling her husband what she needs and wants.

To accomplish their goals in this area, we first have the participants relax down to a 1 or 2 on the SUDs scale, using whatever relaxation technique is comfortable for both the therapist and patient. Second, we introduce a neutral image (such as a benign street scene or a lemon being cut) to accustom them to imaging not only with vision, but also with smell, taste, sound, feel, and kinesis. Third, the subjects are re-relaxed, if necessary, and then asked to vividly image the least frightening of their scenes. If their anxiety begins to rise too high, they are told to go back to relaxing themselves before returning to the stressful image or going to the next step in imaging the full situation. When they can both image the situation and maintain relaxation at no more than a 2 on the SUDs scale, they go on to the next step, using the same procedure. Wolpe has made SD a true art form, and I strongly recommend reading the original source for this eminently practical yet immensely creative technique.

Donald Meichenbaum (1977) has used some of Wolpe's principles in designing stress inoculation (SI). His psychological concept follows the medical idea of inoculation — giving a weak dose of the actual disease to allow the healthy system to build antibodies to fight it. For this reason, he has the individual develop a set of powerful messages to himself or herself which the healthy mind can have available when "stress" tries to enter the psyche. Meichenbaum divides these self-messages into those imaged in the following order: (1) before the confrontation, (2) when feelings start to build, (3) when feelings overwhelm, and (4) when it is all over. Before the SI, have participants choose one or two situations with which they feel they are not dealing well and a set of self-messages for each of the stages of the confrontation. Again, it is advisable to read the original source in order to glean the masterful nuances of this technique for dealing with both anxiety and anger.

SI begins with muscular relaxation and then moves to images of a peaceful meadow. Next comes a rehearsal of positive, powerful self-messages. For example: "I am confident, in control, and the master of my fate; whatever happens, I can handle it; I make good decisions, and I will consistently make the best decision possible in any situation." Then the participant brings an image of the uncomfortable scenario to mind, while continuing to repeat the powerful, confident words. At this point, it may be a good idea to go back to the meadow and more relaxation. Then, he may return to the scene, saying, "I am relaxed and calm; whatever is said and done, I can handle it; just take a deep breath and relax; it's okay." The subject may go yet another time back to relaxation and a deep sense of peace and calm, and then return to the scene and make further masterful statements: "I am handling this calmly, no blowing up or freaking out for me! Keep a focus on what I have to do; look for positives and don't jump to conclusions. I'm doing wonderfully!" Then it's time to relax again before returning to the scene and continuing to affirm: "I've done a wonderful job. I can really be pleased with the progress I'm making. I didn't get exactly what I wanted, but I've learned a lot. Good for me!" Have participants mentally pat themselves on the back for the way they handled the situation, then let them return to the meadow, feeling good and powerful.

Another type of imaging, cognitive restructuring (CR), has been promulgated by Aaron Beck (1979) and his colleagues, including David Burns

(1980). In his research Beck found that a group of depressed people using tricyclic antidepressants and a depressed group using only CR did equally well, with the CR group faring slightly better in the long run than the antidepressant group. These findings and others are changing the face of psychiatry and opening the field of behavioral medicine to new psychological options.

Although CR is essentially a left-brain practice, it provides a bridge to emotions and right-brain images. Beck and Burns explain this in designing the ABCs of behavior: A is the activating event, which we frequently think is the "cause" of C, the consequent emotion. However, there is an intervening factor, B, or the belief, which makes all the difference in what C, the consequent emotion, will be. Although this is in a certain sense a simple idea, it brilliantly adumbrated the biochemical work of Candace Pert, by saying: In essence, how we think and believe has *everything* to do with how we feel and how our bodies respond to situations. If we can identify the belief and change that belief, we can change how we feel emotionally and physically. Translating this into imagery terms: The way in which one believes is essentially one's window on the world, one's world view or world image. When one changes beliefs, one changes images, so it follows that when one's image of a situation changes, one's feelings change and one's body changes accordingly.

I have made a large chart of Figure 3 (in many ways a horizontal version of Figure 2), which reflects the idea that one's beliefs are windows through which one interprets the world. Section A (activating events) is comprised of "kitty cats" or essentially neutral events in the environment which one identifies as stressors. Section B deals with those beliefs which act as panes of glass, varying from rose-colored denial to wavy distortion to a clear view of the outside world. Section C represents the possible physical, emotional, and behavioral consequences of each belief complex. These ABCs provide an easy paradigm through which participants can take responsibility for changing the beliefs that precede and affect their feelings and physical reactions. (Incidentally, *Thoughts and Feelings*, by McKay, Davis, and Fanning, is a wonderful resource for exercises in CR.)

Terri, a 41-year-old woman with lymphoma who had been in and out of remission for over eight years when she came to GETTING WELL, is an excellent example of someone for whom CR worked well. She was unsure of the salient factors in each of her remissions; however, she was aware that exacerbations came when her personal life went out of control. When she entered the program, her life was at an all-time low, and her oncologist thought she had very little chance of making it through the flare-up she was experiencing at the time. Although Terri was nearly as discouraged as she had been in the middle of her fight against drugs and alcohol several

Figure 3. The ABCs of Stress

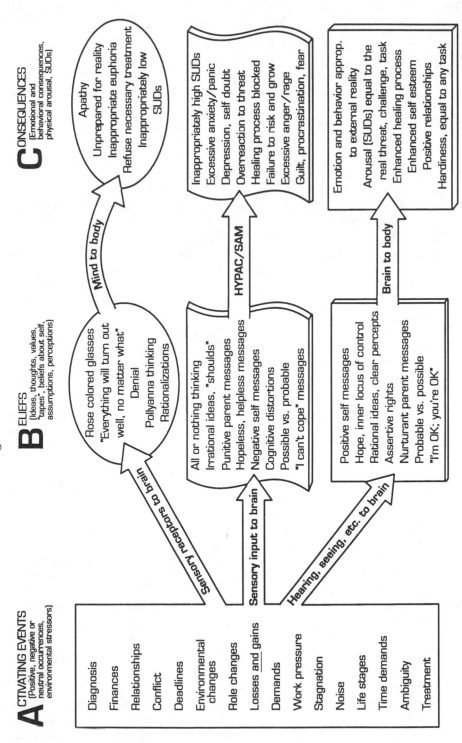

years earlier, a part of her remained determined, and she was particularly encouraged by the effects of cognitive restructuring and stress inoculation upon her handling of a bad relationship and her questions about her own sexuality.

It was wonderful seeing Terri begin to identify problem areas of her life and make some sense out of the chaos in which she was mired. First, she began to look at the dysfunctional beliefs and negative self-messages keeping her self-image ugly and powerless. Then, as she began feeling more worthy and powerful in her imagery and self-statements, she followed through in actual behaviors vis-à-vis the significant others in her life. I see her experience at GETTING WELL as getting a handle on the behaviors and images that were probably responsible for her previous remissions. She had all the resources within her; GETTING WELL merely facilitated her tapping into them. And, yes, against all odds, Terri did go into remission and has stayed in remission during the nearly three years since she enrolled in the program.

Identifying Personal Stressors

Identifying the "kitty cats" in one's life is the focus of several stress management sessions during the program's four weeks. Tubesing and Tubesing's handbook, *Structured Exercises in Stress Management* (1983), has some nice exercises to identify stressors. I also use the Holmes and Rahe Social Readjustment Rating Scale (1967), which gives a numerical weight to life events as disparate as the death of a spouse or going on vacation. The total on this scale allows us to predict with great accuracy the possibility of an illness recurring over the next year. Although this scale is not new and has been overused, it does sensitize the patient to the idea that life events which occurred one or two years *before* the illness may have had some impact on its emergence. My main problem with the Holmes and Rahe scale, however, is that it assigns numerical weights to situations without regard to an individual's *perception* of those situations.

When identifying risk factors of stress, it is important for the participant to see that short-term, traumatic stressors can cause damage, particularly if there is a great deal of rumination thereupon. However, it appears that the "little things" intricately interwoven within negative lifestyles tend to do the most emotional/physical damage. It is also vital that individuals be aware of which factors they can change and which ones are beyond their control. Reinhold Niebuhr's petition for "the courage to change those things which can be changed, the serenity to accept those things which cannot be changed, and the wisdom to know the difference," is an excellent guideline for stress management.

Our participants especially like Tubesing and Tubesing's "Stress Juggling Act," in which the authors provide a drawing of a clown juggling 10 "balls," with another half-dozen lying about on the floor. In this exercise, individuals are asked to identify on paper all the stressors they are juggling, as well as the ones they have let fall. While doing so, they are asked a series of questions about each ball: Is it something you want to continue juggling? Is it something you can control or modify? What goodies do you get from keeping a particular ball in the air? How does your body feel when you're juggling all of these? What parts of your body signal stress and tension in you? After stressors have been identified, the concept of eustress vs. distress is introduced. This is based on Selye's (1956) idea that while a great deal of stress is destructive, some stress makes life exciting and worth living. During group discussions of the insights gleaned from this exercise, profound understandings usually occur.

I also use Wolpe's SUDs scale as a way of evaluating stressors. It is possible to use a 0–10 scale or a 0–100 scale, depending on the length of time available and the precision desired in evaluation of the stressors. This is particularly useful in identifying situations which are quite relaxing, as well as situations that evoke panic, thus providing insight not only into stressful situations, but also into ones that can be excellent stress management models or images.

In addition, we often use journaling as a tool to determine problem stress areas. For example, we may ask that participants list as quickly as possible 100 things that bother them. Of course, there is some repetition, but the results of these nearly stream-of-consciousness lists are sometimes quite surprising.

Invariably, Carl Simonton's speculation that significant, unusual stress is suffered from six months to two years before the diagnosis of an illness is proven to be a reality with our participants. Although there must have been exceptions to this hypothesis, I cannot bring any to mind. I frequently charge myself with having created a Procrustean bed, of forcing data into a particular form to suit my own needs. In this case, however, when a person appears at first glance to be a counter-example, it takes only a few days for the stressors to begin making themselves known.

Bob, an easygoing university professor from North Carolina, came into GETTING WELL with a diagnosis of metastatic prostate cancer with cardiovascular complications. There was nothing upon which he could put his finger in the prior couple of years that might have been a major stressor, except the usual political hassles endemic to universities. During his first week at GETTING WELL, however, it came out that Bob's siblings had decided among themselves that he was elected to have their aging mother live with him and his wife. Taking on the mother was what any Southern gentleman should do with grace, but under his smiling surface Bob was angry. He was angry at the brothers and sisters who took no part in her care, and he was angry at his mother, who became the center of attention in the household. Queried as to when all this took place, Bob suddenly took on a strange look. "It was about a year before my diagnosis," he said.

During the time he spent in the program, Bob learned that he could be a gentleman, a loving son, and a devoted husband, while allowing his needs to be important. His mother is still with them; however, a couple of his siblings are now taking on a great deal of her care, making it possible for Bob and his wife to do the traveling they enjoy. Things aren't perfect, but Bob is feeling really good about his life. (Bob's metastatic cancer going into full remission was also a nice side effect.)

Although such stories offer definitive proof that identifying stressors is effective therapy, we must be very careful about trying to fit participants into our own cognitive boxes. The participant does not need to be confronted with our personal philosophy of precipitating stressors (no matter what we may think!). The patient's problems and hidden stressors always seem to emerge eventually, and it is so much more meaningful for the individual to have his own epiphany, rather than be fitted into our preconceived notions.

Changing Distorted Images and Cognitions

Figure 3, "The ABCs of Stress," will be useful in this section on cognitive restructuring. The main point of CR (and of stress management in general) is that stress is not found in the environment but is created within the individual. The environment is essentially neutral; one's images, thoughts, and beliefs can create stress or joy or peace, depending on how sensory stimulation is handled by the assessment areas of the brain.

Although it varies from group to group, an introduction based on points covered earlier in this chapter is usually employed. To illustrate, I ask participants to imagine a man opening the door of the group room and merely leaning in and smiling. Even a simple, almost neutral, act such as opening the door and smiling may elicit a variety of responses. I take the role of perceiving the act as being intrusive and feeling furious. On the other hand, Rebecca (here I name someone actually in the group) is happy and content to see the man. What makes the difference in our very different responses, I ask. The man is not *causing* the stress. If he were, Rebecca and I would have responded similarly. After all, it is the same man and his relationship to both of us is the same (he's a stranger), yet I was enraged, while Rebecca was happy and expectant. Therefore, the difference must rest within Rebecca and me—perhaps in the way we think and what we believe. I continue in the role of the angry victim by stating that I am a very cynical person. I tell the group that I believe people are never nice for no reason, that if a person is nice to me, he obviously wants something.

I then point out that this *stranger* had the audacity to smile at me for no reason, so he must want something from me, and I'm absolutely furious at his nerve!

On the other hand, I point out, Rebecca looks at the world in a sanguine way. She believes people are basically good, that if people are nice to her, it means they find something agreeable about her or her appearance. As a result, she felt really good inside when the man smiled at her. Imagine the differences in our physical response, based on the different ways in which we view the world! I was flooded with cortisol, adrenaline, and other catecholamines, while Rebecca was probably pumping out endorphins and other salubrious chemicals that enabled her body to function better and her mind to feel happier. In winding up, I point out to the group that this scenario indeed proves the world "out there" to be essentially neutral. We are responsible for the perceptions or feelings which create stress or peace within ourselves.

Perfectionism

Most people who enter the program are perfectionists in major areas of their lives. And I must admit that we therapists in the program are not immune to the promises and pitfalls of perfectionism. Perfectionism has served most of us well in many ways, making us acceptable to our families, helping us get through school, and sometimes helping us achieve other goals. However, when push comes to shove, perfectionism can be insidious and cruel, may keep us from attaining our goals, usually doesn't lead to happiness, and certainly doesn't enhance relationships. In fact, David Burns (1980) suggests the important lesson perfectionists must learn (perfectly) is that success in life may come in *spite* of perfectionistic standards rather than because of them.

Perfectionism can be seen as the basis of Type A behavior, as well as of the "nice guy" profile of many cancer and autoimmune disease patients. It is endemic in our mainstream culture, so much so that many people are proud of being perfectionists, despite the condition's devastating effects on the body and quality of life. In group we point out that a person who continually strives toward impossible goals not only will miss the journey of life, but will also rarely experience satisfaction and pleasure in accomplishments, taking only a momentary enjoyment in them before moving on to the next challenge. We explain that perfectionism is an all-or-nothing business — you either make the grade or you're a failure.

Initially, most participants deny being perfectionists, until we administer one of the perfectionism tests from Burns' invaluable book, *Feeling Good: The New Mood Therapy*. Test items include such statements as "If I try hard enough, I should be able to excel at anything I attempt," "I need to be right," and "An average performance is bound to be unsatisfying to me." Further, following Burns' teaching, we frequently invoke the Socratic method by gently asking, "Why would it be upsetting to you if you did goof up? What would it mean to you?"

For many people, getting rid of old beliefs, destructive to health and happiness as they may be, is like an amputation. With this in mind, we as therapists must go about this process carefully, with consideration for the person's loss and assistance in replacing the amputated belief with a more satisfying and healthy one. Perfectionionism presents a tough problem not only because it is such a mainstay for most "normal adults" in our society, but also because it seems almost a part of the DNA of most of us who are health-care providers. In protecting our own perfectionistic standards, we must avoid getting into a *folie à deux* with participants, or we run the risk of shortchanging them and ourselves.

After having participants identify perfectionistic beliefs and styles in their lives, challenging these distorted beliefs and replacing them with more salubrious ones, I like to do an imagery exercise. In this exercise, participants imagine what it would be like if they no longer had to deal with perfectionism: how their lives would change, how they would feel about themselves, how they might tackle things differently, etc. I encourage them to run a mental movie of their lives henceforth, where all-or-nothing thinking and perfectionism are not a core of their belief systems. I then suggest they act out this movie for the next several days to see how this new way of thinking works in "real life."

Handling Criticism

Handling criticism goes hand in glove with the lesson on perfectionism. Actually, criticism is an activating event on the ABC chart (Figure 3), and perfectionism is a major distorted belief that can create physical and emotional havoc when one is faced with what appears to be a rebuke. The behavioral consequences of dealing poorly with criticism include avoiding challenges and closeness, limiting one's life, or even believing something is terribly wrong with oneself—personality, body shape, or whatever.

To an individual with poor self-esteem, almost any statement may be construed as criticism, even a compliment, so it's a good idea initially to see how group members define criticism. After this introduction, we observe how a passive belief system ("I'm no good" or "I must be totally perfect and totally approved by every significant person") affects the emotions and body. We find that an aggressive belief system ("I must be 100 percent, and I'm furious when someone finds I'm not" or "What right does that dweeb have to criticize me?") churns up the stress chemicals and can lead to inappropriate behavior. On the other hand, an assertive belief system ("Just because my performance isn't perfect doesn't mean I'm unworthy" or "I can learn from feedback from others") may even lead to feeling good about oneself and have a neutral or even positive effect on the body.

Although receiving criticism is a sensitive topic, it is frequently overshadowed by the discomfort felt in giving criticism. In the latter case, a person may avoid criticizing others by stuffing his or her feelings and letting them build up until they explode in outbursts destructive to relationships. Guilt almost always accompanies that particular scenario. We like to focus on the empathic assertion formula (reflecting understanding of the other person's feelings, yet saying directly what is needed) or the feeling assertion formula for giving criticism. It is efficacious at this point to divide the group into dyads and let members both give and receive criticism using their own "scripts." Imagery work or stress inoculation similar to that which I previously described is effective in moving the learning from the cognitive arena into emotional territory.

Handling Guilt

Guilt is another *bête noire* for optimal functioning of the physical organism: It can keep the endocrine system busy spurting hormones 24 hours a day! It comes as no surprise that guilt is a major form of "manipulation" in our society, and that the proud product of our culture, the psyche of the "normal" adult, is actually pervaded by guilt.

Guilt is so important that GETTING WELL tackles it both in stress management training and in other sessions (e.g., high-level awareness). In stress management, we deal with guilt in a rather analytical manner. For example, we assume that we were not born with guilt but learn it from our early caretakers and educators. We then focus on the internalized "critic" and the ways in which everyone's societal/parental programming promoted its growth within.

First we look at the factors that determine the strength of an individual's guilt, factors such as the degree to which issues of taste or safety were mislabeled as moral imperatives, the frequency and intensity of criticism, and the frequency with which punishment was tied to parental anger or withdrawal. In their helpful book, *Self Esteem*, Matthew McKay and Patrick Fanning suggest that we hang onto those painful guilt messages because they occasionally motivate us to do something that we would not otherwise do. For example, nagging at oneself to work harder on a project will *occasionally* result in a job of which one is proud. Yet we put up with so much misery for that once-a-year or sometimes a once-in-a-lifetime "victory."

Behavior therapy tells us that the most powerful reinforcement schedule is one employing variable reinforcement. This is much more powerful than positive reinforcement received every time the behavior is presented. For example, we know if we put a couple of quarters into a cola machine, a soft drink will emerge, but we don't stand around all day putting quarters into a vending machine even though we know we will be rewarded every time we do. Bring on a slot machine, however, and many people will begin feeding it quarter after quarter with little or no immediate reward, hoping for the jackpot. We point out to the group that people invest in guilt in the same way they invest in the slot machine. Although guilt occasionally elicits a reward, one must ask if the emotional pain and the physical turmoil are worth it.

Homework for this session consists of writing down the negatives the critic is feeding to the individual. The therapist must urge the participant not to feel guilty about the number of negative messages encountered in a day's time. As a second step, the individual may confront the critic's negativity by shouting (inwardly), "That's a lie!" or "You're not telling me the truth!"

Another exercise that participants and I like is imaging the critic or the guilt on one's shoulder. It may be slimy, green, and yucky, or a mean, filthy, little being, or anything representing the symbol of guilt for the person. In this imagery the guilt is seen whispering or shouting messages into the person's ear. When the individual gets fed up, he or she pulls the guilt off the shoulder, throws it to the floor, and stomps it to oblivion. Bits of the slime may remain, which can be pulled off and smashed also. This exercise elicits laughter and is extremely valuable in shifting perceptions.

"Shoulds"

"Shoulds" are the fodder from which guilt is created. It's been my observation that the ugly, dangerous guilt does not emerge from things people *should* feel guilty about, such as killing someone or cheating someone out of money. It's not disobedience of the Ten Commandments that brings the problems; rather, it is violation of the Eleventh Commandment, "Thou should always be the perfect spouse and parent," or the Twelfth Commandment, "Thou should always live up to others' expectations," or the Thirteenth Commandment, "Thou should always do any activity thou tryeth perfectly."

Most shoulds have been generated by our need to feel loved, to belong, to please parents, teachers, and/or peers, and to feel good about ourselves. All too frequently, they are values and beliefs based on our needs rather than on some higher morality. Yet we frequently treat our shoulds as somehow coming from God or some other supreme ethical authority. However, most people's shoulds are internalized control measures taken by peers, parents, and culture to manipulate behavior. It is amazing how much personal power is given to those shoulds.

The first step in breaking the tyranny of the shoulds is to identify them. Then comes an examination to decide which of the shoulds reflect deep and healthy values and which reflect a loss of personal power from trying to be "a good little girl or boy." The next step is challenging the shoulds and perhaps revising them from "always" or "never" statements into personal preferences. We suggest that, rather than seeing them as ironclad, the participant ponder how each "rule" fits the specific situation and its outcome.

A nifty little imagery exercise has self-esteem confronting the horde of shoulds. We suggest the participants visualize self-esteem as a judge who decides the fate of the shoulds, or we encourage them to design their own confrontations. The most interesting and creative images are done by the members themselves with very little direction from the therapist. Processing what each participant imaged is always fun, and it's enlightening when each has been the director and producer of his or her own inner drama.

Learned Optimism

One of our therapists, Carolyn Peterson, M.S., M.A., has designed a Sunday morning stress management session centered around the work of one of her (and my) heros, Martin Seligman, and has been kind enough to let me use her "script." She has found his audiotape, Learned Optimism (a companion piece to his 1991 book), to be an excellent instrument to conveying the vast importance of his work to individuals in a quick, easily understood, and participatory manner.

Peterson describes some of Seligman's early experiments with dogs related to learned helplessness, which he has used to teach humans to live more optimistically. She then explains:

Seligman is concerned with our "explanatory style," a method learned in childhood and adolescence for explaining setbacks to oneself which determines whether we rise above failure or become one with it. It consists of three crucial dimensions: permanence, pervasiveness, and personalization. Persons with a pessimistic style believe that bad events will last forever, while those with an optimistic style believe they are temporary. Example: "You never talk to me" (permanent); "You haven't talked to me lately" (temporary). Pessimistic persons make universal explanations while optimistic persons make specific ones. Example: "Books are useless" (universal); "This book is useless" (specific). Pessimistic persons blame themselves while optimistic persons blame other people or circumstances. Example: "I have no talent at poker" (internal); "I have no luck at poker" (external).

At this point Peterson administers Seligman's optimism test. She then says:

> If your scores indicate that you tend to respond pessimistically, you can take heart, for Dr. Seligman offers exercises for training oneself to think optimistically. Borrowing from the "ABC model" of theorist Albert Ellis, he shows how patterns of thinking can result in predictable outcomes. *Adversity* can be almost anything from a crying baby to a leaky faucet. Your *beliefs* are how you interpret the adversity. The *consequences* are your resultant feelings and actions. *Distraction* and *disputation* are intervention techniques: to distract, you interrupt your thought pattern; to dispute, you argue against your beliefs. *Energization* is the relief and release one feels after successfully disputing the beliefs and changing the consequences. Learn to identify your beliefs as they appear and apply the ABCDE formula to them. As Seligman says, "Learned optimism works not through an unjustifiable positivity about the world but through the power of non-negative thinking."

Peterson goes on to discuss some of Seligman's examples and gives the participants homework assignments from the book or tape. She concludes:

> Since the core of pessimism is helplessness, since helplessness is a major form of stress, and since stress suppresses the immune system, you may be able to enhance your health by learning and practicing these techniques for becoming optimistic.

Emma, a 45-year-old woman with a rare, "fatal" liver disease, was hard to persuade that she belonged at GETTING WELL. She worried about the cost, although her insurance fully covered her stay in the program; she felt she should not leave her husband alone, though he was far healthier than she; and she felt guilty doing something just for herself and her own health and enjoyment, because she thought she really had not "earned" it. Emma was awaiting a liver transplant, and we finally convinced her that she could wait just as conveniently and perhaps more productively at GETTING WELL.

From the beginning, Emma manifested great resistance to any penetration of her ironclad belief system, which was full of shoulds, guilt, perfectionism, pessimism, and fear of criticism. After a week we were beginning to question our initial intuitive feelings that she belonged in the program. Around day nine, we did the guilt exercise. As Emma began to rid herself exuberantly of the green, slimy guilt on her shoulder, she exclaimed with tears in her eyes, "I don't have to shoulder this garbage anymore!" After that crack appeared in her armor, the rest of her rigid beliefs began to crumble, and Emma's skepticism started to fade. As she felt more and more comfortable, the truth came tumbling out: Her "perfect" marriage was an iron prison, her life seemed empty and meaningless to her, people always disappointed her, and she was deeply disappointed in herself. (Because this is not an atypical pattern, it's one of the reasons we require a *minimum* of 14 days in the program.)

Once her cognitive restructuring and personal reconstruction began, everything started falling into place for Emma. Emma's husband chose not to take an active part in the program with her, and she reluctantly accepted the fact that he was not going to change. Despite this, Emma was radiant as she declared, "Sure, I'd like him to change, but he isn't going to. But it's very powerful knowing that I can change what's inside me, so I don't have to suffer because things aren't the way I want them to be."

She delighted in being "mediocre and enjoying it" in areas in which she had previously been guilty and perfectionistic, and this attitude change, in turn, enabled her to be less disturbed by criticism. As time went on, Emma became not only deeply involved in life, but also thoroughly enjoyed it. Her physician was amazed by the startling change in her liver enzymes, and we delighted in seeing her previously yellow eyes turn blue-white once again. During the year-plus that she has been in the follow-up group, Emma's eyes are her Pinocchio's nose, as they tell the world whether or not she is following her truth. Of course, she continues under the care of a physician; however, when she sees her eyes beginning to yellow, she looks at her dysfunctional beliefs and at how she is perceiving her situation instead of looking in the medicine cabinet. Although she is active in her liver transplant support group, it is quite likely that she may not need the surgery, and she now exudes optimism and joy rather than her earlier wariness. Indeed, she has created a miracle.

Handling Anxiety and Panic

With the diagnosis of life-challenging illness, many competent, "normal" people develop severe anxiety, agoraphobia, and sometimes full-blown panic disorder. All of these states are characterized by difficulty in dealing with ambiguity or the unknown. Of course, there are many control issues involved, particularly in the case of those with an outer locus of control. In dealing with this anxiety or panic, we focus on relocating the locus of control *within* the person—essentially trading control of people, events, and body for inner power.

A number of years ago some colleagues and I developed the REAP (see Figure 4) method of dealing with anxiety and panic. With a few changes, it can also be used to handle anger or other difficult emotions. REAP is an acronym for: (1) Recognizing and accepting the anxiety, (2) Evaluating the anxiety and the distortions that may be making it worse, (3) Acting or employing some anxiety-reducing behaviors, and (4) Preventing anxiety by assuming some lifestyle changes that will increase peace of mind. Figure 4

Figure 4. REAP the Benefits of Anxiety

Anxiety, or fear, is a gift we are given at birth. The fear/flight response is a survival mechanism. It has the same physiological and emotional responses whether the anxiety is real or imagined. We can learn to REAP the survival and life-enhancing effects of fear and minimize the harmful sickness-producing aspects. Use the energy of anxiety for positive accomplishments. Remember—stress under control gives our lives stimulation, excitement and feelings of accomplishment.

Recognize and accept—Learn the "symptoms" of anxiety and accept the fact that you are anxious without belittling yourself. Remember that it is human to feel anxiety. It's okay to feel anxious. No putdowns!

depersonalization	indecisiveness	negative self-messages
rapid heartrate	avoidance	fatigue
shortness of breath	overeating	restlessness
feelings of unreality	crying	faint feelings
perceptual distortions	"shoulds"	preoccupation
voice shaking	insomnia	sweating
burst of adrenaline	panic	low self-esteem

Evaluate
1. Take a SUDS level. The evaluation itself may bring the anxiety down.
2. Is it real or imagined anxiety?
3. Can I do something about it. Can I really make a change? Or do I need to accept what is happening and "float" or let go?
4. Is it "probable" or merely "possible"? Am I being too "creative"? Have I adequately evaluated the situation as far as its probable reality?
5. Evaluate cognitive distortions. Does my belief system match reality? Are my self-messages accurate or do they reflect an unrealistic pessimism?

Act—Employ some specific anxiety-reducing behaviors
1. Relaxation, deep breathing, letting go, "floating."
2. Exercise—Take a walk, jog, bike, tennis, etc.
3. Change to nonwork activity—take a reading, relaxation, exercise, social break instead of a coffee break. Give yourself a change of pace!
4. Divert the anxiety—give yourself something else to worry about! Do a puzzle, solve a word problem, concern yourself with someone else's problems, do some sewing or woodworking.
5. Face something you have avoided—the phone call you need to make, the "homework" you need to do, the person you need to see, the confrontation that is essential, whatever small or large thing about which you have procrastinated.
6. Be nutritionally sound. Cut down on caffeine, refined sugars, and additives that may give you "flashes" of anxiety or panic.
7. Change an ingrained behavior pattern. Make a positive change in your habits. Begin being assertive with a family member, start saying no to friends, start eating breakfast every morning, etc. Make changes that get you in control of your life. You are in charge—start feeling in charge!

Prevent—Assume some lifestyle changes that will reduce overall anxiety
1. Regular relaxation, aerobic exercise, good health diet.
2. Regularly evaluating and changing distorted and negative thought habits. Learn to relabel each situation. Keep a set of positive "flash cards."
3. Regularly focus on the task at hand, rather than focus on anxiety feelings.
4. Relieving the fear of the unknown—more training, reading on the subject, learning a new skill, talking with others with similar difficulties.
5. Regularly building your social support system, being assertive, being open and honest with friends, family, and acquaintances.
6. Regular stress inoculation. Rehearse situations ahead of time, either in imagery or practicing by yourself or with someone else.

shows the REAP handout—admittedly dense and solid, but still a wonderful left-brain anchor for a terrorized right brain.

People tend to fight anxiety, which seems to make them even more anxious and panicky. The trick to "conquering" anxiety is to let go, to float with it, flow with it, and even welcome it into one's being. I use the analogy of a wave coming toward a person. If the individual fights the wave and tries to stop it, he or she will surely be bowled over by it. However, if the person floats with the wave, he or she can ride it to the crest and down, until it gently dissipates on the shore. When one can change an inner belief and come to know that ambiguity, change, or anxiety are okay—that they can actually be "friends"—wonderful things begin to happen. Most importantly, personal power begins to take the place of the need to control.

Although 53-year-old Shanna was dealing with chronic pain, her main reason for coming to GETTING WELL was her debilitating panic disorder. She was frankly too scared to even *begin* working on REAP. While John Shaffer was doing a workshop on transformational fantasy for our patients, he took Shanna into her "anxiety room," where she had a full-blown panic attack. He then skillfully guided her into handling the attack with her own powerful imagery skills, letting her know that the power she possessed, which allowed her to create such a momentous physical reaction from an image, could also create peace and well-being for her. This experience gave Shanna a safer unconscious foundation to begin work on some of the REAP strategies, and she started making wonderful progress. When she returned home to Ohio, the psychologist who had referred her to GETTING WELL called and asked, "What sort of a magic pill do you have down there? Shanna's progress is remarkable, and she and I are beginning to make great strides." Shanna still has a great deal of work to do; however, as she continues with her therapist in Ohio, she is already beginning to live her new life.

Handling Loss and Depression

My associate for many years, Phil Toal, designed a wonderful stress management session on handling loss. He defined loss as "any change that is perceived as one having less than before the change." This includes the loss of loved ones or friends, the loss of physical functioning, or the loss of a familiar lifestyle. In his sessions, Toal followed Elizabeth Kübler-Ross' (1969) stages of loss: (1) shock and denial, (2) anger, (3) bargaining, (4) depression, and (5) acceptance.

Identifying the physical symptoms of grief seems to be important in helping participants accept the fact that they may be experiencing loss.

For example, people may feel a hollowness in the stomach, tightness in the chest, tightness in the throat, oversensitivity to noise, a sense of depersonalization, lack of energy, muscular weakness, dry mouth, and shortness of breath, but not be aware that these are physical symptoms of grief.

Toal has suggested that participants (1) accept reality, actualize the loss, and experience the pain, (2) adjust to an environment in which the loss is apparent, (3) eventually withdraw the emotion and reinvest it, perhaps into a new goal, (4) focus on the loss, not on the circumstances of it, (5) get as much comfort and support as possible, (6) realize that feelings of shock, injustice, and unfairness will delay recovery, and that one must give oneself permission to grieve, (7) put off major decisions that don't have to be made immediately, (8) maintain contact with a physician, (9) face up to feelings and accept feelings of helplessness (but see that one is not helpless), (10) assimilate both cognitive and emotional components of what has happened, (11) be patient with those who say the wrong thing, and (12) realize that it is okay to express grief.

During this process, Toal points out that grief comes in waves, that even after one has accepted the loss there may be periods of profound sadness which may actually preserve the positive aspects of what was lost.

Daryll, a 35-year-old musician and composer, was devastated by MS nearly 18 months after his first wife died from leukemia and a month or so after he had married again. He had been through "all the stages of grieving" during his first wife's courageous fight for her life, and had looked forward to a new life in his marriage. Unfortunately, his MS became worse, and finally his wife had to support him, which in turn began to create disharmony in the marriage. After Daryll entered GETTING WELL, he began dealing with the loss of his first wife, as well as his loss of role and functions engendered by the MS. At one point he admitted that he had been depressed for as long as he could remember. He recalled the traumatic death by drowning of a younger sister and how neither he nor his parents had ever totally dealt with her death. Running and hiding became a life pattern in handling loss and disappointment.

When Daryll's wife came for a week's visit in the program, it was obvious not only that she had many issues of her own to deal with, but also that the marriage faced great difficulties. Although Daryll had made wonderful personal strides of grieving his sister, dealing with his first wife's death, and handling the devastation of MS, he was not prepared for the loss of his marriage. However, he and his wife separated several months after he returned home. Daryll nevertheless continued to work on the principles he had learned at GETTING WELL, and when I talked to him by phone not too long ago, he was quite optimistic. "I'm really surprising myself," he told me, "I thought I couldn't physically get along without her, yet I'm doing well. I'm still working through the stages of loss, but I am facing things, not hiding. I feel this is a transforming experience rather than just a loss. I'm sad, but I feel good!"

Lessons for the Author/Clinician

My training as a clinician was in many senses traditional but with a strong behavioral influence. Despite the move from the mentor-student relationship of more traditional models toward the partnership of therapist and client implicit in behavior therapy, a discreet distance continued to be *de rigeur* in the therapeutic situation. Then, as GETTING WELL began to materialize, I realized that the only authentic therapeutic relationship had to be a human-human one. Not only must the therapist be the teacher, but he or she must also be the student. In this section, I will share the lessons I have learned as a student of GETTING WELL, a novitiate in becoming fully human.

With a couple of decades of teaching assertiveness, cognitive restructuring, and anger/anxiety resolution under my belt, I felt I could deal fairly well with most things that might come along as I developed this program. Despite my convictions, however, many times I was forced to say to myself, "This *really* is a saber-toothed tiger" or "This is a *true* calamity, and there is very little I can do about it." In taking on the design and implementation of this program, I find I have taken on the burdens and blessings of a life-challenging condition. I don't want to discourage anyone interested in implementing such a program, but major challenges (and also major joys) have become a part of my daily life. In order to survive physically, emotionally, psychologically, and spiritually, I've had to struggle with and change major ways of thinking.

One of my own struggles has been with "perfectionism." Although my family never openly pushed perfectionism (e.g., "We don't care what your grades are, we just want you to do your best"), the message was "With your potential, you can do anything in the world you want to do." Thus, I saw that it was okay for my clients to change their perfectionistic strivings into "average" performances, but it certainly was not okay for me to do so. In addition, I strongly believed that letting go of my grandfather's adage, "A job worth doing is worth doing well," would somehow be letting go of Grandad, whom I had dearly loved. (I actually found that giving up Grandad's injunction gave me more room to embrace my memories of him as a fun-loving, creative explorer of the unknown.) But it's hard to give up perfectionism, because most of us believe that if we do so, we'll become incompetent at best and bag ladies at worst.

It took awhile for me to realize that "A job worth doing is worth doing," no matter how incompletely. For example, I had to convince myself that it's worth playing the guitar just to enjoy yourself, it's okay to take a book back to the library after reading only nine pages, and you're still a good human being even if you didn't convince that physician of the benefits of the program. Gradually, I discovered that the truth is *you actually may become more "competent" when you're not worried about being perfect!* There's another plus: I have to admit that I like to be liked, so it's nice to find that people actually like me more when I make mistakes and am flawed, but human, than when I'm "perfect."

I'm getting better at cognitive restructuring, too. I spent most of my working career at a major hospital where I felt protected and where there were no extreme "highs" or "lows." I got along with just about everyone and, even though I felt somewhat limited in my creative life, I knew what to expect. Going out on my own as a "private contractor" was quite a contrast. I remember someone saying, "If you don't take risks, you won't have much fear; of course, you won't have much of anything else either." I took those risks.

After a couple of debacles with the administration of the new hospital and with "trusted" associates shortly after I started GETTING WELL, I realized two things: (1) These incidents were perhaps the very best thing that could have happened for the program in the long run, and (2) I never wanted to feel that devastated and destroyed again in my life. What a pity, I thought, that there is such a painful time lapse before one realizes that there is a "pony in the manure." I made up my mind to label any future "disasters" as "the best thing that has ever happened to me." That may sound a bit like Pollyanna, but it has worked! And it has turned out to be true in virtually every case.

The overall stress management lesson I have learned is that what's out there really *is* neutral, and I alone am responsible for the stress I experience. This responsibility gives me power, for now I can perceive the environment in whatever way is most useful and least painful for me. I can change what's happening in my body merely by changing my beliefs, images, and perceptions. And this is the lesson I want to role model for participants in GETTING WELL.

6

Stress Management II: Assertive Communication, Survivorship Skills, and Goal-Setting

If people would dare to speak to one another unreservedly, there would be a good deal less sorrow in the world a hundred years hence. — *Samuel Butler*

He that respects himself is safe from others; he wears a coat of mail that none can pierce. — *Henry Wadsworth Longfellow*

If I am not for myself, who will be for me? If I am not for others, who am I for? And if not now, when? — *The Talmud*

In the preceding chapter we established that the basis of stress management rests on one's ability to change one's perceptions about distressing life situations. This chapter continues that emphasis, while offering some valuable tools for shifting one's environment, if that is possible. Although communicating assertively almost always requires an image of oneself as powerful, valid, and worthy, that sense of worthiness can be developed by practicing behaviors which would naturally emanate from that image of worthiness. In other words, images and behaviors have a feedback loop very similar to the bodymind loop, and one can intervene at a variety of places on that loop to create shifts.

Assertive communication, conflict resolution, handling the stress of life-challenging conditions, survivorship skills, and goal-setting are all part of the logical, left-brain infrastructure, which hopefully will provide a strong basis for a shift to that healing right-brain epiphany: "I *really am* a worthy, deserving, loving, lovable, precious human being." We *all* deserve to feel that.

Most of the tools in this chapter are simple ones—so simple that we, as professionals, may overlook them or believe they are too basic for the high-level-functioning individuals with whom we are working. I have consistently been amazed at how these simple assertiveness lessons have struck resonant chords with the most knowledgeable of participants, propelling them to a higher level of awareness of their own personal power and healing potential. Because this book is written for health-care professionals with such a range of training, the stress management exercises are described in detail. Although such detail may be excruciating for some, it will be helpful to others.

Assertiveness Training

Wolpe found that when people openly and honestly express their needs, feelings, and desires, while respecting the feelings and rights of others, their subjective units of discomfort (SUDs) are lowered dramatically. Wolpe alluded to the idea that when people suppress their feelings, they suffer high levels of anxiety, discomfort, or depression, as well as physical problems. For this reason, assertiveness training and communication skills became an integral part of behavior therapy and, later, of behavioral medicine. The concept of assertiveness (as opposed to aggression or passivity) fits beautifully with GETTING WELL's philosophy that achieving health and wholeness involves allowing oneself to image and become who one was born to be, and to love and nurture oneself unconditionally—the basis for giving unconditional love and respect to others.

Depending on the group, we may spend more or less time on the basics of assertion, such as differentiating among aggressive, passive, and assertive behaviors. An important point is that almost any behavior can be considered assertive if it is freely and openly *chosen*. The essence of assertiveness training is learning to act and feel not by default, but with choice. Ideally, we respond to the world from a core belief in our own worth, resourcefulness, and power.

Formulas for Assertive Communication

At some point in the 28-day cycle of stress management training we teach formulas for assertive communication. The first formula, the simple assertion, has one step: It is simply an open, honest, direct statement of a request, an opinion, a question, a feeling, or a need. For example: "No," "I like the way you did that," "I need some help."

The second formula, the empathic assertion, has two steps: (1) showing understanding and recognition of the other person's feelings, yet (2) assertively stating what one needs. For example: "(1) I can tell that you really care what happens to me, yet (2) this is a decision I need to make for myself." This is a particularly powerful assertion because it forces one person to really get into the thoughts and intentions of the other, and possibly to perceive the goodness of his/her intention—or at least the validity of his/her position. Taking the other individual into consideration requires less boldness of the novice and creates a win/win situation.

The third formula, the feeling assertion, has three steps: (1) non-accusingly describing the situation or the behavior in question, (2) stating one's feelings (*not* one's opinion), and (3) asking for a change. For example: "(1) *When* I am criticized in front of others, (2) *I feel* embarrassed and hurt. (3) *I'd prefer* that if you need to tell me something you do it in private."

The fourth formula, the confrontal assertion, has four steps: (1) ask for private time to talk to the person, (2) point out the facts in a non-accusing manner, (3) check areas in which you may not understand the situation, and (4) ask for the changes you need. For example: "(1) I need to talk to you privately. (2) It seems to me that our communication is not what it has been in the past. I've noticed that you watch TV while I am telling you about my day. (3) Maybe I'm being supersensitive, but we just don't seem as close. Am I off base? (4) I'd like to find out what the problem is so that we can get our relationship back on track." This formula can be expanded to deal with major relationship difficulties.

We may offer a series of vignettes or have the participants come up with their own situations. (Practicing one's response in a variety of formulas is empowering and stabilizing, particularly for those who feel their lives are falling apart at the seams.) After the vignettes, participants are asked to image a difficult assertiveness situation and practice imagery responding to this situation assertively. Further, we ask them to practice using these formulas with other participants, family, and friends until the formulas become part of their lives, helping to create images of themselves as powerful, resourceful people.

Assertive Rights

Getting people in touch with their assertive rights is a crucial part of assertive communication. We list on the board the rights group members feel they have as people. We may add some of the rights gleaned over the last couple of decades from books on assertiveness, as well as from clients. After we talk about the importance of making these rights available to oneself as well as to others, we ask each person to choose a right he or she has some difficulty accepting. Then we conduct a group relaxation and request that participants image themselves as totally accepting the rights they have chosen in all aspects of their lives. Following that we ask: How does it feel? How do you behave? What do you say? How do others respond to you? How does your life change?

I usually give the group three to five minutes to explore the possibilities. Then I suggest, "Imagine that this right has now been taken from you. What are your feelings? What is the effect on your body, on how you present yourself?" etc. Allow no more than one minute to explore this, then bring back the imagery of accepting the right and suggest that they "act as if" they have that right for the rest of the day. Remind them, too, that if this imagery practice is done only once a day for the next week, this right can be theirs for the rest of their lives. After the exercise, we process the feelings. It is always surprising how much emotion is elicited by taking away the right after it has been given. Although this exercise requires only a few minutes, it is amazing what images of empowerment and resourcefulness it brings forth (if it is practiced).

Making Requests, Expressing Feelings

People who always smile, never tell anyone their troubles, and neglect their own needs put themselves at risk of becoming ill. When feelings are repressed over a long period of time, the body frequently pays a price. Expressing needs and feelings is a major tool for reducing stress and the resultant physiological arousal. (While making this point in the group, it may be useful to refer to Figure 2 [p. 72] and reiterate the toxic effects of stuffing feelings). Being able to express needs and feelings builds the image of the self as valuable and okay.

We discuss the benefits of being able to express oneself honestly and directly to family and friends, as well as to physicians and other caregivers. Participants often come up with ideas, such as being able to request a change in the environment, to ask for help, to ask for information or advice, to ask for intimacy, or to request a "fair shake."

We explore the rights involved in expressing oneself freely, including the right to make requests, the right to express feelings and opinions, and the right to be told "no" without feeling unworthy. People hesitate to express their feelings or needs because they feel that they don't have the right or because they are afraid to hear "no" as an answer. The "myth of obligation," wherein the other person will not be able to say no and will resent the requester for having obligated him or her, may also prevent people from making requests. The "myth of the good friend" may be another roadblock: This myth suggests that if another person really cared for you, he or she would know what you need and feel without your having to ask; if you have to ask, it makes filling the request without value. As we examine factors that keep people from making requests and expressing feelings, we find significant blockages to their fully becoming themselves; therefore, these factors need to be thoroughly probed.

Refusing Requests, Saying No,
and Taking the Pressure off

Bernie Siegel (1986) has found that the patients who are the most uncooperative, refusing to put on the standard hospital gown or asking all kinds of questions before submitting to tests, are the ones most likely to be survivors. Accordingly, long-term survivors have "poor" attitudes, say many physicians and nurses. Siegel found that these so-called "problem patients" were also rapid healers, that long-term survivors possessed the most active immune systems.

There are other advantages to being able to refuse requests. These include: choosing one's own priorities, saving energy for the important things, developing an inner locus of control, and avoiding the buildup of stress chemicals that compromise the immune, cardiovascular, gastric, and other systems. Among other benefits, patients may receive better medical and other professional care, because doctors and other professionals may actually respect assertive behavior (although they may initially be annoyed by it).

We usually ask people to consider the consequences of *not* saying no, such as having a lack of self-respect, feeling like a victim or pawn, having no time to accomplish priorities, or feeling angry and resentful. We try to elicit the rights involved in refusing requests, such as the right to say no without feeling guilty, the right to choose one's lifestyle, the right to make decisions about one's body, and the right to decide whether one should live up to the expectations of others. Participants are asked to image themselves saying no in a variety of situations, being direct, and honestly expressing wants, desires, needs, feelings, or reservations. We also review the assertive communication formulas and try them on for size in refusing requests.

Assertive Communication and Receiving Messages

Clear communication is an essential element of stress management. Figure 5, adapted from Gottman et al. (1976), is a blueprint of the communication process. Although the figure's message is simple, and most of us have internalized its meaning *most* of the time, problems frequently materialize when the image of the intention of clear communication has disappeared.

Good communication takes place when the *intent* of the message equals the *impact* on the listener, when the *content* matches the *feeling* message of the communication, and when *leveling* and *editing* are both employed when sending the message.

Leveling involves making a direct statement of what one thinks, feels,

Figure 5. The Communication Process (adapted from Gottman et al., 1976)

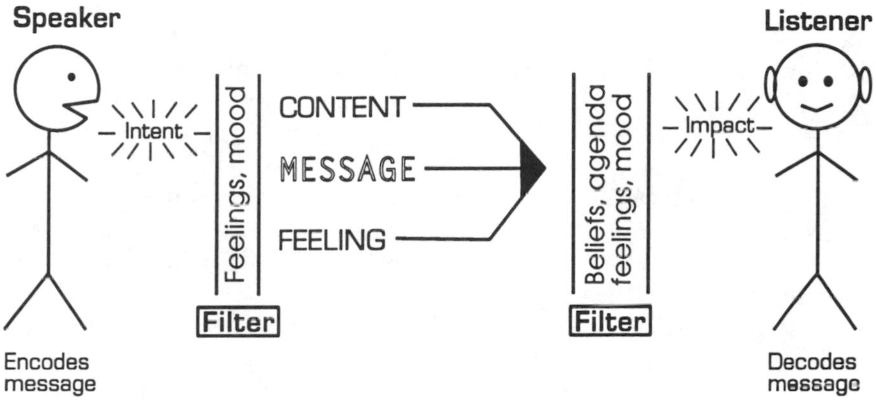

Speaker   **Listener**

— Intent — | Feelings, mood | CONTENT — / MESSAGE — / FEELING — | Beliefs, agenda feelings, mood | —Impact—

Filter   Filter

Encodes message   Decodes message

or wants in a situation—for example, expressing oneself at the time rather than letting grievances build, being appropriate in the time and place chosen for leveling, claiming ownership of one's feelings, and liberally using empathic assertions as described above. Editing, on the other hand, involves removing incendiary elements that shut down communication, such as statements containing *always, never, should, ought,* etc., insults, "mind reading," and changing the subject.

Receiving the message accurately involves active listening, the use of open-ended questions, empathic reflection, being aware of past experience that may distort the reception of the message, and attending to one's body language.

We usually discuss sending the message and receiving the message on different days. Of course, both lessons are most effective if group members use their own situations as communication examples. I've found it quite helpful for participants to get a mental picture of the above communication paradigm and, with their eyes closed, fit their particular communication problem into the model, particularly attending to their own "filters." We are often amazed at what comes up in our members' imaginations, from a "bear of anger" preventing the completion of a message to "thinning gas" not allowing a message to be expressed with its full intent.

Expressing and Handling Anger

Several of our stress management sessions deal with the issue of anger. Society gives mixed messages about anger, most of which suggest that anger is not to be expressed, especially by women, or that it can be expressed only through limited avenues. It is my belief that the suppression or bottling and inappropriate expression of anger are major factors (both cause and effect) in chronic and life-challenging conditions. I think there is some truth, although far from a cause-effect connection, to the idea that different styles of emotion characterize different disease processes. For example, hypertension and rheumatoid arthritis clearly seem to involve underlying anger. Heart disease patients may openly express anger and hostility. (However, this may be a defense against a deep hurt or a "broken heart.") I have known several multiple sclerosis patients who were admittedly so angry they could kill. Is the muscular immobilization of the disease protecting them from acting out their rage? I don't know, but I have seen incredible connections between a person's feelings about and style of handling anger, on the one hand, and the disease that person has, on the other. Be aware there is a difference between my making that connection and putting that onus on the person. In general, I find pronouncements of this sort (or any attempt to put an individual into a category) to be absolutely counterproductive. Given a safe environment, participants will invariably make these connections themselves.

At GETTING WELL we assume that emotions are repressed at the expense of the body and the psyche. And, because of our cultural "rules," anger is most frequently the emotion repressed, suppressed, or redirected. During our sessions, we initially make the point that anger is a natural emotion and is, in fact, a basic survival tool, without which we would be dead in a matter of hours. Our society's efforts to be "elite" and "above the animals" have forced its members to renounce anger or to channel it in ways that are destructive to their bodies or to mankind. We make the point that when we can recognize anger and express it appropriately, then it neither develops into disease nor explodes inappropriately.

Because it is frequently difficult for group members to recognize anger, the first order of business is to have them identify signs of anger within themselves, such as voice volume, muscular tension, pounding heart, withdrawal, or rapid breathing. After anger has been recognized, we make the point that it is okay to be angry. Next, we look at beliefs that can exaggerate anger or affect one's ability to deal with anger—for example, "The world should be fair," "It's awful if things are not the way I want them," or "People and situations should turn out better than they do." Participants then identify their own constellation of irrational beliefs and observe the ways in which those beliefs skew their emotional and physiological reaction to the anger.

At this point, challenges to the irrational beliefs are developed (cognitive restructuring). These challenges may take the form of creating new self-statements about one's beliefs or about how the person can handle the anger situation. Some examples are: "Easy does it. Remember to keep your sense of humor and laugh at yourself if you can," "The world isn't fair and things aren't always going to turn out as you wish, but you can handle it," or "As long as I keep my cool, I'm in control." Then we have the participants look at the consequences of their altered beliefs. It is important for people to write down their new ABCs under the old dysfunctional ones. This is a powerful, left-brain activity with the potential to change participants' images and the paradigms for handling anger.

After the cognitive restructuring, we look at possible ways to deal with anger. For example, we consider the possibility of redirecting anger through physical activity or journaling, drawing, or writing a letter (which will be burned) to the object of the anger, tearing up old phone books, or beating pillows. The patient may choose relaxation therapy, or decide to take a shower, where screaming and crying can be done to the heart's content. Of course, the most appropriate solution is expressing the anger directly to the source, using one of the formulas for assertive communication. We encourage people actually to rehearse in group what they wish to say; if there is time, we may use stress inoculation or systematic desensitization.

The work we do on anger in stress management tends to be mainly "left-brain." A variety of other techniques for handling anger show up in Chapters 7, 8, 12, 16, and 17.

Expressing and Handling Tender
Feelings and Compliments

Although expressing and accepting anger is quite difficult, it is almost as tough to communicate tender feelings and accept compliments. Again, we look at the beliefs that make expression or acceptance difficult, beliefs such as, "I'll make myself too vulnerable," "They're trying to get something out of me," or "They don't know how bad I really am."

In this part of the exercise, we allow plenty of time for our "compliment circle," giving each participant an opportunity in the "hot seat." As we go around the circle, each of the other participants gives one or two positive expressions of feelings to the one in the hot seat. The receiver is allowed only to say "thank you" for the compliments and must resist the urge to contradict or diminish what has been said. This is a potent exercise from both perspectives, because it gives the sender practice in finding something positive about the person, whether superficial or insightful, and it is a positive exercise in acceptance for the receiver. Participants often start out feeling extremely uncomfortable about this session, but it usually ends with tears of joy and feelings of tenderness all around.

Lola is an excellent illustration of the healing powers of assertiveness. Lola, a 68-year-old woman diagnosed with lung cancer, emphysema, and heart disease, was quite ambivalent about entering the program since her husband, who'd had a crippling arthritic condition for 40 of the 48 years of their marriage, could not manage without her. "I've tied his shoes for him every day for nearly 40 years," she explained. "I don't think he can get along without me." We suggested, since her physician had given her six months to live, that maybe it was time for her to take care of some of her own needs. "It is *my* time," she kept murmuring under her breath for the remainder of the interview, "I need to take care of Lola for a change."

A major step in her assertiveness training was deciding to enter GET-TING WELL despite protests from her husband (but with the support of her children). She became an ardent student of assertiveness; it seemed as if she had just discovered that the world was round instead of flat: "I really have the right to think that? You mean my needs are just as important as anyone else's? It's really okay to have the anger I'm feeling? I really do deserve to have good things happen to me?" Things came to a head quickly when she found that her husband, who had worn carpet slippers for the first few days she was in the hospital, actually put on his shoes and tied them himself for the first time in over 30 years. Lola's anger was a sight to behold! She steamed, then exploded, as she realized that she had been "used" over the years. Whether her anger was justified was not the point; her expression of that long-stifled rage made an unbelievable difference in her breathing ability.

Although at our insistence Lola's husband attended a number of sessions with her, he remained distant from the group, arms folded across his chest. This precipitated more anger and frustration in Lola, since she felt her efforts at appropriate assertive communication with her husband were falling on fallow ground. Recognizing the neglect of her needs and feelings over the years, she began seriously to rethink her nearly half-century marriage. Marital therapy was not terribly successful; yet it made Lola aware that, although she could not change her husband, she didn't want to return to being a doormat. After many anguished days, she decided to stay with her husband but determined that she was going to start leading her life the way she wished—no matter what! This was her decision, and it was a good one. For the several months before they went back to their home in the Midwest, Lola lived her choice. Lo and behold, her husband started changing and the relationship began to improve. They even had several sessions focused on how they could improve their sexual relationship. When Lola returned home, X-rays could find no sign of her lung tumors, and her emphysema had improved to the point that it was not a problem.

Lola is a good example of behavioral/emotional changes that are followed by changes in the body. After eight or nine months at home she lapsed into her old passive behavior of living according to others' expectations and not making choices in her life. Noticing her emphysema worsening, she returned to GETTING WELL for a couple of weeks. As she restated her assertive choices and worked on her anger, as well as many inner child issues, her wheezing and puffing subsided, and she returned home to her husband. They began going out dancing together, the relationship improved, and Lola's health was good. Over a year went by before Lola's health began to take a downhill turn. Over the phone she shared her dismay at how hard it was to be herself in her marriage with her husband and the entire social network of her small, conservative, Midwestern town working against her. "I'm getting tired of fighting and it breaks my heart not to be who I am," she said sadly. As you may guess, a number of weeks later she entered the hospital for her heart condition, where she died peacefully.

Conflict Resolution

I have found that, with the major exception of Type A cardiovascular patients, most people with life-challenging illnesses avoid conflict. As GETTING WELL participants frequently say, "There just isn't anything good about conflict." Thus, the first task of this session is to find the positive in conflict and to have each participant determine his or her style of handling conflict, from running away to trying to smooth it over to fighting back. Lois Hart's book, *Learning from Conflict*, is a helpful resource for this session.

In the case of conflict, the behaviors of the persons involved make perfect sense from their frame of reference, and there is some reward in maintaining the behavior. To break the pattern the therapist may want to bring forth a number of techniques that have been used before, such as systematic desensitization, stress inoculation, and cognitive restructuring. We also like to divide participants into groups of three or four and behaviorally rehearse maintaining a mood, a feeling, an opinion, or a course of action in the face of someone's negative remarks or feelings. In another game we use, the participants may admit an error, a weakness, or a problem without feeling inadequate as a person.

I've also found it extremely useful to use a transformational fantasy exercise wherein the individual goes to the "conflict room" and meets with the person with whom there is conflict. With an eidetic Gestalt flavor, the therapist then suggests that the individual be in the shoes of the "adversary," experiencing his or her feelings or thoughts about the situation. Although this is a simple exercise, it produces frequently surprising and always useful insights.

The idea of hanging in with conflict rather than avoiding it or trying to pour oil on it frequently becomes a "real life" issue in group therapy and can be dealt with in even greater depth in that setting.

Shirley, a 28-year-old nurse whose blood pressure and diabetes frequently got out of control, stated during an exercise, "There is absolutely nothing that *anyone* can find that is good about conflict." Shirley had grown up in a family where verbal and physical abuse was the norm among parents and siblings. As an adult she tended to walk out when situations — with friends or on the job at the hospital — became confrontational. She never let this behavior interfere with her care of patients; yet she was constantly at odds with her peers and supervisors, which certainly did nothing for her health or her enjoyment of life. At the same time, Shirley tended to be especially sensitive to personal slights or even the slightest hint of breach of trust.

As might be expected, Shirley developed "issues" with most of the counselors at GETTING WELL and avoided the individuals rather than leveling with them and risking conflict. At GETTING WELL Shirley was finally caught in a situation from which she could not escape; although she grudgingly admitted in session that maybe there was some good in conflict, she continued to flee these feared situations. As time went on, however, she began to return to the scene of various "conflicts" and to tell each individual involved about her perceptions of the "incident" (frequently the person had not realized there had been an "incident").

Shirley worked on her conflict phobia with a number of strategies, including stress inoculation and transformational fantasy. Gradually, she was able to stay on the scene, to tell others what her feelings and perceptions were, and to hang in there until the situation was resolved. When she was able to see the conflict through, she began to realize that increased understanding was a much more likely outcome than rejection, abuse, or hurt feelings. Staying "to finish the job" at GETTING WELL took immense courage on Shirley's part, but when a friend at the hospital said she thought that after three weeks at GETTING WELL Shirley was better than ever — even better than after her three years with a psychiatrist — she decided the pain of change was worth it.

On Becoming a Survivor

Victor Frankl (1959) noted in his moving works about the spirit and hope of the survivors of the holocaust that he suspected people had not survived by accident — that their beliefs, their way of processing the world, had affected their survival. Psychologist Al Siebert became interested in the personalities of survivors when he joined the paratroopers after finishing school in 1953. His trainers were the survivors of a platoon which was nearly wiped out during the Korean war. He realized that it was not luck alone that enabled these individuals to survive; their personalities, their philosophies, and their attitudes toward life had something to do with it. His long-term study of survivors and their characteristics described in *The Survivor Personality* is helpful in facilitating participants' learning these qualities.

Carl and Stephanie Simonton (1978) have found that Frankl's and Siebert's survival characteristics are remarkably similar to those found in patients who did well in their program. These patients generally have successful careers which they enjoy, and they remain employed during illness or return to work soon after. They are receptive and creative, but sometimes hostile, due to having strong egos and a sense of their own adequacy. A high degree of self-esteem and self-love, intelligence, and self-reliance, as well as a strong sense of reality, also characterize these individuals. They don't *need* to be included among others although they *value* such interactions. They tend to be nonconformists, they are unprejudiced, and they appreciate diversity among other people. Those who are developing survival traits seek solutions to problems rather than lapsing into depression, and they interpret those same problems as redirections rather than as failures. They also truly feel they cannot afford the luxury of negative thoughts.

One of the goals of GETTING WELL is to help people develop resilience and adaptability and to acquire the confidence that will allow them to become survivors. Siebert (1985) has found that the survivor personality can be learned, although it cannot be taught like history or math. He conceives of the process as a psychological and neurological maturation — a growing-up that paradoxically involves remaining a child, that is, childlike but not childish.

In his writing, Siebert enumerates a number of signs that show a person is reaching a synergistic, survivor level of functioning. They include:

- Empathy for others, including opponents
- The ability to see patterns in relationships
- Recognition of intuition as a valid source of information
- Good timing, especially when speaking or taking an action
- The ability to see early clues about future developments, and to take action concerning those developments
- Cooperative nonconformity: refusing to be controlled by improper laws or social standards, yet choosing to abide by them most of the time for the sake of others — unless attempting to change them
- Being comfortable in complex, confusing situations that others find bewildering and frightening
- Keeping a positive outlook and confidence in adversity

- The ability to absorb new, unexpected, or unpleasant experiences and be changed by them
- A talent for serendipity: the ability to convert what others consider accidents or misfortunes into something useful
- The feeling of getting smarter and enjoying life more as you get older

Because Siebert's guidelines really say it all, we usually let people mull over these ideas, discuss them, and ask themselves how they can transform these left-brain concepts into the consciousness of a survivor. These changes can be facilitated by practicing imagery in which the participant images himself as he wishes to become. In this particular session the confrontation of habits and behavior becomes the most important charge of the therapist. At some point, we may see the "aha" indicating that the individual has moved from the "rules" of survivorship into the emotional stance which really creates a survivor.

Sandi Green joined the GETTING WELL program in early 1988, after having been sent home from her unsuccessful metastatic breast cancer treatment. Her physician at Memorial Sloan-Kettering had suggested she get her affairs in order, because it was obvious to him that she had little time left. Sandi told us she did not accept his prognosis, that she was going to be a survivor, and she wanted us to teach her how! "I'm not ready to die." she stated flatly, "I have too many things I want to do. I want to learn everything you know about surviving because *I'm going to do it!*" Sandi already had many of the characteristics of survivors; further, she eagerly grasped the tools we offered her in the area of learning to be comfortable in difficult and confusing situations. She was beginning to trust her intuitions and to make imagery a way of life.

Sandi was trained to be a nurse, but had gone into real estate due to its financial rewards—for which she was paying a terrible price emotionally and physically. Her goal in life was to go back into nursing and eventually to work at GETTING WELL, but there seemed to be little likelihood of that—with her radiation-damaged ribs and the cancer in her shoulder bones. Still, Sandi courageously took a look at all aspects of her life and made some tough "survivor" decisions, such as ending one particular code-pendent relationship which had kept her in emotional turmoil. "I want someone to take care of me, but if I am to survive, I really have to take care of myself!" she said firmly. She took other steps to reinstate her confidence in herself and her intuition, began to look at all situations in her life as learning experiences, and continued to expand the image of herself healing and surviving. A few months after Sandi finished the GET-TING WELL program, I received a call from her from New York City. She had gone back to Memorial Sloan-Kettering for a checkup, and was told that 27 of her 28 tumors had disappeared. "I did it! I did it!" she cried enthusiastically over the phone, "I told you I would do it, Dee!"

Our lives touched occasionally over the next couple of years, as Sandi worked as an information nurse on a hospital line and ran a cancer support group for a while. Interestingly, when she became soft on her survivor skills, the cancer would return; then, as she got back on her survivor track, she would go into remission. Over a year ago I received a call from Sandi, who was working with the Visiting Nurse Association and had gotten the idea that we might be able to work together. GETTING WELL was in a hospital setting at the time, which made it unworkable. With our move to outpatient, nonprofit status, however, Sandi's dream of being a nurse and working with GETTING WELL has finally been realized. In addition, she is writing a book chronicling her cycles of healing. You can imagine the inspiration she is to those newly diagnosed individuals who may be feeling their lives slipping away! Sandi is a true survivor's survivor.

Handling the Stress of
Life-Challenging Conditions

For many people, the diagnosis of a life-challenging condition is the most dreaded occurrence imaginable. It may open a can of worms dormant for decades; it may bring fears of death or unmitigated suffering; or it may incredibly sensitize one to the joy of life and the moment.

The first step in dealing with the negative reactions is to uncover the feelings the patient may have had at the time of diagnosis and prognosis. Among these feelings are denial, despair, self-pity, anger, resentment, and guilt. Remember that whatever the participant felt or is feeling, those emotions are justified and need to be expressed. There are no "bad" feelings or "wrong" ways to deal with a diagnosis. It is interesting to look gently at the person's emotional evolution and to discover his or her current mental attitude.

In this process, Bernie Siegel (1986) likes to ask four questions. The first question is: "Do you want to live to be 100?" Interestingly, most people do not. Perhaps they do not want to take responsibility for making those end years of high quality. Whatever their reasons, it is provocative to find out why people fear living so long.

The second question is: "What happened to you in the year or two before your illness?" I am fascinated by people's denial of the background of the disease. For example, one young woman unequivocally stated that nothing unusual had happened in the 18 months before she was diagnosed with systemic lupus—nothing except that her fiancé cancelled their large wedding the week before it was to take place, and the child she was carrying was stillborn! Her case was not unusual. We find that invariably there is unusual stress with long-term consequences almost immediately preceding the diagnosis of a tumor, MS, a heart attack, diabetes, an arthritis "flare," and virtually every chronic or life-threatening illness. The point is not to bring blame on the person for not handling stressful situations well in the past. Rather, the point is to allow the person full awareness of his or her past activities so that he/she might choose to change life patterns or to perceive the world in a different way in the future.

Siegel's third question is: "What does the illness mean to you?" Does it mean death or merely a formidable, but not insurmountable, challenge? Here actions usually speak louder than words. For example, Jackie was told by her physician that her breast cancer had metastasized to her brain, yet she continued with plans to pull up stakes and move to a new community and a new job that she loved. That decision certainly gave a loud and clear message to her being, and she spent some of the most joyful months of her life in that new situation.

The fourth question is: "Why did you need the illness?" Obviously this question must be asked with all the gentleness, perception, insight, and understanding the therapist has. Participants—indeed, all of us—are uncomfortable thinking that a disease may meet some psychological need. However, the truth is that it usually does. It may provide permission to do what one wants to do but has been too busy to start, or it may make it easier to say "no." Illness may give us time off to meditate or to chart a new life course, or it may in some way be an excuse for failure.

Sometimes it becomes easier to get attention and love when we are ill; on the other hand, having a disease may make it easier for us to accept love, express feelings, and be honest with ourselves and others. And many find the illness an acceptable way to die—a socially acceptable "suicide." I think it is important to express these ideas as possibilities for the person's consideration rather than to force them upon him. A light, tentative hand can prevent the person from "blaming" himself for somehow "creating" the illness and enable that person to pull back his power and make choices about participation in and responsibility for life.

Anne was in the program for less than the required 10 days because she wanted to gain some strategies to get her through surgery scheduled within the week for a tumor on her larynx. She was violently resentful (though she had to express her resentment in a whisper) that we would even ask her why she needed her illness. I soon began to question my decision to let her come into the program for only a week, although we were somewhat able to resolve the situation before she left. Several weeks after the surgery, which doctors expected would leave her without a voice, this 35-year-old woman called me and said in a whisper, "I think I know what you were talking about. There are a bunch of things that I need to say to people, but I'm afraid I'll destroy them if I do. I want to come back and work on that." And Anne did come back, nearly nine months later, and finish the program. Her larynx was fully healed, and she finally learned to put a voice to the anger she had choked back for years.

Goal-Setting

Envisioning and realizing satisfying goals are important to one's health and self-esteem. Setting goals for one's life reinforces self-responsibility and defines intentions and commitment. Having goals actually tends to facilitate creativity and personal insights. Of course, goals can also be limiting and, like outcomes, may become more important than the process of living itself. For that reason, in our goal-setting session we begin with an old exercise that helps to generate clarity about life purposes and meaning. The exercise involves participants' taking two minutes to write down all they would like to accomplish in the next three years. In the following two minutes, they write what they would like to accomplish specifically in the next year. Then we have them pretend that in six months they will be struck dead by lightning and ask them how they would live until that time (other than buying rubber-soled shoes and getting out of Florida!). From the items that emerge we may have them choose one or two as long-term goals. Then we have participants write several short-term goals which will lead to the long-term goals. After they identify barriers they may encounter as they attempt to reach their goals, they are asked to choose a first action step.

It is quite useful either before or after the development of the short-term goals to see the long-term goal in imagery. In other words, the participants see themselves having achieved the goal, imagine how they feel and what they are doing, see how people respond to them, and visualize their surroundings. When that image becomes clear, have them run the movie backwards to "see" *how* they arrived at their goals; alternatively, they can image themselves taking their first action step and moving toward the goal through their sub-goals.

Janice was afraid to set goals. She had rarely gotten what she wanted out of life since childhood and the systemic lupus which was ravaging her body appeared to be more of the same bad news. In the stress management session on goals held during her first week in the program, her paper was blank, and she felt anguished. Over the next few days we started with her successive approximations of long-term goals. For example, we had her set the following goals: saying an affirmation five times before three o'clock, finding in a magazine three things she would like to do, or being assertive with her husband at least once in the next 24 hours. When she combined her self-esteem work, transformational fantasy work on identifying blockages to her goal-setting, and expressive therapy work in her "image book," she was able to start setting goals, albeit reluctantly at first. Our suggesting to her that having a blueprint for a house made it more likely that the finished house would be what she wished (yet could be changed at will) helped her move toward solidifying goals. In the process, it also helped to solidify her life.

Lessons for the Author/Clinician

The rise of assertiveness training in the 1970s was inviting to me. My ideas about relationships and communication had jelled in the 1950s; however, I was attracted (although sometimes dismayed) by the excitement and new honesty of relationships in the 1960s. The concept of assertiveness seemed progressive, yet balanced. My acquaintance with and admiration for Dr. Joseph Wolpe were no small part of my intrigue with the emotional and physiological power of openness, directness, and honesty. A colleague, Karen Licklider, and I designed numerous assertiveness training groups for women, nurses, and business people—and practiced the tenets in our own lives and professional relationships as well. The concepts I learned allowed me to deal gently with my dear mother-in-law, who felt that graduate school and working as a therapist were just a momentary madness for me and that sooner or later I would realize that my calling was baking cookies and having dinner parties.

We usually teach what we most need to learn, and certainly facilitating assertiveness and stress management courses made it possible for me to sing my own song in the midst of conflicting family and societal expectations. I can credit our assertiveness courses with giving me the courage and confidence to risk everything on starting GETTING WELL years later. Nonetheless, the lessons had just begun. Being in such close communication and contact with participants, there were no closets in which to hide my passive or aggressive inclinations. It meant being real, honest, and direct in ways I had never experienced before. I have to admit that much of my new behavior was inspired by not being caught short by the patients; however, as it became more a part of my life, such behavior felt really good and right. I still have some of my precious "closets," but more and more are opened each day. I know I am a better therapist for it—and also a more joyful and peaceful human.

One of my shortcomings has been the avoidance of conflict or any unpleasant encounter. As a result, I've worked hard to avoid such situations and have surrounded myself with people who will do my "dirty work" for me (and who probably don't appreciate being in that role). In developing GETTING WELL, I ran into a number of situations in which I had to face conflicts and challenges — otherwise the program would have suffered immeasurably. So I boned up on my empathic assertions and confrontive assertions, and practiced stress inoculation as well as a great deal of relaxation and imagery. To my surprise, facing those situations resulted in deeper communication rather than hurt feelings. As a result, I have an incredibly powerful feeling that I can handle anything that comes my way, and that everyone will walk away feeling better about himself or herself.

I'm still learning from GW's lessons in stress management, and I believe sharing the lessons I am still learning in assertive communication is valuable in helping participants dissolve the barriers to fully realizing themselves. It may be particularly valuable for them to realize from their "leader" that one never really "gets there," but that we as humans are in a continuous process of creating and becoming.

7

Group Therapy

Jesus said, *If you bring forth what is within you, what you bring forth will save you. If you do not bring forth what is within you, what you do not bring forth will destroy you.* — *The Gospel according to Thomas*

All of us struggle with issues that in many ways are very different. Yet when we look a little deeper, we find that others' issues are not unlike our own. We have so much in common. Whatever the issue is, the fear is that we'll be rejected. So we often hide it and pretend to be something we're not. — *Dean Ornish*

Perhaps there is a positive way to feel all emotions. It seems to me that all emotions serve a purpose and are potentially life-affirming. Perhaps it is not so much the emotions themselves as the way we deal with them that either is or is not life-affirming . . . the only bad emotion is a stuck emotion. — *Rachel Naomi Remen*

This daily process group focuses on styles of interacting, expression of feelings, instilling of hope, being in the "here and now," gaining and giving of social support, facing conflict, and being one's own person. The group is seen as being a microcosm of a person's social experience. In other words, individuals will relate to others in the group in much the same way that they relate to others in the "outside world." For this reason, group is a laboratory which not only allows each person to see how he or she relates to others but also provides that person with a safe place in which to change the image of his or her relationship to others and the world and to be fully himself or herself. I consider the process group work to be one of the most powerful therapies when done well, so the most experienced clinicians on our staff conduct this daily session.

Guidelines for the Group Process

My bible for group therapy is Irvin Yalom's *The Theory and Practice of Group Psychotherapy* (1985). Although this volume may contain more information than necessary about how to run a therapy group, it gives one a grasp of the myriad dimensions of group therapy, without which the group may become pedestrian or even countertherapeutic. *Critical Incidents in Group Therapy*, by Donigan and Malnati, gives a nice overview of four schools of group therapy *and* tells how each school would handle the crises that are endemic to the therapeutic group process.

If one plays it too safe in group, one can expect that chit-chat or "interesting conversation" will be the rule of the day, rather than the therapy that needs to take place. On the other hand, group is not the place, in my opinion, for the swashbuckling therapist to whom nothing is sacred. That style does not work well with our population, since participants "turn off" very quickly when confronted too blatantly or pushed too hard. Few of these people have been in a therapy group before, and that actuality needs to be respected. Initially, it is hard for them to look at the group as a whole, as a system within itself. So when things seem to be getting a little off base, we'll ask, "What's happening in group?" This gives members a chance to look at the group as a painting in progress, and to analyze what they see.

One of the most difficult jobs in group is getting at feelings and being empathic with participants without allowing the group to become a place for endless "war stories" and "doctor bashing." It is often a tough call as to what is therapeutic or cathartic and what is antitherapeutic and will further attach the patient to his own bitterness and helplessness. Sometimes, when the patient seems to need to tell and retell his or her story to the detriment of the group, we will give writing that story as a journaling assignment and try to bring the person back to the here and now by asking about present feelings: "How did you feel when we told you to write your story rather than to tell it again in group?"

Another major problem occurs when the group is finding it difficult to move beyond safe, idle chatter and get down to business. Although group should be safe, fun, positive, humorous, and growth-producing for the facilitator and members, it is the facilitator's job to keep discussions on target. Asking what's happening in group or why members are choosing to stay on a safe level and not address significant issues frequently results in a shift of the group's focus and attention away from extraneous subject matter and onto the business at hand.

Expressing Feelings

Expression of feelings is an issue with virtually every participant who comes into the program, as well as perhaps with every card-carrying member of our culture. I believe that the main reason heart disease, cancer, diabetes, and other chronic diseases have become "diseases of civilization" is the manner in which our culture teaches us to deal (or not deal) with feelings. Evidence has shown (e.g., Pennebaker, 1990; Schwartz, 1990;

Shedler, 1992) that repression of feelings promotes unhealthy conditions and expression of feelings has a salubrious effect on the body.

We are finding more often than would be expected by chance that people with cancer and life-challenging diagnoses who enter GETTING WELL have experienced some serious childhood trauma. This trauma includes acute physical, emotional, or even sexual abuse, which the victim has shoved so far to the back of his or her mind that it may not even be recognized. Several times in group we have had participants exclaim, "Oh, now I remember what happened to me!" and a tale of long-ago abuse or incest tumbles out. Others have been dimly aware of things that "weren't right" happening to them. I remember one group of six or seven men and women, ages 39 to 70, in which every one had experienced sexual abuse as a child.

Different conditions are described in the literature as having different emotional "profiles" (e.g., LeShan, 1959; Simonton et al., 1978; Temoshok & Dreher, 1992; Williams, 1989). My experience has been confirming in this regard. This is *in no way* an attempt to put people into emotional boxes according to their conditions; yet it may indicate to the therapist fertile fields in which to dig at appropriate times in group. For example, cancer patients tend to suppress feelings of anger and other "negative" emotions, expressing only feelings that they feel will be pleasing to others. Frequently, even their oncologists are not aware of the depths of their depression, helplessness, fear, and despair.

Cardiovascular patients seem to express their anger easily; yet it sometimes appears to be a cover for deep hurt, fear, and *perceptions* of early parental abandonment or rejection. There may also be issues of competition and deeply hidden sensitivity to comparison and rejection, which are secondary to the hurt/fear issues. MS, rheumatoid arthritis, lupus, and other autoimmune diseases appear to cover a rage which is frighteningly close to the surface but which the individual fears acting upon. A number of times I have heard insightful people with an autoimmune condition say, "I have so much anger that it scares me to even think of expressing it." I wonder sometimes if part of the condition is a mechanism to keep that overwhelming anger from being physically expressed. People with diabetes sometimes have low self-esteem and an acute sensitivity to what is said to them. It seems they have difficulties expressing feelings for fear they will get feedback from others which will in turn hurt their feelings.

Intellectualization of feelings is a defense that crosses the lines of diagnosis and seems almost indigenous to the population that seeks out the program (as well as to the therapists thereof). The comparatively high educational level of participants, as well as the admiration of intellectualization by the culture, may account for the widespread use of this defense.

Since group may be the setting where the individual's style of dealing with feelings is most clearly evident, having a loose handle on these general styles is helpful in promoting expression of a wide variety of feelings. In group people can experience and express a full range of feelings — from hurt, joy, guilt, affection, anxiety, anger, and sorrow to sexuality, love, boredom, and playfulness. As a daily preamble to group we try to give participants license to identify and express feelings they have found difficult in the past. We point out that many of us have learned to insulate ourselves from the feeling world *because that is what we had to do to survive as kids.* We indicate that as adults we have a wider range of choices to call upon. We also invoke "the morality of the body," and the research suggesting that in order for one's body to be healthy one needs to feel *comfortable* expressing *all* feelings. In other words, for our bodies to perform optimally, we may *choose* not to express a feeling in a given situation, yet that needs to be a choice, rather than a feeling that it is socially incorrect to do so.

In 1976 James Elliott published a valuable book of reproducible handouts for group members, which I found to be quite useful for "setting the stage" for process groups I facilitated in professional settings. While one does not want to limit group interactions with one's preamble, a preface starts the group with a thrust rather than allowing the members to indulge in time-consuming, unproductive groping for what the process is all about.

In the handout, "What You Can Get from Your Group Experience," the Institute emphasizes the value of being able to initiate feeling issues in group, of being honest with feelings rather than playing the social game, and of learning about blocks one may have to closeness and intimacy. Learning to give and receive honest feedback and becoming more sensitive to the ways that others communicate feelings, particularly attending to nonverbal factors such as posture and facial expression, are other important avenues to explore in group.

You will undoubtedly encounter a great deal of resistance when you encourage people to make contact with their inner feelings, so you must remember to honor that resistance or denial and deal with it gently but effectively. Many people are afraid of experiencing "negative thoughts" for fear of hurting their bodies by acknowledging anger, fear, etc. They believe that "you don't have the luxury of a negative thought" and work hard to maintain their cheerful facade. Pat Norris gives a wonderful counter-example: "If I stand here and have a spike through my hand, what is the most negative thing I can say about the situation? Is it that it hurts or that it might get infected and make me sick? No, the most negative thing I can say is 'I don't have a spike in my hand.'" Her point is that when one embraces the reality of the situation or the feelings that are present, then one can do something about them. Denying the feelings or situation renders one helpless.

All of us play many kinds of games to make it seem that we are expressing our deepest feelings when we really are not. One of the most beautiful "scams" is making a wonderful "feeling assertion," which is, when push comes to shove, a blatant judgment or opinion. It goes like this: "I feel like you're handling that whole situation wrong." If the "I feel" is followed by "like" or "that" or anything except a feeling word, it is *not* a feeling statement. This is a really tough, but important, distinction for group members to make; nevertheless, it is essential that they do so for the preservation of the group process.

Another defense is substituting a "comfortable" emotion for a more difficult one. For example, I believe that we women often say "I'm hurt" when we mean "I'm angry." There are a number of "anger-suppressing" illnesses where this also applies. At GETTING WELL we don't argue this point, but we do suggest that the person attempt to substitute the difficult emotion for the comfortable one for a few days and see if it "fits." Sometimes it doesn't; however, going through the exercise frequently elicits a shift in perception for the individual.

Annie, who was dealing with diabetes among other conditions, spoke with a small voice and consistently reacted to comments and situations by displaying either hurt or numbness. When we asked her to try anger on for size during situations in which she previously experienced hurt, she agreed to do so. However, she found it impossible to find any anger within herself for the first few days. Later, after someone made a jarring statement in group, her face lit up. "I felt a little bit angry when he said that," she noted. "That was really neat to feel." With this tiny window open, we were able to revisit Annie's emotionally abusive childhood and help her deal with the rage she felt toward her parents. Opening herself to anger allowed her to move out of the victim role; it entitled her to be angry without guilt and to shift, ever so slightly, toward feeling better about herself. There was still much hard work to be done, pain to be suffered, and anger to be felt; however, Annie left the program feeling that the direction of her life had been changed. Her volatile blood sugar levels began leveling out, and she found that she could stay stable with considerably less insulin.

With people who tend to express a great deal of anger and seem overreactive to their environments (Type A style), we suggest that when they feel angry they explore the possibility that they are actually afraid or hurt. Initially, the reaction is to deny the possibility that hurt or fear has ever been a major part of their lives; yet the seed has been planted. Days later, sometimes in an individual session, the seed begins to sprout, and the person begins to talk about the incredible hurt or fear he or she has been covering with anger.

Alf is a 60-year-old, big, burly, bear of a man who came into the program with brittle diabetes and cardiovascular disease. A financial situation caused by unscrupulous real estate lawyers had catapulted his life into one rage reaction after another and his health into life-threatening symptoms. He felt alternately helpless, furious, vindictive, homicidal, and suicidal. Because his health was so precarious, he sent his wife up north to deal with the business situation, and he came to GETTING WELL. Of course, his wife was not handling things to his satisfaction, so when he finished his diatribes about the lawyers he would start a litany of complaints about her.

It was hard to cut his stories short and have him focus on how *he felt*, rather than shifting the blame for his poor physical and mental health onto circumstances and other people. When he finally stated that he felt angry, we asked him to go back over his life decade by decade and recount a time he had felt the same way during each decade. Returning to his very first decade, Alf burst into tears and wailed, "Why didn't anyone know that I was there? Why didn't anyone love me?" Then he opened up and began talking about a childhood in which he felt he didn't exist for his mother. Even the family album contained only one picture of him. There were numerous photographs of uncles, cousins, parents, and siblings, but only one of him.

Therapy finally reached the real issues behind his rage: the hurt and grief over not being seen or acknowledged by the ones who *should* have loved and cared for him. He began to see his wife in the new light of what had happened to him as a child and to realize that neither she nor other people nor other situations were *causing* him to feel or act a certain way. He found a portrait of himself as a young, handsome entertainer which he brought into GETTING WELL and put on the mantel over the fireplace. It was touching to see Alf's face as his GETTING WELL family acknowledged and admired the picture daily for the week it was there. And the visiting nurse who was monitoring his diabetes while he was in the program said, "I don't know what has been going on psychologically with Alf, but what's happened with his diabetes is surely a miracle."

Alf's story reinforces the need to deal responsibly with one's feelings as a part of the group therapy task. There are a number of other sessions which go into the didactic aspects of self-responsibility—of recognizing that one's feelings are generated by one's own perception of the situation rather than by the situation itself. The main task in group is being sure that this responsibility is put into words. For example, when someone says, "He made me mad," the therapist needs to have the person change the statement into a self-responsible assertion, such as "I feel angry when . . ." or "I find myself feeling mad in circumstances of this kind."

Sometimes reminding participants that they give a great deal of their precious power away when they let themselves be pushed around by others' feelings or actions allows them to rethink the idea that their environment is responsible for their feelings. Holding each individual, and no one else, responsible for his or her own emotions allows people to express and hear feelings without the emotions being a crowbar for manipulation. This paves the way for more honest communication in the group and allows the members to be close without losing autonomy and self-esteem.

Social Support as Healing

Giving and receiving social support is a healing experience. As we have seen with Spiegel et al. (1989), social support may be a factor in extending life; in addition, a number of studies (e.g., House, Robbins, & Melzner, 1982) have shown that helping others enhances the immune system. The Institute for Noetic Sciences has as one of its main tenets the idea that altruism is an essential element of our human potential and that the exercise of altruism leads not only to spiritual wholeness but also to physical health.

Although the daily therapy group is not a "support group" in the usual sense, one of the main missions of this group is, indeed, social support. GETTING WELL is, as a whole, a deeply supportive experience, and the heart of that experience is the daily process group. The group process tends to concentrate "the work" among the members rather than placing all responsibility on the leader. Participants begin to see other members as valuable resources in dealing with their personal issues, and each individual has the opportunity to see himself or herself as intimately connected and deeply valuable in the lives of others. The group members are a rich reservoir of support and information, so the facilitator needs to be sure the focus is kept on the group members rather than on himself or herself. Members will inevitably ask the advice or opinion of the group leader first, and it is a wise facilitator who replies, "There are a number of people who know you well here in the group—what about asking them?" Yalom suggests that events which strengthen bonds between group members make the group and the healing experience more powerful.

In David Spiegel's (1991) research groups of breast cancer patients, mutual support was encouraged. He found that a great deal of caring evolved among the women in the intervention groups. He was struck by how often the issues of death and dying came up, and how the group helped each woman recognize that even a problem as overwhelming as death could be handled better when it was talked about and broken down into a series of smaller problems. He noted that most patients were not afraid so much of death as of the process of dying. Many of the problems with dying were issues concerning control over their treatment, pain management, and loss of physical abilities and functions they valued. In group discussion about the specific problems within the big issue, the group helped its members "detoxify death."

Spiegel's groups also helped members learn how to deal with problems in physician-patient communication, worked on enhancing family support, and helped members regroup their social networks. They gave up superficial "social" interactions with negative or nonsupportive individuals and became intensely involved with one another, visiting each other in the hospital and just "being there."

Although, for whatever reason, the death and dying issue generally is not a major one in GETTING WELL groups, the deep connection between members both while they are in the program and long afterward is typical. I think especially of the "Dream Team," which congealed during a week when, surprisingly, we had only men in the program (at that time based in a psychiatric hospital). These six men, aged 35 to 75, had disparate diagnoses, including MS, arachnoiditis, metastatic prostate cancer, HIV, and chronic pain, and certainly were "nondangerous" patients by anyone's standards. They championed my struggles to get doors unlocked, grounds privileges reinstated, and some measure of freedom for them. As a result of their bonding for a "cause," their pain and other symptoms dropped away, and they really felt as if they were living life again. (As a caution: fighting "outside forces" can be antitherapeutic if done in old, dysfunctional ways; however, such fighting can also be an excellent lesson in relabeling and in cognitive restructuring.)

Unfortunately, the hospital did not care for the Dream Team's self-assertive attitude, which precipitated a move of the program—on three hours' notice—from a desirable location in the hospital to "the pits." However, the Dream Team (and other members they had picked up with time) demanded a trip to Epcot since they would lose a full day of therapy during the move. The hospital complied, and within a couple of hours they were off, wearing their new rainbow GETTING WELL t-shirts and riding in the psychiatric hospital's van with "The Dream Team," taped to the side.

The Dream Team men have stayed in contact with each other—helping each other out in difficult situations, consoling the family of a member who died, being available by phone for a member who divorced, and generally sharing a beautiful, special, unconditional love.

Facing Conflict

Inevitably, when feelings are being expressed and people have different opinions, conflict may erupt in the group. In fact, conflict is inevitable in the development of a group, and its absence may be a sign that the group is not doing all it should be. Most group members fervently pray that conflict not come forth, for all the same reasons they have denied and suppressed feelings as well as avoided conflict for most of their lives. For the therapist to go along with this charade (and it's tempting to do so) is ineffective or bad therapy!

Our particular population seems to be exceedingly sensitive to expressed anger and almost phobic of conflict. For this reason, group members may demand guarantees of safety before they bring forth their deepest thoughts and feelings—the assurance that they will not be "punished" for trying out new ways of relating in the group laboratory. Although warranties cannot be given to concerned *individuals*, the group needs to be as safe as possible, and each person should be assured that that his or her feelings will be respected and that he or she can handle whatever comes up in group.

People need to know that, although group is ultimately a *safe* place, it is not always a *comfortable* place. Still, the firm foundations of safety and support must be adequately established for the patient *before* conflict and discomfort are allowed to enter the group situation. *After* these foundations have been established, we can encourage members to express their feelings—not with guarantees of protection, but with assurances of growth if they see the situation through.

We have found that the most therapeutic way to handle conflict when things get hot and heavy in the group situation is to stop the process and examine what is happening in the here and now. Yalom suggests a statement such as: "We have been expressing some deep and heavy feelings here in group. To keep us from overloading, let's stop and look at what we are doing, and try to understand what is going on, and where these powerful emotions are coming from." Here the therapist may wish to reiterate the concept of responsibility for one's own feelings and respect for the feelings of others.

Although conflict in group may be uncomfortable for everyone, the potential for growth is rich. I sometimes feel like a parent in these contexts: wanting to protect my child against hurt, yet also wanting the child to build the emotional muscles necessary to deal with the world effectively and powerfully. This is another of the many fine lines that must be walked, a place where we need to be aware of consequences while moving forward confidently in the direction our intuition leads.

Laurie, a 38-year-old woman diagnosed with chronic fatigue syndrome, seemed to spend much of her life pouring oil on the waters of conflict. She found it difficult to voice a direct opinion, always hedging so that no one could disagree with her; yet she was exceptionally able to give advice to nearly everyone. The atmosphere in group grew more tense as Laurie spent long, precious minutes of group time explaining herself as well as deflecting her anger through advice-giving. Finally things blew up in group (as had happened frequently in Laurie's life), and she was stunned and amazed that once again "people were turning against" her.

This was an opportunity for the facilitator to talk about directness, honesty, and taking responsibility for one's feelings. Members of the group began giving Laurie feedback: "I want to get to know you better, Laurie, yet sometimes it seems that your advice is like a wall around you. I feel really frustrated when I feel that wall come up," and "I like it when you say how you feel, and I like it when you let me express my feelings without my thinking that I'm upsetting you." The group lovingly gave Laurie an image of how her behavior might be affecting others—a pattern that was evident in her family and social life. It *was* uncomfortable, yet it led to an epiphany for Laurie which opened large doors in both her individual and family therapy. The biggest miracle was the shift in her relationship with the group, however. She was at last truly one of them, as well as being one with herself.

Instilling Hope

Norman Cousins, in *Head First: The Biology of Hope*, describes a number of studies showing the way in which the mind changes ideas and expectations into biological realities. The most startling studies involve the placebo effect, wherein people are told what to expect from a medication but are given a placebo instead of the medication. For example, British physician J.W.L. Fielding told 411 patients they could expect hair loss from the chemotherapy that was about to be administered. Thirty percent of the patients received placebos instead of chemotherapy and actually experienced hair loss although their pills had contained no medication. And Henry Beecher of Harvard observed from his studies that the greater the anxiety or pain, the more effective the placebo.

George Solomon, Lydia Temoshok, and their colleagues (1987) have evaluated the psychological characteristics of AIDS patients who have lived far longer than expected and functioned at a very high level. What they have found is suggestive that positive attitudes, adaptive coping, and hope can strengthen components of the immune system in a way that offsets the loss of helper T cells and the resultant physical havoc.

Ronna Jevne notes, "If someone is ill, they are interested not in the many who die, but in those who survive." Her book, *It All Begins with Hope*, is required reading for anyone facilitating a group of this sort. It is a collection of stories by patients diagnosed with life-challenging conditions with whom she has had contact in her work in Alberta, Canada. These are stories of hope by simple people "in some stage of becoming remarkable."

Ronna points out that there *are* problems with hope; our challenge as helpers is to encourage hope which is helpful.

Hope is frequently experienced in the logical, cognitive domain, yet it is most powerfully experienced in the symbolic, ideational, or unconscious spiritual sphere. Hope that embraces physical or material outcomes certainly has a place in the lives of us all. Nonetheless, when situations get really tough or are truly unbearable, it is necessary to shift to those deeper, more spiritual provinces of hope—hope in the most profound sense—in order to survive physically, emotionally, psychologically, and spiritually. This is the hope of which Al Siebert speaks in his studies of survivors. It is the hope of the survivors of the Holocaust epitomized by the works of Victor Frankl, and it is the hope expressed by Vaclav Havel when asked if he saw a grain of hope anywhere in the 1980s. His reply was:

> Hope is a state of mind, not of the world. Either we have hope within us or we don't; it is a dimension of the soul, and it's not essentially dependent on some particular observation of the world or estimate of the situation. Hope is not prognostication. It is an orientation of the spirit, an orientation of the heart; it transcends the world that is immediately experienced, and is anchored somewhere beyond its horizons. . . . Hope, in this deep and powerful sense, is not the same as joy that things are going well, or willingness to invest in enterprises that are obviously heading for . . . success, but rather, an ability to work for something because it is good, not just because it stands a chance to succeed. Hope is definitely not the same thing as optimism. It is not the conviction that something will turn out well, but the certainty that something makes sense, regardless of how it turns out. (Symynkywicz, 1991, p. 23)

Havel's conviction that hope is the sense that life has meaning despite the tragedy and absurdity that surround us is what we try to convey and shape in ourselves as well as in our participants. Typically, most of us have learned a meaning of hope that has to do with good outcomes and not with our own inner power and spirituality. Indeed, shifting one's core imagery to "whatever happens, I can handle it and find meaning in it" is a belief we try to foster in the group situation. When that belief is taken to heart, ripples occur throughout a person's life.

Dan came into the program well after liver cancer had overwhelmed his body. Determination was certainly one of Dan's long suits as he daily slammed the cancer cells (which he saw as tennis balls) outside of his body and into the other court. He continued his daily tennis (both in actuality as well as in imagery) for several months before he said, "I'm losing the battle." His depression concerning outcomes deepened until a brilliant member of the staff tapped into the spiritual aspects of hope. Dan, having once been a priest, was no foreigner to this aspect of his being, and began an inner spiritual rebirth. He continued his inner and outer tennis; however, his focus became more clearly on meaning, and how that meaning manifested in each moment. The beautiful relationship he and his wife had became deeper and more meaningful. Even though the disease was progressing, he began emanating an aura of light and healing and peace. He and his wife decided to take a vacation of several weeks, visiting friends and tennis resorts, even though Dan was no longer able to play tennis. Three weeks later, we got a call from his wife saying that Dan had been hospitalized with a stroke. Within a few days, he died. However, Dan *truly* lived until he died, and I have the feeling that with his death an even greater healing took place. The changed thrust of his hope allowed him to live his life with much more fullness and meaning, and to prove beyond a doubt that death is not a failure.

Ronna Jevne (1991) talks about what we can do to enhance hope. She has some excellent suggestions, which I have modified for the group situation:

Share hope stories. These are stories told by the facilitator or by the group members themselves. While there are many hope stories, people seem compelled to tell worst-case scenarios to individuals facing a challenging condition. Although group members are often more sensitive than the general public, they are not always, so it is the group facilitator's challenge to help members change the negative into the positive.

Look for hope models. All of us have someone who can be a "hope model" for us, whether a television personality, a mythic character, or someone with whom we have had contact. Jevne suggests that participants may be able to take on the role and the strengths of the hope model when their own hope falters. In taking on a hope model, however, one must be looking at hope in the deepest sense of the word—not just whether the model lives or dies. I consider Gilda Radner a wonderful hope model, yet the unenlightened will argue that, because she died, she cannot be a model of hope. Of course, I feel that is a benighted point of view; yet a facilitator needs to be able to handle that argument, if it should arise.

Encourage hope images. Jevne suggests that images of an anticipated state or outcome can help a person focus his energies in a healing direction. Sessions in imagery or expressive therapies focus more intensely on developing such images, and frequently in group we give an assignment to be completed in one of those other sessions.

Build hope bridges. Jevne points out that hope is experienced in the present but is inextricably connected to the past and the future. She suggests bringing the person's strength and wisdom, either or both of which have brought success or satisfaction in the past, into the situation the person is presently facing. Frequently, people do not consider their illnesses as similar to problems they may have successfully dealt with in their professions. But their illnesses *are* similar, so they must learn to call upon the skills they have applied in the past to create a bridge to the future.

Sustain your own hope. As caregivers, we frequently find our hope wearing thin, meaning we, too, need to have a vision of the future. On this subject, Jevne states, "Having a vision allows us to measure our progress not only by the events of a single day, but also by our contribution to the greater picture. Having a vision is a way of reminding ourselves of the important questions: 'Why am I here? What am I really doing? How am I allowing myself to get sidetracked?'" (p. 171).

Lessons for the Author/Clinician

Group therapy has been an exuberant teacher for me. Although some of the lessons have been honed during the the past several years, I really began learning them nearly two decades ago when a colleague and I started a women's group, which ran continuously for nearly a dozen years. My background as a philosophy major led me to believe that if you read enough books or reasoned in an enlightened way, all problems could be solved—that emotions were encumbrances one occasionally had to put up with in living the life of reason. Indeed, although people or situations *could* make one angry or anxious, one had merely to control people or situations in order to avoid those uncomfortable emotional aberrations.

I also thought there were answers to every question if one simply researched enough, and there was a "right way" (the rules for which were *somewhere*) to conduct therapy and to live life. If one really thought hard enough, planned ahead assiduously, and controlled one's environment and feelings enough, one could have a safe and secure (i.e., happy) life. And life *was* good. I had a handsome and loving husband, two wonderful children, a nice house, a great job, good friends and colleagues, and the affection of my clients. Yet remembering back to those years, I can see that any glitch in the system created serious emotional upheaval for me, so that I felt rather helpless until I could get the situation back under control.

It's great to have been in that space, because a majority of the people who come into our program are clones of me at that time of my life—even though *their* "safe" lives have been blown to pieces by the diagnosis of a life-challenging condition. And although I do not feel it is particularly therapeutic for us as facilitators to hold ourselves up as models per se, I do believe it is immensely useful to have this background, as well as our own struggles, which we can share. It certainly helps us to know more intimately what participants are dealing with in making changes; moreover, the participants can realize that we are all in this endeavor together.

The major lesson I learned in my early days in group was to take responsibility for my own feelings. Actually, this was a shift that had pragmatic beginnings because group simply wasn't manageable if we did not assume that a behavior or an honest feeling a person had was not going to hurt someone else. It took away the ability to blame someone else or put the responsibility on the world for what happened to me, yet gave me a curious sense of power and peace within myself. Although this was a beginning for me, it was not until I began the GETTING WELL experience that I accepted the gift of responsibility for my life as well as for my feelings. It really came down to being pushed around by events, people, and disappointments, and being plowed under—or taking responsibility for my feelings and choosing how I would respond and still survive. At first, it was an intellectual choice, but now, I am glad to say, it is a part of my intuitive underpinnings.

In my earlier group, I always played it safe. Luckily, the co-therapist was more daring than I, so the group probably did not suffer terribly. Early on at GETTING WELL it occurred to me not only that the participants could not afford to give up growth for safety, but also that I had to give up safety for growth. For example, I had already made the uncharacteristic move of giving up my safe, stable job and risking my life's savings on the dream of creating the type of comprehensive program I felt was really needed for people with life-threatening conditions. And while that move was real enough, I think my belief at the time was that my new situation would soon be nearly as safe as my old job had been. (That, indeed, was a fantasy!) However, because growth does not occur in comfort zones for therapists, participants, or programs, it was clear I had to go for broke. At first, this meant intellectually relabeling crises as challenges, but soon a deep, intuitive chord within me was struck, and it became hard to imagine myself handling threat in the old way. This does not mean there are not discouraging times or moments when I feel like giving up, but even those occasions are now a spur to try a new direction or face a challenge that I previously had been afraid to face. It is freeing to realize that safety is a terrible burden to maintain and that it's not much fun either!

By staying in comfort zones for the better part of my life, I had avoided conflict like the plague. In the women's group, I frequently was the one who poured the oil on the waters and tried to avoid conflict at all costs. At GETTING WELL, my associate director assumed the major responsibility for handling conflict situations both in group and in the program. However, when he resigned, I had to deal with the conflict or have the program go under with me. Given those circumstances, conflict looks absolutely beautiful!

Two little epiphanies hit me at the same time several years ago and helped me crawl out of the hole where I was hiding from conflict. The first was the realization that most people would return to some kind of conflict situation when they left the program. So if GETTING WELL were only a *haven* for its graduates, it would not be serving them well in their real lives. What they needed was to experience conflict and build their emotional muscles for dealing with it appropriately. Secondly, I realized that conflict could be relabeled "communication," and could be a useful tool to enable relationships to become closer.

With these ideas in mind, I began to look at conflict as a game in which both parties, using the skills GETTING WELL teaches, can be winners. This became knowledge for me, not only at the intellectual level, but also at the emotional and intuitive levels. I find I am now able to walk into many new arenas without the frightening shadow of conflict turning me away at the gate. And I've discovered more recently that if one is not afraid of facing conflict or even bids it welcome, it does not rear its head as often and is not so scary when it does.

It may be comfortable to keep the group under control as one might do in a didactic group such as stress management, and it is sometimes tempting to turn the process group into a focus group, because things aren't working out or there are threats of explosion. While such action may be appropriate at some times, I've found the whole point is lost if one takes responsibility for the process away from the members. At the risk of losing safety for myself, I've experimented with letting the group members carry the ball. The results are wonderful! They really can handle their issues beautifully if allowed the freedom and permission to do so. This is another "letting go of control" issue which I found scary at first but which became a powerful and freeing experience for me and for the groups. I can honestly say that the beauty, relief, and power of letting go in the group process has extended into virtually every corner of my life.

8

Relaxation, Imagery, and Meditation Training

Imagery is the universal language of the unconscious.
— *Frances Vaughan*

Imagery is real. The stuff of the world is mind stuff and everything that comes out of mind. One of the forms of mind, one that is inherently transitory, is matter. Images last. Matter withers away. — *James Fadiman*

Tell yourself that everything you visualize is already there. Every *thing* is energy. Everything vibrates at its own level of reality. Having a thought about what you'd like to see happen for yourself, it is nothing more than connecting the two frequencies together to make the reality happen for you. — *Wayne Dyer*

Imagery training is a daily staple of the GETTING WELL program. This session may include relaxation training with imagery, meditation techniques, and transformational fantasy. (Since our staff's training with Dr. John Shaffer, transformational fantasy has become such an integral part of imagery at GETTING WELL that it will be the subject of Chapter 9.) Imagery training is the one time during the day when we might focus on the diagnosis and the direct use of techniques that may affect the person's physical problem. Anees Sheikh's *Anthology of Imagery Techniques* is a splendid resource for the clinician looking for a style and philosophy that will offer optimal advantage to the client and the highest degree of comfort to the therapist.

We accept the hypothesis that imagery is the blueprint for all voluntary behaviors and exerts a preeminent influence on involuntary physical, emotional, and mental behaviors. Imagery takes place all the time in the individual, whether at a conscious or unconscious level. Images may provide healthy blueprints for one's life and body, or they may supply destructive designs for body and spirit. We do not teach a person to image; however, we do facilitate changing from images destructive to health and well-being to those promoting a healthy body and a quality life.

Although we may at times interchange the words, the concepts of "visu-

127

alization" and "imagery" differ. Pat Norris (1988) describes visualization as a consciously chosen visual instruction to the body. It deals, as one would guess, primarily with the sensory modality of sight rather than the totality of sensory information. Imagery, on the other hand, arises spontaneously and involves all the senses. Jean Achterberg (1990) aptly describes imagery as thought with a sensory quality. That sensory quality could be sight, smell, texture, taste, kinesis, feel, sound, or the "felt sense" of Eugene Gendlin.

During this session a combination of techniques is likely to be used, depending on the therapist, the needs and levels of the participants, and the issues of concern at the time. Relaxation, guided imagery, breath work, unguided imagery, transformational fantasy, and meditation-type work may be used in the same session; for clarity's sake, however, I will discuss these in separate sections.

I like to precede each imagery session with a five- to ten-minute rationale for imagery or relaxation training—giving good left-brain reasons for this essentially right-brain experience. We may talk about neuropeptides, examples of successful imagery experiences of participants, the power of the mind-body connection, or some bit of research that has just come to the fore about imagery or mental processes. I usually talk about John Schneider's research, which suggests that the person who tries too hard at imagery, relaxation, or meditation is not as successful as the person who takes a playfully relaxed and curious, "let's see what happens" approach to the process. We also emphasize that there is no right or wrong way in this experience. (It may be necessary to reiterate this many times and in many ways.)

Relaxation and Breathing

Relaxation and deep breathing are wonderful physiological inhibitors to the stress response. In turn, when physical relaxation is in place, there is a concomitant message to the mind and emotions to relax.

Pat Norris has stated that if she had to choose only one stress management technique to teach, it would be breathing. In her fine mind-body program at the Menninger Clinic in Topeka, Pat places a major emphasis on breathing. She suggests that when we breath deeply from our abdomens (as a sleeping baby or cat might do), we send a very different message to our psyches from the one given by shallow, tight, chest breathing. If one can breathe those slow, deep belly breaths during times of crisis, the situation is stripped of its destructive anxiety and the flooding of stress chemicals. In essence, this is a major way for us to intervene in the mind-body cycle: When we change what the body is doing, we change what the mind is thinking and feeling.

A member of our staff, who has studied breathing at Menninger's to reduce the stress that exacerbates her systemic lupus, has designed a weekly session in breathing techniques and hand-warming at GETTING WELL. This hour, focused solely on breathing, includes both didactic and experiential work. During the stress response the blood supply (heat) is channelled away from one's hands and feet, leaving them several degrees colder than the rest of the body. Conversely, during the relaxation response, blood vessels in the hands and feet dilate and their warmth is a measure of the relaxation's depth. She gives little hand-held thermometers to participants to provide biofeedback on the effectiveness of their breathing and the profundity of relaxation.

Nadine, a 40-year-old woman nearly confined to a wheelchair from multiple sclerosis, learned to make an eight-degree difference in the temperature of her hands, according to her thermometer, and began to have feeling in her feet for the first time in years. Through the use of controlled breathing techniques, she was able to make her chronically cold feet comfortable and warm. It was unbelievably empowering for Nadine to realize that she was able to create noticeable physical effects from her own efforts. This session, using a technique that shows a demonstrable effect of the mind on the body, has frequently shifted core beliefs of skeptics and of those who have previously felt powerless in their lives.

Elements of breathing are an integral part of relaxation training, which in turn is a basic step for effective imagery. Many people come into the program so physically tense that it is virtually impossible for them to have a good imagery experience. Progressive relaxation, which was developed decades ago by Jacobson (1938), is useful with these patients.

As a preface to the technique, I say something like this:

> I am going to teach you a technique called progressive relaxation in which you will be instructed to alternately tighten and relax the various muscle groups in the body. The reasons for using this particular technique are at least six-fold. First, in tensing the muscles we learn to recognize muscular tension. Often, we are so used to feeling tension in particular muscle groups that we do not even realize we are tense. Now at least we can know the tension is there and recognize it.
>
> Second, we begin to recognize what a relaxed muscle feels like. Some of us have kept some muscle groups, such as those across the shoulders, so tight over the years that we have no idea what a relaxed muscle in that area feels like. Third, in tensing the muscle quite tightly and suddenly letting it go, you create a deeper relaxation than by simply trying to relax the muscle. Fourth, you begin to learn firsthand the connection between muscular tension and emotions. As you tense your brow, for example, you may notice feelings of worry or anxiety that emanate from the tightening. And as you relax and let go of that tension, you may notice a feeling of peace or comfort taking its place.
>
> Fifth, you may realize that you are responsible for the tension in your

body and that you are responsible for relaxing your tension—that you are, indeed, in charge of how you feel in mind, body, and spirit. Sixth, you learn to gain control by letting go. As you go through the exercise, some of you may find it difficult to let go at first. This is not surprising, because most of us have been taught to hold on tight all the time because we might lose control. However, you will soon see that when you let go of tension in your body, you actually gain power—to change your body, your mind, and your life. Deepak Chopra (1991) suggests that there is more self-control in letting go than in trying to control your body by force.

Now, take a deep breath, down deep into your abdomen and hold it there for a few seconds. Now let it go, all of a sudden, and feel all the tightness and tension leaving your body on your breath. . . . Now let your eyes close gently if you wish, and take another deep abdominal breath . . . hold it . . . and let go of all the tension, feeling every muscle in your body relax as far as it can.

We are going to take a journey through the muscle groups of your body alternately tightening them and relaxing them. First, tighten your fists in a tight ball . . . tight . . . tight . . . now recognize that tension. What does it feel like . . . tight . . . tense. Now totally let go of that tension and let your hands just hang there just like a rag doll's . . . so relaxed . . . so calm . . . so tranquil. What does the relaxation feel like? Notice the difference.

As the therapist goes through the various muscle groups, each group can be tensed and relaxed once or twice. Twice is more effective; however, in the interest of time I usually do each group only once. I usually have people tense for seven seconds and relax for ten or more seconds, my voice tensing during the tightening, and then slowing and reflecting a sense of peace and serenity with the relaxation. I also like to interlace the six "purposes" of progressive relaxation with the patter that accompanies the exercise. If one has the six goals in mind, there is really no need for a script. In fact, I believe the exercise is much more effective if the facilitator is actively tensing and relaxing his or her own muscles and the accompanying talk is in response to what is happening within the therapist.

After the fists we move on to "tighten the hand again and flex the biceps . . . and as you relax, let your forearm and hands be like wet, warm dishrags lying there just so relaxed . . . " (etc.). The exercise continues:

Now put your arms out as if there were a wall in front of you, bending your hands back at the wrist and pushing against the wall . . . tight . . . tense . . . (etc.).

Let your shoulders hunch up at your ears . . . feel the tension . . . know exactly what that tension feels like . . . now, slowly rotate your shoulders to the back . . . keeping the tension up . . . rotate them down . . . to the front . . . and now back up to your ears . . . now, all of a sudden, let them relax and feel the warm relaxation like a floodgate opening, and experience the serenity and peace . . . (etc.).

Tighten your chin to your chest, and notice the tension—remember if there are places where you are injured or have pain, do not put full tension in those places. This exercise should not hurt. As you are experiencing the tension in your neck . . . notice how rays of tension go into your back and chest . . . now, slowly, keeping the tension up, slowly move your head to the right side . . . to the back . . . to the left side . . . and back down on your chest again . . . remembering that you're in charge of this tension. . . . Now, relax! . . . and feel that tension draining away . . . you're in charge of this relaxation . . . (etc.).

Wrinkle your forehead . . . tight . . . tense . . . notice that when you tense these muscles in your brow, there is an emotional reaction . . . possibly anxiety . . . possibly apprehension or fear . . . notice how the tension is eliciting these emotions. . . . Now, relax! . . . and notice, amazingly, when those muscles are relaxed, your forehead is as smooth as a forest lake during the summer . . . and those uncomfortable feelings simply disappear . . . and let these muscles relax even further . . . (etc.).

Close your eyes tightly [*however, remind people with contact lenses to be careful*] . . . feel the discomfort and the tightness . . . you may notice color . . . tense colors . . . possibly stabbing reds and blacks . . . be aware of the tension that is creating these feelings and colors . . . tight . . . tense. . . . Now, relax! . . . and feel your eyes becoming soft and hazy . . . notice the colors you're experiencing now . . . peaceful colors . . . tranquil colors . . . as your eyes relax even further . . . (etc.).

Now, I'd like you to do several things at once. Pull your lips back in a tight smile, clench your jaw, and push your tongue hard to the roof of your mouth . . . feel the tension . . . notice the feelings . . . anger . . . anguish . . . your throat is so tight that no words can escape . . . tight . . . recognize this tension. . . . Now, relax! . . . and notice the difference . . . the uncomfortable feelings have flowed away with the tension . . . your throat feels warm, and moist, and so relaxed . . . as if you could say anything you wished . . . as the warm relaxation flows in . . . placid . . . calm . . . tranquil . . . so relaxed . . . (etc.).

Now, focus on your breathing . . . breath in deeply . . . now, hold it . . . hold it for about seven seconds . . . feeling the tension build in your chest and back and shoulders . . . tight . . . tense . . . be aware of how much tension you may store in this area . . . you create this tension . . . and now let the breath go . . . and feel the relaxation flooding into your chest and upper back as you let the tightness go out on your breath . . . and realize that you have created this beautiful relaxation . . . (etc.).

Focus now on your solar plexus . . . and imagine that someone is ready to throw a hard ball into the center of your body . . . tighten up so that it won't hurt you . . . muscles tightening . . . like a metal shield . . . to protect your organs . . . and feel the tension . . . and notice the feeling that goes with that tension . . . apprehension . . . fear . . . concern. . . . See if that tension has a familiar feel to it . . . and now totally relax that area . . . the danger is gone . . . and feel the relaxation come in like a warm, melting sun . . . so relaxing . . . so calming . . . and notice that those scary feelings have simply disappeared . . . as you let those muscles relax even further . . . serene . . . calm . . . (etc.).

Now, sit in your chair as hard as you can . . . feel the tension spread to your whole pelvis . . . buttocks . . . lower back . . . (etc.).

Push your feet onto the floor as hard as you can . . . feel the tightness coming up through your legs like a spring . . . feel the tightness . . . study it . . . understand it . . . (etc.).

Let your legs extend out in front of you . . . and point your feet back

toward your face . . . feel the tension on the under sides of your legs . . .
like tight rubber bands . . . tighter . . . tighter . . . notice the places you store
tension . . . (etc.).

Now, tighten all the muscle groups in your whole body and hold the
tightness for about seven seconds . . . now, let go . . . and let your whole
body relax . . . so relaxed . . . and tranquil . . . and serene . . . (etc.).

We are now going to revisit all the muscle groups and let the muscles
relax even further . . . if there is any residual tension . . . let it go . . . relax
further and further [*repeat this general idea with each of the muscle groups
revisited*] . . . first, your hands . . . arms . . . head and scalp . . . face . . . throat
and neck . . . shoulders . . . chest . . . solar plexus . . . pelvis . . . thighs . . . lower
legs. . . . Now, scan your body for any tension that is left . . . any residual
tension . . . and simply let it go . . . and let the relaxation fill all the spots the
tension used to be. . . . Take another deep breath . . . and as you let it go,
your body will become twice as relaxed . . . and be totally aware of what it
feels like to have your whole body completely relaxed.

And now that your body is relaxed, we can begin to let your mind relax. . . .
Imagine a set of ten steps in front of you. . . . As you descend these steps,
your mind will become even more relaxed . . . ten . . . relaxed and calm . . .
nine . . . more and more relaxed . . . eight . . . so serene and calm . . . seven
. . . six . . . more and more relaxed, but calm and focused . . . five . . . four
. . . so heavy and relaxed . . . three . . . two . . . totally tranquil . . . one . . .
totally relaxed. . . . Now, step onto the path ahead that leads to a special
place that is all your own. Follow the path to your special place whether it
be by the sea, in the mountains, in a forest, by a river . . . or it may be up in
the clouds . . . or may be in some place that exists only in your imagination.
Allow yourself to be in that special place . . . and spend some time exploring
it . . . its colors and shapes . . . textures . . . sounds . . . smells . . . tastes . . . its
feeling. You can have it any way you would like it to be . . . can bring in
anything you like . . . just the way you want it. And spend some time letting
your mind relax totally. . . . If you would like to anchor your special place in
your mind, simply rub your thumb against your middle finger as your anchor
. . . and you might be happily surprised when you do this an hour from now
. . . a day from now . . . or a week from now . . . that your special place will
come back to you in its entirety . . . just as it is right now in your mind's eye
. . . when you use your anchor . . . rubbing your thumb against your middle
finger.

When you get ready . . . but stay as long as you wish . . . we can go back
down the path to the steps and begin to climb the steps . . . one . . . very
relaxed but more alert . . . two . . . three . . . calm and relaxed . . . four . . .
five . . . serene, but more focused . . . six . . . seven . . . tranquil, but energized . . . eight . . . nine . . . eyelids becoming light . . . eyes beginning to
open . . . ten . . . step off the stairs . . . eyes open . . . relaxed but refreshed
. . . knowing that for the next few hours . . . you will have a wonderful, relaxed energy that will allow you to do whatever you wish . . . knowing also
. . . that you have created this feeling within yourself . . . you're responsible
for it . . . and you can renew this feeling anytime you wish . . . merely by
doing the exercise . . . going to your special place . . . or just by using your
anchor.

I do not always use the full progressive relaxation; instead, I may use
brief (few sentences) muscle relaxation along with the steps down to the

special place and use the special place where the person develops his own imagery. Full progressive relaxation, however, is a wonderful tool for a person who is having problems relaxing or getting into imagery.

James, a 62-year-old physician with cardiovascular disease, had a terrible time with imagery. He labored to obtain the images that he believed would be helpful to his condition, but they just wouldn't come. Finally, it occurred to us to use progressive relaxation, which was metaphorically consistent with James' personal belief that one had to *earn* relaxation. The idea of working to tense the muscle groups before one relaxed them was ideologically more palatable to James than just relaxing. Actually, it took only a couple of progressive relaxation run-throughs before he could effectively use the anchor to relax himself totally. He began to see relaxation less as a matter of losing control than as a way to gain personal power.

Meditation, Mindfulness, and Yoga

Meditation, mindfulness, and yoga techniques are most commonly used in the high-level awareness session, although we have a special group to teach meditation and yoga techniques once a week. Some programs (e.g., Jon Kabat-Zinn's program at the University of Massachusetts Medical Center, described in *Full Catastrophe Living*) have meditation as the major focus of the whole program—with excellent results. We encourage those participants who are so disposed to initiate or continue meditation practices on their own time.

The main reason pure meditation practices are not a daily part of the program is time. A secondary reason is that most people who enter the program have such a strong Western enculturation that a sudden shift to the inner Eastern style is very difficult for them. Additionally, we frequently encounter participants with fundamentalist religious views who want nothing to do with yoga, meditation, or hypnosis. Certainly the philosophy of mindfulness, yoga, and meditation is integral to what we are teaching at GETTING WELL, and although we do not provide comprehensive training, we do provide a way for participants to embrace meditation and seek further training.

Nearly 20 years ago, a psychologist presenting at a regional meeting of the American Psychological Association read a "meditation" that moved me deeply. I had the forethought to tape the session. After laboriously transcribing the exercise from a poor tape, I used the bits and pieces of it for years with good results. Nearly 15 years later, I came across it again in Dr. Frances Vaughan's exceptional book, *Awakening Intuition* (an absolute *must* for anyone in this field), and discovered it had been developed by Lester Fehmi, Ph.D., of the Behavioral Medicine and Biofeedback Clinic of Princeton. I have found Fehmi's Open Focus exercise to be an ex-

tremely effective bridge among the areas of relaxation, imagery, mindfulness, and meditation. Talking to Fehmi, I have become fascinated with
his translation of consciousness into space to effect a flow, balance, and
connectedness that is the basis for healing the mind, body, and spirit.
Open focus can be seen as an altered state of awareness in which denial
processes are dropped, thus promoting alert tranquility, normalization of
physiological processes, and performance optimization. Fehmi's work is
most compelling, and worth close perusal, and I deeply appreciate the
permission he has graciously given me to use Open Focus.

The Open Focus exercise consists of a series of questions to stimulate your
imagination of objectless experience, and to broaden attentional scope of
focus in an effortless and relaxed way. For example, "Can you imagine
the distance or space between your eyes?" By distributing attention over a
distance, volume, region or space in the body, one naturally lets go of internal and external objects of sensation as the apprehended focus of objective,
separate attention.

This exercise is in the form of a series of questions; the answer to each
question is your experiencing what it asks. (Allow approximately 15 seconds
between images.)

Is it possible for you to imagine or can you imagine —
    . . . the space between your eyes . . . ears . . . throat . . . shoulders . . .
hips . . . thumb and first finger on each hand . . . first and middle finger on
each hand . . . middle and fourth finger on each hand . . . the space between
all your fingers simultaneously . . . that your thumbs are filled with space . . .
    that the region between the tips of your fingers and your wrists is filled
with space . . . between your wrists and your elbows is filled with space . . .
between your elbows and shoulders is filled with space . . . between your
shoulders is filled with space . . .
    that the space inside your throat is coextensive with the space between
your shoulders and your shoulders and arms, hands, and fingers . . .
    that the regions inside your shoulders, and the regions between your
shoulders and fingertips is simultaneously filled with space. . . .
    Is it possible to imagine the space between your toes . . . that your toes
are filled with space . . . that your feet and toes . . . the region between your
arches and your ankles . . . between your ankles and your knees . . . between
your knees and your hips . . . between your hips is filled with space . . .
    that your lower abdomen . . . lower back . . . is filled with space . . . that
your body from the diaphragm down is filled with space . . . that the region
between your kidneys . . . inside your kidneys . . . between your navel and
your backbone . . . inside your stomach . . . inside your rib cage . . . between
your ribs . . . between your shoulder blades . . . between your shoulders and
your ribs . . . inside your neck . . . between your shoulder blades and your
chin is filled with space . . .
    the space inside your lungs . . . inside your bronchial tubes as you inhale
and exhale . . . the space inside your throat . . . your nose as you inhale and
exhale . . .
    that your jaw . . . cheeks and mouth . . . tongue . . . teeth and gums . . .
lips are filled with space . . . that the region between your eyes and the back

of your neck . . . between the bridge of your nose and back of your head . . . between your temples is filled with space . . . that your forehead . . . brain . . . spine is filled with space . . . that your whole head is simultaneously filled with space . . . that your whole head and your face are simultaneously filled with space . . .

that your whole being fills with air when you inhale and your whole being is left filled with space when you exhale. . . .

At the same time that you are imagining the space inside your whole body, is it possible for you to imagine the space around your body, the space between your fingers and toes, behind your neck and back, the space above your head and beneath your chair, and the space in front of you and to your sides . . .

that the boundaries between the space inside and space outside are dissolving and that the space inside and the space outside become one continuous and unified space . . .

that this unified space, which is coextensive inside and outside, proceeds in three dimensions, front to back, right to left, and up and down . . .

that, at the same time you imagine this unified space, you can simultaneously let yourself attend equally to all the sounds that are available to you, the sound of my voice, the sounds issuing from you and other members of the group, and any other sounds that you may be able to hear . . . that these sounds are issuing from and pervaded by unified space . . .

that at the same time you are attending to the space and the sounds you can also attend simultaneously to any emotions, tensions, feelings, or pains that might also be present . . . that these sensations and perceptions are permeated by space . . .

that at the same time you are aware of the space, the sounds, emotions and other body feelings, you can also be simultaneously aware of any taste, smells, thoughts, and imagery that might be present . . . that you also can now admit to awareness any sensation or experience which was inadvertently omitted thus far, so that you are now simultaneously aware of your entire being, of all that is you . . .

that all your experience is permeated and pervaded by space . . .

that, as you continue to practice this Open Focus exercise, you will increase your ability to enter into Open Focus more quickly and more completely and more effortlessly . . .

that, as you continue to practice this Open Focus exercise, your imagery of space will become more vivid and more pervasive . . . and your ability to imagine space permeating all of your experience will continue to be vivid and ever-present. (Fehmi & Fritz, 1980, pp. 29–30)

Guided Imagery

Although a major section of this book is devoted to guided imagery, the most effective imagery in the long haul is imagery that the participant has designed himself or that unfolds as it is happening, such as occurs in transformational imagery. Guided imagery is fine as long as it serves as a means to that end, yet it is perhaps not the most effective end in itself. The wonderful tapes of Bernie Siegel, Diane Keck, Emmett Miller, Carl Simonton, Adelaide Davis, and others serve a purpose by leading someone to imagery, expanding that person's idea of the parameters of imagery, and being easily accessible. In particular, giving someone a tape of a guided imagery to use before chemotherapy or after surgery is convenient and helpful.

Jumping into asking people to design their own imagery or even presenting them with an unguided imagery can lead to confusion and frustration. Therefore, it's best to begin by presenting a guided imagery to let them know what the process is about. Using guided imagery may give participants useful images from which they can create their own, as well as a secure handrail on a stairway which eventually will take them where they need to go.

At GETTING WELL we encounter certain conditions which seem to be accompanied by impaired dream life and inability to image. It is not clear whether the problem lies with the condition itself or with the personality characteristics that may shape the condition. Jeanne Achterberg has noted that people with autoimmune diseases seem to have a reduced ability to generate their own imagery, and therapists at GETTING WELL with rheumatoid arthritis have noticed differences in their own ability to image and to remember dreams since the onset of their symptoms. For these individuals, guided imagery may be necessary until the missing link is found or the walls of repression are dissolved.

Guided imagery is also useful for the therapist who has not facilitated imagery or relaxation long enough to feel comfortable doing it without a script (or a tape). Twenty years ago when doing relaxation or imagery was a "big deal," I even experienced some stage fright before a session in which I planned to so some of this "strange" stuff. Using a script or someone else's tape made it easier for me until I became comfortable using extemporaneous guided images with my clients or groups. Since then I have regularly made guided imagery tapes which I have duplicated for various focus groups dealing with issues such as panic disorder, stress management, and behavioral weight control. Although there is an element of imagery in these tapes, their focus lies mainly in cognitive restructuring and support when facing an eating, panic, or stress crisis.

At GETTING WELL, each participant receives an "anthology" tape of imagery for cancer, self-esteem, or letting go, depending upon his or her physical diagnosis. Adelaide Davis, our resident expert weaver of rich images, has recently recorded several tapes that embrace a variety of conditions, which are available to the public as well as to participants.* While

---

*See the Resource Guide at the end of the book for a listing of these and other useful audiotapes.

these guided imagery tapes serve the purpose of introducing a person to the imagery process, they are only the beginning of the journey, because a person who stays solely with tapes and guided imagery will find that his or her personal growth and healing is stunted. Nonetheless, guided imagery and tape recordings are far better than nothing at all.

One of the problems with guided imagery, whether on tape or created for the individual by a therapist, is that it encourages an outer locus of control. Participants sometimes say, "This person is an expert whose images are better than mine." Not infrequently, clients panic because a relaxation or imagery tape wears out or breaks. As crutches, tapes and guided imageries need to be put aside as the *major* imagery focus as soon as possible. The process needs to be internalized so that the person doesn't need a tape, a quiet spot, or a special time — the new imagery needs to become a natural part of every thought.

Glenda, a high school teacher, decided to divorce her husband of 22 years the day she went in for surgery for colon cancer. "He's been a pain in the ass for the last 15 years, and if I'm going to live, I've got to get rid of that pain," she said. Unfortunately, surgery, chemotherapy, radiation, and even divorce did not prevent her cancer from spreading. We met Glenda immediately preceding her trip to the National Cancer Institute for her third round of experimental treatment. "It's a real bitch!" she exclaimed. "I walk into my motel room in Maryland, and I immediately get deathly ill and start throwing up — and I haven't even started getting the chemo." We worked with her on imagery that afternoon, and I promised to make a tape for her to use on the plane the next day.

As luck would have it, the next morning a television crew was swarming through our offices and group rooms (converted hospital rooms), and the only sanctuary was the tiny bathroom in my office. I made Glenda an ambitious 30-minute tape with a musical background while sitting on the toilet, with the tape recorder on the sink, the tape player on the tile floor, and the TV crew moving equipment and shouting orders outside the door. I used the Simontons' imagery as a skeleton, expanding on the beneficial effects of the treatment, etc. I dubbed the tape, Glenda picked it up on her way to the airport, and three weeks later I heard from her. "You won't believe this," she told me excitedly, "but I just sailed through my treatment this time. I didn't get sick in the motel room; as a matter of fact, when I walked in the room, I felt a heavy load fall off my shoulders, and I actually felt *better than I had in a long time!*" (I never knew if it was the tape or her laughter over the image of me perched on the toilet lid, juggling tape recorders and healing messages, that did the trick!)

Glenda became proficient with imagery, and at the end of her clinical trial she was the only one in her "class" with a *full* remission. When others in the class asked the professionals in charge what the difference was, they were told that it *might* be the imagery she used in conjunction with the treatment. Glenda, however, was *convinced* that it was her imagery, which allowed her experimental treatment to do what she hoped.

Unguided (Participant-Generated) Imagery

Ideally we gently probe the problem, work with the individual on generating imagery, and plan as a team an expansion of the person's own imagery. Several individual sessions—apart from the group—are necessary for the person to begin formulating the most effective imagery for himself or herself. In the group situation, I like to experiment with imagery that has a little structure but still allows the person to devise his or her own images. For example, I may ask that people go to some part of their body which is experiencing a problem and see the problem as a symbol, using whatever image comes to them. I then suggest that they evolve a healing symbol with special meaning to them and allow the healing to take place. We teach "veterans" to ignore our own slight guidance and go in their mind's eye wherever they wish.

I usually suggest that outside noises or commotion should merely serve to deepen the relaxation being experienced. We never have had, nor probably ever will have, a situation in which the environment cooperates with a sense of peace. There will always be a lawn mower running, a carpet cleaner operating, or a physician demanding to see his/her patient right at that moment. I tell participants (with tongue in cheek) that we have planned these interruptions so they can hone the experience of being able to relax/meditate or to image, *no matter what is happening*. I explain that almost anyone can relax when the situation is quiet and peaceful, but to be able to relax during chaos is a powerful skill.

I cannot emphasize enough the importance of getting participants connected with their own intuitive imagery process. It certainly is more work for the therapist to give over control to the individual, yet it is crucial to do so. The results—enhancement of the mind, body, emotions, and spirit of the participant—speak for this choice.

Jetta, a young woman in her late twenties, came into the program with more than 50 active tumors in her abdominal region and, as one would expect, a dismal prognosis from her physician. She was, in addition, on high dosages of morphine-based medication for the pain. She was very concerned about what would happen to her preschool daughter in the event of her death, and wanted to stay alive "just a little longer." Under her self-effacing demeanor there was a brilliant, creative mind. Jetta, a self-described "neatnik," designed an elaborate image, seeing the immune system as the housekeeping service for a large hotel. The tumors became the dirt and disarray found in the many rooms of the hotel.

As the supervisor of housekeeping, Jetta kept her crew of maids scurrying, making the daily rounds of all the rooms. If a room could not be completely cleaned during a visit, the door was locked so that none of the filth could sully the hallway or other rooms. The cleaning crew would be sent back to those locked rooms to finish up the job when the other rooms had received at least a thorough once-over. There were many twists and turns to the scenario—rather like a detective novel; however, the clever maids eventually triumphed over dirt and some surprisingly messy guests. By the end of the 28 days, Jetta was feeling wonderful. She was able to control her pain with an occasional aspirin, and her next visit to her physician several weeks later showed that 50 percent of her tumors had disappeared and those that were left were diminished by nearly 50 percent. Nearly two years later, her oncologist announced that Jetta had experienced a "spontaneous remission." Jetta took a bit of humorous umbrage at the statement. "This wasn't spontaneous. I worked hard for this remission, and I'd like some credit!" she exclaimed.

General Considerations in Designing Imagery

It is difficult to sort out my mentors in imagery, since the basic philosophy was internalized (without source references) many years ago. Certainly the Simontons, Jeanne Achterberg, Patricia Norris, Anees Sheikh, Martin Rossman, and John Shaffer have been enormous influences, but exact attributions, for the most part, have long since been lost (though certainly not my gratitude for their influence).

One needs to be aware that imagery goes on at all times in our beings, at both the conscious level and the unconscious (maybe even the cellular) level. It is first necessary to explore the imagery already in place concerning disease, health, values, fears—what the person sees occurring in the body, and as many aspects as possible of an individual's world view. Any guided imagery must be syntonic with the individual's core beliefs. Imagery cannot be effective unless it is in line with the person's deepest values and does not contradict that person's world view. For example, Jetta was a "flower child" and was deeply disturbed by imagery that had the immune system brutally slaying her cancer cells. On the other hand, her "cleaning crew" got the job done in a way that was syntonic with her values. Another interesting example of imagery that had to be customized was a tape I made for a panic disorder group years ago. In the taped imagery, one reached his or her special place by going down an escalator. As it turned out, at least a third of the group members were petrified of being on an escalator! We eventually were able to work the escalator into a therapeutic experience, but at the time it destroyed the effectiveness of the imagery.

Similarly, guided imagery must be idiosyncratic and must reflect deep personal meaning and metaphor. (In the next chapter, this aspect will be explored more deeply.) Pat Norris, whose book, *Why Me?* (written with Garrett Porter), tells the odyssey of facilitating Porter's development of his life-saving Star Wars imagery, suggests that ready-made visualizations from a therapist or on commercial tapes are of limited value and have a place only where they tap into the unique unconscious desires, preferences, and values of the individual. For example, Jetta's wonderful cleaning and organizing imagery would be wasted on me, yet was exactly right for her.

Particularly with immune deficiency diseases such as cancer and HIV, the disease symbol should be seen as weak, less intelligent, non-menacing or nondangerous, smaller, less active, and less defined than the image of the healing process. With autoimmune diseases, the disease symbol may in the beginning be seen as wild, burning, and raging—but eminently tamable, reversible, or manageable. For example, for Jetta the dirt or untidiness of the hotel rooms was mainly an inconvenience or a job to be done rather than an overwhelming task. For individuals dealing with clogged coronary arteries, the atherosclerosis is simply unintelligent "gunk" to be reamed out by a Roto-Rooter®. When the disease is seen as powerful, the power of the metaphor needs to become a therapeutic issue. For example, Syd's arteries were clogged with a concrete-like substance that was unmovable. As we began to explore issues, he began to see connections between his father's stoic emotional messages to him and his inability to express deep feelings. When we began to resolve these issues, the concrete plaque started dissolving into a more pliable and removable substance.

The healing symbol needs to be seen as powerful, intelligent, active, vivid, focused, competent, and large. With autommune diseases, the healing symbol might befriend and tame the immune system without vitiating its protective attributes for true invaders, or the symbol might selectively teach elements of the immune system how to behave. As might be expected, healthy cells need to be seen as powerful and invincible, while unhealthy functions or cells need to be seen as weak and malleable. If an anatomical image is to be used, it needs to be physiologically correct. Even deeply metaphoric and symbolic images need to be crafted along these lines for the end result to be in tune with the needs of the body.

Medical treatment should be visualized as eminently effective—with healthy cells protected from the radiation or chemotherapy designed to destroy the unhealthy cells. In cardiovascular disease, one might see surgery or antihypertensive medication as giving the body a jump-start on dealing with physical problems, making it easier for the bodymind to pump out more nitric oxide for relaxation or to break down plaque on arterial walls. In autoimmune diseases, treatment to suppress the immune system can be seen as quite selective—acting only on the elements that need suppression without creating negative effects in other functions of the body. For example, Jetta used the image of her pain medication jump-starting the endorphin release valves in her body, which she imaged as a sprinkler system putting out the "fires" of pain in her hotel rooms.

The concept of restoring balance should be intimately entwined with all images. Imagery is powerful! Frequently, medical science does not know exactly what is happening, and we could be doing damage by imaging an incorrect theory. The bodymind is incredibly intelligent, so it may be that we need to leave the exact process of what to do up to our own "control center." In all imagery concepts of *balance* and *wholeness* should come into play most powerfully. Jetta's imagery was metaphoric rather than anatomical, yet deeply embedded in its unfolding was the sense of balance and of her "hotel" returning to an image of a perfectly working system.

Wayne Dyer (1989) suggests that willingness, rather than determination, perseverance, and trying hard, is the most important factor in imaging. This is in line with John Schneider's (1989) research indicating that when a subject works too hard at imagery his or her blood results show fewer changes than blood results found in the person who images in a rather playful manner. If imagery has not worked, Dyer feels one needs to ask oneself, "What is it that I am unwilling to do?" Although he is speaking of visualizing successes in life rather than of physical changes, this provocative question may be helpful to some people.

For best results, the disease image needs to be seen as *completely* gone and the body perfectly healthy at the end of the imagery session, and the patient should affirm that everything he or she imaged is already in place. In our experience, when the image of *mostly gone* is left, the message is picked up by the body. In other words, loving one's disease and not wanting to have it *completely* gone may allow the body to accept the disease and create a pleasant place for it to evolve. The image is a blueprint for what is to happen, so *be sure the blueprint is what you want!*

Some of these tenets are arguable; however, these guidelines have worked for our participants and are supported by the work of other experts in the imagery field. At GETTING WELL we are always open to new ideas and eager to hear of guidelines that have worked for others.

Lessons for the Author/Clinician

I have never felt that I was a "natural" at imagery, relaxation, or meditation, although I have actually put them to use most of my life. My big lesson has been that it works if I do it! The need to "put my money where my mouth is" prompted me to include imagery and meditation in my own daily life. Although at the beginning I was imaging only because I was too embarrassed to admit to participants that I was not, it soon became a part of my daily routine. (This is an example of the positive actions that sometimes arise from guilt!)

I began by using a generalized imagery similar to the "Color Imagery" you will find in Chapter 25. This imagery involves breathing healing color into various parts of the body and breathing out "dis-ease," negativity, or discomfort. One of my first projects was elbow warts, which had grown back after surgical removal. I had the healing color go everywhere in my body except to the roots of those warts, and I literally starved them into dissolution within a couple of weeks.

When a cold or sore throat threatens, I simply have my immune system flood those extraneous viruses with exactly the dose of immune cells needed to send the invaders running. With aches or pains, I use either my colors or a transformational fantasy technique in which I go directly to the site of the pain and symbolically soothe it. I use imagery often and am continually amazed at how well it does *work*.

In imaging myself and my life as I would like for it to be, I found that I was held back from seeing things happen as I would wish by the niggling superstition that if one wished for too many good things, one was tempting fate. And there was another "irrational belief"—that I would be less disappointed if the magic event didn't happen if I had not imaged it as happening. Although the evolution of these beliefs into more productive ones has been going on for a long time, GETTING WELL has helped me throw over their last traces. I can now easily image an audience thoroughly enjoying one of my talks or wonderful opportunities coming the way of GETTING WELL, without feeling arrogant or even slightly delusional. And amazingly, things continue to happen the way I image them!

9

Transformational Fantasy

The psyche, or some higher aspect of mind, creates an ongoing fantasy story within our lives—a drama with which most of us never communicate. . . . The play, however, has no set script—the person experiencing the fantasy improvises as he/she changes with the spontaneous development of the plot. —*John T. Shaffer*

We need to ride our images as one would ride a giant eagle soaring up and down, wherever they take us . . . our creativity does not consist in being right all the time but in making all our experiences, including the imperfect ones, a holy whole . . . who knows what lies beyond our images until we trust them enough to ride them fully, even into the darkness and into the depths like a seed in the soil. —*Matthew Fox*

All of us use these transformative modalities in everyday life to varying degrees. . . . But we generally use many of our innate abilities in a dissociated fumbling and unconscious way. Conscious transformative practice builds on the half-conscious practice of life in general. —*Michael Murphy*

D r. John Thomas Adams Shaffer is a genius! He studied with Carl Rogers at the University of Chicago, received his doctorate in theology, became fascinated with Assagioli's psychosynthesis, and developed a whole new field of "directed daydreams," "guided imagery," "symbolic visualization," "twilight imagery," and "guided fantasy," which he chose to call "transformational fantasy."

I was first introduced to TF a number of years ago at the Third World Conference on Imagery in Washington, D.C., in a workshop with Dr. Shaffer and Dr. Jack Birnbaum, a psychiatrist from Canada. Without any of the hoopla of trances or extended relaxation, Birnbaum asked us to "be at a place in your body where there is a problem." To my amazement, people were there! With Jack's guidance, one person was talking to a sore and churning stomach, and another one was repainting a room full of guilt—and by the expressions on their faces and the gestures they were making, I could tell that they were actually there. And I was there, too, vividly seeing a problem that was gnawing away at me. Because I found it difficult to hurt or destroy the little creature that was nibbling away, I was able to take him gently out into a forest and set him free. (And the gnawing

143

problem was gone!) If this workshop had not been led by professionals who I knew had the consummate respect of major clinicians in the field, I might have felt I was at a "healing" tent meeting without the usual theatrics.

An epiphany took place that evening, although I had no idea what it meant for my life or for GETTING WELL. The next year I attended a training workshop for professionals which Shaffer conducted in Boston, and discovered that this brilliant, distinguished scholar was also a kind, funny, generous, unassuming, gifted teacher—and a special human being. After that workshop, I began seriously incorporating TF into GETTING WELL, and for the last several years, Shaffer has come to Florida to train our staff and work with our patients. We remain in awe of the results we see from TF, of its ability both to diminish negative physical symptoms and to help participants deal with unconscious emotional issues such as guilt and resentment that may be impeding the healing process.

TF is certainly a right-brain technique, and left-brain techniques such as writing and even speaking do not do it justice. Of all the techniques discussed in this book, TF is the one least suited to being conveyed and taught verbally, yet it is the one most conducive to creating sudden insight. Experience is the only way to truly learn TF, and I feel it is worth whatever it takes to study with Shaffer in St. Louis if one is really serious about transformational fantasy and PNI.

Transformational fantasy is much more than a strategy or a technique. It is a philosophy and a process in which the therapist is merely a facilitator or a companion in the participant's own fantasy. In working with this fantasy process, Shaffer asserts that

> . . . the psyche, or some higher aspect of mind, creates an ongoing fantasy story within our lives—a drama with which most of us never communicate. This fantasy story is like a series of scenes from a mystery, or acts from an ongoing play. The play, however, has no set script—the person experiencing the fantasy improvises as he or she changes with the spontaneous development of the plot. Solving the plot of the fantasy symbolically usually produces a transformation which yields a solution to a real-life problem. The transformation is part of a process that avoids any kind of predetermined framework. (1986, p. 325)

Shaffer frequently refers to his work as "psyche-drama," with the subject being not only all of the main actors but also director and producer of the play and the facilitator being the drama coach and stage manager.

Setting for the Fantasy

Shaffer suggests using a calm and peaceful room that is dimly and soothingly lit. (I have found, however, that this ideal setting is not necessary for the process to work.) He begins by giving an explanation:

What you are about to experience is similar to a dream because you will be caught up in your fantasy as you are in a dream. You will have a very real sense of "being there." You are not "creating" the dream. Instead, it just happens, entirely of its own accord. You will experience the fantasy from two points of view. One part of you is caught up in the fantasy experience. At the same time, another part of you is objectively looking at the experience and is able to report both feeling and content to me without shattering the fantasy. You will be able to live completely inside the fantasy, and at the same time, you and I will be sharing. The simplest way to understand what fantasy is like is to experience it.

Close your eyes. Relax in your own way as much as possible. . . . Breathe deeply several times using your diaphram. . . . You are walking down a strange road or strange street. Look around and observe where you are. As you walk along, you come to an unusual house. . . . Tell me about it when you are ready. . . . (1986, p. 326)

Shaffer notes that most subjects have little difficulty entering the fantasy quickly, even in a group situation. I have frequently done this image in a group setting, and after members have explored their houses, we process what each person has experienced. Sometimes there are barriers to getting into the scene or perhaps some aspect of the fantasy that was frightening or blocked. When these barriers occur, I ask the person to go back inside and together we process what is happening. Frequently I can facilitate the individual's calling upon some inner resources to help unlock the scene. At first I felt uncomfortable doing this, and of course, so did the individual! However, I am finding that the more my attitude is "this is the way this exciting strategy is done," the more it is accepted by participants. According to Shaffer:

Most subjects have little or no difficulty entering the fantasy quickly. Some report in immediately. Others may take up to a minute. The reporting involves a surprisingly easy process of disengaging the conscious mind. If the person does not report in fairly soon, the therapist asks, "What's happening?" In a few instances, the subject may have trouble seeing the house or in experiencing the particular stage setting agreed upon. If this happens, the guide begins where the subject is. He/she asks what the person is experiencing and seeks to help him/her in exploring it. Generally, the subject in a fantasy is able to slip into and out of altered states of consciousness at will, in a way that allows him/her to interact creatively with his/her own internal resources. (1986, p. 325)

Using the house image is a good way to get started in a group setting. After "setting the scene" and letting group members explore the house, I ask them to come back to where they started, and we process the images:

PATIENT: It was a really unusual house, not really strange, but not your ordinary house. But . . . and this didn't feel really good, there was a lot of junk in the yard. It just ruined the looks of the place.

GUIDE: How would you feel about going back inside and taking a closer look?

PATIENT: Yeah . . . I'd like that. (*closes eyes and after a few seconds begins to describe the scene again*)

GUIDE: Tell me a little about the junk. Do you recognize it? What's it doing there?

PATIENT: Hmmm. Most of it I don't recognize . . . but I do see an old frazzled rabbit that my brother used to play with . . . what's that doing there?

GUIDE: That's interesting. What's it doing there? Could you ask it?

PATIENT: I've always hated that rabbit. Whenever my brother wanted something, he got it. And if he didn't, he had "Rabby" to comfort him. I was told I was too big to have a stuffed animal.

GUIDE: Go ahead and ask "Rabby" what he's doing in front of your house and what he means to you.

These questions led to unresolved issues the individual had with her brother. There was not time to go into the other pieces of "junk" that sullied the yard of her house, but the stage was set to deal with them at a later time.

A wonderful aspect of imagery is that when a change is made in the "unconscious" imagery a significant change also occurs in how one sees oneself in the world. Another individual, Roma, a first-rate nurse, saw the house as a broken-down shack:

ROMA: It's just a heap of wood and wire and rubble. It's not worth a whole lot.

GUIDE: Hmmm. What does it remind you of? What meaning does it have for you?

ROMA: I guess it sort of reminds me of myself and my life. The place is liveable, but just barely.

GUIDE: Is there anything that you'd like to do with it?

ROMA: Well . . . yes. But it's such a big job, I'm not sure I can do it myself.

GUIDE: Is there someplace where you could get some help?

ROMA: I don't really think so. . . . Hey, I'll bet my grandmother would help.

GUIDE: What about asking her? She might have some friends who would give you a hand.

ROMA: I think my grandmother will be enough . . . with me. Now let's just tear down this old wood and start putting things together the way they should be. (*The whole group could observe the work which was going on by the expression on her face and the movement of her hands.*) . . . Yes, this is nice. The old wood has a history, so we still want to use it, but we're getting a lot of new wood. It's a nice little cottage now, and Granny is putting some finishing touches on it, and it's okay.

When Roma came back to the group, she looked as if she had lost five years from her face and appeared more relaxed than I had seen her in a long time. "That is amazing," she said. "I really feel much better about myself. It was simple, yet so amazing." And, Roma is right. TF *is* simple, and even after years of using it, so amazing.

The Role of the Facilitator/Guide

The therapist will generally be the guide in TF, although in some groups trained by Shaffer the members serve as guides for each other. I have found that to use TF effectively, one needs a guide to facilitate getting through the inevitable blocks—a person simply cannot do this on his or her own. The "guide" is more like a Rogerian facilitator than someone who controls or guides the action of the subject. The facilitator is the drama coach and stage manager for the psyche-drama. To quote Shaffer:

> The subject's partner in fantasy actually *follows* him/her closely. The guide's principal task is to understand all the nuances of what the subject is experiencing within fantasy. From time to time, the guide may need to ask questions for his/her own clarification. In this sense, it is the subject who is leading the guide in order that the latter may participate meaningfully in the experience. This feeling of mutual participation is basic to the success of fantasy.
>
> The second task of the guide is to communicate his/her understanding of what the subject is saying and experiencing. This is different from the first form of clarification, in which the guide seeks to understand. In the second task, the guide translates his/her understanding into the subject's terms. This process helps to reassure the subject that the guide is following sensitively and knows what is going on. Such a translation of understanding is important in helping the subject gain insight into his/her own feelings as the process unfolds.
>
> The final task of the guide is to help move the experience along. In the early sessions especially, the subject does not know what to expect in guided fantasy. He/she has no idea of the creative possibilities of his/her own resources. This is especially true in dealing with strange and unexpected events or objects having a symbolic quality. The guide assists by offering various procedural aids to expedite the subject's progress: "Talk to the house. Tell it you want to be friends," "Ask the monster for help," and "Be the dark pit." The guide assists the subject in experiencing the full depth and breadth of his/her fantasy.
>
> Sometimes the subject becomes blocked and does not know what to do. In this case, the guide simply can wait and see what will happen. The subject usually experiences some cue within the fantasy and a new direction and

movement emerges. Many times, however, the subject is really blocked. Experiencing and then overcoming the blocking may be the most important thing for the subject. As this happens, the client gains confidence and experience in taking control of his/her life.

Although the guide strives to experience the emotional feel of the subject's fantasy, he/she must maintain his/her objectivity. He/she needs to be able to survey the emerging plot, or plots, of the fantasy in order to be able to help the subject when blocking of some kind occurs. In such a case, the guide's sensitivity to the subject's present state, along with his/her memory of what has happened earlier, enables him/her to give good procedural guidance. In addition, the fantasy experience tends to be self-correcting as far as the guide is concerned. The subject will either ignore or refuse a suggestion that is not consistent with the inner movement of the fantasy. . . .

We have seen how the psyche becomes a spontaneous storyteller. Like the waters of an underground spring which flow to and fro and finally bubble up through fissures in the overlying rock, so the psyche's "plot" seeks to bypass conscious and unconscious resistance. There appear to be two functions of this blocking. A learning dilemma, that is, a problem to be solved, is the most common reason for the appearance of a block. The psyche seems to be testing the will or the strength of a person. In doing this, it also forces the individual to stop and really become acquainted with the whole area. Then he/she will discover many reasons for the block, and this discovery opens up many new possibilities for growth and learning.

A second function of a block is best illustrated by the ending of the old Looney Tunes® films: "That's all folks!" The psyche, for some reason, is closing out the fantasy experience. It is my hypothesis that the psyche carefully protects the person from going too far, too fast in a fantasy. We have come upon this phenomenon many times. Gloria experienced both the "That's all folks!" ending and one of an entirely different kind. She was on a path leading to a desired goal, when she was suddenly confronted with a large plastic shield blocking her way. Nearby was a ladder; she placed it against the shield and climbed up. To her surprise, the ladder curved backwards and unceremoniously deposited her behind where she had started. Not to be outdone, she began to dig a tunnel under the shield, but instead of coming up behind the shield, she came up in front of her starting point. With more stubbornness than ever, she looked for another way. It appeared that there was a path leading off to the left around the shield. She followed the path, but it brought her back to the starting place again! At this point, she gave up with the remark, "I guess I'm not supposed to go out there today."

Another type of blocking, which appears to be a signal of the psyche to stop, is blackness, or a light so bright so that one cannot see. Such hindrances appear often in fantasy but usually last only for a single episode. Indeed, by the time the person comes back to the next session, the block may be completely gone. When structures of resistance are encountered, it may be necessary to call upon the resources of the guide. Sometimes his/her role is to get the subject to do what he/she at first doesn't want to do. (1986, pp. 328–329, 341)

Shaffer has given the example of a man whose nightmares involved a room wallpapered with live snakes, the bites of which he was constantly dodging and avoiding. He suggested to the man that he let one of the snakes bite him. As the snake was "biting" the patient, he stroked its head and found the snake actually liked him. After the TF experience, he never had his snake dream again.

A major goal of TF is to facilitate the building of inner resources. It is important that the guide not take over as director of the person's inner drama; however, when the person seems hopelessly blocked the guide might tentatively say, "Would you be interested in trying this as an experiment?" Usually, given enough time, participants come up with their own solutions. People are incredibly creative in their inner dramas if we give them the time and latitude to be. To this end, it is imperative that the facilitator remain calm and avoid jumping in too soon, which might hinder the individual in creating his or her own solution.

Basic Staging Areas for Transformational Fantasy

There is an uncounted number of stages on which the unconscious fantasy unfolds from the faithful "head center" to what Shaffer calls the "cosmic board of review." We, as therapists, have our creative fun in helping the client examine staging areas of which he or she might never have dreamed. And I want to point out that TF is fun and playful, even in some of the most serious situations. Four or five staging areas are fundamental to getting started and will keep one going at a basic level until experiential training is possible.

I like to use the head center as a starting place. It is located between the right and left hemispheres of the brain and is equidistant front and back, up and down. It is home base, a comfortable place from which one can go in all directions, forward, backward, up, down, right, or left. Sometimes people keep their inner child or some other inner guide there. It's a safe place, a place of balance, and can be whatever the individual wants it to be.

The right and left hemispheres are rich staging areas that can be reached from the head center. Even without knowledge of "right-brain/left-brain" languaging, people most frequently see the hemispheres as quite different from all sensory angles.

The "hallway of the mind" goes back into the past and contains virtually every experience and sensation one has ever experienced. It is a wonderful place to reexperience and explore parts of one's past that are impinging on the present. The back corridors of the mind are a laboratory in which one can literally transform the drama of the past and change thoughts, beliefs, and behaviors for a fuller and more joyful life in the present.

The body in general or the particular area of a physical problem is another rich staging area. Although at times the therapist may wish to designate a specific area for the person or group (e.g., the heart center or the solar plexus), I usually let participants make this decision.

The "control center" of the brain may be a staging area in itself, or one might have a "control room" in the back corridors of the mind. The control center may be the place where computer printouts concerning what's happening in the cardiovascular, immune, endocrine, or other system can be read, and knobs turned, keys punched, and levers pulled to effect change in the system.

Using Transformational Fantasy in a Group Setting

Although transformational fantasy is used extensively in individual therapy at GETTING WELL, I also use it in group sessions where members can enjoy and gain from one another's images. The creativity and improbability of the images that come forth seem to give license, entitlement, and vitality to the process for everyone.

Most people very quickly become comfortable at entering and leaving the imaging process and soon do so quite easily. As work is being done with one person, others may continue with their own process or may follow what is transpiring with that individual. Following are some demonstrations of transformational fantasy in a group setting.

Head Center, Left and Right Hemispheres

GUIDE: Take a deep breath, and let your whole body relax. When you get ready, be in your head center. As you know, your head center is between your right brain and your left brain, and equidistant up and down, front and back. Take some time to explore your head center (*long pause*). How large is it? ... colors? ... shape? ... smells? ... How do you feel in your head center? ... Would you like to change your center to feel more comfortable to you? ... Perhaps furnish it, bring in more light, paint it ... whatever you would like to do (*long pause*). When you are finished, could you visit your left hemisphere? You may find you have a pathway there ... or you may want to simply be there. ... Now take some time to explore your left hemisphere (*long pause*) and perhaps you see the gift which is there for you (*pause*) and now find your way back to your center and into your right brain ... and explore it as you like (*long pause*). How is it different from the other side? ...

size? . . . colors? . . . What's going on there? (*pause*) Can you find the gift that is there for you in your right hemisphere? . . . When you are ready, be back in your head center . . . and come on back to the room in your time.

Processing this little bit of business may take many forms, and soon you as a therapist will be comfortable with your own style and intuitions. I might go around and process each person's experience, and if an individual has had difficulty in entering one of the hemispheres or in moving back and forth, I ask the person if he or she would mind going back inside to the place of difficulty: "I'm trying to get into my right brain through the tunnel from my head center. . . . The tunnel to my left brain was big and bright . . . but this . . . it's small and crowded and dark. . . . I just couldn't get into my right brain."

GUIDE: Just impossible to get through. . . . Could you ask the tunnel what the problem is?

PATIENT: Hmmm . . . (*laughs a little*). The tunnel says it's never used, so why should it have to keep in shape? It almost seems a little angry.

GUIDE: Could you be the tunnel and tell me how you're feeling?

PATIENT: Well, yes, I am angry. That prissy left brain gets all the business and all the attention. I'm supposed to stay in readiness for when you decide to throw me a few crumbs? No way!

GUIDE: Could you be yourself again?

PATIENT: That's really funny what the tunnel said. I guess I do use my left brain more than my right. I didn't know that there were hard feelings (*pause*). Tunnel, I really would like to use you more because I'd really like to get into my right brain more. Would you let yourself become larger so I can get through? (*pause*) Look at that, it is getting larger . . . I think I'll try it (*pause*). It's like being on a rope bridge, sort of squishy and swaying. . . . If I hold onto the sides I can walk. . . . It's not easy but I'm getting there. . . . Now I'm there. . . .

Juanita, a beautiful young mother with a brain tumor, said, "I couldn't get into my head center at all. I just couldn't concentrate because of this terrible pain across my shoulders." She was asked to be where the pain was and describe what she experienced. "It's like a piece of heavy metal . . . it's not shiny . . . it's dull and thick and hard." ("Is there anything you can do about it?") "I don't think so. It is so thick and powerful . . . no . . . there's nothing I can do." (Someone in the group asks if she can change it to something else.) "Well, maybe I can do that . . . yes, it's changed to wood . . . actually it's balsa wood like I use for my crafts. . . . Well, I can do something about that . . . I'll just sand it down to nothing . . . (*long pause*).

("What's happening?") "Boy, I'm really getting this down to size . . . it's almost nothing (*pause*). There it goes. Wow! That's really something. The pain's gone . . . it's just not there. I can't believe this!"

As we were doing this exercise, Gert, a 60-year-old woman with severe asthma, started coughing, and sneezing violently after being in her right brain. I was concerned that she might have a bad cold, which would not be good for the two severely immune-impaired individuals who were present that day. "No, I don't have a cold," she said, "but I sure am allergic to all the black grass that I saw in my right brain." And she sneezed several more times. I suggested that Gert go back into her right brain and see if there were anything she could do about it. "Ooooh. That black grass is really awful stuff (*pause*), but I have a hose here and I can just hose it away (*pause*). There it goes down into the gutter . . . all of it (*pause*). Oh, look at that. There's a rainbow . . . a beautiful rainbow forming in the mist from the hose. . . . That's really nice!" There was not a hint of a sneeze or a sniff from Gert the rest of the day. A week later I reminded her of the power of the bodymind that she had shown the week before, and Gert allowed that she was taking only a fraction of her usual dose of allergy medication and felt great. "I feel that I do have some control," she said with a pleased smile on her face.

I point out that obstructions are gifts, that these are places where we can really learn something about ourselves. The real therapy is done when blockages (resistance) are uncovered and dealt with. Rather than responding to the disclosure of a blockage with "that's too bad," I am more inclined to say, "That's great. Now we really can have an adventure." I try to process as many blockages as possible, although group flow or time considerations frequently require that I ask members to hold onto the image of the blockage until later in the day when their individual therapist can help with it. Remember, there is no need to "finish the job" on the spot. After all, the blockage has been there for years, and it will be there when we return to it several hours or even a day or so later.

Hallways of the Mind

After finishing what needs to be done in this preliminary exercise, I may ask members to go back into their head centers and from there into the back corridors of their minds. I point out that my guidance is really a jumping-off point for them rather than a prescribed way for them to image. They are encouraged to do it their way, and they are free to go in whatever direction they wish. For example, I use the word "room" for convenience, yet in their own mind's eyes members may have an outdoor scene or something else entirely, which is great. In other words, they are encouraged to use the structure as a handrail, not a cage. I usually say, "As you go back from the head center into the hallways of the mind, you may notice that there are rooms on either side of the hallway in which are stored virtually every thought, experience, feeling, and sensation that you have ever had. On every door there is a label, and as you walk down the hallway look at the labels on your doors as you go by . . . love? . . . guilt? . . . anger? . . . joy? . . . and many more that you see as you explore your corridor."

At this point I may suggest that members of the group notice a door to which they are drawn "that seems to have some importance for their lives right now," and have them explore that room. Or I may guide them to a specific door. The process can be explored in many different ways; what I am presenting is merely a way that feels comfortable to me, has been effective in group settings, and gives a little structure without impinging on the creativity and meaning of an individual's idiosyncratic process.

I generally guide participants in the following manner:

As you continue exploring the hallway of the mind, see if you can find a door marked "anxiety" or "fear." . . . When you find it, open the door to the room and see what is behind that door. . . . Examine the room. . . . How do you feel as you look in the fear room. . . . Then start exploring the room if you feel comfortable doing that (*long pause*). You may notice over in a corner that there is a picture . . . could you take a look at that picture? . . . You may need to brush dust off the picture or bring it into focus (*pause*), and you may wish to ask yourself what the meaning of this picture is in the anxiety room (*long pause*).

And when you are ready . . . explore the room a bit further. . . . You may be surprised to find a person in the room . . . or an object . . . of whom you have questions or to whom there are things you need to say . . . and this is a good time for that to happen. . . . This may be scary for you . . . so if you like, you can bring in someone to help you out or even to say it for you—for example, your inner child or your inner guide. Now, go ahead and ask that question or say what you need to say in whatever way is most comfortable for you (*pause*) and experience the response of the person or thing you are addressing (*pause*) and there may be more questions or things you wish to say (*pause*). Now, be the person or thing you have encountered, and how do you respond to what you have asked or said (*pause*). Now, be yourself again, and respond (*pause*) and again be the person or object . . . and just let this dialogue go back and forth . . . and really listen to each other (*long pause*). Before you leave this person or thing . . . would it be possible to find some resolution to your issues? (*pause*) And to show that resolution by a hug or some other gesture? (*pause*)

And when you're finished, bring your attention back to the room. . . . What's wrong with the room? . . . What needs to be done? . . . Where do you want to start? . . . Remember to bring in any help that you need, and now really get to work getting this room exactly the way you would like it (*long pause*).

When you come to a stopping point take a look at the room. . . . Is there anything else you'd like to change . . . anything else you would like to do before we go back? (*pause*) When you get ready . . . and have thanked every-thing and everyone who has helped you . . . and particularly remember to thank the blockages, the barriers or the resistance you encountered . . . and when you have thanked all parts, come back out into the hallway . . . back to your head center . . . where you may wish to spend a few moments think-ing about what has happened to you (*pause*) and then back out to the present.

In the processing, there are frequently problems and blockages in the hallway of the mind. Patients say things like, "It was dark and dangerous. I feel uncomfortable going in there." ("Would it be possible to do something about it?") "Well, I don't know . . . oh look, there's a book of matches. I'll light a match . . . hmm . . . that doesn't help too much. Maybe I could make my match into a torch. . . . Yes, that's better . . . it doesn't look as dangerous . . . it even looks quite pleasant. Now, I can move on."

I remember one participant, a young pharmacist, who found something unexpected waiting for her: "I just can't go in there. There's that tiger again blocking my way in the hall. I'm really scared of him. He looks ferocious enough to destroy me." ("What is he doing there?") "He's just there looking mean and hungry." ("Could you ask him what he's doing there?") (*pause*) "Now that's interesting. He says he's protecting me. I never thought of that . . . protecting me." ("Would you be able to thank him for protecting you and perhaps give him a pat?") "Hmmm . . . now that's not so bad. His fur is really soft, and he seems to be purring—if tigers purr (*pause*). Isn't it funny, he's really my friend, and I didn't know it until now . . . that's *really* interesting." Making friends with her tiger allowed this young woman to begin exploring areas of repressed emotion essential to her healing process.

There are frequently blocks to entering a "room" which represents heavy emotions such as fear, anger, or guilt. At this point participants will often say, "I can't bear to open the door" or "I have the door open, but there's no way I'm going inside." It is the guide's job to help the subject detoxify the situation or mobilize his or her own resources for facing whatever is inside. Questions such as, "Could you open the door a crack and just peek inside?" and "Is there a transom above the door through which you can look?" will begin to ease the person into the scene. "Is there someone special to you who could hold your hand as you go into the room?" or "Would you like the members of the group to be there with you to support you?" may help the person call forth his own support for the job ahead.

Sometimes the patient will say, "All I can see in the room is black . . . there's nothing else there . . . just the black." "Blackness" and "nothing" are frequent blocks which may be softened by requesting that the subject ask the nothingness what it is doing there or that he or she inquire of the blackness what purpose it is serving. A patient may then reply, "The blackness says that it is protecting me by not letting me see what is there. I guess it is protecting me from even worse fear." At this point, encourage the patient to have the blackness let him or her see exactly what is in the room, and if it is too terrible, let the blackness cover it up again. When the person is able to see what is in the room (frequently it is a childhood fear the individual had completely "forgotten"), the problem can be worked through and excised from the rest of the baggage the subject has been carrying through life.

"When I opened the door to the fear room," said Marcia, a 33-year-old social worker with a recurrence of breast cancer, "I saw a big black locomotive belching black smoke. It was the face of fear, and I felt terrified. I really wanted to run, but this time I thought I'd just stand there and let it do its worst.... Oh! There's a white light engulfing it. Wow! (*pause*) and just look at it now. It's a multicolored little train . . . with every color you can imagine (*pause*) and it's taking me to an adventure in the future. I don't know what the adventure is, but I'm excited about it." This was a major epiphany for Marcia—seeing the ambiguity she so feared as an adventure. A few days later she conquered another major fear by appearing on a television show where she said, "I know this may sound a bit strange, but my recurrence has changed my life in a very positive way. I'm not quite sure where it is leading, but I am really happy and excited about it."

Staging Areas of the Body

Transformational fantasy is a powerful strategy for dealing with the presenting physical problem, be it pain, a tumor, a systemic infection, an autoimmune disease, or an immune deficiency disease. It is an excellent way of tapping into how the person sees and interprets physical occurrences and of changing the emotional and psychological aspects of what the person is experiencing to become consonant with the healing process. We have seen very powerful work done with TF, work which not only facilitates the medical treatment, but also has a direct impact on the disease itself.

Although one could use a number of different ways to set the stage, such as a relaxation exercise or one's "special place," for the sake of continuity let us use the head center. Such an exercise might go like this:

> Be in your head center . . . take a moment to explore this safe, comfortable
> space . . . your home base (*pause*). As always, if there are changes you would

like to make ... having it larger ... smaller ... lighter ... more comfortable
... go ahead and do that right now (*pause*) and now settle back comfortably.
Could you think of a physical problem that is bothering you? ... And right
now find yourself wherever in your being that this problem manifests itself
... seeing the problem as a symbol ... or a metaphor ... and seeing the
symbol of this physical problem arising before your eyes ... color ...
shape ... smell ... sound ... texture ... and even taste. Even if the symbol
does not make much sense ... just let yourself go with it. It can be as simple
or as complex as you like ... just let it come forth as it is (*pause*). Now take
some time to explore the problem ... see what it is doing ... understanding what has gone wrong ... what's not right? (*pause*) And if you like,
you can ask the symbol of your problem why it is there ... what are the
positive intentions for you ... and await the response (*pause*). And then, if
you wish, you can ask the image of the condition what it is that you can do
to allow it to go away ... and await the response (*pause*) and you can continue this dialogue as long as you would like (*pause*). And when that is
finished, allow an image of the healing process to begin to develop. ... This
may involve a symbol of whatever medical treatment you are receiving ...
and may also include images of the many healing forces in your body ... or
the image of healing may be in terms of metaphor or symbols or colors ...
or whatever is presented to you. If you are having difficulty having an image
of healing come forth, you may wish to visit the control center that is
involved with your disease. For example, you may want to go to the control
center for the immune system ... and read the printouts ... and see just
what it is that is needed to restore a healing balance to your system ... and
allow that answer to come in the form of symbols or colors or sounds (*pause*).
It may be helpful to see the healing symbols as much larger, more powerful,
more vivid, and more intelligent than the image of the problem. ... Now let
the healing begin (*long pause*). And when the healing is completed—and be
sure that every trace of the problem is gone in your imagery—you can begin
to clean up the debris that is the result of the healing process ... and perhaps let this debris find its way out back into the universe where it may do
good for someone or something else (*pause*) and let the sense of healing fill
your whole being—mind, body, and spirit (*pause*). And when you are ready,
return to your head center, where you may wish to ponder what has just
taken place (*pause*). And then when you're ready, come on back out.

This imagery (which I owe to my training with Martin Rossman and
John Shaffer) provides a structure for the person to do his or her own
work relatively unfettered, yet includes suggestions that may allow a powerful healing experience. Of course, the most important part is processing
the fantasy and helping participants deal with blockages in the process.

Vera, a 38-year-old woman with chronic fatigue syndrome, saw her illness as "an engine room, filled with blackened, greasy engines. There is
black oil and grease everywhere ... sprayed on the walls, all over the floor,
and the sludge over all the engines is thick and awful. There's at least an
inch of sludge and grease on all the engines, and they just can't work, and

if they do, they go sooo slowly. It's hard to know what to do (*long pause*). Oh, look over in the corner . . . there's solvent and rags . . . clear stuff that will dissolve all the grease (*pause*)." ("What's happening?") "It's doing a really good job. . . . My goodness, those engines are actually shiny, stainless steel under all this gook. That's pretty amazing . . . " ("Are you finishing up the job?") "I've gotten a good start on things but I don't feel like doing it all now. It's a pretty big job . . . and I'll work on it in bits and pieces." This reflects Vera's style of doing things slowly, but surely. And she will get the job done, in her own time.

Todd, a 33-year-old man whose adrenal cancer had metastasized to his lungs, reflected his physicians' pessimism about the chances that his chemotherapy would work. His initial imagery symbolized his tumors as black, ugly skulls and crossbones with his treatment making pusillanimous efforts to dissolve them—certainly not a good situation. On his third day in the program, transformational fantasy reflected a positive change, as he said, "I can see where the spots are on my lungs . . . and this energy—it's hard to describe—is welling up in me and it shoots up toward the top of my head. And it bounces off . . . it was all shiny and light at the crown of my head . . . and the energy became shiny and light . . . and bounced back with an incredible force and now goes back to my lungs . . . and now it's spraying into my lungs like a fire hose. . . . It's really powerful in my right lung and it just blasted away all the spots. . . . Pow! . . . Uh oh, it's not doing too well in my left lung . . . it lost power (*pause*). Huhh . . . there's a fire hydrant. Let me just unscrew this plug (*pause*). There it blows! (*pause*). Now my left lung's clean too. . . . They're all gone. . . . Isn't that something? Yeah."

Todd still has a tough road ahead with his treatment; however, he is presently in an experimental study, which his physicians had not thought would be possible. Although the outcome is still unclear, all our bets are on Todd's coming through with flying colors.

Lessons for the Author/Clinician

Much of my training in graduate school was Rogerian and behavioral. In practice I have tended toward behavioral techniques because they seemed to get the job done effectively in an efficient manner. Since working with John Shaffer and transformational fantasy, I have a new respect for the work of Carl Rogers and the effectiveness of client-centered therapy. I realize that my predilection for behavioral methods reflected control issues within myself that had not been resolved. I also realize that, although behavioral methods get the job done, what the "real job" is may not be apparent. Behaviorally, we may do quite well in dealing with the task that superficially presents itself, yet it may even be antithetical to the real healing task.

A major lesson for me was learning that we gain power by letting go of control. In transformational fantasy one never knows what is going to happen. Nothing you expect to happen does. The unexpected is what one can expect. And if one is trying to maintain control of the process, *nothing* happens. It was hard for me to trust the process *and* to trust myself to go with the flow wherever it led and to deal with whatever happened. It involved giving responsibility for the therapeutic process to the client, where it belongs.

Perhaps because I came to the field of psychology and psychotherapy relatively late in life, I always had a nagging feeling that I didn't know quite as much, or did not have as natural a talent for the field, as those who had been there since undergraduate days. Being a companion-guide with other humans in their own self-transforming odysseys and realizing that the answers are within them (not within me), has somehow effected a shift that allows me to be a partner rather than an "expert." It has allowed me to "sing my own song" and accept my own constellation of talents and intuitions just as they are. These days I expend less energy comparing myself to others.

TF has also opened my eyes to the rich, incredibly creative inner lives we "ordinary" people have. I have such a feeling of awe after having processed a transformational fantasy group! I feel so honored to be privy to the splendid, colorful, even frightening, images that are brought forth— and I am astonished at how creatively individuals are able to heal themselves when they have access to their own unconscious. The result is that no one will ever look "ordinary" to me again; now I consistently see the extraordinary in my fellow humans.

10
Exercise and Nutrition

What is it that makes it so hard to determine whither we will walk? I believe that there is a subtle magnetism in Nature, which, if we unconsciously yield to it, will direct us aright. — *Henry David Thoreau*

The inner intelligence of the body is the ultimate and supreme genius in nature. It mirrors the wisdom of the cosmos. It is our duty to the rest of mankind to be perfectly healthy, because we are ripples in the ocean of consciousness, and when we are sick, even a little, we disrupt cosmic harmony. — *Vedic verse*

Living in tune with nature is having healthy desires that match what you actually need. As nature made you, what you need and what you want should not conflict. At the source everyone has healthy desires. To make the right choices is easy — once you begin to listen to your own deepest nature. — *Deepak Chopra*

It is our intention at GETTING WELL to give participants skills to intervene at as many points as possible in the mind-body loop, in order to enable them to make optimal use of their inner resources for living beautifully and healthily. Nutrition and exercise are important modes for making changes at the physical level. Such changes resonate throughout one's emotions, body, and spirit. Judith Wurtman's provocative book, *Managing Your Mind and Mood Through Food*, suggests that what one eats affects one's emotions and mental functioning, as well as one's body, in numerous ways. An even better case can be made for exercise, which positively affects emotional dimensions such as depression, anxiety, and locus of control, and enhances overall physical function.

Over the two decades during which I have been designing and implementing outpatient hospital programs heavily based on nutrition and exercise (e.g., stress management and behavioral weight control), I have found that the solution to changing the lifestyle of an individual rests in changing the mindstyle, the imagery, or the consciousness of that person. It requires a shift in awareness to significantly change one's nutrition and exercise programming. No amount of warnings, imprecations, or positive reinforcement will create change unless there is a modification in consciousness.

159

However, when that change takes place, the details of what one eats or of how often one exercises fall into place as if by magic.

Both exercise and nutrition have heavy-duty cultural significance for most of us. To choose not to eat meat, to turn down food loaded with sugar and fat, or even to insist on getting a daily three-mile walk frequently evokes eye rolls, laughter, and even the contempt of people from whom one would like approval. Happily, the consciousness of the culture regarding exercise and nutrition is shifting; however, for those with life-challenging conditions it is sometimes difficult to do what one needs to do for one's body (and mind and spirit) and still keep the pre-diagnosis social structure intact.

Sometimes, but not always, one's diagnosis alone is enough to keep pressures at bay. People don't generally force a piece of birthday cake on a diabetic, for example; yet they will insist that a cancer patient, a heart patient, or a person with MS eat something loaded with fat. Breakfast meetings of service organizations still serve up mounds of buttery scrambled eggs, bacon, and sausages—with bran muffins as the concession to heart health. (It is as if the bran muffin somehow will dissolve all the cholesterol in the rest of the food!) Meeting breaks usually mean coffee and donuts, and dinners out almost guarantee a flood of fat and calories. Family or co-workers with their own agendas may actively campaign against daily exercise at whatever level, saying, "You don't spend enough time with me," "You look pretty silly doing that funny walk you do," etc. Therefore, unless one's image of the personal advantages of good nutrition and daily exercise is quite clear and one's vision is connected with a new consciousness, it will be extremely difficult to effect healing changes at the physical level.

Using Imagery for Adherence and
Compliance to Aerobic Exercise

Aerobic exercise is a magic bullet. There is perhaps no better prevention lifestyle to prevent the emergence of a variety of ills, from osteoporosis to heart disease (Clausen, 1977). Research has indicated that regular aerobic exercise may even reverse the ravages of already established conditions, such as diabetes and hypertension. Although years ago I presented aerobic exercise in quite a specific sense, I have moved to fewer charts and rules. For example, I encourage a daily 30- to 45-minute walk at a brisk, but comfortable pace—making exercise an integral, pleasant part of one's life rather than being overly concerned about getting one's heart rate up to a certain level. Research is showing that aerobic benefits occur even at lower heart rates, as long as the duration of the activity is extended. The point is to make exercise enjoyable and non-obsessive. Excessive exercise or chronic exercise stress may be counterproductive for both the immune system and the cardiovascular system (Hoffman-Goetz, Keir, Thorne, Houston, & Young, 1986). All too often, personality styles of participants lead them to overdo a good thing.

Many participants already exercise on a regular basis. Our job is to help them keep it up and enjoy it even more. For the cardiovascular or controlled-diabetes patient regular aerobic exercise is a lifeline, and further research is showing significant benefits for those with cancer, autoimmune diseases, and other life-challenging conditions. Cancer patients usually can exercise more than one would expect; however, it is important for them to check with their primary physician before making significant change in an exercise program.

Changing one's lifestyle successfully usually requires a change in perceptions. First there may be an intellectual shift, usually influenced by new information that totally changes the logical picture of things. For most of us a decision to "become aerobic" is a left-brain shift. We want to lose a few pounds, sleep better, feel less tired, or have fewer colds, and exercise is a logical way to accomplish this. After the exercise habit is well in place, we may find that exercise itself engenders feelings of being in shape or in control, and may even have shifted our consciousness and our sense of connectedness. This almost guarantees that the behavior will continue as a part of one's blueprint for the rest of one's life. Therefore, the first step in "converting" someone to exercise is to present good, intellectual arguments—to build a strong image of the benefits of aerobic exercise.

Covert Bailey's amusing, yet knowledgeable, little book, *Fit or Fat*, was the catalyst in a dramatic shift in my own thinking about exercise. It not only secured a permanent place for aerobic exercise in my own life but also made me a vocal advocate (some call it "zealot") for aerobic exercise in all my programs, from panic disorder and stress management to behavioral weight control. Because of my belief in the central importance of exercise in the life well lived, I chose a few years ago to get a master's degree in exercise physiology and wellness.

Group members find that having a printed list of the benefits of exercise renews the image of its advantages when memory begins to fade a little or when a bit of extra sleep seems much more inviting than a 30-minute walk in 40-degree weather. Participants are encouraged to glean benefits from the following list which fit their particular lives or conditions and to create their own lists. I also suggest to members that they not only image the way the "benefits" look in black and white but also create an image of what is actually happening to their bodies as they are exercising and visualize the benefit happening at the moment.

Aerobic exercise:

- Is a major prevention factor for heart disease (Acierno, 1985; Ornish, 1990), cancer (Eichner, 1988; Paffenbarger, Hyde, & Wing, 1987), diabetes, and "all-cause mortality" (Paffenbarger, Hyde, Wing, & Hsieh, 1986).
- Increases endurance both physiologically and psychologically. It decreases stress-related fatigue. It also decreases the feeling of fatigue often associated with dieting or calorie restriction, and it resolves the "exhaustion without exertion" phenomenon. Participants become more active because they *are* more active. Their enthusiasm and zest for life increase as their aerobic capacity increases.
- Increases respiration and pulmonary functioning. It also increases lung capacity and allows more than four times the normal amount of oxygen to be available at the cellular level (McArdle, Katch, & Katch, 1981).
- Is a natural anti-stress experience. It increases levels of brain norepinephrine (similar to the action of antidepressants), which results in an improved psychological outlook. It is a natural tranquilizer and antidepressant. Fifteen minutes of brisk walking produces more relaxation at the muscular level than a tranquilizer (Morgan, 1985). Aerobic exercise may be the treatment of choice in minor depression and can be helpful even in major depression (Buffone, 1984).
- Decreases resting blood pressure and heart rate. In the case of abnormally low blood pressure and heart rate, aerobic exercise moves the rate toward normal. It strengthens the heart muscle, allowing it to beat more strongly and pump more blood per beat. A lower heart rate is a sign of a more efficient pump — it can do the same job by working less hard and should last longer (McArdle et al., 1981).
- Is a natural diuretic, so water retention problems are lessened.
- Increases insulin efficiency and is recommended in the treatment of Type II diabetes. Aerobic exercise also increases the sensitivity of insulin receptors in each cell, so that less insulin is required to transport sugar into cells to be used as energy. It may even *prevent* the occurrence of non-insulin-dependent diabetes (McArdle et al., 1981).
- Increases circulation and the number of capillaries available to feed muscles and other tissue.
- Reduces obesity, which is implicated in cancer (Eichner, 1988; Henderson, 1987; Siiteri, 1987), heart disease, diabetes, and other life-challenging conditions.
- Lowers serum cholesterol and triglycerides. It increases high-density lipoproteins (HDL), an anti-risk factor associated with lower incidence of cardiovascular disease.
- Is recommended for building stronger bones, better posture, and healthier skin. Walking (and running) provide the stimulus to keep

the bone mass at a high level, minimizing the likelihood of osteoporosis (McArdle et al., 1981).

- Reduces arthritis pain, alleviates chronic lower back pain, and reduces menstrual discomfort.
- Is ideal for the "Type A" behavior type, as it is a natural outlet for tension, anxiety, and aggression.
- Increases the release of endorphins, which are natural morphine-like pain killers 200 times stronger, drop for drop, than morphine itself (Buffone, 1984).
- Is associated with reducing risk of cancer in humans (Frisch, 1985) and tumor reduction in animals (Holloszy, 1985). Increased beta endorphin enhances lymphocyte proliferation (Gilman, Schwartz, Milner, Bloom, & Feldman, 1982); increases leukocytes, neutrophils, and platelets (Masuhara, Kami, Umebayasi, & Tatsumi, 1987); and increases interleukin-2 and interferon (Cannon et al., 1986; Eichner, 1988), both of which are connected with prevention and treatment of cancer.
- Has a calming effect upon the mind, significantly reduces anxiety (deVries, 1982; Hatfield, Goldfarb, Sforzo, & Flynn, 1987), and contributes to better sleep.
- Contributes to the adoption of positive lifestyle choices such as improved diet, weight reduction, alcohol moderation, and smoking cessation.
- Increases resistance to disease and infections. Raising the core body temperature benefits the immune system by increasing endorphin production, which in turn increases production of certain lymphocytes (Friedlander & Phillips, 1986). The increase in body temperature also debilitates or kills foreign cells and cancer cells. Exercise also increases intestinal motility, the lack of which is implicated in some cancers (Cordain, 1986; Keeling & Martin, 1987). And it provides increased transportation of antibodies to the sites of infection and disease (McArdle et al., 1981).
- Increases substances vital to wound repair (Dinarello, 1985; Gimenez et al., 1987).
- Dissipates substances such as cortisol and catecholamines (Friedlander & Phillips, 1986), which are associated with depression of immune function (Riley, 1981) and cardiovascular damage (McArdle et al., 1981). It puts a governor on the response of the adrenal gland (Mathur, Toriola, & Dada, 1986; Sapse, 1984).
- Reduces immune system compromise in response to emotional assaults such as the *diagnosis* of AIDS or cancer (N. Hall, 1993a).
- Puts a brake on muscles wasting from cancer or AIDS. Cancer reduces the ability of the body to use fat stores for energy; aerobic

exercise helps reverse the process and allows one to lose fat without the accompanying loss of lean muscle mass.

- Helps build lean muscle mass, which uses ten times the number of calories as body fat (Bailey, 1977).
- Uses calories without depleting vitamins, minerals, or protein, as very low-calorie dieting does.
- Increases stimulation to the right hemisphere of the brain, allowing for greater creativity, particularly during the exercise (Buffone, 1984).
- Builds self-esteem, confidence, a sense of joy in being in charge of your life, an enhanced ability to enjoy the senses (including taste), an awareness of physical well-being, a feeling of independence, and self-responsibility (Buffone, 1984).
- Is a delightful, rewarding activity in itself. It can be made as stimulating and pleasurable as eating, smoking, or drinking alcohol—becoming a positive habit.
- Allows one to turn inward, to be in touch with what it feels like inside oneself, to be connected with one's body and with the miracle of life and being.
- Can be used as a meditation connecting one with others, the planet, and the universe.

Imaging the benefits actually happening as one is exercising is a powerful "in the moment" incentive. Seeing one's increased temperature as boiling and destroying every cancer cell in the body, seeing the fat dissolve from one's body in sweat, or seeing insulin receptors in every cell of the body becoming exquisitely sensitive to the smallest amount of insulin so that less is needed—such images supply a powerful blueprint, as well as a "construction crew" to get the job done.

Adherence to and compliance with exercise regimens are crucial factors in the establishment and continuance of this health-enhancing behavior (Clausen, 1977). A rule of thumb among exercise physiologists is that it takes 90 days to make an activity a part of one's lifestyle, although the hardest work takes place in the first three weeks of habit change. Using the imagery of *outcomes* or benefits of the exercise experience is a good place to start, since many people are motivated to start exercising to make changes in physical functioning such as lowering blood pressure and blood sugar or reducing fat stores. However, I find that outcomes motivate only for a short period of time; in order to make exercise a part of one's life, one must become deeply involved in the *process*—not just in the effects.

Imagery is quite effective in helping the individual focus on the process. I found the image of myself as a large cat—a magnificent jaguar, moving sleekly, smoothly, and powerfully on the lakeside path—to be energizing and compelling. Using the exercise period as a time to go within and meditate—or to experience the very beating of one's heart, the flow of the blood, the pressure of the ground against one's feet, the feel of muscles contracting and extending and of molecules of oxygen going to every cell, and the breeze playing across one's skin—expands the consciousness of the moment. One participant used her walking time to be totally in the moment and to see the world as a baby does for the first time—moving mindfulness. Others use the time to listen to tapes or have a close time with a significant other. Our follow-up has indicated that "process walkers" have a much higher adherence to a daily regimen than "outcome walkers."

Using Imagery to Implement Dietary Change

Nutrition occupies one of the most politically and emotionally charged arenas of scientific inquiry. Although the Framingham Study (Dawber, 1980) suggested that diet and obesity may play some role in heart disease, it was decades before the American Heart Association and the American Medical Association conceded there was sufficient evidence that nutrition plays a role in heart disease to develop even the most modest of dietary guidelines. Nathan Pritikin (1979), who developed a very low-fat, vegetarian, low-sugar, low-salt program for heart patients, was dismissed as a fanatic by the scientific community. A decade later, Ornish and his colleagues published a study in *Lancet* indicating that a similar diet (approximately 10 percent fat and 75 percent complex carbohydrates) actually reversed coronary artery disease, while the coronary blockage of those controls following the American Dietary Guidelines (approximately 25–30 percent fat and 40 percent carbohydrates) increased blockage. Yet the conservative medical establishment remains skeptical of the power of nutrition, and our national dietary guidelines are slow to change.

Although the concept that diet and nutrition may influence cancer is not new, this relationship has received surprisingly little focused attention. Before the 1982 report, "Diet, Nutrition, and Cancer," from the Committee on Diet, Nutrition, and Cancer of the National Research Council appeared, American scientists, physicians, and nutritionists were hesitant to state openly that diet was involved. British epidemiologists Doll, Muir, and Waterhouse suggested as early as 1970 that diet is the number-one cause of cancer, accounting for 35 percent of all tumors (with smoking ranking second at 30 percent).

In researching my exercise physiology thesis, *Lifestyles, Mindstyles, and Cancer* (1988), I found that nutrition is clearly related to the development of cancer in a number of different ways. Excessive fat, animal protein, sugar, obesity, nicotine, and alcohol are implicated in the development and promotion of cancer (Buzby, 1980; Weisburger, 1986). On the other hand, fiber, beta-carotene, cruciferous vegetables, vitamin E, vitamin C, selenium, and other minerals (iodine, zinc, and iron) are associated with decreased incidence of cancer (Coem & McNamara, 1980; Goodman, 1984; Newberne & Suphakarn, 1983). In addition, from animal studies there is strong evidence (e.g., Horvath & Ip, 1983; Kalamegham, 1984; London, Murphy, & Kitowski, 1985; Menkes, 1986; Sporn & Roberts, 1983) that beta-carotene and vitamin E not only inhibit, but reverse, tumor growth.

Although the research has arrived from different sectors, I find it interesting that optimal diets for heart disease, diabetes, multiple sclerosis, obesity, and cancer have virtually the same elements. On this basis we feel comfortable at GETTING WELL doing generic nutrition education; however, we in no way try to do clinical nutrition (suggesting specific foods for specific problems). We strongly advise our participants to keep their physicians informed of any significant changes in diet, since too few calories may be ill-advised for cancer patients or certain foods or classes of food can interfere with treatment (for example, vitamin C interferes with the action of some chemotherapies).

Many people come into the GETTING WELL program following particular nutritional regimens — frequently ones that are "unproven" or alternative. While we make no attempt to interfere with their choices of nutritional lifestyle, we may suggest they take a close look at what they're doing if it seems health-threatening, e.g., fasting while losing critical muscle mass or eating only one or two foods. The problem with most alternative nutritional programs is that they are unnecessarily (in my eyes) limiting in the choice of foods allowed and tend to create an obsession with "doing it the right way." I feel particularly disturbed when a person chooses not to join GW because participation would not allow enough time for elaborate food preparation. Nevertheless, we respect the person's right to make choices about his or her lifestyle, and we honor the power of the placebo effect in believing what one is eating is healing. A person who is uncompromising about his or her alternative nutrition or treatments is unlikely to choose GW, and the relationship probably would not work out well. At the same time, a number of individuals whose standard treatments have failed have managed to integrate some rather strange alternative nutritional regimens successfully into the program and their lives.

Cara, a nurse in her fifties, had undergone several years of treatment for metastatic breast cancer, at which point her oncologist felt there was nothing more that standard treatment could do. She opted to go to a treatment center in Mexico where she became involved in a rather complex nutritional program of juicing and dietary supplements. Although it meant some compromises in her regime, Cara joined GETTING WELL. She amiably took good-natured teasing about the rather vile-looking liquids she consumed, such as a blend of juiced calves liver and vegetables; however, participants gained a respect for Cara's nutritional knowledge, spurring them to focus more positively on what went into their own systems.

After she successfully completed GW, Cara's physical condition improved to the point that standard treatment was again indicated. Cara's physician did not approve of her eccentric diet; however, he was willing to cooperate in letting her participate in planning her own treatment. She continued with her nutritional plan, along with intermittent treatment with chemotherapy and radiation. Although her cancer would come and go, she felt her "treatment combo" gave her body the best shot. She lived her life with direction and clarity for years, living out her desire see her grandchildren born and to know them and be a part of their young lives.

The GETTING WELL nutritional guidelines (Figure 6) are broad enough to encompass all but the most esoteric nutritional philosophies. For example, a person on a macrobiotic diet would have no difficulty with the thrust of our guidelines, although there may be categories from which he or she would not make choices. A strict macrobiotic diet would have a more limited range of choice about specific vegetables, methods of preparation, and "organicity" of substances, yet the basic nutrition is the same. Even Cara's alternative diet, with only a few exceptions, fell within our plan.

Concerns about unproven dietary regimens include the fact that frequently preparation of foods literally takes most of a person's waking hours, dietary constituents are inclined to be expensive, the regimes tend to separate people from their natural social support systems, and most put an undue focus on the nutritional aspect of the healing process rather than on truly living well in all dimensions. All the evidence I have seen suggests that nutrition is important in the healing process; however, it is far from *the* most important factor in health, healing, or life.

Before I started GW, I thoroughly read the literature on alternative nutrition (and did mainstream dietary research as well). There is a great deal of the absurd in the former; however, other evidence exists which seems convincing from a scientific point of view. We definitely have only just begun to learn all we need to know about nutrition and the "unproven" theories that abound worldwide. For example, when our delegation visited the College of Traditional Medicine in Beijing, we found that a major thrust of their inquiry was scientifically investigating the active properties of the hundreds of herbs used in traditional Chinese medicine and bringing the rigors of Western science to that ancient healing art. Homeopathy has brought forth some intriguing and scientifically validated principles, and physicians such as Dr. Virginia Livingston have expanded

Figure 6. GETTING WELL Nutritional Guidelines

Legumes, Grains, and Nuts
2–3 or more servings from *each* column (high in fiber, protein, protective indoles, selenium, vitamin E)

Whole grain bread and rolls	Garbanzo beans
Bulgar	Black-eyed peas
Brown rice	Black beans
Whole wheat pasta	Lentils
Oatmeal	Split peas
Whole grain hot and cold cereals	Soybeans
Whole wheat matzoh	Azuki beans
Millet	Other dried beans and peas
Wheat berries	Almonds and other unsalted nuts*
Steel-cut oats	Sesame, sunflower, and other seeds*
Barley	Peanut butter, sesame butter*
Rye berries	(White potatoes)
Corn	Mung beans

Fruits and Vegetables
2 or more servings from *each* column (high beta-carotene, protective indoles, vitamins C and A, fiber)

Beta-carotene rich	*Cruciferous vegetables*	*Fruit (esp. red fruit)*
Carrots, carrot juice	Broccoli	Melons
Spinach	Cauliflower	Bananas
Greens	Brussels sprouts	Oranges
Sweet potatoes	Kale	Strawberries
Deep green lettuces (not iceberg)	Cabbage	Grapefruit
Broccoli, kale	Chinese cabbage	Mangoes
Summer squash, zucchini	Collard and turnip greens	Apricots
Winter and acorn squashes	Chard	Papaya
Green pepper	Red cabbage	Blueberries, other berries
Beets	Escarole	Apples
Pumpkin	Okra	Figs
Tomatoes	(Eggplant, mushrooms,	Peaches
Asparagus	onions, garlic)#	Plums

Milk Products (optional)
Not necessary in adult diet, yet may add variety.

Buttermilk (from skim milk)	Low-fat cottage cheese
Low-fat milk (1%)	Low-fat yogurt
Nonfat dry milk	Skim-milk cheeses
Skim milk	Skim-milk and banana shake

Poultry, Fish, Meat, and Eggs (optional)
1–2 servings for non-vegetarians. Vegetarians should eat added servings from legume and grains group

Cod	Chicken or turkey (no skin)
Flounder	Very lean beef, pork, veal*
Shellfish	Egg whites
Halibut	Water-packed tuna
Salmon	(Chicken or beef liver, only occasionally.
Pollock	High in vitamins, minerals, but high in fat)*
Rockfish	

*High in fat   #Not cruciferous vegetables, but important in the diet.

All foods on this list should be appropriately steamed, broiled, baked, or boiled without fat. No frying!
Optional supplements: Multivitamin with zinc, B12, and iron; 500–1500 mg vitamin C; 200 IU vitamin E; 20,000 IU beta-carotene.

other possibilities in the area of nutrition. John Steinbacher established the Cancer Federation a couple of decades ago to fund and support intelligent research into alternative theories of nutrition. His organization has become a major source of funding for scientists investigating nutritional theories in the area of cancer and is responsible for expanding our scientific horizons in many areas of cancer research.

I become concerned when proponents of alternative nutrition push their theories as the *only* way to health and even actively *discourage* people from seeking other avenues of healing such as standard medicine and even PNI. Make no mistake, there are both charlatans and well-intentioned people out there promoting questionable programs. Yet, we must not throw out the baby with the bathwater by being too quick to label as quackery anything outside of the mainstream in nutrition.

Therefore, we maintain an open mind to what our participants themselves have investigated in the area of nutrition, and we provide a set of guidelines that have been gleaned from the *accepted* scientific literature. With the exception of wheat and rye berries (available in bulk at health food stores), everything on our list is available in regular grocery stores.

Weekly, we present a lesson that often creates a left-brain nutritional shift. It starts with our showing a fake nine-ounce steak and playfully suggesting that if we eat the steak it will go directly to lean muscle mass in our bodies. Of course, that is false. We then illustrate how the body will break the steak down into component amino acids. Those amino acids will then convert in the body to muscle or other tissue (much as the cow formed the steak).

We then ask participants to guess how much grass, grain, and soybeans the cow had to eat to produce this nine-ounce steak. Pulling out a ten-pound bag of grains and soybeans, we let people see the large amount of complex carbohydrates it takes to produce an eight- or nine-ounce steak for our consumption. We explain that we have the same abilities as cows to convert complex carbohydrates (grains, vegetables, and legumes) into protein for our bodies, and we do not need meat to live. We then show the protein equivalent to the steak in our own consumption of legumes and grains with a food model (three-quarters of a cup of black beans over a cup of brown rice). We direct attention to the fact that the beans and rice contain less than half the calories of the steak, have virtually no fat, cause no leaching of the body's calcium during digestion, and are quite filling and delicious.

Frances Moore Lappe's book, *Diet for a Small Planet*, changed my thinking about food almost 20 years ago; it is a wonderful source of ideas and recipes for protein-complementing. It states that, in essence, proteins are formed from amino acid building blocks that combine in an almost infinite variety of ways. Animal protein contains all of the 22 amino acids necessary for tissue building. Although the amino acids that come from plants are exactly the same as those from animal sources, there is no *single* plant source that contains all the essential amino acids. However, all the amino acids (including the critical amino acids, lycine, tryptophan, and methionine) are present in some form in vegetables, so that by combining different vegetable sources we can have high-quality protein easily available. For example, grains are high in tryptophan and methionine but low in lysine, while legumes are high in lysine but low in tryptophan and methionine. When grains and legumes are merged, a complete protein is created. As a result, we see that animal protein is optional in a healthy diet!

More recently GW purchased the video *Diet for a New America*, which explores how our food choices affect not only our bodies but also our planet. Although its focus is on raising one's consciousness, this powerful video dramatically creates a new image for excellent nutrition, lower on the food chain. In addition, it creates an awareness that every food choice we make reverberates throughout our lives and the life of our planet.

When we present the GETTING WELL Nutritional Guidelines, which are included in each participant's notebook, we emphasize that they are *only* guidelines — if one is, for instance, allergic to tomatoes or if one's clinical dietician has suggested the elimination of tomatoes, then one should not eat tomatoes! We also point out that, even though in general it may be preferable to exclude most meat and dairy products, an individual may not be ready to let go of those foods entirely. For these cases, we offer the best choices in the particular categories. We suggest that one have a wide variety of choices of foods which are very low in fat; high in fiber; high in complex carbohydrates; low in sucrose; and high in selenium, anti-oxident vitamins C, E, and beta-carotene; high in protective indoles, potassium, and calcium.

In the category of legumes, grains, and nuts, we suggest that participants work up to at least three servings (approximately one-half cup) from *each* column. It is important to choose equally from the two columns in order to complete the essential amino acids, which are only partially available in legumes and partially available in grains, yet complete in the combination of the two. We also point out that very small amounts of dairy or meat/fish will complete the proteins in both grains and legumes. The focus is on having complex carbohydrates as the backbone of one's diet rather than the slab of meat most Americans are used to. Participants are usually warned not to make the changes too quickly, since the body (and the family) may not adjust well to them. "Evolution rather than revolution" is a particularly good admonition when an entire family's eating habits are involved.

Fruits and vegetables should be as close to their natural form as possible (with the exception of carrots, which need juicing or moderate cooking to release their nutrients). I have read the literature on both sides of the fence about the importance of vegetables and fruits being "organic." Although I have found no compelling health-related evidence for eating only organic products, I applaud a move to more natural control of insect damage and recycling of wastes for fertilizer.

Beta-carotene has been implicated in both the prevention and the reversal of cancer and heart disease. I have not seen any evidence of problems of beta-carotene "overdose" from beyond the skin having a yellowish cast. Although I believe a multivitamin with B-12, zinc, and iron is a good option for vegetarians, I have a prejudice against massive supplements, since it is so easy to upset the balance of the body, and micronutrients in the natural sources may be as important in empowering the given vitamin as the vitamin itself. For the most part, one should go to the natural source for one's nutrition rather than depending upon a capsule. Natural sources of beta-carotene, for example, contribute a great deal more than just beta-carotene to the diet (e.g., fiber, B vitamins, vitamin E, etc.); however, those very foods inhibit *absorption* of beta-carotene, so a booster supplement may be considered. Sources of beta-carotene include sweet potatoes, greens, summer and winter squashes, tomatoes, asparagus, and of course, carrots.

We believe that carrot juice is such a rich source of beta-carotene that we have had a juicer for the use of the participants (or the hospital dietary department) since our first day of GW. We have found that including an apple with each pound of carrots produces a drink delectable to even the most resistant of palates. To boost the power of the carrot juice, we suggest that participants image the passage of the carrot juice into their blood streams, dissolving cancer cells, changing the character of HIV cells, atomizing coronary artery blockages, replacing the myelin sheath on nerves, reducing inflammation, and calming any painful sensations.

Cruciferous vegetables (so named because of the cruciform shape of their flowers) include the cabbage family, broccoli, cauliflower, Brussels sprouts, kale, chard, collard and turnip greens. They, too, are high in beta-carotene (the vegetable form of vitamin A), in addition to protective indoles — substances protecting against cancer and a variety of other conditions. Two or more servings either raw or slightly cooked are suggested. It helps to visualize these foods balancing the body's immune system, cleaning out cholesterol lined arteries, moving food quickly through the digestive tract, maintaining appropriate blood sugar, and fighting infections.

Fruit is an excellent replacement for desserts and makes a delightful snack. The sugar in fruit, fructose, is metabolized differently from sucrose (common sugar) and is less destructive for diabetics. In addition, fruit provides more "sweet" to the taste per calorie, is not "empty calories" as is table sugar, and is a source of water soluble fiber. Fruits that have red juice, such as watermelon, strawberries, and cherries, are especially protective against cancer, according to the *Tufts University Diet and Nutrition Newsletter*. Citrus fruit is high in vitamin C, which not only increases the body's ability to fight infection but also tends to neutralize certain carcinogens in other foods. If a person takes a vitamin C supplement, we strongly suggest that it be taken with a natural form of ascorbic acid, since research suggests that the natural micronutrients are essential for the effectiveness of vitamin C.

If supplements of vitamin C are taken, one must be quite careful to take the same amount every day. Vitamin C is not stored by the body, so if an individual is taking a daily supplement of 1000 mg. of vitamin C, the body becomes accustomed to flushing the unused portion out of the body daily (maybe 900 mg.). If a person misses a day or so, the body continues to flush out the 900 mg., at the expense of vitamin C necessary to the body's functioning. Inconsistency of dosage over a period of time is likely to result in pin-point scurvy.

Dairy products, poultry, fish, and meat are optional in the diet. A majority of Caucasian adults and up to 90 percent of adults with African origins are lactose intolerant (Whitney & Hamilton, 1984). Therefore, milk products may be actually damaging to a large proportion of adults. Meat, fish, and poultry are not necessary to good health, and in excess can be harmful. Based on these facts, we urge participants to use only small amounts (if any at all) of animal proteins as a seasoning for complex carbohydrates rather than as the focus of the meal. If an individual is losing a great deal of weight, it may be imperative to include animal proteins to increase caloric intake; however, most people can find good sources of calories in the complex carbohydrates. If an individual is having problems maintaining a normal weight, we make sure that a physician or clinical dietician is working with the person.

There are many cookbooks that provide delicious recipes with little or no meat or dairy products. My particular favorites are *Jane Brody's Nutrition Book*, *Jane Brody's Good Food Book*, Robertson, Flinders and Godfrey's *Laurel's Kitchen*, and Nikki and David Goldbeck's *American Wholefoods Cuisine*. Dr. Dean Ornish's *Program for Reversing Heart Disease* provides excellent menus as well as tasty recipes, which are as appropriate for the person with lupus, MS, chronic fatigue, or cancer as for the individual with heart disease. Dr. Ornish's research indicates that the people who follow his nutritional guidelines most closely have the most reversal of blockage. Most writers on nutrition pussyfoot around what really works because they fear people won't adhere to a diet with 10 to 12 percent fat in it. I appreciate the fact that both Pritikin and Ornish stick to their guns and present revolutionary changes in diet that actually lead to increased pleasure in eating and the consumption of a wider variety of good foods.

In our present outpatient setting we all bring our lunches. Almost every day the lunch hour is a nutrition inservice with sharing of new discoveries in healthy eating, whether it be a delectable sandwich spread made from ground garbanzos and garlic, juiced carrots, or a crockpot of *Getwellsuppe*. This easily prepared soup makes a superb centerpiece for nutrition education since it embodies virtually all the principles of the GETTING WELL Nutritional Guidelines—very low fat, combined legumes and grains, high fiber, high beta-carotene, and cruciferous vegetables. Additionally, having the delicious smell wafting through group rooms all morning and consuming the soup in an atmosphere of joy and camaraderie give participants a headstart on shifting nutritional images better than any cookbook could.

As with exercise, a shift in consciousness and imagery about nutrition promotes lifelong changes as opposed to the short-term changes evoked by following a "diet" to lose weight, reduce blood sugar, reduce cholesterol, or prevent cancer. I am opposed to "dieting" because it creates a deep image of deprivation, giving up one's power, and investing in an outer locus of control. And, in my two decades of working with people in nutrition-based programs, I've found that "diets" not only don't work but also cause physical damage, a sense of helplessness and low self-esteem, and a poor quality of life. On the other hand, when participants eat mindfully, imagining each morsel bringing new life and health to every part of the body, a new consciousness emerges. What we eat is an important and necessary part of our lives, and I believe that it should be done with the image of robust joy and with the idea that we are choosing to bring a wide variety of delicious foods to our diets rather than depriving ourselves of what we want most.

As we were discussing a planetary consciousness the other day, a participant said, "I was trained to 'take dominion over all other living things,' to eat other living creatures, and to exploit the planet. I'm remembering myself enough to realize that this is not my essential self. I have no problem with other people's choices about what they eat, but I am realizing a part of the real me by making changes in what I eat."

As we eat lower on the food chain and experience the new consciousness that arises from that experience, we are indeed effecting healing—for ourselves, for the other humans on this planet, and for the planet itself—and we are connecting most profoundly with the universe.

Lessons for the Author/Clinician

Exercise occupied a negative place in my life from the time that I was excluded from my seventh grade basketball team by my gym teacher because of my height. Although I was on my high school tennis team, we never played anyone, since there were no other tennis teams in the state.

We generally used the time at the tennis club to reinforce our smoking habits or catch up on gossip rather than practice our serves or strengthen our backhands. I was a master at escaping required gym classes in high school and college, and would look with sophisticated disdain at any activity that might generate sweat. I really got back at that gym teacher!

It was not until I was forming behavioral weight control classes at the hospital's center for life management in the late 1970s that I became intellectually convinced that exercise was the major key to weight management. I also realized that, if I were to have any influence on the people with whom I was working, I needed to have exercise become a part of my life. I started jogging (which I really did dislike), ran on an injury, and got myself in a miserable pickle. I found, however, that walking was something I really enjoyed, and I actually became proficient enough in race walking in the early 1980s to place in a couple of races (and not just in my age category). I found, however, as Alfie Kohn would have predicted, that my pleasure in walking was nearly ruined by my walking to compete, and with great relief I entered no more races.

For the three months requisite to establish a new lifestyle I had to force myself, with guilt as the stick, to continue my aerobic walking; however, I haven't missed more than two days in a row in the nearly decade and a half I have been exercising (although I once switched to an exercise bike for the duration of a sprained ankle). I have discovered a part of my essential self I had discarded because of the wounds of competition and feel profoundly that I have taken back my power in this area of my life. I feel I have given my body a legacy even greater than stopping smoking many years ago, and have allowed my soul the gift of creation and awakening—the wonderful remembrance of my animal nature. With the stretch and contraction of muscle and sinew, I become a true creature of the planet and a vital cell in the body of the universe. My morning walk is an experience of mindfulness, of my spirit awakening with the light of the sun, of connectedness with my mate, or of union with the grass, waves, trees, and herons of the Florida landscape. I feel alive and awake in every sense.

As a child I learned to eat meat as most of us do; however, when I was four my family moved to an orange grove they owned in order to ride out the last years of the Depression. "The Grove" was a paradise of bucolic charm complete with wild rabbits, a cow on whom I could practice my cowgirl riding skills, and a yard of chickens for eggs—and alas, for Sunday dinner. My enlightened parents had impressed upon my sister and me the reality that animals were raised not only for the milk and eggs they produced but also to feed the family when their producing days were over. "Pets," of course, were an exception, and I quickly found that no pet would be put on the chopping block. Thus I named, thereby making pets of, a prodigious number of the chickens, and my father honored the lives of my large pet family of Chidden, Shirley, Chickie, etc.

One Saturday, after the weekly execution, I perused the chicken pen for my special ones, and Shirley was missing! "You've broken Shirley," I said, confronting my father in tears. "You promised not to make her broken."

"I'm sure I couldn't have killed Shirley, dear, but tell me exactly what she looked like and I'll check," he comforted me. I described Shirley's face down to the little freckle she had under one eye. Daddy checked the heads, and, indeed, he identified Shirley. He sadly admitted that he had inadvertently killed Shirley, and he and Mother joined me in mourning. My wise mother took me into her arms and reminded me that she and my father loved me—and that Shirley had loved me as much as I had loved her. In fact, Shirley had loved me so much that her highest purpose in life was to sacrifice herself to feed me and help me grow. My imagination was captured by that beautiful thought, and the next day my grief was allayed by helping Mother with the ritual of preparing Shirley for dinner. At Sunday dinner, I presided at the dining room table, offering Shirley around to the to the family: "And, what part of Shirley do you want, Mother? Would you like Shirley's leg, Daddy?"

As the sacrament of Shirley came to an end, I remember musing upon its beauty and then telling my parents earnestly, "I want you to promise, that if I ever get broken, you will have me for dinner just like we've had Shirley."

I remember a look of dismay crossing my mother's face, but I don't remember my parents' exact answer. It probably embodied the truth yet allowed me room for my illusions. In the next few months there *were* some subtle lessons on cannibalism imparted, and I seriously turned over in my four-and-a-half-year-old mind the distinction between eating human animals and other animals. As I think back, that day was a crossroads in my life—an inchoate realization that I would always need a lot of help in keeping myself convinced that it was okay to eat other creatures and that the death of animals was of little import to most people.

Even now, a part of me is amazed at our culture's ability to hypnotize us into indifference about animals sent to the slaughterhouse for our tables or young people sent to war for their country. It seems that the same move to separate us from our true being, our oneness, is in some sense responsible for our apathy or denial. *Diet for a Small Planet* opened me to the possibility that one could eat much lower on the food chain and be adequately nourished. I continued to eat meat because it was socially quite impossible for me to avoid it; however, at least I was allowing into my consciousness my disgust at the conspicuous consumption (and waste) being practiced at the then-popular steak houses.

In the past several years at GW, the idea that I can eat not only deliciously and healthily but also in line with my primal conscience and instinct has been a revelation. It is such a relief not to feel the inner turmoil that I have felt in the past when cutting up chicken, preparing steak, stuffing turkeys, slicing ham, or even steaming crabs. I relish the idea that my choice to eat meat only occasionally probably opens up over an acre of farmland that can grow grains and legumes for human consumption rather than for feeding cattle—that it may well be contributing to the healing of our planet. GETTING WELL has taught me that I don't have to feel embarrassed or a little stupid to feel as I do. I am remembering myself, and it feels good—it feels right.

11

Laughter and Noncompetitive Play

Celebrate your life. Bring pleasure into it whenever you can and see that pleasure as truth not as some secret sin. When you begin to blossom and glow and dance down the street just because you are happy . . . then you are free. *—Emmanuel's Book*

Human life is basically a comedy. Even its tragedies often seem comic to the spectator, and not infrequently they actually have comic touches to the victim. Happiness probably consists largely in the capacity to detect and relish them. *—H. L. Mencken*

I have not found a shred of evidence to support the common assertion that competition is an inevitable part of "human life." . . . Competition— no matter in what amount it exists—is always destructive. Healthy competition is a contradiction in terms, and the ideal amount of competition is *none*. *—Alfie Kohn*

Laughter and noncompetitive play are so important in the healing process that we reserve at least an hour a day for humor and playful activities. Although this session may seem a bit frivolous, it is perhaps the most difficult one for a large percentage of our participants. When one considers the personality and early training of the typical participant, who is nearly always adult, logical, left-brain oriented, concerned about competence, competitive, goal/outcome oriented, etc., such difficulty is not surprising.

Laughter and Play (L&P), as we call the course at GETTING WELL, is the antithesis of several of the guiding concepts of Western culture, which we feel contribute mightily to death and suffering. Competition vs. cooperation, separateness and individualism vs. unity and support, and one-upmanship and put-downs vs. humor that is creative and loving are life-and-death issues not only for the body but also for the mind and spirit. Because Western culture teaches us to image our world and our relationships through the dark glass of competition, people who enter the program have spent decades immersed in a competition/individualism consciousness. As a result, they may need to hear some good left-brain, logical arguments stating that competition produces physical and emotional (as well as spiritual) effects which are counterproductive to their getting well in the deepest sense.

The most cogent argument for many participants is that competitive images and intentions, in general, produce stress chemicals which retard the immune system and erode the cardiovascular system, while cooperation and support produce endorphins (which have an enhancing effect on all bodily systems).

Arguments revealing the destructive emotional and spiritual effects of the competitive consciousness are also numerous. Alfie Kohn, the author of *No Contest—The Case Against Competition*, contends that there are ways to have fun that do not involve attempting to triumph over other people. However, from our earliest social beginnings in Western culture we are taught to be for ourselves at the expense of others—the game of musical chairs at our preschool birthday parties is an excellent example. Kohn points out that "survival of the fittest" does not involve competition by its nature, and that, in truth, cooperation is the best way for this astonishing concept of evolution to take place. Kohn (1990) posits that "competition is destructive and counterproductive not merely in excess; it is destructive not merely because we are doing it the wrong way; it is destructive by its very nature" (p. 13). He continues by suggesting that several consequences of competition have led him to the view that it is always destructive.

Further, Kohn states that competition does not predict success. In fact, researchers have shown repeatedly that cooperation predicts ability to learn more than competition or individualized attainment does. Indeed, the more complicated the task, the worse competition fares when stacked up against cooperative approaches. Personal need to compete hinders success because it creates anxiety (*fear* that someone else will do better), which distracts the person from doing the best job possible. Cooperation, on the other hand, allows people to share their powers and skills in a way that competition does not. And, lastly, competition undermines intrinsic motivation. Often, when people who used to find something interesting and rewarding in itself begin doing it for the money, or competitively, they suddenly lose interest in the behavior itself.

Kohn also indicates that competition destroys self-esteem. He points out that the emotional needs we try to meet through competition (e.g., "I'm OK," "I'm a winner") are actually exacerbated by that same competition. In other words, possessing a high self-esteem becomes contingent upon whether one can "beat out" other people. One's self-evaluation becomes dependent on having other people to beat and on having other people *see* one win over others—which has nothing to do with a strong sense of self. Kohn further states, "The genuine alternative to being number one is not being number two. It's being able to dispense with these self-defeating rankings altogether" (1990, p. 19). Additionally, competition poisons relationships in that it encourages a separation consciousness. Following this line of thought, Kohn suggests that we are envious of winners and contemptuous of losers—and suspicious of just about everyone else as a potential rival.

In L&P, we replace a competitive intention/image with a model for cooperation—doing something just because it is enjoyable, being able to laugh without putting down oneself or someone else, and helping each other solve "problems" rather than vying to be a "winner."

The very essence of humor and play is perceiving a situation in a different way, a cognitive shift, a small epiphany. In fact, I sometimes refer to L&P as "epiphany training." Being able to make those perceptual shifts and imaging an everyday situation with a new consciousness seems to make us more open to shifts on universal, eternal issues. And when our minds are experiencing joy, laughter, love, self-acceptance, and peace, we create a splendid blueprint for our bodies and biochemistries to follow.

Clifford Kuhn, M.D., a professor at the University of Louisville School of Medicine, is quite articulate about the benefits of humor in achieving one's full humanity. "Humor is not just a series of jokes—of strategies to make people laugh," says this delightful psychiatrist with a twinkle in his playful blue eyes. "When humor is used to share ourselves with the essence of another, it is enormously healing. It is another model of therapy—an art" (1993). Clifford Kuhn has been a sparkplug in the UL Arts in Medicine program, which seeks to actively use the arts in addition to standard medicine in the recovery process. When he is not integrating programs for tapping into the healing creativity of individuals, Dr. Kuhn "does gigs" for comedy clubs all over the country.

Someone who has recently received the diagnosis of a life-challenging condition may feel there is "very little to laugh about." Elements of lifelong depression, catapulted to reactive status by the diagnosis, may have turned the "pleasurestat" down even further. I've had the privilege of observing Cliff Kuhn in consultations with several cancer patients who were having a tough time dealing with their diagnoses. It was almost magical how he empowered patients in shifting their perspectives, even to the point of enabling them to chuckle a bit about the absurdity of life. Indeed, we may choose to be very careful about using humor when dealing individually with the participant who is depressed or who is grieving the losses implied in a diagnosis; however, the L&P session "demands" that we laugh whether we feel like it or not—and that session is required.

Hank was one of the first patients in the program. He had survived several years of metastatic colon cancer, terribly botched abdominal surgery, and near-death experiences. Although he had a darkly sardonic humor about the physical roller coaster he was riding, he considered "playtime" to be a total loss. "Listen, I worked hard to become an adult, and I'm not ruining it all with this," Hank retorted when told that Laughter and Play was a "required course" at GETTING WELL.

"You *have* to take it," we said.

"We'll just see about that," he muttered.

Thus began a good-natured battle of wills, with Hank "needing" to take a nap or having a doctor's appointment at one o'clock when L&P was normally scheduled. The GW staff is unexcelled in its persistence and perversity, however, so we started scheduling L&P on an extremely flexible basis — like whenever Hank showed up! He finally capitulated and agreed to come, but still refused to participate. Instead he would lock himself in the bathroom during Blind Man's Bluff, make end-round plays during Simon Says, and generally engage in outrageous antics to out-smart the therapists. Soon Hank became the most engaging feature of L&P for everyone, including himself. As a result of his rebellion, he became the playful imp he had never been allowed to be and started having the time of his life. Hank's beginning openness to the childlike part of himself allowed him to explore during other therapy sessions the blockages to the healing process that his demanding childhood had erected.

Physiological Benefits of Laughter and Play

Dr. William Fry, Jr., a psychiatrist affiliated with Stanford University, has studied laughter for over 30 years. In a 1979 address to the Annual Convention of the American Orthopsychiatric Association in Washington, D.C., he made a case for laughter's being an important factor in major health issues, such as heart disease, cancer, and cardiovascular accidents (CVA).

Fry has found that humor and laughter give specific antagonistic relevance to several of the major risk factors for heart disease; for example, they diminish the physical tension which contributes to stress and is a part of the web of causality for coronary disease. In addition, laughter is antithetical to the rage and sudden intense anger which may precipitate heart disturbance. Mirth diminishes the impulses of hostility, and since anger demands a serious attitude, humor expels the tightness and severity necessary for anger.

Although Fry admits that the cancer picture is an extremely complicated one, he suggests that humor and mirth are palliative, reducing the pain and mental anguish involved in this condition at least momentarily.

In addition, he suggests that depression may be an etiologic substrate in the onset of cancer for some, and that humor and depression are incompatible, because laughter and play relieve the "devitalizing grip" of depression. He also adds, tentatively, that our impulse to enjoy mirth may "oppose vulnerability to developing cancer."

Fry admits that the contribution of humor and laughter is a mixed one for CVAs, since some strokes have reportedly occurred during mirthful laughter (probably associated with the temporary increase in blood pressure during laughter). However, laughter does create the conditions necessary to combat the circulatory sluggishness associated with strokes attributed to brain artery blockage or the clotting associated with stasis of blood circulation.

On the same subject, most people are familiar with Norman Cousins' use of laughter to deal with the pain and debilitation caused by ankelosing spondilitis. He found that just 20 minutes of hearty laughing allowed him two hours of pain-free sleep. Studies undertaken since the publication of *Anatomy of an Illness* indicate that the neuropeptide beta-endorphin is drop-for-drop 200 times more effective than morphine in reducing pain — and does not produce the side effects. For example, Cogan et al. (1987) found that laughter is as effective as relaxation training in increasing pain thresholds (reducing discomfort) and is also very effective in the management of stress through tension reduction.

Both laughter and play exercise the lungs, stimulate the circulatory system, and increase oxygen in the blood. Mirth and laughter have been compared to a good sneeze: First, muscle tension increases in anticipation of the punch line; then the chest, abdomen, face, arms, and legs get a workout; heart rate, breathing, and circulation are speeded up; then, after the climax, the pulse rate and blood pressure drop below normal and skeletal muscles become deeply relaxed. In fact, Norman Cousins (1979) called laughter "a form of internal jogging."

Laughter and noncompetitive play increase endorphins, not only decreasing anxiety and depression but also activating the thymus gland and generally increasing immune system activity (Gilman et al., 1982). Dr. Lee Berk (1989) found that another way in which laughter may exert an influence on the immune system is by reducing cortisol, which in turn affects the synthesis of interleukin-2. He discovered that those who watched a humor video (Gallagher) had significantly increased lymphocyte proliferation and natural killer-cell activity, and that even *anticipation* of the "good-natured humor" brought significant drops in epinephrine levels.

Psychological Effects of Laughter and Play

William Fry and Waleed Salameh have edited an interesting volume called *Handbook of Humor and Psychotherapy* (1987), which indicates that humor is a powerful tool for use in therapy for people with mild-to-moderate depression, anxiety and panic disorder, and most adjustment disorders. Loss of one's sense of humor and sense of playfulness are prime symptoms (and maybe causes) of burnout, depression, anxiety, and "dis-ease." Bringing play and humor back into the picture for afflicted individuals often starts their recovery/healing process.

Humor and mirthful play may be contraindicated for those with severe depression, recent loss, or psychoses, and are usually not appropriate until the therapist has investigated the situation and established a relationship. In my experience, however, an attitude of lightness and humor appropriately used can melt resistance and help people grapple with their defenses. A light nonthreatening approach frequently can move therapy much more quickly and pleasantly than a serious, ponderous approach. And of course, it is so much more fun and so much more educational when a point is made with a belly laugh than with a serious nod. If humor feels uncomfortable to you, by all means, don't force yourself to use it. However, I have found through presentations made to professionals all over the country that those of you attracted to this field invariably have a fine sense of the ridiculous. You just don't have to hide it anymore!

Perhaps the most important psychological effect of humor and a playful attitude is the increase in the overall quality of life for those who can image in this "alternative" manner. With the pairing of the expected and the unexpected, laughter promotes cognitive flexibility. Having a playful and humorous eye and attitude gives one optional ways of looking at a situation—no matter how absurd. Even if the alternative arrived at is outrageous, it is *still* an option, and one is no longer backed against the wall with no choices.

One cannot laugh and play and catastrophize at the same time, because laughter tends to put situations into perspective, forcing one to realize that every situation—no matter how tragic—has some humor in it. Certainly humor and play make it easier to cut overwhelming situations down to manageable size. Further, as people develop the cognitive flexibility which humor and play promote, they may create a different set of images about themselves, the future, and the past—and these images may transform their lives. When we laugh, our perception shifts. We let go of feelings of judgment, blame, and self-pity to embrace a more extended knowledge of ourselves and of others. Deliberately taking the time to amuse and be amused allows us to absorb change which otherwise would be overwhelming.

When people can be playful and laugh at themselves, they are able to begin to let go of perfectionism—and enjoy themselves as wonderful, perfectly fallible humans. We find that play and humor are terrific tension-releasers for hostility, anger, anxiety, fear, irritability, adultness, and feelings of overresponsibleness. Above all, being able to laugh and play increases the joy in life, sends "live messages" to the right brain, boosts self acceptance, and makes life fun.

Laughter/Play as an Integrative Process

Dr. Walter O'Connell (1987) describes a wonderful, humorous psychotherapy, "natural high therapy," which he calls the humorist's game of games. He points out that humor employs both visual and verbal means, such as brief, incongruous, unexpected, condensed situations, to bring us to an awareness of sudden shifts in meanings. Additionally, humor and play involve the concept that anything can be something else. O'Connell uses humor and playful interchange to strengthen the ego, to dissolve destructive defenses and ego restrictions, and to challenge the limits to a person's achieving a natural high. His method uses humor and playfulness to synthesize and integrate the therapy experience—that is, the life experience.

I particularly appreciate (and use extensively throughout the GW program) O'Connell's use of aphorisms to bring home his points. For example: "Nothing is crazier than the assertion that the well-adjusted Western man is sane," "The sayings of saints get inscribed in stone by the same forces that resist their evolutionary implications," "Don't cry over spilt shit: Make it into fertilizer," "Embarrassment is a type of vicious vanity," and "Most of us do not want control over our lives: We merely want control of people and conditions that we allow to control us" (pp. 76–77). Somehow the humorous twist hammers home the point. A decade ago, when I was facilitating cognitive/behavioral weight control programs, I found that a single *Cathy* cartoon did more good than an hour's lecture on changing cognitions about eating. My framed *Far Side* cartoon with the big ship in flames, the little ship in flames, and the survivors in the water shouting, "We won! We won!" explains the concept of a Pyrrhic victory better than I could in 486 words.

We use humor and play to integrate all aspects of the program and all parts of life. Sometimes our biggest laughs are during the serious business of transformational fantasy. The incredible juxtapositions of our unconscious images take on outrageous, playful, psychotic qualities, which are enjoyed as much by the subject as the group. Curiously, the laughter also seems to dissipate some of the discomfort in relating one's deepest images, while allowing the person to perceive and "confess" his or her foibles with greater ease.

Carl Simonton has a policy that his Pacific Palisades program can be interrupted at anytime (except during imagery) to tell a good (or not-so-good) joke. We have a rule at GETTING WELL that one can ask for a standing ovation from the rest of the group (as long as it is requested assertively). These rules convey the idea that nothing in the program is so serious that it cannot be appropriately interrupted for a laugh or some playful activity. We believe that the same rules apply to life. (My daughter Rosalind made quite a name for herself by asking for standing ovations in the lunchroom of her large high school.)

Laughter, Play, and Creativity

Laughter and noncompetitive play increase right-brain activity, creativity, and a healing, childike attitude. When we look at the characteristics of the creative process, we find powerful similarities to the processes of humor and play. Creativity is frequently ambiguous and nearly always incomplete. It is a sensuous process that involves all perceptions and the wholeness of the mind, body, and spirit. Childlike qualities of curiosity and wonder, as well as the ability to assemble ingredients no one else has thought to combine, are characteristic of creative thinking and L&P. Just as humor and play are the exact opposite of the closed, rigid, and judgmental, so creativity means openness and receptivity.

When we watch children at play, we marvel in their creativity. A pan is not just something in which to boil peas; it is a drum, a hat, a bank, a chair — it can be almost anything. As adults we become tied to labels such as "pan" or "coat hanger," failing to see more than a fraction of the possibilities. At GW one of our playful exercises is to think of as many uses as possible for a coat hanger. Over the years, participants have come up with at least a hundred uses of a coat hanger, from roasting weenies to creating topiaries.

We are all born creative and playful and creatively playful, but at an early age that creativity and playfulness are trained out of us. "That's not the way to play with that toy," "Quit fooling around and win," and "Don't you ever do anything except play around?" are the messages of our culture. In order to please the "giants," we give up our playfulness and creativity to embrace the rigid models of the culture. To assist our participants in returning to their earlier creativity, we play a number of the commercial games (e.g., Whatzit) designed to go beyond the conventional ways of interpreting a situation. We also have sessions in which puzzles are used to jog our mental rigidities (e.g., the nine-dot puzzle, and enigmas such as "8D − 24H = 1W" [eight *days* minus 24 *hours* equals one *week*]). Of course, it is important that these puzzles be done noncompetitively and in a way in which everyone wins. Sometimes pointing out that children do much better than adults with these puzzles gives some of the more rigid adults the idea that solutions come more easily through letting go than through learning more.

For many, mirthful play triggers muscle memories of the child they were decades earlier. When we spark the consciousness of our childhood, we may recreate the extraordinary healing powers we had as children. Even more important, we activate that beautiful curiosity and joy we experienced during childhood. "When I'm playing, I'm immediately transported back to summer days in upstate New York, when I was so taken by what I was doing that time stood still," said one participant. "It was, *and is*, pure and engulfing joy."

For others, there was little levity as a child. Molly, a 64-year-old woman with breast cancer, stated up front, "I don't remember playing as a child. I was the oldest of eight children, and we lived on a farm. I was always too busy taking care of the other kids or doing chores to play or have a good time. Anyway," she continued, "playing just wasn't in my parents' scheme of things. In fact, I never had a birthday party, and I don't even remember ever getting a birthday gift from my parents." During a transformational fantasy session she was able to remember her child-like desire to play, and gave herself a wonderful birthday party in her "play room." With the help of the other participants, she set about recreating a normal, playful childhood. Cohorts taught her how to play jacks, Drop the Handkerchief, and Red Rover. Kite-flying day was pure bliss for Molly, and wreaths of smiles replaced her usually dour demeanor. "I feel so much lighter," she said several days later, "It's almost as if my spirit is soaring like my kite did the other day."

The Daily Schedule

We have a fairly loose structure for L&P, but there are elements we feel are important to include daily. For example, L&P is usually comprised of joke telling, juggling, and game playing—with the only rule being that one can take nothing that happens between 1 and 2 p.m. seriously. While this session *focuses* on laughter and noncompetitive play, we make it clear that the attitude of humor and playfulness should be incorporated in all of GETTING WELL's sessions, as well as all of life.

We also have an excellent library of humorous videos, from *Candid Camera* to Billy Crystal and Gallagher, which we tend to schedule at times other than the official L&P session. We feel it is important for everyone to be actively involved in the L&P happenings rather than merely watching—this is especially true for facilitators. We also "require" everyone to bring in a joke each day, which provides an impetus to go looking for amusing stories and to keep an expectant ear out for a good joke. We maintain a library of joke books, old *Reader's Digests*, and a card file of all-time favorite jokes. Frequently, our most shrinking violets become some of our best story-tellers by the end of the four weeks.

Of course, we make it clear that humor is not to be used to put down another person, race, religion, sexual preference, or nationality. If one is telling an "ethnic" joke, it must be about one's own "eth." For example, I can tell blonde, WASP, Scotch/Irish, English, Welsh, or Scottish jokes (or fit other ethnic jokes into those categories). There are many ethnic-type jokes that are genuinely funny in themselves, and we find they do not suffer when converted to the background of the teller. If the joke does suffer from such a change, it is probably of the kind of humor that separates us from one another and is not healing.

A couple of years ago, when trying to render some of our tasteless gems "tellable," the group decided to use a strategy which we had once employed in the Brigham family to clean up otherwise abhorrent jokes—that is, to use a college dean as the target. My professor husband was tilting with university administration at the time, and certainly no brief could be found for any college dean. Our group during that period included a professor from the University of Florida, and she concurred that nothing was too bad for deans. So we had a wonderful two weeks with college dean stories! (Have you heard the one about the college deans who were out ice-fishing? They carefully hacked holes in the ice and put their lines in, but got no bites. The deans then hacked new holes, but again got no bites. This went on for about an hour, and the college deans decided to ask God what was wrong. After they invoked divine guidance, there was a loud rumble and a voice from the heavens boomed out, "This is the manager of the arena. Will you please get off the ice!!") It was a great two weeks of dean jokes which screeched to a halt when our professor was called out of group for an important phone call. When she returned, she said, "You guys aren't going to believe this. That was the university administration and they want me to consider becoming dean of my college."

As people begin to know each other (often before), raunchy, sexual jokes start coming out, and there is usually a well-reared participant who finds these shocking. Personally, I think they are therapeutic. Lewis Mehl, M.D., Ph.D. (1990), of the University of Arizona in Tucson, points out that the mainstream culture of the United States represses humor concerning many natural physiological human functions such as sex in a way that no other culture does. This may be our culture's way of remaining disconnected and aloof from natural animal processes. In Mehl's own native Lakota culture (certainly one more connected with nature and the natural healing energy flow), no natural function was verboten for creating humorous stories for all ages. I was particularly taken by the "dirty coyote" stories told in his childhood. Those stories usually starred a wily male coyote who would go to any ends to lure females into his den and impregnate them. We find some major therapy taking place as the looks of disgust at "those terrible jokes" begin to fade into smiles, then laughter, and finally, attempts to tell a similarly saucy story.

Although I usually temper my jokes if I know that someone in the group has been sexually abused as a child, I usually find that tiptoeing is unnecessary. Sexual humor has frequently been used surreptitiously by those abused in an attempt to get a handle on the situation, to distance themselves from it, and in a sense, mentally to control the abuser. For example, Shirley had been unable to talk in group about her early sexual abuse, even though we suspected it was a part of her history. At first we were all very careful about our stories, because Shirley never told a story with the least shadow on it. Then we found that, instead of speaking up, she was writing stories out or giving other participants the page number of a joke that captured her interest—and they were sizzlers! As we therapists ended our moratorium on off-color humor, Shirley also began to *tell* her stories, with much blushing and embarrassment at first, and then as a member of "the club." Finally, in group therapy, she felt desensitized and protected enough to tell her "secret," and the healing began.

After joke time we usually juggle. I was taught to juggle by Carl Simonton at a workshop called "The Healing Power of Laughter and Play" nearly a decade ago. Juggling is one of those things one never thinks he or she will be able to do, and people usually don't even try to learn for fear of failure. We have a juggling bag filled with colorful nylon scarves and juggling "balls" (two-inch cubes of corduroy which I have made over the years and filled with lentils or rice). If you are going to use juggling as part of your program, I suggest you obtain the authoratative book on the topic, *Juggling for the Complete Klutz* (Cassidy, 1978). To learn to juggle, one must live with constant failure—dropping balls. The way one accomplishes this is to define the "drop" as a strategy as important as the "toss," and *practice* the drop. One starts by juggling with one ball or one scarf and tossing it from hand to hand. (That's juggling! All the rest, up to and including six running buzz saws, is just icing on the cake.) After the art of tossing the object from one hand to the other has been mastered, we move on to two objects and then to three. If people can tolerate the "failures" and just enjoy the experience, it is amazing how quickly they become adroit at juggling two or three balls. But if a person chooses to stay with just one object, we consider that a success, too.

Nat, a 28-year-old school teacher, had survived a serious form of meningitis at age 12, which left the right side of his body spastic. Only with difficulty could he extend his right arm or open his tightly fisted hand. I was tempted to forgo the juggling while he was there because of his problems with balance and muscle extension. Nonetheless, the group moved into juggling before I could suggest an alternative, and Nat, good sport that he was, gave it a try. The first couple of days were excruciating for him. He could catch the ball but found it difficult to release it. He finally got the one-ball toss and moved to the two-ball toss. He would practice after hours, intending and imaging his right hand's letting go and opening, until after nearly 10 days, the two-ball toss was finally conquered. For Nat, this was akin to climbing Everest! Unbelievably, by the end of the four weeks he could do one round—sometimes two—of three-ball juggling. His physical therapist remarked on the exceptional changes that had taken place in his coordination and extension while he was in the program. And just looking at Nat's face as he juggled, we knew a miracle was occurring.

Although some may exist, I know of no exercises as good as juggling for building skill and self-esteem, for letting go, and for just being in the moment. Perfectionists resist it viciously, probably because it gives them license to have fun and cease worrying about results and outcomes—in the process of wonderfully healing the wound of perfectionism. There is no being in the past or the future when one is juggling, for one can be intent only on the moment. Juggling (and dropping) for 15 minutes works up a good sweat and probably qualifies as aerobic exercise. For people in wheelchairs (even with limited arm mobility) a one- or two-ball toss gets the juices moving and helps them feel they are part of the world again. And it allows GETTING WELL to make at least one promise to prospective participants—not only will your life be better, but you will also learn to juggle!

On nice days, we may take the juggling outside and combine it with playing with our giant parachute, blowing big bubbles, or flying kites. Our goals with these somewhat esoteric activities are to have everyone fully participating despite physical challenges, feeling good about themselves, and totally connected with everyone else.

Playing with the four-color parachute is a favorite L&P activity. A staff member usually has people warm up by moving the parachute up and down while holding onto the handles. Depending on the physical condition of participants, she may have "everyone wearing blue" or "everyone with brown shoes on" run under the chute and change places, or she may place a ball on the parachute and enlist a cooperative effort to bounce the ball in a certain way. After these initial activities, she encourages the players to create their own games with the chute, and everyone is off and running. This play is good exercise in addition to being amazingly energizing—particularly for those whose physical condition or pain usually do not allow them to be active. Having one's pain disappear during the parachute antics is also a powerful reminder to everyone of their inner ability to control pain.

The rest of L&P time is usually devoted to indoor games such as Pictionary, charades, or Whatzit. Of course, we redesign the rules so that the game is cooperative and noncompetitive. In fact, the rules of any game can change if a participant wants to play the game a completely different yet noncompetitive way. Safari is a favorite game, in which members must guess the class of items the leader is taking on safari in order to be allowed to go along. This game could be quite competitive, but we have redesigned it into a cooperative venture. The leader says, for example, "I'm going on safari and I'm taking a cow and a table [things with four legs]. Who'd like to go with me?" Group members take turns trying to guess the category: "I'd like to go on safari and I will take a pair of shoes and a chair. Can I go on safari?" Because the person has not guessed the category, the leader says, "I'm sorry. You can't go on safari." The next person may say, "I'd like to go on safari and I'm going to take a dog and a cat. Can I go on safari?" And the leader answers, "Yes, you can go on safari." This continues until everyone has an acceptable pair of items to take on safari. The group enthusiastically works and gives hints to get everyone on the safari as quickly as possible. Then a new leader volunteers and starts a new category (things with eyes, things that start with the initials of one's first and last name, things that are red, things that live in the ocean, etc.). In addition to being fun, this game forces people to think in new ways, relabel old concepts, and see things in new ways.

To become a true, initiated member of GETTING WELL, one must have the key to the arcane mystery of Black Magic, a game that needs a facilitator and an accomplice. The facilitator states, "This is an exercise which demonstrates the powers of mental energy. We are going to send [accomplice] out of the room and choose an object for that person to guess." The accomplice leaves room, and participants choose the object; then as someone goes for the accomplice, members are reminded to image the object clearly. The facilitator points at various objects in the room, asking, "Is this it?" and the accomplice says "no" until the *object after a black object* is pointed out, and the accomplice says, "That's it!" to the oohs and aahs of the group. We play this game until everyone in the group has caught on—usually this requires many creative guesses as to how it is done and several games of Red Magic or Green Magic. We typically play Magic several times a month so that everyone has been "in the dark" and has served as facilitator or accomplice.

Yuri Geller's Two-Finger Lift is a favorite trick and a total mystery that was introduced to us several years ago by a patient who had seen Geller perform this feat on television during a lunch break at GW. (He was subsequently forgiven for watching commercial TV rather than a healing video during lunch.) Five people are needed for this experiment, one who sits in a chair and four others who lift. Care must be taken that there are no physical problems or pain that will be disturbed by this. A first round involves the four lifters hooking their two index fingers (pointing from otherwise grasped hands) under each of the arms and the knees (one person on each arm and knee) of the person sitting in the chair, and then trying to lift the person. Rarely can even the lightest individual be budged.

Before the next lift, the lifters silently put their hands "in a stack" over the liftee's head, one at a time, without touching. Person one puts out his or her right hand, person two places his or her right hand about an inch above that of person one, and so on. Then in the same order, everyone adds their left hands (not touching) to the stack. Silently, the hands are removed in the reverse order from which they were placed, and each person gets his or her two index fingers in place and lifts. Miraculously, the person is lifted quite easily. It does not seem to matter how large the liftee is or how strong the lifters are. During the first round it feels as though the liftee is solid mass, but in the second round the liftee seems almost to float up. And this is not a set-up! It is a beautiful enigma which, although done in the sense of fun, brings mysteries to ponder when we are exploring more serious territories such as transpersonal imagery and the healing energies of therapeutic touch.

"Changes" enmeshes the person in finding a partner, spending 60 seconds looking at the other person, and memorizing everything about that individual. Couples are then asked to turn back to back and make five changes in the next 60 seconds. When they turn back, each person identifies the changes he or she sees in the other for a couple of minutes. Then we ask the couples to turn back to back again and make five more changes. (By example, we encourage creative change—such as exchanging shoes with a nearby person, putting on glasses we don't normally wear, etc.) Depending upon the circumstances, we may ask the group to make five more changes. The point of this exercise is that we can always make changes—even when pushed to the wall—and sometimes even a small shift in perception, a tiny change, can create a miracle.

"Elbow fruit hop" is one of my favorite Playfair games; I use it at GW and at conferences with large groups of people. A person names three things: first, a part of the body to be touched (e.g., elbow); second, a category from which one item can be chosen (e.g., fruit or animals); and third, a way of moving around (e.g., hop or skip). People move in this style (e.g., skipping, finger to hip, calling out "greyhound") until someone yells "Stop!" and names a new trio, for example, "eye, automobile, walk backward." The game continues until someone calls out "elbow, fruit, hop" which ends the game for everyone. Participants loosen up with this game and enjoy seeing others and themselves being ridiculous.

In searching for these and other noncompetitive games, I have found *Playfair* by Matt Weinstein and Joel Goodman to be invaluable. *Playful Perception* (1984) by Dr. Herbert Leff provides inspiration not only for

L&P activities but also for expressive therapy and high-level awareness pursuits. Leff, a psychologist and photographer, presents numerous intriguing exercises for cognitive flexibility and consciousness-raising. For example, he suggests imagining new uses for things around you, viewing the world as if you were an animal, or seeing objects around you as the *tops* of structures going deep underground and guessing what these buried structures are like. Although starting with activities such as "seeing everything around you as alive," these exercises quickly draw one in to the profound shifts in perceptions required in "imagining what it would feel like to be the whole universe" or "regarding everything as *perfect* exactly the way it is each moment." Indeed, one is struck by how fun and play are the seeds of epiphanies.

Lessons for the Author/Clinician

I am so glad Norman Cousins stated many years ago that laughter is a healing process. By contrast, the somewhat analytical philosophy under which I was trained suggested that humor was a rather spurious defense mechanism. To use laughter in a therapy session was completely in sync with my own instincts, but unfortunately was considered to be the ultimate insult to Freud the Father. Guffaws emitting from the sacred therapy room caused black looks from one's colleagues. Yet, in my family of origin, a sense of humor was a mandate for membership.

My father, an esteemed educator (who is now in his mid-nineties), had exceptional goals for his students, which were met consistently because he never quit being a kid himself. He tells the story of the boys who were tussling and showing off at the lake in front of the school in the 1930s, when a couple of them fell in and were drenched. These bedraggled creatures presented themselves to my father, begging for something dry to put on. "Well, men," he said, "you've broken the rules, and you have a choice. Either you can take off all your wet clothes and go around with *nothing* on, or you can use a couple of these Santa suits which are nice and dry to finish out the day." I believe that the choice was for the Santa suits! These men still keep in touch with my father and still tell him how humorously and meaningfully this "punishment" touched their lives.

A number of years ago I learned a ploy which is not only good for a laugh, but which has also created innumerable shifts of consciousness for me. Whenever I found myself in the middle of an impossible situation, I would create a stage play of it in my mind's eye and sit in the front row to watch it unfold. The play nearly always turned out to be a comedy. Turning a harassing situation into a play or a TV sitcom allows me to detach from the situation at its worst and usually creates a flash of insight or a new way of perceiving "reality" which is easier on my body and spirit. This technique has become such second nature that I can start chuckling at the twists and turns of a "day from hell" and how I'm going to weave it into a tale for my family—while I'm still in the middle of it. Unfortunately, sometimes when things really get rough, I forget that I have this skill. Writing this paragraph reminds me that I can recreate my reality with humor—if I will just remember to do so!

As I have mentioned, throwing my lot with GETTING WELL has thrust me into a world that at times seems overwhelming and has placed me in the company of people who, frankly, have tried to bully us. Early on, I realized that if GW and I were to survive, I had to rid myself of feelings of intimidation and eventually forgive those individuals. But before forgiveness could take place, I needed to cut those people down to size and to feel that I had some power in the situation.

For example, I was forced to have at least weekly contact with the two doctors who threatened to destroy the program, and I despised the feelings of helplessness I felt in their presence. At lunch one day, as we watched them come through the line, my small staff and I decided to disempower them in our own minds with humor. We began imaging the large one in diapers underneath his slightly mussed professional attire, and the nattily dressed smaller one as wearing under his suit the most glorious, sexy, black lace women's lingerie one could imagine. Lunches surely took an up-turn as we had heated discussions about whether today's bra and garter belt were from Frederick's of Hollywood or Victoria's Secret! Meeting one of these men in the hall or elevator took on new and hilarious meaning, and despite the gravity of the situation, we were no longer helpless. Many months later, a friendly member of administration said, "I knew what was going on in that situation and how terrible it must have been for you, but what really amazed us was how cheerful and gutsy you guys were about it all." (Isn't it amazing what a little black lace will do!)

Finally, let me say that the L&P session is also a wonderful respite during a demanding professional day. When any of us is having a less-than-great day, we check ourselves into the L&P session and laugh the problems away!

12

High-Level Awareness I: Taking Responsibility for Pulling Weeds in Our Gardens

Real change takes place within our souls; the real change takes place when the unfolding of our souls reflects in some deep, mysterious way the unfolding of the universe. Then it is—when an individual person dares to live within his or her truth—that the world is changed, forever. —*Jeffrey Smynkywicz paraphrasing Vaclav Havel*

The process of letting go of what is completed or outgrown is absolutely essential in affirming life. One cannot engage with life if one is caught by the past sadness. Grief is not harmful. It is the lack of connection with ongoing life that is harmful. —*Rachel Naomi Remen*

What I find most fascinating and personally rewarding in this work is how illness can be a catalyst for addressing the emotional and spiritual dimensions of living. —*Dean Ornish*

High-level awareness is the session during which we focus upon philosophical and spiritual issues. It is the time each day when participants try to expand the depth and breadth of their personal awareness and get in touch with their full human potential. I like to characterize high-level awareness as the highest common denominator of human spirituality—the essence and ethics that thread through all religions and other forms of human spiritual tradition. Just as the 28 sessions of stress management teach one how to survive, so the 28 sessions of high-level awareness teach one how to thrive. The session is not religious, yet we suggest people add the frills and lace of their own faiths to the core concepts that we present. We make it quite clear that the ideas presented are not Truth with a big T, but possibilities which each individual can try on for size.

We certainly do not advocate making a clean sweep or throwing away *all* old beliefs. However, we do encourage examining beliefs and holding them by choice rather than default—finding beliefs that further our images of the good, whole, luminous, creatively gifted creatures we all are. Living with a new belief or image for an hour or two, or a day or two, can create powerful insights, as well as shifts in the way people perceive the world, often changing that perception so it is never the same again.

As we know, beliefs, thoughts, and ideas form or are formed from our images. Our images about our limitations or potential, about separation from or connectedness with ourselves, others, and the universe, and about our helplessness or power form the blueprint not only for how we live our lives but also for how our bodies function. In order to create change in participants' awareness, we consistently employ imagery, transformational fantasy, and meditation, using those tools to tap into unconscious beliefs, connect with the universal, and create an emotional shift. These shifts, in turn, create fertile grounds for the epiphanies and personal miracles that we see daily in the program.

Here I will try to give you an idea of how we present the sessions, as well as a feel for the philosophy, theories, and principles which underlie high-level awareness. While many of you will be familiar with the thoughts and hypotheses we are presenting, others may be less familiar with this particular area. For that reason, I am including a plethora of ideas, just as our folders for each session contain far more material than one would ever consider using for one lesson. Since many of the ideas are new to participants, we generally lecture the first 20 to 30 minutes of the session and then move to a more interactive style. With an active group, the facilitator may not get past the first two paragraphs of the lecture before the group is off and running. Of course, the point is not to include everything that "should" be in the lesson but, rather, to use the material as a jumping-off place for participants' own philosophical and spiritual awakenings. Certainly, high-level awareness could be addressed just as well in many other different ways; this is merely the manner in which *we* present the material.

Pulling the Weeds of Isolation and Separation

A number of the new breed of scientist/philosophers, such as Joan Borysenko, Dean Ornish, and Larry Dossey, identify separation or lack of connectedness as one of the major stressors of our civilization. Dr. Dovey Gamble, a well-known therapeutic recreation researcher, refers to those stressors as "cross-graining our lives."

Charles Tart (1987) relates the story of a man who was dissatisfied with his health and his life and decided to plant a garden of wonderful vegetables and beautiful flowers in his back yard. With great excitement, he went to his local garden center, where he chose seed packets of splendid vegetables and glorious flowers, in addition to bags of rich fertilizer. As he approached the checkout counter, he saw a wise neighbor, told him about his plan, and asked him what he thought of it. The neighbor considered for a moment, then said, "I know the plot you're talking about and it's overgrown with weeds, so it certainly doesn't need the fertilizer. In fact it's so choked with weeds that none of your seeds would be able to grow. What you really need are hoes and shovels to get rid of the weeds so that your seeds will grow."

Like this man, we need to "cultivate our gardens," to pull the weeds of guilt, resentment, blame, attachments, helplessness, judging others, etc., before the seeds of connectedness and unity can be planted and thrive.

Examining Cultural Norms, Conditioning, Identification, and Consensus Trance

Dr. Tart's exceptional book, *Waking Up*, discusses overcoming the obstacles to human potential, a process in which we need to accept a couple of givens. We must accept, first, that we have a basic nature or essence, and second, that we have an acquired nature. Whatever our basic nature is, it has been subjected to an enormous amount of bending, shaping, and repression in the course of our becoming an acceptable member of our culture. This indoctrination is so subtle and so powerful that it is hard for an individual to know what is essence and what is acquired nature. This lesson may oversimplify the enormous complexity of our genetic inheritance and the fact that we are born with different affective/temperamental potential in order to make the point that one can change what one has learned and does not need to be a victim of the past. To assist in differentiating between essence and acquired nature, group members take a look at several of the culture's most powerful tools—conditioning, consensus trance, and identification—and begin to tease out what is essential self from what is acquired self.

Let us assume that we are born a wonderful, shining little being, full of power and the potential to be everything a human can be. Frequently, such creativity and potential don't fit in with our parents' desires or the culture's needs, so the conditioning process begins almost at once, as we are rewarded for being the little kid our parents want us to be and punished for being the little kid we want to be. We learn pretty quickly that our needs aren't important, that we eat when our parents want us to, sleep when *they* need a rest, and refrain from expressing our feelings about the situation. A whole system of conditioning takes place at the preverbal level, as we are rewarded for "proper" behavior and punished for "deviant" behavior. Because this activity *is* preverbal, we have no words to describe what has happened to us, so that it lies in the unconscious area of our senses and emotions. When we realize that most of our truly important feelings about ourselves were conditioned, we are in a better position to begin at least to identify the "weeds" from that conditioning.

It may seem that we are making parents malevolent actors in a drama to rein in the creative infant and not taking into account individual differences, and a discussion of these issues usually comes up. Sometimes in helping people see their lives in a different light, I believe the end justifies making a dramatic teaching point. The inevitable paradoxes (and even outrage) this method engenders move individuals to thinking the issues through more thoroughly and coming to their own resolutions.

Tart discusses the consensus trance, in which the hypnotist is the culture and the subject is us. Each of us is born into a culture with a consensus about how things are and how they ought to be. As soon as we are born, the culture begins to pick and choose among our potentials, some of which are encouraged and some of which are actively discouraged and punished. Consensus trance induction is a process of shaping the behavior and the consciousness of that little bundle of potential into what is "normal" or what fits society's norms. Dr. Tart points out that if you are very lucky, and most of the characteristics of your essence are ones that happen to be valued in your culture, the induction is smooth and free of conflict, and your adult life will be "normal" and successful. For example, if you are short-tempered and aggressive and you happen to be born into a culture that prizes warriors—you're okay. However, if your essence is short-tempered and aggressive and you happen to be born a woman in a culture where women are supposed to be docile helpmeets, there can be *major* trouble.

The consensus trance involves years of repeated induction and reinforcement of the effects of previous inductions with no suggestions to wake up. For that reason, in order to become aware, we must be cognizant of the machinations of the consensus trance, and in a sense see that the seemingly important things we are taught are merely the "quaint notions of the particular tribe one was born into, not necessarily universal truths" (Tart, p. 88). However, most of us are so much a part of the trance that it is hard to see its content. Becoming aware of the trance and of the power of television/motion pictures to affect one's beliefs and behaviors, as well as the power of a parent giving a nonverbal message to a child, can help one tease out the trance from the essence.

Identification is another powerful source of control of the individual. Tart defines identification as the attachment of a "this is me" quality to certain aspects of experience, thus creating the sense of an ego. Any item of information to which the "this is me" quality is attached acquires a great deal of power and arouses strong emotions. Identification is a chief source of attachments and is a process of defining oneself as a mere fraction of the person one was born to be.

The truth is that most of us identify with anything: our names, our bodies, our possessions, our family, our jobs, our country, our causes, our gods, our fingernails, etc. To illustrate the power of this identification, Dr. Tart uses a wonderful exercise. He places a paper bag or box in the middle of the room. Then he asks his students to identify with the bag, "to think of it as 'me,' to love the bag and attend to the bag in the way they attend to themselves" for several minutes. Then, without warning, he stomps on the bag. I have done this myself, and I can tell you that the reactions are amazing. They range from anger at me to hurt, from shock to personal anguish, wonderfully illustrating how easy it is to give a sense of identity to anything and to give up personal power at the same time. When teaching the power of identification, one must remember the adage: "The map is not the territory." When we empower the map, the representation, we give away our personal power.

Homework for this session consists of journaling about the factors in one's personal conditioning, consensus trance, and identification—trying to sort out the essential self from the conditioned personality. We ask that people begin observing themselves—not analyzing or putting themselves down, but merely examining. This is particularly difficult, because one tends to see the map and not the territory itself. To begin with, we ask people to start writing and see where it takes them. Later, there will be exercises for getting in touch with the essential self.

Pulling Weeds of Guilt, Worthlessness, "Shoulds," and Shame

None of us is born with a conscience as standard equipment. It is nurtured and molded by our culture and hopefully reflects (and inspires) the highest values of human civilization such as justice, altruism, responsibility, and honesty. Conscience, which is frequently connected with the deity, is a powerful force in the affairs and feelings of humans and may be the spiritual glue that pulls life together and gives it a sense of meaning. Unfortunately the power of conscience is sometimes corrupted and used as a weapon to gain control, causing guilt, shame, "shoulds," and resultant feelings of worthlessness to emerge. Not only do our parents use guilt and shame to keep us under control, but we also quickly learn to do the same to others. Abundance of guilt pretty well ensures that one will be depressed and unhappy, as well as more susceptible to degenerative diseases. For all of these reasons, this is a particularly important cluster of weeds to extirpate.

In this session it is helpful to distinguish guilt and shame that serve a healthy purpose for the individual from guilt and shame which are destructive and pathological. In *Self-Esteem*, McKay and Fanning have an excellent section on guilt as the pathological critic. Joan Borysenko's *Guilt is the Teacher, Love is the Lesson,* and Charles Whitfield's book, *Healing the Child Within* are splendid sources in this area. Guilt and shame are processes that have an enormous impact on how we feel about ourselves, our relationships, and our spiritual lives.

Guilt, the pathological critic, is the negative inner voice that attacks and judges, blames for things that go wrong, lashes out if the individual does not live up to a long list of "shoulds," and compares him not only to others but also to himself — always finding him lacking. People with a high level of guilt tend to feel more worthlessness and shame, which Bowen White (1990) defines as the fear of being seen as flawed — of being disclosed. At GETTING WELL, we stress that the critic is created so early in one's existence that it is difficult to realize one is not born "worthless, guilty, and ashamed." We teach, rather, that the experience of socialization by one's parents and institutions has created these emotional weeds. In the normal family, a four-to-one ratio of punitive expressions compared to positive statements exists — a norm heavily on the side of criticism.

With these hypotheses in mind, we process the idea and the actualities of guilt, shame, and worthlessness among the group members. Starting with the hypothesis that at birth we are luminous, good, creative, and powerful little beings, we suggest taking a look at the education process in each participant's particular family or subculture. How do we differentiate healthy "shoulds," guilt, and values from the destructive variety? How did participants learn guilt and shame? What are the rewards of continuing to feel guilt (the need to feel accepted by critical parents, the need to achieve, the need to feel right)? Invariably, the discussion is rewarding. Open individuals who freely discuss what happened to them in their families frequently pave the way for more repressed individuals to remember bits and pieces of what happened to them. We make it clear that this is not a parent condemnation session — that parents did the best they knew how — since many people hide their guilt to protect their parents. (There will be other times when it is appropriate to express anger or rage at parents; however, such expression is not the point of this session.) Participants are given homework of journaling that evening with the idea of uncovering sources of guilt, shame, and unworthiness.

Although the religious issue of "original sin" frequently arises, we don't try to tackle theological issues. (I tend to believe, however, that this issue has a great deal to do with disease and malaise in our culture.) Michael Fox, a Dominican priest, has written a lovely book, *Original Blessings,* which gives philosophical and scriptural support for the opposite hypothesis. Following his thinking, we simply ask participants to try on for a few days the hypothesis that we were created from a pure and beautiful spirit to see if it *works* or feels good. In most cases, the original sin idea is not a consciously held doctrine. Rather, it is a vestige of early religious or cultural Puritan ethic training and holds no particular spiritual meaning in the present, although it powerfully affects the way we feel about ourselves.

To assist participants in identifying destructive guilt and shame, we use a guided transformational fantasy exercise in which we have them go down the back hallways of their minds into the "guilt room." As they enter the room, we suggest that they see a bookcase (or some other symbol) which holds the volumes of their guilt, "shoulds," and shame, as well as all of the other reasons they feel bad about themselves. We then have participants explore their guilt library, reading off the titles and opening the books if they wish. They may also want to bring an inner guide or a wise, friendly mentor with whom they can discuss some of the guilt books and decide which ones they are ready to get rid of. There may be several books which they prefer to put back on the shelf and explore later in expressive therapies or journaling. In some areas of guilt, group members may want to make amends. This could involve bringing the wronged people into the image or making an action note of something they need to do "in the real world." At the end of the exercise, we ask participants to decide what to do with their discarded books—sell them, burn them, tear them up, get rid of them in some manner that seems right.

In processing this imagery, remember that it is particularly important to key into the feeling level of the guilt, shame, or unworthiness. Many issues need to be continued in individual therapy sessions.

Pulling Weeds of Resentment, Bitterness, and Lack of Forgiveness

People dealing with life-challenging illnesses cannot afford the luxury of being resentful, bitter, or unforgiving. In fact, none of us can afford the physical, psychological, and emotional sequelae of bearing old hurts. Remember, resentment is not the same as anger. The latter is generally a short-lived emotion which is natural and survival-oriented, while resentment is a smoldering, long-term, restressing process which works on the mind and body 24 hours a day.

In the group setting we process the ideas of resentment and forgiveness, asking people to give examples of resentment they are carrying or situations they have not forgiven. Invariably, we find most people are blocked from pulling the weeds of resentment and bitterness because they feel that doing so would allow the involved party to "get away with something." Thus, they endure the terrible emotional and physical burdens of bitterness and resentment because they cannot bear to let the other person off the hook. A number of years ago I came across a statement which has been a wonderful help in this area: "When you forgive people, it does not absolve them from responsibility for what they have done. It does not excuse them. It simply frees you from being affected in a harmful way." I have made a small sign of this adage, and it remains on the bulletin board in the group room. Frequently group members realize that their resentment keeps them attached to the situation, that in actuality the other person is leading them around by the nose because of this attachment. Suddenly they understand that the other person usually isn't feeling bad; only they are. When this understanding occurs, they are eager to let go of the bitterness and resentment.

In the books I have mentioned (Borysenko, 1990; Whitfield, 1987), there are many good exercises for overcoming bitterness and resentment. An exercise I have used for years has the participants identify an old hurt, another person's culpable behavior, or a distressing situation they have replayed again and again in their minds. We use a relaxation procedure to still their minds, and then ask them to create a clear picture of the person toward whom they feel resentment. After a long pause, we ask them to picture good things happening to that person — perhaps receiving money, love, attention, or another such reward. After another long pause, we ask the group members to be aware of their own reactions and remind them that with practice seeing good things happening to persons toward whom they feel resentment will become easier. At the end of the exercise, we have the members become aware of how much more relaxed and less resentful they feel, and we suggest that they will carry this new understanding with them.

After the imagery is completed, we let the group members process their experiences. Remember, participants may need to forgive themselves before they can completely the forgive others. We find that this exercise usually allows people insight into their resentment. For example, the resentment may allow them to play the victim or feel sorry for themselves without taking responsibility for changing. The processing may also allow them access to their difficulty in admitting anger in the first place. When the processing is completed, it is sometimes helpful to repeat the forgiveness exercise and note the changes.

Pulling Weeds of Attachment

Don Pachuta (1989) has stated that all human misery might be traced to attachments to things outside one's being — that, in essence, when one invests heavily in material goods or relationships or one's physical form in order to give meaning to one's life, disappointment and misery are likely to follow. For example, if we were to become attached to our beautiful new sports car and build our lives around it, and then it were to be "totaled," we would be devastated. Of course, Pachuta does not mean that to become enlightened we must give up material things or relationships.

He does mean, however, that we should not give things or relationships life-and-death power over us.

Let us assume we are born with an incredible amount of potential and power. Continuing with this paradigm, in our relationship with our caretakers we give our "power cards" away, dealing them out in exchange for love, security, acceptance, control, and comfort. Unfortunately, when our power begins to reside outside of us, we are bereft of that energy which is the essence of our inner healing power, and we begin to see ourselves as helpless or powerless.

In the session we initially focus on uncovering those attachments to which we give our power. One of the most common attachments is to material goods and money. A person may feel worthless without the right kind of car, house, clothes, etc. Attachments to other people—situations in which one needs to "own" another person or feels useless and hurt if rejected by that individual—are a source of codependency. Attachment to winning or being number one is a powerful and destructive force in our culture. Certainly most of us can identify with the attachment to "being right" or to certain philosophical ideas and beliefs, and many of us have an attachment to the past and its iron-handed role in making us what we are today. The attachment to blaming others or to judging others is also a powerful emotional force in our culture, and attachments to food, alcohol or drugs seem almost epidemic. Attachment to one's form—believing that one's body (fat/thin, black/white, healthy/sick) totally defines the person—invites a lifetime of suffering, confusion, and distress.

The main focus of this session is the identification of areas of attachment in each person's life. For many, this session opens whole new vistas of self-knowledge and self-discovery. For example, during one session I realized how attached I was to having people spell and pronounce my name properly, Lola realized how much she defined herself by what she weighed, Frank's job (from which he had been forced to retire due to his cancer) was a major way in which he judged his self-worth, and Nina's X-rays were the key to her happiness or misery. As the session continues, people become more open in admitting their attachments to how their children are living their lives, to being perfect, to their prejudices, or to the host of other concepts to which they give the power to run their lives.

We frequently have participants draw a "genogram" of their attachments, indicating their size and power and the proximity of the attachments to themselves. As people recognize their own attachments in others, their genograms become larger and more complex. They are often surprised and even overwhelmed by the amount of personal power they have given away and by how much control they have given to their attachments—even in some instances, literally giving up their lives.

We have a very simple exercise, based on Jill Jackson's empowerment workshops, which is enormously effective *if it is performed*. The exercise involves making a simple statement about each attachment: "I'm taking my power back from _____ right now!" The practice becomes even more potent when it is written down. Jill suggests that participants first make a list of perhaps 20 attachments headed by the statement: "I have given my power to _____." My own list, created at a workshop in 1989, included my having empowered expectations of outcomes over which I had no control, to achieving, doing, and accomplishing rather than being, and to the belief that I'm not good at math. In another list headed by the statement, "Viewed from my place of empowerment, _____," one takes back his or her power by stating, for example: "I am learning to love what the universe presents rather than demanding that the universe present what I love," "I am empowering who I am rather than what I can do," and so on. I encourage participants to carry their lists with them, so that when they experience "suffering" they can identify the attachment behind it and take back their power from the attachment. I've found that my own list is like a journal, making me aware of where I have been and the transformations that have taken place.

Pulling Weeds of Codependency, Helplessness, and Powerlessness

This section could be subsumed under attachments; nevertheless, I find it valuable to confront the giving away of power from as many angles as possible. We humans have a tendency to say, "Oh, that really isn't my problem," unless the nail is hit on the head. John Bradshaw's book, *Healing the Shame that Binds You*, and Charles Whitfield's *Healing the Child Within* are valuable resources for this area.

Identifying the weeds that are entangling and choking one's garden of health is indeed a difficult job, because their seeds go back to one's preverbal existence, and there are sometimes no words for these weeds—only inchoate feelings and sensory data. However, when one gets these weeds to the level of conscious images, they can be extirpated at the imagery level without great difficulty.

In guided imagery, I suggest the image of identifying what is a weed and pulling it from the soil of one's garden. I make it clear that this is my image and that if another image is more helpful for the individual, he or she should feel free to use it.

As you begin to relax . . . let yourself become aware of a specific weed in your garden of enlightenment. Can you see that weed as it has entangled itself in the soil of your body, mind, or spirit? . . . Be aware of how it looks, of how its roots go deep in your body or mind . . . of perhaps seeing its stalk and leaves extending beyond your crown center . . . if you wish (*long pause*). And, do you have a name for that weed? (*pause*) Having sensed the weed and how its roots are implanted in the soil of your being . . . do you have a sense of anything you need to do to allow those roots to come up more easily? (*pause*) Such as dampening the soil with showers of compassion? Or loosening the soil with the cultivating power of understanding? . . . And, when you get ready to pull the weed or when you have asked perhaps a spiral of light energy to vacuum it out . . . let it begin to happen (*long pause*). See the roots begin to give . . . gently . . . go gently . . . so that the roots come out intact . . . and feel that weed begin to move . . . and to begin to come (*long pause*) and finally out . . . out of your being, and out into the universe where it may serve a good purpose (*pause*). Now, check where the weed was . . . be sure that all vestiges of roots are gone . . . and notice that where the weed was is now filled with the golden light of love and power. . . . And, it feels wonderful! . . . And, when you get ready, come back to the room, feeling full of power and light and love.

Cassie, a successful businesswoman in her mid-forties, said that all she wanted was to get her life back under control. "Everything was in order until this cancer came along and blew my life to the winds," she stated. But as Cassie began examining her life, she realized that she had invested her personal power heavily in control, material goods, and codependent relationships. Merely identifying the fact that power and control are nearly opposites opened her eyes to the rigid structure that had to be in place for her to feel "in control." The cancer was a hand grenade thrown into Cassie's rigidly ordered life. As she began to identify her attachments, which ranged from "people doing what I expect them to do" to "my house must always be clean" to "my MRI must show positive change," she was astounded by the amount of energy it was taking to keep her attachments in order.

Actually, her orderly approach to her affairs allowed her to be assiduous in identifying and listing where she had given up her power and in creating statements to re-empower herself. Cassie first looked closely at her relationship with her children and at her failing, codependent relationship with her drinking husband. In three weeks, she had turned her perspective inside out — with the power now on the inside. In the several years since, she has become a powerful woman rather than simply a woman in control. She has divorced her husband and learned to create newfound depths in her relationships with others. She is relaxed about herself and watches life with a curiosity about what is going to happen rather than with a need to control those events. Her metastatic breast cancer flares up occasionally, but she uses those exacerbations as a signal to weed her garden. Her physicians openly state that her incredible attitude has changed her prognosis. I like to believe that Cassie's taking back her power totally regenerated her inner healing mechanisms.

Letting Go, Gaining Inner Peace

The concept of "letting go" is presented as a major conduit to gaining a sense of inner power. "Letting go" means choosing not to need to hold onto things and people, not to become hooked by what is "out there." It is one of the greatest paradoxes of life that we are connected to all other humans, yet we do not *have* to be attached to people and things in order to feel whole.

Although the concept of letting go is a core concept of the teachings of Jesus, it is perhaps one of the most difficult ideas for members of our culture to embrace. To implement letting go, we must flow with what is encountered rather than oppose and judge those around us. This involves looking at the world in a completely different way from what we were taught. Rather than indulging the judgments we were trained to make, we should send a loving thought to the person driving thoughtlessly on the interstate, for example. Seeing yourself in a cooperative effort on this earth rather than in a competitive one or seeing yourself in a new relationship with your "possessions" or body is another way of letting go. Spending some time daily just being—without any attachments—is a way of practicing letting go. When you let go, you remove the need to prove yourself right or others wrong.

Peace Pilgrim (Ryan & Travis, 1981) describes some symptoms of letting go and attaining inner peace, which include a tendency to think and act spontaneously rather than thinking and acting based on fears created by experience, the unmistakable ability to enjoy each moment, a loss of interest in judging others and interpreting the actions of others, and an increased susceptibility to the love extended by others, as well as the uncontrollable urge to extend love.

At the 1989 Third World Conference on Imagery, Don Pachuta presented on Sunday morning a session called "Inner Peace." He shared with the audience two devices which he claimed would automatically bring peace. He told us that as one does not have to believe in a saw for the saw to cut, we did not have to believe in these devices for them to work. We just had to practice them once a day and our lives would be changed. The first device was a simple mantra, "Let go, *your name*," to be said over and over for three minutes a day during deep breathing exercises.

The second device was a meditation called "Effective Prayer," written by one of his AIDS patient who had since died. It is a powerful affirmation of connectedness and letting go and gratitude which we have used at GETTING WELL as a guide to move one toward high-level awareness. Rather than being a prayer for certain outcomes, it is an effective vehicle for releasing attachments and for "sending light energy" to various people and endeavors without judgment or without specifying outcomes. I find it is most effective when personalized. For example, when resentments are released to the light, it is helpful to specify the resentments one is working on at the moment. I like to use it as a working imagery exercise—actually seeing the weed of resentment being pulled out of my being and sucked up into the universal light. When one is sending light to various people, it is important to send it also to those with whom one is at cross purposes, rather than just to those one likes. Some people may wish to insert Christ Light, Jehovah Light, or Buddha Light.

EFFECTIVE PRAYER

1. I release all of my past, negatives, fears, human relationships, resentments, inner-self, future, human attachments, and judging to the Light. (Be specific as you are doing this.)

2. I am a shining, radiant, Light being.

3. I radiate the Light from my Light center to all parts of my being. (This is a good time to do some healing imagery.)

4. I radiate Light from my Light center to everyone. (Actually see each person surrounded by light and love and appreciation—especially difficult people and "enemies.")

5. I radiate the Light from my Light center to everything.

6. I am in a bubble of Light and only Light and Love can come to me and only Light and Love can be here.

7. Thank you, God, for everything, for everyone, and for me. (Be specific about the people and things.)

Taking Responsibility for One's Life and Health

We humans continue to look "out there" for answers to our health, our happiness, and our meaning in life. This session focuses on a recurrent theme in the healing process: taking responsibility for one's thoughts, feelings, and life—all of which imply taking one's power back. Ryan and Travis (*The Wellness Workbook*) and Ardell (*High Level Wellness*) have been my guides in this area for over a decade. Their material is lively and quite adaptable to whatever level group one may be addressing. Self-responsibility is a core concept in their views of high-level wellness and awareness.

At GETTING WELL, we begin by pointing out to the group that most of us have accepted since our earliest years that someone else knows what is best for us. We have given up our power to our parents, to our teachers to choose what we should learn, to our politicians to decide the direction of our country, and to our physicians to determine what our minds and bodies need. Certainly, experts are important in all areas of our lives, yet we tend to shift *all* the responsibility to somebody or something outside of ourselves. By this time, group members are usually eager to contribute ways in which they or others shift responsibility outside themselves.

Frequently, members bring up the point that taking charge of one's life and health means taking calculated risks and making choices, the consequences of which one must be willing to live with. This is a good place to reintroduce the idea that taking responsibility for choices which result in increased stress or illness does not mean blaming oneself. Blame creates a burden that causes guilt, which in turn increases stress. It is important to call attention to the fact that self-responsibility is not the same as blame, fault, or guilt. Taking responsibility is a gift, not a burden, and is actually a liberating act. Taking responsibility implies that one has input into his or her life situation and can choose to keep it the way it is or to change it. Taking responsibility involves accepting the right and the power to decide one's destiny and making a conscious commitment to one's own well-being. Self-responsibility implies becoming skilled at knowing the difference between what is beyond one's control and what isn't and realizing that we are the source of what we are and that we do not need to blame others.

Of course, it goes without saying that accepting responsibility for one's health does not mean failing to seek the help of a physician (any more than one would try to fix one's own TV when an expert repair person was available). It does mean asserting one's rights as a customer in the medical economy, asking questions, seeking other opinions, and feeling that one knows oneself better than anyone else does.

Self-responsibility really comes down to truly connecting with and trusting one's intuition and the inner messages from one's body. It involves providing the body with the best conditions (nutrition, exercise, rest, etc.) to heal itself and respecting the body for the powerful and magnificent gift that it is. It means being good to oneself and having love and compassion for this wonderful being.

Ardell provides a list of "positive states of whole person being" which participants enjoy discussing. He suggests that self-responsibility and wholeness involve "high self-esteem and a positive outlook, a foundation philosophy and a sense of purpose, humor, support, and concern for others and the environment, conscious commitment to well-being and excellence, an integrated lifestyle, the capacity to cope and learn, deep roots of connectedness, effective communication, and integrity" (1979, p. 105). Similarly, Ryan and Travis list the components of self-responsibility and self-love:

- Tuning into your own inner patterns and recognizing signals your body is giving you.
- Discovering your real needs and finding ways to meet them.
- Realizing that you are unique and *the* expert about your self.
- Making choices. Being self-assertive.
- Creating the life you really want, rather than just reacting to what seems to happen.
- Expressing emotions in ways that communicate what you are experiencing to other people.
- Creating and cultivating close relationships with others.
- Trusting that your own personal resources are your greatest strengths for living and growing.
- Allowing disease to be a constructive and positive experience.
- Responding to challenges in life as opportunities to grow in strength and maturity, rather than feeling beset by problems.
- Experiencing yourself as a "Wonderful Person."
- Loving yourself and exercising compassion for your weaknesses.
- Realizing your connectedness with all things.
- Celebrating yourself, others, and the world in which you live. (1981, pp. 3–4)

As an exercise in taking responsibility for one's health, we ask people to write in their notebooks five major life changes or stressors that occurred six to 24 months prior to the onset of their illness or recurrence/exacerbation. We then suggest that they examine how they participated in each stressor — either how they created the situation or how they responded to it (by putting others' needs first, ignoring their own mental, physical and emotional limits, etc.). If the events were outside their control, such as the death of a loved one, were there alternative ways of reacting (fully grieving, seeking support, etc.)? After these events have been discussed in small groups, we ask participants to write down five major stressors they are experiencing at the present time, to explain how they are reacting to each, and to consider alternative, healthier ways of perceiving.

After discussing the aspects of self-responsibility, we use an imagery exercise demonstrating how the person would feel and be if he or she could accept all aspects of self-love and self-responsibility. "Future pacing" — having participants see themselves in various situations in the future as they feel this new way — helps participants internalize their new insights.

Identifying the Benefits of Illness

This session carries the concept of self-responsibility a step further. In our culture, feelings and emotional needs are not given a great deal of importance, so frequently illness becomes a way to express those needs or have them met. It is probably rare that a person consciously *decides* to become seriously ill in order to have fewer demands in his or her life, to receive increased love and affection, or to take time away from work. Yet on an unconscious basis illness may be a metaphor for something needed in one's life.

A case in point is Janice, who was committed to being everything her own mother was not. With her husband, Janice, whose lupus made it inadvisable for her to conceive, adopted a little boy. She bravely conceded that flare-ups of her lupus occurred when the demands of parenthood became overwhelming. In fact, she recounted times when her emotional inability to say "no" to PTA requests for cookies had brought on a flare-up that made it *physically* impossible for her to make the cookies. "I'm really using my illness, or my illness is using me," Janice said. "It's giving me permission not to do something I *think* a good mother *should* do. I'll bet that if I learn to say 'no' it's going to make a difference." And it did make a difference, although it involved a great deal of therapy and work on Janice's part. Only when she was ill was it acceptable for her to drop the pressures and responsibilities of "perfect" motherhood and simply take care of herself without guilt or having to justify or explain herself. As she became more in tune with her needs and her ability to get her needs met assertively, the number, intensity, and frequency of her flare-ups dropped dramatically.

Being able to recount a number of stories like Janice's helps us soften participants' resistance to the idea that they may have some part in the inception and continuence of their condition. It is important to point out here that accepting some responsibility for the illness gives one more options to make healthful changes, just as Janice did. As I've mentioned before, this session needs to be handled gently, for there undoubtedly will be someone in the group who is not ready for this step in self-responsibility. In this case, the facilitator might suggest that the reluctant one playfully try the hypothesis on for size. Disease or pain is a high price to pay to solve problems that could be altered by giving oneself the permission or license to meet one's needs legitimately.

I question Louise Hay's (1984) belief that one is 100 percent responsible for one's illness. Her chart, attributing specific diseases to particular emotional/spiritual patterns, is interesting; for example, she suggests that high cholesterol is fear of accepting joy. Judgments such as this can be dangerous in the hands of those looking to see how the "patient" brought on his or her disease. On the other hand, it is frequently enlightening for participants themselves (if they choose to do so) to take a look at the chart and consider the possibilities. Hay also asks a series of questions which may be quite useful to members, depending on the openness of the group. For example, "What problems does this illness resolve? Why *this* illness at *this* time? Whom do you need to forgive? What is the truth that needs to be told? What is happening in your life?" Similarly, Al Siebert (1993) likes to ask, "If you wanted to develop a fatal illness on purpose, what would you do?" Questions like these elicit a great deal of thought and insight about self-responsibility among most participants. It is important to realize that we *are* in charge of our states of being, we have *learned* to be the way we are, and we have the incredible capacity to learn to be another way or to create new patterns in our lives.

During our group discussion of needs that might be met through illness, we list those benefits of illness on the board. We then ask participants to list in their notebooks five or more of the most important benefits they have received from a major illness in their lives—such as not having to meet others' expectations, getting out of a problem situation, or using it as an opportunity to take time out to re-group. We then have members meet in small groups or dyads with the intent of sharing thoughts and adding to the list. We encourage them to write down alternative ways of getting the benefits they have listed, with the small group's input. The final processing with the whole group usually reveals a number of learning experiences about choices that are available in living life in a healthier way rather than relying on illness.

Relabeling, Reframing

The focus of this session is on giving participants experience in changing negative labels they may have applied to events (concomitantly stirring up stress chemicals) into neutral or positive formulations which are less challenging to the autonomic nervous system.

Relabeling is the art of calling a spade a club. Most occurrences in our lives are neutral, yet we create meaning for these events by the labels we give them. For example, a red light is only a clump of metal and glass emitting light waves of a certain length. Nonetheless, the meanings and associations we apply to a red light are varied, but usually negative: "Damn, I'll be late to work, and I might be fired," "Nothing ever goes right for me!" or "I can't stand waiting." In this exercise, we may have members suggest what happens to the sympathetic nervous system chemicals when this kind of label or interpretation is applied to a red light, or the facilitator may choose to use the chart of Figure 2 (p. 72) to explain the process.

We point out to participants that they can choose to give a negative label to a situation (and have a corresponding unhealthy response) or they can choose to give a neutral or positive label to a situation (eliciting no response or a positive response). At this time, we ask the group to come up with positive, healthy responses to a red light. These may include realizing that: It's a way of controlling traffic and preventing me from being in an accident; it gives me an opportunity to practice my relaxation; it allows me a respite, permitting me to reaffirm my goals or do my self-affirmations; or it gives me a chance to put my makeup on before I get to work. During this exercise, I usually tell the story of the traffic light near the hospital where I worked, which would always turn red as my husband Bob was taking me to work. Nearly every morning I would rant and fume because that light was going to make me late and ruin my day. Finally, I grew tired of feeling angry at the beginning of each day, and Bob and I decided to relabel the light. We labeled the light as a signal to have an extra-long, delicious smooch, and we began pulling for it to turn red as we approached it. "Come on, turn red, turn red," we'd say enthusiastically. And with that shift, it began to be a pleasurable game.

Moving on with our session, we turn to the example of losing one's job. On the blackboard, we put "Job loss" at the top and let the group call out the negatives which loss of work entails. We explain that this is accepted as a negative event in our culture because of the Puritan work ethic, and discuss how culturally colored it is. The participants can usually get a board full of negatives, such as depression, anger, defeat, helplessness, hopelessness, fear, and finances. We then erase the board and ask them to fill the board with positives about losing a job. They hesitate at first, usually mumbling that there's nothing good about losing a job, but then they begin to come through. This subject may hit very close to home with most members since their pain or diseases have interfered with their jobs and professions—almost to the last person. As they struggle to relabel, members begin to suggest that it might mean a time to reevaluate one's life, a time to slow down and focus on family, or a chance to change directions—possibly doing something more fulfilling, etc.—and soon the board is full of rather wonderful possibilities.

Next, we may have the group come up with a word that creates a great deal of anxiety in most of the members, but this time we only go through the "positive process." *Disease, cancer, death, divorce,* and *loss* are common choices. The group usually begins to develop a facility for finding legitimate silver linings. We then ask them to write in their notebooks the three most stressful words in their personal vocabularies right now, and to go through this same process on their own.

Pain is another difficult concept that is frequently put forth for relabeling. Pat Norris has provided cogent, yet lyrical, ways to relabel pain:

Pain is a good friend of ours. It lets us know that we have encountered something sharp or hot. Pain is asking for help, and we need to say, "Thank you pain for reminding me to send blood flow or white blood cells into that area of my body or to send love to that place. Thanks unconscious for letting me know that you're scared so I can comfort you." (1992)

In his book, *The Survivor Personality*, Siebert suggests that survivors develop their talent for serendipity, which he defines as converting misfortune into a valuable experience. This could be thought of as relabeling a harmful or damaging stressor as a strengthening, beneficial event. Siebert indicates that the negative physical impact of virtually any situation can be reversed by asking a series of "serendipity questions": What can I learn from this? What is this teaching me that is useful for me to know? Why is it good for me that this happened? Next time something like this happens what will I do? What is amusing about this? What might I do to turn this around and have it end well?

Often, we can look back at our "disasters" from a year's perspective and see how they were actually the "best thing that ever happened." But at the time of the occurrence, the pain and anguish we experienced were not necessary, and certainly they were not good for our bodies. When we learn to ask Siebert's serendipity questions *at the time of the disaster*, and thereby immediately to relabel the situation, we give ourselves power to avoid unnecessary anguish.

If there is time, we may go through a reframing process, as described by Bandler and Grinder (1975). Neurolinguistic programming (NLP) assumes that any situation, behavior, or even health problem originally had an unconscious positive intent for the organism—that it helped one to survive at a time when things were tough. Although the event or behavior may have quite negative implications in the present, the original unconscious intent was good. For example, someone may have begun smoking to feel more sophisticated and mature in a situation in which he or she felt vulnerable or callow—the unconscious intent was good but the behavior was eventually destructive.

The first part of the reframing is identifying the behavior or health problem needing to be changed. Then communication is established with the part of the person that was responsible for the problem. It is suggested to the person that the problem be separated from the positive intention of the part responsible for the problem, and the part responsible is to let the person know what the positive intent or the payoffs or the benefits to the person are. Then it is suggested that the individual go to the creative part of himself or herself, which has always been helpful in so many ways throughout life, and ask for several alternatives that will provide the needed payoffs. Then the part responsible for the problem can choose one or two of these new ways in which the positive intent will be fulfilled without harm to the individual. An ecological check determines if the alternative patterns are acceptable to all parts of the person. Spending some time imaging ways in which this new insight will affect future behaviors (establishing new blueprints) concludes this powerful exercise.

Lessons for the Author/Clinician

Developing the high-level awareness component required exposing myself to a plethora of ideas—some mainstream wellness concepts and some more esoteric and recondite. My goal was to present a wide range of possibilities gathered with an eclectic spirit. At its inception, high-level awareness was almost a scholarly exercise. Indeed, while the life-challenging aspects of GETTING WELL became clear to me rather quickly, I continued to use my old, faithful tools—intellect and determination—to resolve virtually every issue in my or the program's path. And although the actual clinical work and interactions with patients were stimulating and satisfying, my life was beginning to fray badly around the edges.

For example, there were daily skirmishes with physicians and other professionals who unfortunately wanted us to compromise our principles so they could get a piece of the financial pie (while we received virtually nothing). Run-ins with the hospital administration over space or nursing services were a constant aggravation. *Something* was always in chaos or confusion, and my personal life reflected it all. I would spend long hours awake at night, feeling terrorized or completely out of control of the situation. I was so preoccupied, in fact, that I didn't sense how miserable and ignored my husband of over thirty years felt. I cannot begin to relate the intensity of the pain that we both were experiencing. But even while I realized that these problems wouldn't be solved by intellect and determination, I continued to cling to my time-worn strategies as I dug myself deeper into a hole. Finally, a light went on, and I knew I couldn't continue without a change. Over a period of time I took a close look at where I had given my power away. I examined the effectiveness of my main coping strategies, determination and intellect, and wondered what their reverse would accomplish.

I spent a long Memorial Day weekend pondering where I had empowered my attachments. For instance, I had given a great deal of power to fearful projections about the future; to feeling I had to be understood by everyone; to controlling rather than accepting; to *resistance* to being invalidated, overlooked, and ignored; and of course, to achieving and accomplishing goals rather than experiencing the unfolding of my life. These brief phrases hardly begin to give any idea of the struggle it was for me to recognize these blockages—as well as the ones mentioned earlier in the chapter—in the flow of my being. Finally, I wrote affirmations from my place of empowerment:

- I release my attachment to fear to the Light. I choose to focus on the joy of the moment rather than fears of the future.
- I take back my power from having to be understood. I understand my motives and the universe does, too. That's enough.
- I empower myself to accept and let my source guide me. I see controlling as directly giving up my power. I empower acceptance as my choice over controlling.
- I empower myself to go beyond the *resistance* to being invalidated, overlooked, ignored, or misunderstood. I realize that what I resist persists, what I accept flows.
- I empower the only real and lasting commitment in life to be the joy of living. I choose not to create ends to replace that joy.

I released these and a number of other attachments during that weekend. As I am writing this from the smudged pencil entries in my journal, I realize the major turn I took in my life that weekend and remember the feeling of peace that pervaded my being. I felt the deep knowledge that, whatever the outcomes, I could handle them and find meaning and opportunity in them. Of course, I still have my strategies of determination and intellect, but now I can also choose empowerment through letting go and knowledge through emotions and intuition as well as intellect.

Many of the same issues continue to crop up in my life; however, I can always choose to let them go rather than to let them destroy my peace. This knowledge really turned my life around! For one thing, my marriage began to flow in directions in which both Bob and I could find love and joy. I began attracting really interesting people into my life, and doors were constantly opening—I felt as if I were living again. It's as if in losing my way, I found it. Of course, with GETTING WELL, life will always have an interesting complexity, and I find that I must frequently realign myself. At these times, I like using the "Effective Prayer" quoted earlier in this chapter to keep the weeds pulled, the ground cultivated, and the seeds of peace planted in my garden.

13

High-Level Awareness II:
Planting Seeds of Intrapersonal
and Interpersonal Connectedness

In rediscovering the missing parts of ourselves and becoming psychologically whole, we simultaneously mend our souls and become spiritually
whole. The flower of psychospiritual growth is loving-kindness and compassion, the ability to suffer *with*, to leave the limited sphere of personal
concern and enter into the life of another. — *Joan Borysenko*

All suffering is caused by the illusion of separateness, which generates
fear and self-hatred, which eventually causes illness. — *Barbara Brennan*

Forgiveness is not about what we *do*, it is about the way we perceive
people and circumstances. The underlying and often unconscious beliefs
that we hold about ourselves and human nature influence and ultimately
determine our ability and willingness to risk, to trust, to love, and to
forgive. — *Robin Casarjian*

One's beliefs are the basis for one's self-images, as well as one's
images about the world and about the unseen. These images, in
turn, are powerful blueprints for one's body and one's life. Our
culturally imposed beliefs can be quite limiting to our human potential. In
explaining this, I like to use the example of a tiny embryo pumpkin just
off the blossom, which if put into a bottle will grow to the size of the
bottle—but no larger! GETTING WELL participants who are fighting life-
challenging illnesses need every resource and avenue of potential healing
available to them, so we use every path possible to expand their consciousness. Thus, high-level awareness is a gentle club used to break the "bottle"
and tap into their areas of power and potential, allowing them to grow to
their fullest.

A teacher who was in the program recently cited an education study
determining that there were 110 distinct areas of human potential. Unfortunately, however, our culture and educational system honor and tap into
only *10* of those areas of potential. With this in mind, we use high-level

214

awareness to present a smorgasbord of ideas, beliefs, images, and behaviors which help participants connect with as many of those additional 100 uncultivated resources as they wish.

Our intrapersonal images (how we see our essential selves) determine our interpersonal images (how we see others and our relationship with others). Shifts in consciousness in these areas are crucial to the healing process.

The high-level awareness sections are presented to participants in the form of mini-lectures followed by group discussion. Our materials include far more than any one facilitator would use in an hour's session, so that facilitator is free to shape the lesson. We tell our therapists not to feel the need to include everything, for that would only overwhelm the participants (as well as the facilitators). We have tried to include multiple ways of viewing the subject, since each group is different and requires an individualized approach.

Sowing the Seeds of
Connectedness and Unity

Dean Ornish (1990) states, "Anything that promotes a sense of isolation leads to chronic stress, and often to illnesses like heart disease. Conversely, anything that leads to real intimacy and feelings of connection can be healing in the real sense of the word: to bring together, to make whole." Larry Dossey, Jeanne Achterberg, and Joan Borysenko have concurred that isolation is perhaps the major stressor of our society and that connectedness and unity with oneself and powers beyond the self are the core of the healing process.

Borysenko divides connectedness into three areas: intrapersonal connectedness or one's relationship with oneself, interpersonal connectedness or one's connection with other people, and transpersonal connectedness or one's unity with a power greater than the self. I have chosen to use her divisions as a way to organize the smorgasbord content of this section.

Seeds of Intrapersonal Connectedness

Connecting with oneself and loving oneself is a key task in the healing process. Louise Hay says that loving/accepting/approving ourselves exactly as we are is essential to having everything work, from our relationships and our health to our financial status. It is a fact that people who connect intrapersonally, who love themselves and their bodies, abuse neither themselves nor others.

Studies (Borysenko, 1990a) looking at the relationship between guilt and self-esteem have shown an exceptionally strong correlation between high guilt and low self-esteem. When we find guilt in people about having "caused" their diseases, we invariably find self-esteem problems. To work on why they "shouldn't feel guilty" rather than on the real problem of their poor connection with themselves is essentially fruitless. However, when we make headway with the self-connection and facilitate feelings of worthiness, the guilt problem drops away.

This same research has also found that the way people feel about themselves influences their experience of God. The study took place in a small New England town where all the subjects belonged to the same parish, had been brought up with the same catechism, and therefore had the same religious training. It was found that those scoring low in self-esteem on a psychological test saw God as powerful but punitive, "a malevolent Santa Claus." On the other hand, those scoring high in self-esteem considered God to be abundantly loving, compassionate, bountiful, and forgiving.

Our beliefs, thoughts, and feelings about ourselves are crucial to our health and happiness; and beliefs, thoughts, and feelings can be changed, if one is willing to take the risk. The therapist must encourage participants to be gentle, kind, and patient with themselves as they learn these new ways of thinking and being.

Accepting, Loving, and Finding Compassion for Oneself

One of the major tasks of the GETTING WELL program is enabling participants to love themselves; to see themselves as radiant, loving, lovable, good, and powerful beings; to accept themselves; and to be connected with the luminous center of their being. Connecting with oneself is a prerequisite to connecting with others and connecting transpersonally, yet is extremely difficult to accomplish. Accepting and loving ourselves just the way we are is a theme that threads through high-level awareness, expressive therapies, and group and individual sessions, as well as those on stress management and laughter and play.

One may ask why it is so difficult to accept on the emotional level that we are okay just the way we are. Again, we must look to our enculturation. As infants, we look up to the giants leaning over our cribs and ask, "Who am I and what am I doing here?" And the giants give us answers in words, looks, body language, and other nonverbal ways, both clearly and ambiguously. The message seems to be: "If you fit into the mold we design, you *may* be okay; however, if you don't fit you're sure not to be okay." One may think we're talking about the design of a dysfunctional family; however, we're talking about what is *normal* in our society in the best "loving" homes. Our society makes it very easy for us to feel terrible about ourselves and inculcates enormous resistance to our loving ourselves.

We suggest that participants consider scenarios which occur in many native cultures or animal families: The young one is nurtured and cosseted; the infant is a part of the natural flow of its family and of life. Its every need is being attended to by its parent(s), so there is no need for extended crying or discontent. As a result one rarely finds low self-esteem among jungle creatures, nor is low self-esteem endemic in more primitive cultures as it is in ours. Cheetahs, for example, don't wander around wondering if they are worthy. Aborigines probably don't have nagging doubts about living up to parental expectations. Yet it is rare to find an individual in our culture who feels naturally good about all parts of himself or herself (although we all tend to think that everyone else but us has high self-esteem). These examples may be challenged from a strictly scientific view; however, like myths, they provide a resource for reconceptualizing human dilemmas — in this case that one of self-worth.

As we try to establish license or permission among participants to feel worthy and good about themselves, we also ask them to imagine the far-reaching emotional and physical effects of feeling worthy or unworthy. An important point to make here is that it is fairly easy to feel good about oneself when things are going well — the trick is to have the seeds of worthiness so deeply planted and well fertilized that one feels worthy and compassionate toward oneself even and *especially* when events are not going well.

After eliciting the participants' ongoing beliefs about their core selves, we suggest that they choose affirmations which will move them toward more positive and realistic feelings about their worthiness. Some examples are: "My life is full of love and acceptance. I am secure. I believe in myself. I radiate poise and inner strength. I accept myself unconditionally. I am lovable. I believe in myself more and more every day. I have high self-esteem and self-worth. I deserve the good things in life. I radiate inner confidence."

Then we have participants try a powerful little exercise in group and commit themselves to practicing it before they go to sleep at night for the next week:

> Get into a comfortable position, close your eyes and relax. Take several abdominal breaths and begin concentrating on the affirmation you have chosen. Imagine the words and imagine yourself accepting this affirmation. Repeat the suggestion 10 times, keeping count by slightly moving the fingers on each hand from the little finger to the thumb. When you are finished, allow yourself to fall asleep gently.

(Remember that affirmations should encompass the desired result, be specific and clear, be worded positively, and use colorful, active words and images. Suggestions are usually most effective when they involve gradual rather than sudden change.)

A mindfulness or meditation exercise is a powerful way to embrace one's radiant inner self. Joan Borysenko, Ellen Langer, and Jon Kabat-Zinn have excellent ones in their books; however, a favorite of mine is Charles Tart's "Musical Body," which we modify to practice in group. First, we put approximately 15 minutes of slow instrumental music on the tape recorder. Then we instruct participants as the music begins to play:

> Take a minute or two to just relax. Now listen to the music with both of your feet. Put your attention on whatever sensations are in your feet and gently let the music be there too. Gently put your mind in your feet. Sense whatever is there, and hear the music there. . . . Enjoy the music in your feet and the sensations in your feet. . . . After about a minute, move your attention up into the calves of your legs, then from your ankles to your knees. Pay attention to whatever sensations are there, and hear the music there. Enjoy the music in your calves and the sensations in your calves. . . . At about one-minute intervals, go through your body . . . genitals, pelvis . . . belly . . . chest and back . . . shoulders . . . upper arms . . . forearms . . . hands . . . neck . . . and face scalp. Then focus on the inside of your head for a minute or so. Then listen to the music in your heart. Strong, positive feelings will probably result here. . . . Finally, spread the sensing and listening to the music and any positive feelings associated with your heart throughout your whole body. After a minute or two of this, let your attention relax and just drift into a relaxed state for a few minutes until the music ends . . . and you get up slowly. (1986, pp. 280–281)

Differentiating Between the Societal Mask and the Real Self

Dr. Tart says that we "value, defend, and cling to our personality, even when it has characteristics that cause suffering. The characteristics of our personality do set us up for suffering" (1987, p. 163). Personality comes from the Latin word *persona*, which is a mask used by actors. As our essential selves become more and more overlaid by the plaster layers of cultural expectations and demands, and as we surrender the power of our real selves, our masks become thicker and begin to obscure our essences. To survive, we frequently believe that we need to separate from our true being — to be what we are not, to survive for the moment. Depending on the length and complexity of our survival, by the time we approach adulthood it is very difficult to differentiate between our personae and our true essences.

Earlier, we spoke of "pulling the weeds" and recognizing the power of conditioning, the consensus trance, and identification as a means of understanding society's contribution to the mask. In this session, the focus is on remembering who we really are, on remembering the self in its full, shimmering essence.

I have found Les Fehmi's "Open Focus" exercise (see Chapter 8) to be excellent for self-remembering. I also frequently use Dr. Tart's self-remembering and self-observation exercises as a splendid way to expand the consciousness deliberately, so that the whole is kept in mind simultaneously with the specifics of consciousness.

The self-remembering exercise involves sitting in a chair, becoming quite comfortable and relaxed, and focusing on the sensations in the right foot for about 30 seconds—really being there. Then, leaving attention on the right foot behind, focus on the lower half of the right leg for 30 seconds, and then for 30 seconds each on the upper half of the right leg, right hand, right forearm, right upper arm, left upper arm, left forearm, left hand, upper half of the left leg, lower half of the left leg, left foot. (At this point there is a broadening of the senses, and the exercise moves into a form of self-remembering called sensing, looking, and listening.) After sensing the left foot for 30 seconds, broaden the focus of attention to both feet, then both legs, both hands, both forearms, both upper arms. Now spend 30 seconds or so sensing the entire pattern of sensations in your feet, legs, hands, arms all at once. While continuing to sense your legs and arms, actively listen to whatever sounds are around for 30 seconds, and then, while continuing to listen and sense your arms and legs simultaneously, let your attention broaden even further, open your eyes and actively look around so that you are simultaneously sensing, looking, and listening. You are now remembering yourself.

Dr. Tart speaks of the difficulties in self-remembering, one of which is the "flabby muscle" of our attention. He says our attention is a muscle that rarely gets used because our mental machinery has been automatized and conveys our attention along an automatic path. To strengthen the "attention muscle," we must use it over and over in all kinds of situations so that it grows stronger.

One of my favorite attention exercises involves having the participants take a 15-minute walk outside the house and act as if they were space aliens dropped onto a strange, new planet where everything is different. We suggest they bring back souvenirs (a twig, a leaf, a piece of Spanish moss, a beer can) to the group from this visit, and tell stories about their findings. Although the attentional focus is outward, the effect is to move members more deeply into an understanding of their essence and their creativity—in addition to strengthening attention muscles.

Recognizing and Expressing Feelings

This session, taken from Tubesing and Tubesing's *Structured Exercises in Wellness Promotion*, focuses on the exploration of emotional responses to a variety of situations, on identification of personal response styles, and on expanding participants' vocabularies of feeling words. First, the importance of feelings as a component of the whole person is discussed. We point out that mentally healthy people are characterized by a capacity to feel deeply, by a sensitivity to feelings in themselves as well as others, by an openness to experiencing feelings, and by the possession of a wide range of feelings they can express.

Then we discuss the reasons that people limit their feelings. For example, people confuse *experiencing* emotion with *acting* on it, and so may suppress feelings of anger for fear that they will act on that anger. Because our culture has a great deal to say about those emotions which are "good" and those which are "bad," most of us spend large amounts of energy keeping the bad emotions in the basement. From what I have seen, when people repress *one* set of emotions, they generally repress all of their emotions. For example, someone who is unable to express feelings of anger is likely to be hindered in the expression of joy.

In this session, we present a situation and ask participants to name the feelings they would have in that situation. We say, for example, "Your significant other angrily stomps out of the house, slamming the door so hard that the house shakes." We fill the blackboard with the plethora of emotions elicited from the participants, emotions ranging from anger to fear to amusement. We then note that the situation itself did not cause the emotions; rather, the emotions were caused by the interpretation of the situation. We also point out the wide variety of emotions elicited by the situation, from depression-type emotions to anxiety-based emotions, and we emphasize that *all* the feelings were okay to have.

We follow this by having the group members come up with one or two more vignettes and go through the process again. Afterward, participants are asked to write down their own five most favorite feelings and their five least favorite feelings. We ask the group to come to a consensus (without the facilitator's help) on their most favorite five and least favorite five feelings. Finally, we ask each member to choose one or two feelings he or she would like to be more open to and to search out at least two opportunities during the next day to experience those feelings. (For example, someone might wish to be more open to anger or to compassion.) Participants are asked to note the outcome of their experiences and report back the next day.

Empowering the Self: Finding One's Own Truth

We all were born with great sources of power, which tend to dissipate as we try to please those around us and to fit into the cultural "bottle" into which the embryo self is thrust. In attempting to be "normal" in a somewhat pathological culture, we tend to lose ourselves and to give away much of our power. This session focuses on re-empowering the self, finding one's own truth, and creating a life that is consistent with this truth. Gershon and Straub's book, *Empowerment*, is a valuable resource for this high-level awareness session.

To discover how they currently experience personal power, we tell participants to ask themselves, first, what allows them to feel powerful in their lives, and second, in what ways and in what situations do they *not* feel powerful. We then suggest that they take a few minutes to write their answers in their notebooks. After they have done so, we write on the board the ways in which they feel powerful. For the most part these feelings of power fall into three categories: (1) doing things such as exercising, drawing, working, or making something; (2) being a certain way, such as having a sense of humor, being insightful, being hopeful in adverse situations, or being in the moment; and (3) having power in relationships, such as being sexually attractive, having people look up to you, helping others learn, or being one others seek out for advice.

Gershon and Straub point out that the first two ways make up personal power and, when balanced, allow one to have access to the full range of his or her power—the yin and yang of being both active and receptive. If, however, the primary way in which one feels powerful is either having power over another or empowering another, this may be a false sense of power, in that it is not coming from within oneself. When one needs another person to activate that power, the need distances one from the source of power which springs from within. At this point, we encourage the group members to discuss this concept of personal power and to begin asking themselves what their own personal truths are.

Gershon and Straub suggest that there are seven sources of personal power that help sustain personal growth over time, and we discuss each source in this session. The first is the *commitment* or the willingness to stick with one's vision throughout the vicissitudes of life. This involves a deep passion for one's truth and the willingness to plow through the resistances and blocks which prevent its coming to bear fruit. *Discipline* is the second source of power, which involves daily dedication to the vision and the willingness to put one's money where one's mouth is.

The third source of power is a *support system* made up of people dedicated to acknowledging our growth in positive ways yet giving honest, loving feedback when needed. A fourth source is *inner guidance,* tapping into the wisdom within ourselves. This involves becoming still, asking the question to which an answer is sought, trusting one's intuition, and acting on the inner guidance when it is experienced.

A fifth source of power is *lightness,* shedding the heaviness of limiting beliefs and emotional baggage, keeping one's spirit light, and making one's enlightenment an exciting adventure. *Love* is a sixth source of power— loving and being loved. Of course, the primary love relationship needs to be with one's inner self, which in turn makes it possible to have unconditional love for others. The most central source of power is *finding one's own truth* and letting it be the guiding force for creating the life one wants.

Gershon and Straub offer excellent imagery for easing participants from a left-brain discussion of personal power into an emotional exploration and acceptance of self-empowerment and finding their truths. We suggest that members have their notebooks and pens in front of them to journal or draw at the appropriate breaks in the imagery.

> Imagine yourself walking through a bright, sunlit forest. You walk farther and farther into this sunlit forest until you come to a clearing. In the clearing you see a magical palace. You walk up to the palace, and as you enter through the main gateway you see many doors, each of a different color and shape. Pause for a moment to visualize this.
>
> The first door you come to has "Commitment" written on it. Open this door and enter into the room of Commitment. In your imagination begin exploring the room of Commitment. What do you see — images, colors, or shapes? What do you hear — sounds, phrases, or words? And what do you feel — emotions, sensations?
>
> Pause to explore this room for the next few minutes, then record in your journal the images, words, or feelings you discover. As you record in your journal, keep your eyes soft as you move in and out of your imagination. (long pause)
>
> Now see yourself leaving the room of Commitment and closing the door behind you. You are back to the place in the palace with all the doors of different colors and shapes. This time you come to the door marked "Discipline." ... (pp. 50–51)

Have the participants continue in the same way in the Discipline room, the Support System room, the Inner Guidance room, the Lightness room, the Love room, and finally, the Finding Your Own Truth room. When they have finished exploring and writing/drawing about the Finding Your Own Truth room, have them come back into the hallways and go back out the way they entered, pausing outside the doors of each room they explored and thinking of the insights gleaned in each room — Love, Lightness, Inner Guidance, Support System, Discipline, and Commitment. Then suggest they come back through the main gate into the forest and, finally, come slowly out of the forest into the here and now.

Processing this powerful imagery exercise is worth extending the session. Frequently, we will use it back-to-back with an expressive therapy session, using the full two hours. Often, participants are blocked from going into one or more of the rooms, and it may be useful to use transformational fantasy techniques, to go right back in and deal with the resistance or block. If there is time, the facilitator might take the participants back in as a group to redesign rooms that weren't quite the way people wanted them to be the first time.

Changing Core Beliefs

Gershon and Straub and Ken and Penny Keyes (1987) are sources of wisdom for this session concerning core beliefs, which are the base of the iceberg for our consciousness, our behavior, our emotions, and our bodies. Below the level of our awareness, our bodymind is programmed with core beliefs that affect every aspect of the ways in which we relate to ourselves, to others, and to the universe. Like the bedrocks of a river, which determine its direction and flow, core beliefs are the hidden rocks in the river of life. They provide the bed for the river, influence the smoothness or roughness of the flow, lie at the deepest level, and most frequently are unseen. Much of the programming for our core beliefs comes in our childhood—frequently at the preverbal, unconscious level—and is deeply influenced by the beliefs that one's parents hold and communicate through their words and actions. Those early communications penetrate deeply into the child's sponge-like, survival-oriented little psyche, and burrow into each cell of its being. So pervasive are these early beliefs that they continue to be the bedrocks of our existence, even when they have far outlived their survival value.

A core belief is so deeply embedded that one is usually not consciously aware of its existence. For that reason, it is hard to identify those basic beliefs, even though they determine the direction of our lives. Gershon and Straub have a series of questions that help participants break into the hideaways of those beliefs, allow the beliefs to surface, and assist participants in making choices about the usefulness of such beliefs at this point in their lives. "When a misfortune happens in your life, how do you respond?" is a question that gives understanding into what participants believe about self-responsibility. "Do you feel that you are a lovable person?" gives insight into self-esteem, while "Do you believe that you are part of a supportive universe?" reveals beliefs about trust in the universe. The answer to "When something difficult happens to you, is your first response to look for the positive or the negative?" reveals a person's attitude. "Are you anxious when circumstances change and you can't control them?" sheds light on a person's beliefs about control and his or her ability to flow with change. These questions spark the group discussion about their early programming and about core beliefs that inevitably come to the fore.

Recognition of core beliefs is a major step toward being able to change them. The Keyes have an excellent list of "possible destructive core beliefs" against which people can match their own beliefs. Seeing that beliefs such as "I must please others to be worthy," "I'll never live up to my parents' expectations," or "I'll get hurt if I get too close in a relationship" are generally considered destructive gives an individual a new outlook on the usefulness of his or her beliefs. Ken and Penny Keyes also include a page of beneficial, legitimate, self-enhancing core beliefs, such as "I am a lovable and worthy person," "I am learning to flow joyfully in the present moment," and "I can let others love me the way I am," which are alternatives to the destructive beliefs.

For homework we assign journaling about one's childhood and the situations out of which the core beliefs arose, giving details about how the same patterns are repeated again and again as one goes through life. Participants are also asked to observe themselves as they remember painful behaviors or emotions and to trace the origins of the core beliefs underlying the emotions.

Developing an Inner Locus of Control

Numerous studies show that people who believe they have control of their lives have less depression, less hypertension and heart disease, and less vulnerability to cancer and other diseases. Feeling helpless or unable to cope in a situation sets up the most vicious of physiological stress reactions, with the resultant buildup of cortisol and other stress chemicals. (Remember that cortisol is believed to inactivate the macrophages, which are the first line of defense of the immune system.)

The helpless person can be said to have an *outer* locus of control. He or she looks to factors and people outside for help in coping with life. He or she is like a leaf on the river of life—being moved along by the direction of the stream without input or influence or direction. Such people are the ones who depend on their doctors or medicines "to make me well." They are the ones who say, "I could have been a real success if life had not dealt me a rotten hand." On the other hand, the "hardy" individual—the pathfinder—can be said to have an *inner* locus of control. Gail Sheehy (1981) finds that pathfinders take responsibility for their lives, their happiness, and their feelings. They are aware that they have many choices about how they can see the world, and they choose perceptions of the world which bring to themselves and others the greatest benefits. They are the kind of individuals who do not seek to control others; rather, they respect the right of others to make choices about their own lives just as they themselves have the right to design their own lives and perceptions.

This is a good place to open the discussion up to the group and elicit other hallmarks of the individual with an inner locus of control. We ask members which of these qualities they recognize in themselves, and which ones they would like to work to develop. (It might be pointed out that these qualities are almost exactly the ones which Al Siebert found as characteristic of survivors.) Here is the exercise I use:

I like to think of us as beautiful rainbow trout swimming in the river of life. Life is so beautiful, and the water is so clear and cool and clean as it babbles through mountain and wood. And we're enjoying being strong and powerful as we wend our way in the stream of life. . . . When one day right in front of our eyes is a hook [*I draw a fishhook on the board*] with a tempting fat worm on it. The hook might be someone pulling in front of us on the interstate or it could be a spouse saying something he or she knows "drives you crazy." When such things happen we have a choice in what to do. We can choose to bite the hook, become outraged, and let our bodies and minds become mega-stressed, or we can choose not to bite, and instead relax or do nothing. The point is that when we see the hook, we need to stop and ask ourselves "Is it worth dying for?"

We always have a choice whether or not to react. The individual with an inner locus of control will be aware that he or she has a choice of whether to bite the hook or not. Remember, we don't *have* to bite the hook just because it is there.

At this point, we ask participants to think of situations in their lives where they feel there is no choice but to bite the hook. After processing these situations, we try to elicit as many "hooks" that participants can identify as time allows and look at alternative beliefs we can practice when confronted by hooks in the river of life. In the group room we have a picture of a fish being hooked, on which I have written "Is it worth dying for?" This serves as a powerful image for members confronting incendiary situations in their lives and facilitates many insights concerning the power of choice and an inner locus of control.

Inner Child Work

In her book, *The Inner Dance*, Diana Mariechild writes that there is a little child living within our hearts who is the embodiment of love, creativity, curiosity, and joy. This whole, healthy child infuses our energy, allowing us to meet life with a curiosity and a lighthearted playfulness. Our child is a bold explorer. Each situation is new, and there are no preconceptions for our child. By the time we reach adulthood, however, many of us are harboring an inner child who is hurt and afraid and crying out for love and attention. These feelings and unmet needs translate into behavior that is limiting, destructive, and repressive. We may even, as adults, react to neutral situations as though they were in some way as life-threatening as similar childhood situations.

Carla, who was physically and emotionally abandoned as a child, is an example of such behavior. Carla is a beautiful, extremely intelligent, and successful professional woman who appears to have her life under control.

The truth is, however, that she remembers times in her early years when she believed she would not survive until adulthood—so severe was the abandonment she had suffered. As an adult, she finds herself in relationships in which she experiences confusion about love and about which parts of herself are okay to reveal. As a result, she keeps her real feelings and her real self in a dark cave inside and exhibits only the mask which proclaims, "Please, don't leave me, I'll be anything you want me to be." Of course, she tends to attract men with similar masks, and her relationships are doomed to failure almost from the beginning. And with every relationship that collapses, Carla once more becomes her wounded four-year-old self, who retreats further into the dark, "safe" cave.

Unfortunately, Carla's story is not unusual. We hear less dramatic accounts of parent-child relationships, such as ones about parents who want their children to take advantage of opportunities they themselves never had, while unknowingly projecting their own pain and dissatisfaction with their own life circumstances onto their kids. Or we may see adults who as children were silenced by such messages as "Grow up and quit that foolishness," "I can always count on you to embarrass the family," or "Why can't you do anything right?" Whatever the message or learned behavior, this hurt has been brought into participants' adulthood in the form of a silent or wounded inner core.

To combat such problems, we focus this session on providing the tools for re-parenting, for creating a nurturing, rather than punitive, inner parent. We suggest that members take the best qualities of their natural parents, if they wish, and combine them with bits and pieces of the desired nurturing parental behavior they have seen in others. With their eyes closed, participants are asked to fold their arms across their chests and trigger nurturant muscle memory by stroking their upper arms gently—being their own baby. As they picture their nurturant parent creation in their mind's eyes, we ask them to repeat silently to themselves after us, with pauses between each sentence:

> You are my child and I love you. I am very proud of the way you are growing and learning each day. Don't forget how much I love you. I'll always be here to help you. I am proud of you. You are a worthy human being, a most lovable person. I love you for just being you. I'm proud of the decisions you make. It's hard making choices. I really appreciate you for doing so. You're a total success just being you. Your uniqueness is precious and respected. You deserve the best in life. I love you.

This powerful exercise is almost sure to bring forth a few tears from those who say, "I never heard that from my parents." Now they can, whenever they wish!

Alternatively, we may use a transformational fantasy exercise with the group in which we ask members to go to the place in their being where their inner child is, to explore that place, and to make changes if they wish. Carla found her inner child in her heart. Here are the words she spoke during this exercise: "She is in a dark, cold cave and she is so afraid. It is light outside the cave and it is really beautiful, but the infant is afraid of the light. She might be herself, and it's not safe . . . she might really have feelings and do something that would make people leave her." ("Could she look out?" we asked.) "No, it's too scary . . . but look at that window. It's turned into a picture of me and my father. I know that picture. I was acting up that day—just being myself—and my father didn't leave me. I'm out there in that bright light, but I feel so vulnerable." ("What would you like to do?") "I'd like to join the infant in the dark with little Carla out in the light, but Carla feels too vulnerable—she's shaking." ("Perhaps a cloak?") Yes, a cloak. A cloak with a hood that I can pull over my face . . . that's good. Now I can be in the light but be protected. . . . Yes, I think the infant and Carla can be joined . . . yes, that feels okay." ("Could you bring your father in and be yourself with him?") "Yes! . . . I'm pushing *him* around and it feels good. And you know, I'm really beginning to feel some anger now. But the peculiar thing is . . . I don't feel guilty. This is the first time I feel anger without feeling guilty." Carla proceeded to bring in not only her father, but also various men in her life, and she began to express the years of pent-up anger. And then her healing really began!

Seeds of Interpersonal Connectedness

When we have healed what Joan Borysenko calls "the wound of unworthiness," then and only then can we hope to connect deeply with others. Until we have "remembered ourselves" as the truly luminous and gifted beings we are, we continue to wear our personae or our masks, and we continue to be attracted by and attractive to the masks of others—culminating in a painful but deeply meaningless dance of the masks. Interpersonal connectedness demands that we love ourselves, and allow ourselves to be vulnerable—that we open our hearts and souls and be able to trust ourselves so fully that we can learn to trust others.

Connecting interpersonally does *not* mean that we are indiscriminate about those we allow around us. As a matter of fact, it may enable us to become even more selective, since we may be less "desperate" to feed the false demands of our masks. And although we should maintain an attitude of unconditional love, forgiveness, and acceptance toward all those with whom we come into contact, we may certainly *choose* to be around only those persons who are sympathetic to our healing path.

Interpersonal connection means opening our hearts and communicating our feelings to others, as well as empathically receiving the feelings of others. It also involves tapping into the core of our higher selves, tapping into our wells of love and altruism and actively helping others.

Interpersonal Aspects of Illness, Social Support, and Altruism

Dean Ornish writes, "Altruism, compassion, and forgiveness—opening your heart—can be powerful means of healing the isolation that leads to stress, suffering, and illness. In other words, altruism, compassion, and forgiveness are in our own, best self-interest, for they help to free us from our limitations and to empower us" (1990, p. 215).

There are a number of studies which indicate that helping others or exhibiting altruistic behavior has a positive effect on both the immune system and the cardiovascular system. For example, in the Tecumseh study (House, Robbins, & Melzner, 1982), the nearly 3,000 residents of that Michigan town were followed for more than a decade. During the study, researchers found that men who did no volunteer work were two and a half times more likely to die sooner than those who volunteered at least once a week. Anecdotal reports about physicians and other caregivers during the Plague indicated that their resistance to the disease was considerably higher than that of the ordinary citizen. There are a number of other studies indicating that nurses and other caregivers have less likelihood of developing infectious diseases from the population they care for than do others.

Such statistics create an important dilemma. Many of the people who are most susceptible to life-challenging illnesses are those who have made a life out of caring for others rather than for themselves. Their training has been: "You must care for others before you can even begin thinking of yourself." Too frequently, however, the giver is not giving to others out of true compassion; rather, the giver is attempting to make himself or herself more acceptable, more lovable, or more worthy in the eyes of the receiver. Often these generous acts are toted on a secret inner agenda board and can be used to end friendships if, down the road, the receiver refuses a request from the giver. "I am always doing things for others, yet I'm usually disappointed by them in the long run," is often heard from people who appear to demonstrate altruism because they are always "giving" to others. But such a reaction does not demonstrate altruism. This is such a significant issue with participants that we need to clarify the difference during this session. During the clarification process, we find that giving to others and expecting something in return comes from deep wounds of unworthiness and from scars and walls that protect a heart broken in childhood.

This "conditional altruism" points up the necessity to love, accept, and connect with the self *before* viable interpersonal connections can be effected. *Emmanuel's Book* (Rodegast & Stanton, 1985) states, "Love and compassion for others cannot exist until there is a goodly supply for self. How can you feel the love of God if you do not love yourself? Are they not one and the same thing? Until you can accept yourself, you lock the doorway to the expansion you all yearn for" (p. 48). True interpersonal connectedness demands that we love *both* ourselves exactly as we are and others just as they are. Considering our enculturation and the judgments, separation, and defiant individualism of which it consists, remembering our loving, nonjudgmental, essential selves becomes a difficult task.

Choosing Between Love and Fear

We have found that many of the teachings of A *Course in Miracles* open the participant to see the world in different ways and may be touchstones for "aha" experiences. The *Course* teaches that there are only two emotions: love and fear. Love is the emotion with which we are born; it is part and parcel of our essential selves. Fear is an emotion created by our minds and our reactions to our experiences and our programming. For this reason, in any situation we have the choice of love (tapping into our essential selves, our wholeness) or fear (separating ourselves from our essence through resentment, judgment, guilt, or hate). Jerry Jampolsky, M.D., has written a very understandable little volume called *Love is Letting Go of Fear*, which untangles the paradoxes of the *Course* (which I consider to be a graduate course in self-responsibility). Although the concepts presented are puzzling or disturbing to participants, the ideas are fertile seeds of epiphanies. As we present some hypotheses from the *Course*, we suggest that participants not reject them out of hand but act "as if" with them for a while before they decide to toss them out.

There seems to be a growing need to feel inner fulfillment and peace rather than to rely merely upon the external symbols of success. And when one is stymied in achieving these external symbols, one encounters stress, depression, pain, and suffering. Despite our pain, we seem to hang on to the old beliefs, even when it is abundantly clear that they're not working. To experience inner peace means seeing the world in a different way and letting go of those beliefs that are not working.

Jampolsky suggests that most of us are confused about what is real, that most of us base what is real merely on feedback from our physical senses. To confirm this reality we look to what our culture defines to be "normal" and "real." Thereby, we learn fear and separation part and parcel with learning the rules of our mode of civilization.

In presenting this hypothesis to participants, we want them to process the idea that love is eternal, that everything else is transitory, and therefore meaningless. "Fear always distorts our perception and confuses us as to what is going on. Love is the total absence of fear. Love asks no questions. Its natural state is one of extension and expansion, not comparison and measurement. Love, then, is really everything that is of value, and fear can offer us nothing because it is nothing" (Jampolsky, 1979, p. 17).

We throw this idea out to participants for their contemplation: When we can begin to see beyond our belief in reality as defined by our sensing of the physical world, a shift may occur in which we perceive that all our minds are joined, and that choosing to participate in this unity is participating in love and peace of mind. I also like to use the definition of fear found in *Emmanuel's Book*: "a fungus that grows rapidly in the dark places of the consciousness. . . . It is the denial of light and denial of light is resistance to God. It is the falsehood that separates you from God" (p. 107).

Thus, it follows that choosing love is choosing what is true and embraces the perfection of the universe, while choosing fear is choosing the falsehood foisted upon us by our culture. Of course, it should be noted here that the assumption of a "perfect universe" does not imply that disaster is "God's will." (After what is usually a long discussion, we ask participants to present scenarios that test these hypotheses.)

Bertie, a 52-year-old woman with MS, thought a lot of this session was "a bunch of bunk. When you're diagnosed with MS," she continued, "there's no choice in what you feel. You're scared to death. That's the normal way to feel." ("Yes, it's normal," the facilitator replied, "but is it possible to choose to feel another way?") "I guess so." ("How would you have felt if you had chosen to respond with love rather than fear?") "Well, let's see. I guess I wouldn't have felt I was being punished for something. I also might have seen it more as the river rather than as a dam that ended my life. I might even have seen it as sort of an adventure."

With more encouragement, Bertie developed a love scenario that was dramatically different from her fear reaction. Although not totally convinced, she promised to play with the idea. Later, she decided that it was actually a rather practical concept and began to use it on a regular basis. "It's amazing how much better I sleep now and how much more peace I feel inside even though the world out there hasn't changed," she concluded. "It's a little miracle that has happened."

Interpersonal Needs Satisfaction

In this session, gleaned from Tubesing and Tubesing (1983), participants generate a list of people to whom they relate and examine their social connections in view of the expectations and rewards implicit in various levels of these relationships. The facilitator usually opens the exercise by discussing the importance of supportive relationships and of one's health. Important points may be that everyone needs to be loved, valued, and appreciated; relationships tend to happen by chance rather than by planning and building a support system; in order to attract support, people must be willing to allow themselves to be vulnerable and to state clearly what they need and want in a relationship.

Participants are asked to list the names of three or four people of moderate importance in their social lives (neither those who are the most significant nor those who are the least significant). They are then asked to focus on and list the demands placed upon them in these relationships. In addition, we ask them to discern who sets the demand as a requirement (themselves, others, or both); if this requirement were not fulfilled by themselves, what difference would it make (would the relationship still exist?); and finally, what insights occur to them as a result of their answers?

After responding to these questions, participants focus on the rewards in their relationships, listing the specific rewards they expect in each one, along with the percentage of time each relationship gives them these rewards. After some discussion, they decide how completely rewards match up to their expectations.

The facilitator then explains that relationships fill a multiplicity of personal needs, and as he or she lists these needs, participants are asked to identify the person to whom they look *primarily* to meet each need: To whom do you look primarily to listen to you? To give you emotional support? To give you emotional challenge? To tell you that you're good at what you do? To stimulate you? To play with you? How successfully (percentage) does each person you identified fulfill this need for you? For every need that is not fulfilled at least 75 percent of the time, participants are asked to list two or three other persons who could possibly help fill this need.

As participants look over their papers, the facilitator may point out that it is unlikely any one person can meet *all* of our interpersonal needs. Expecting one person to do so lays a heavy burden on that person and sets us up for disappointment. We then discuss how frustrating it is to count on a certain person to meet a particular need and not have that person come through. We explain to participants that when they find themselves feeling isolated and lonely, perhaps they are not getting important interpersonal needs met; it might be a time to assess their support systems and find other people to help fill the gaps. If there is time left, we may identify and plan steps for the development of a personal support network.

Forgiveness, Compassion

Catherine Ponder (1966), a well-known spiritual writer, has said, "It is an immutable mental and spiritual law that when there is a health problem, there is a forgiveness problem. You must forgive if you want to be permanently healed." The *Course in Miracles* says that disease comes from a state of unforgiveness and that whenever one is ill one needs to check out who or what needs to be forgiven. This is a hypothesis worth considering and one which has been borne out over and over at GETTING WELL.

This section is a key one in the participants' healing process, yet the concept is a very difficult one to internalize. What I am presenting may seem repetitive (which may be reflective of my own difficulty in some areas of forgiveness), since I find that coming at the subject from all angles may be necessary in order to make the point. We usually divide the material presented in this section into several one-hour sessions. If you are planning to make only one session from this, we suggest that you present only a few of the points.

In her book, *Forgiveness*, Robin Casarjian conceptualizes forgiveness as "a shrewd and practical strategy" for dealing with intrapersonal, interpersonal, and international situations. Forgiveness is an act of self-interest and self-love. Similarly, she sees hanging onto anger as like holding onto a burning coal with the intention of throwing it at another person—even though all the while it is burning the hand of the holder.

We point out to participants that, when one holds resentment toward another, one is bound to that person or condition by an emotional link stronger than the most powerful steel. Forgiving the person or condition is the only way to dissolve that link and become free. We say that it is sometimes easier to forgive those whom one resents, condemns, or even hates when one accepts this hypothesis: People act in the best way they know how, given their knowledge, insight, or level of consciousness. It also may make it easier to forgive when one realizes that forgiveness does not condone whatever was done or make it right or absolve the transgressor of responsibility; it merely releases the forgiver from the negative consequences of resentment. Forgiveness is not forgetting, either. As one participant put it, "When you forgive, it's like you take a receipt and file it. You don't have to deal with it anymore. It happened, but it's neutral. It's a piece of paper."

Simon (1990) points out that it may be difficult to forgive because it means giving up the illusion that if the incident hadn't happened you would have a perfect life. In addition, it involves letting go of defining yourself as the "good" person or "the poor innocent victim" in the situation and the other person as "bad and reprehensible." Not forgiving also compensates one in a perverse way for having been so helpless and hurt at the time of the incident. It is well to remember, too, that for many participants, keeping the pain alive gives the illusion of protection from a similar situation happening again.

Simon suggests that forgiving is the by-product of an ongoing healing process—the gift at the end of that process. It is a sign of positive self-esteem, a moral right to *stop* being hurt by a situation that was unfair in the first place. When we forgive, we realize that we no longer need our grudges as an excuse for getting less out of life than we deserve or as weapons to punish others. Forgiving frees up energy that can be channeled into discovering our strengths and moving onto better things in life. One of our participants put it well: "When we forgive, it means that we never have to be the victim again."

At this point, group members may want to discuss resentment or anger that may be getting in the way of their relationships with others. It is important that participants not jump over their painful feelings and forgive too quickly. Casarjian (1992) emphasizes that before one forgives, one must own the pain that was experienced in the situation. She says, "Owning the pain is recognizing, acknowledging, and admitting what is true. Once it is owned, the pain of the past can then be turned into the richness of life itself. . . . Our pain needs a safe, appropriate place to be vented and allowed, without judgment, to be" (p. 49). Here it is well to mention that releasing or venting painful memories and feelings doesn't necessarily involve directly confronting those who were unfair or hurtful to you; the feelings of anger, resentment, sadness, and guilt need to be released. Methods for releasing these feelings are found in Chapters 5 and 6.

Just as one need not directly encounter those who were the source of painful feelings, one does not need to make actual contact with the other person involved in order to forgive him or her (although that can be an effective part of the healing process if the occasion arises). The forgiveness process can be done equally well with someone who is alive or someone who is dead. Frequently, participants may not even be aware of what or whom they need to forgive in the past or present. In fact, Ponder feels it is not necessary that you know what or who hurt you; the only requirement is a willingness to speak words of forgiveness and let those words do their cleansing work. She suggests a daily meditation upon these words: "All that has offended me, I forgive. Whatever has made me bitter, resentful, unhappy, I forgive. Within and without, I forgive. Things past, things present, things future, I forgive."

After participants have identified a situation or person they need to forgive, we suggest they repeat this affirmation five times, several times a day: "(Name of person or situation), I freely forgive you. I release you and let you go." The affirmation is most effective if it is written five times at least once of those several times.

Alicia's divorce nearly 15 years earlier was extremely bitter. She certainly had every right to feel hurt and enraged by the years of emotional abuse she suffered at the hands of her husband; however, her relief at her freedom was overwhelmed by her bitterness and sense of having been grievously wrongcd. Some weeks after the divorce, Alicia had her first serious attack of rheumatoid arthritis which continued in crippling intensity for months. Nearly a year later she recognized her illness as a metaphor for the inflamed rage coursing through her body—attacking her from within. Having read some of Catherine Ponder's work, she decided to give forgiveness a shot. At intervals up to 15 times a day she repeated, "John, I freely forgive you. I release you and let you go, and I release myself from my anger at you." As Alicia forgave John, her inflammation and pain subsided, and she was able to put her cane away. Arthritis flare-ups still serve as a reminder to Alicia of the forgiveness she needs to do from time to time, but it is amazing how freeing herself from resentment through forgiveness simultaneously frees Alicia's joints from inflammation.

Like Alicia, most participants find that, when they can forgive, they pull back their power from the situation. They may have felt powerless in the past to solve the problem, but suddenly there is a change, a shift in their perception of the situation. This process is somewhat similar to watching a large boulder crumble, changing from a solid, impenetrable object to a pile of dust. This epiphany is almost invariably followed by a positive change not only in emotional health but also, as in Alicia's case, in physical health.

We tell participants that forgiveness opens the door to compassion, which has been defined as a consciousness of the suffering of others and a desire to help them. Compassion also means releasing the judgments concerning others and ourselves that separate us from the flow of our wholeness. We also explain that compassion requires a connectedness with and understanding of oneself in order to understand and to connect with a wide range of human experiences in others, that compassion is love and a nonjudgmental attitude in action.

The Institute of Noetic Sciences sponsors a project on altruism, believing that love, compassion, and altruism are integral parts of the human spirit, the human essence. In connecting interpersonally with compassion, one is in actuality connecting with one's essential self and, indeed, connecting transpersonally with the higher power of the universe. A *Course in Miracles* suggests that a combination of love, compassion, and connectedness is the equivalent of healing, that in any given situation we can choose love, wholeness, and healing, or fear, separation, suspicion, and illness.

This hypothesis usually creates some lively group discussion. A main objection to putting the thesis inlo practice is the fear that "If I love and trust everyone, I'll be robbed and taken advantage of." Putting aside judgments of others certainly does not mean being nondiscriminating about our lives, however. It doesn't mean we should leave our doors unlocked to thieves or marry someone who is abusive. It *does* mean understanding the background of abuse, neglect, and pain which may have brought such people to the place they are and perhaps saying about them, "There but for the grace of God go I."

Most of us are well trained in being judgmental, because such training allows a culture to maintain control of its members. For example, we are trained to discern the ways in which everyone we meet is different from us in skin color, hair color, gender, socioeconomic status, etc. For this reason, learning to encounter others and our world with compassion requires that we put much of this training aside. We suggest that participants work to achieve this goal by spending at least 30 minutes a day manifesting an attitude of compassion toward each person they see. (I frequently do my practice while exercising around a downtown lake where many of the homeless congregate. It is a powerful experience to shed one's judgments and encounter each human being as a reflection and part of oneself and see both the other and myself as important cells in this body of humanity. Personally, I find this exercise "lightens the load" considerably and brings me a sense of joy and belonging.) When participants bring their experiences back to group, it is indeed the material of which holy moments are made.

We often use an adaptation of Tart's "Remembering Love" (1987, pp. 275–276) exercise to help participants practice compassion:

1. Think about someone who loved you a lot. (Parents may be tricky to use here because of unresolved psychological tensions; however, a grandparent is usually a good choice.) Think about how the person loved you and was kind to you. . . .
2. Realize that you must be a worthwhile person to have been loved so by another. Focus on that rather than on any doubts you have about yourself.
3. Experience the feeling of being loved, of how that person felt in loving you.
4. Now, experience the feeling of loving. Then call up images of other people and give your love and compassion to them.

   a. At first use images of other people who have been good to you.
   b. As you become successful at this, extend the giving of love to images of people who have treated you neutrally.
   c. As you become even more practiced, extend your love to images of people who have treated you badly.
   d. When you feel comfortable with the above, extend your love to images of people with whom your relationship was mixed and complicated, such as your parents.
   e. Now extend your love to all beings.

When I think of paradigms for forgiveness, my thoughts go to Kathy and Jasper Becker, M.D. Kathy and Jap were driving home from dinner with their three children when a young man in a sports car rammed their van while passing them illegally on the road shoulder. The van flipped, and their 14-year-old daughter Loren was thrown out and killed. Although the young driver left the scene, he was eventually apprehended and processed through the justice system. When Kathy was called to help determine his fate, she responded, "Let him know that I forgive him, and I love him," thus starting a process in which the young man was able to rebuild his life, and the Beckers were able to arise from the ashes of the despair surrounding their daughter's death. As a result of this turn of fate, Jap Becker, a prominent urologist in Orlando, retired from his successful practice "to practice true healing." Jap (one of our consulting physicians) and Kathy have founded the Loren Quinn Institute for Attitudinal Healing and are devoting their lives to sharing the healing process of forgiveness.

Lessons for the Author/Clinician

One of my most valuable lessons in the area of intrapersonal and interpersonal connectedness was seeing that my negative judgments about others (including the occasional patient) were actually judgments about myself. Although I recognized that what annoyed me about others were usually mirrored aspects of myself and my behavior that I disliked or rejected, it was a year or so into GETTING WELL before I *knew* this was the case. At that time, I met Kit, a patient whom I could barely stand. I thought she was nosy and always trying to one-up everyone. Additionally, I hated the way she intellectualized incessantly and was uncomfortable with a few more things I could not really put my finger on.

While Kit was in the program we had a high-level awareness lesson on the factors in lack of acceptance and love of others, and I felt that I epitomized the benighted individual in this area. The lesson forced me to take a look at those parts of myself I had rejected and to reintegrate those qualities into a self I accepted more unconditionally. As I did so, I began to see myself reflected in the mirror of Kit, and as I became more at peace with all parts of myself (plus did a great deal of forgiving and "white lighting" of Kit), our relationship became a good one.

My experience with Kit led me to take a closer look at myself whenever I have feelings of animosity or a lack of acceptance toward *any* individual. Although this mirroring device frequently brings me chuckles, it is actually a personal power tool that takes the onus off of others to change to suit me so that I may be at peace in a situation. Since gaining this insight, I've found that my genuine love and acceptance of others have increased exponentially, and I rarely find myself in a situation of major conflict. Not only have I attuned my inner self more to what is occurring "out there," but also I think this change has released a different energy, which may indeed change the way in which people respond to me.

One of the great lessons that GETTING WELL has taught me is that of forgiveness. Although the program itself has been a clinical success since its first day, there have been a series of individuals (and institutions) who have wanted to make money off of GW at the expense of the integrity of the program (at least, that's how I've seen it). When I naively refused to play their game, we were threatened with the destruction of the program, refusal to pay thousands of dollars of hard-earned money owed us, and other subterfuge and despicable behavior. I felt angry, terrorized, and betrayed. As time went on, however, I realized I was in a trap of my own making, and, unfortunately, it wasn't in my behavior pattern to fight my way out. Then as I became more desperate, a lesson came up in high-level awareness. Being aware that I didn't have to condone anyone's behavior or forget that the incidents had occurred, I started the process of seeing the people involved having good things happen to them and then letting go of my own resentment—releasing it to the Light. After I had many such sessions with myself, things finally started to fall into a different perspective, and I began to feel freer from the poisons of resentment.

Although I feel good for having developed an attitude of forgiveness and acceptance of people the way they are, sometimes it has been responsible for my keeping employees with the program who were not working in concert with GETTING WELL's goals. However, this has become less of a problem as I have grown more comfortable with letting people know what I expect and working with them in an empathic, nonjudgmental way. In other words, I can still accept and honor them without having to tolerate behavior or attitudes that disrupt GW. And so the perfect universe becomes an exceptionally curious and exciting place!

14

High-Level Awareness III: Planting Seeds of Transpersonal Connectedness

Literally we say transpersonal means beyond the personal. But it also refers to the transcendental, as expressed in and though the personal . . . it's the link between the personal and that which is transcendent . . . a psychological view of spiritual development, rather than a religious point of view. —*Frances Vaughan*

. . . health is an intuitive perception of the universe as being of one fabric. Health is maintaining communication with the animals and plants and minerals and stars. It is knowing death and life and knowing no difference. It is blending and melding, seeking solitude and seeking companionship to understand one's many selves. Health is seeking out all the experiences of creation and turning them over and over, feeling their texture and multiple meanings. Health is expanding beyond one's singular state of consciousness to experience the ripples and waves of the universe. —*Jeanne Achterberg*

I like the analogy of truth as a mountain with all the different religions as different paths up the mountain. When you're down on the lower slopes, you may argue about the shape of the mountain. But the further up you go, the more you see that there's a convergence, that there are certain values that tend to be common to all traditions. —*Frances Vaughan*

Stanislav Grof (1988) has used the word "transpersonal" to describe transcending the customary boundaries of the personality by the consciousness. Transpersonal connectedness involves building a bridge connecting ourselves with the Source, which completes the circle and reconnects us to ourselves. It embraces the realization that, not only are we within the universe, but also, more importantly, the universe is within us. When we fully tap into our humanity, we tap into our divinity. This hypothesis is based on the fact that most people have had holy moments when they feel at one with something beyond themselves, whether they call it God, energy, the universe, consciousness, holy spirit, Qi, or prana.

One's image of "how the universe is" or "how things work" has powerful mplications as the blueprint for one's life—physically, emotionally, and piritually. It is perhaps the crucial image and the salient consciousness.

Seeds of Transpersonal Connectedness

Ornish (1990) writes:

> This experience of oneness, of an expanded self, has implications on both a cellular level and a global level. In this context, "Love your neighbor as yourself" is a description of truth, not simply a command. All religions, all forms of worship, all types of prayer or meditation are equally valid—there are many paths to the same ultimate truth. Our higher self is limited only by our capacity to experience it. (1990, p. 234)

Here we see the intimate linkage between intrapersonal, interpersonal, and transpersonal connectedness. If God is omnipresent, omniscient, and omnipotent, then we are not apart from God. The *New Testament* states, "Know that you are all Gods," which suggests that God is within, rather than a despot ruling from a throne in the sky. In connecting with the energies of the universe, we find the light or the peace *inside* ourselves rather than outside ourselves. It is in remembering who we really are that we connect with the higher power and are healed in the deepest sense.

Unfortunately, many religions—or people's interpretation of those faiths—are not the conduit to spirituality or inner peace that one would hope. Some even support chaos, guilt, fear, and judgment of others; they do not teach the love and safety of the universe. Yet, according to Einstein, this is perhaps the most important question we need to ask: "Is the universe a friendly place or not?" Although we have no theological axes to grind at GETTING WELL, we feel that believing the universe is a supportive and loving place is more conducive to healing than believing the opposite. Occasionally, our "highest common denominator of human spirituality" beliefs conflict with someone's religion. We're not out to change religious beliefs; however, we do like for people to look at the effect such beliefs have on their everyday life and their healing. We noted earlier that one's sense of self significantly affects how one experiences God or the universe—as friendly and supportive or as punitive and capricious. We have seen that working on the intrapersonal aspect of one's spirituality can have significant effects on the transpersonal spiritual experience, and may help us avoid uncomfortable confrontations in this sensitive area.

Helena had grown up in a strict religious household. "All my parents' social activities were within the church, and until I went to college, all my friends were church friends," she explained. "I followed *all* the rules. I'm really good at that, and I followed the rules to a T: I didn't go to bars, I tithed, I took care of everybody, I didn't have sex, I went to church, etc. I even handled my blood disorder with a certain sense of balance. But when I was told I had HIV last year, I was really angry. Here I am 25 years old, and I've followed the rules all my life, and now this happens to me! I realized then that my church had given me rules, but I really had no spiritual life; I really didn't have anything to fall back on. Now I know following the rules isn't what spirituality is all about." It was beautiful seeing Helena come to life as she began questioning original sin and getting in touch with her inner goodness and worthiness. She is even seeing the HIV as a vehicle for genuinely connecting with others, and she glows as she speaks of her relationship with herself and her spirituality.

Finding Meaning, Finding Hope

As we enter this session, for which we owe a deep debt to Ryan and Travis (1981), we explain to participants that, in general, much of the meaning we assign to our lives in this culture revolves around the roles we play or the jobs we hold. When changes happen in our lives—such as retirement, serious illness, children leaving home—a part of our identity is amputated and we often lose our reason for existing.

Looking within ourselves to find meaning is a difficult and sometimes foreign and frightening process, because we are so used to finding meaning in our "attachments." We tell participants that looking within for meaning means trusting their own intuitions and their own truths rather than trusting a book or an expert "out there." It also involves confronting the present moment rather than looking to the past or the future for meaning. In addition, looking within involves that scary process which is part and parcel of the transformational fantasy experience of directly encountering and making friends with death, pain, disease, and other "monsters" in one's life.

Socrates stated, "The unexamined life is not worth living." However, we sometimes become too serious, analytical, and left-brained about this process. I prefer Marcel's statement: "Life is a mystery to be lived, not a problem to be solved." In other words, to become enlightened, we may need to lighten up! And we surely need to find joy in the moment, to live as if we were going to live forever—or die tomorrow.

Of course, meaning comes from within and involves going to the source—our essential selves. This is not the easiest task, as we have seen, and at this point we ask participants to begin a list of internalized messages about themselves by making two columns in their notebooks and listing in the first column all the roles they play. In the second column, they list adjectives that describe the kind of people they are. (Allow five or six minutes for this and then process briefly.)

Resting on our successes of the past or living for happiness in the future are setups for disappointment. If we live only in the past or the future, we miss the place where life really is—in this very moment. To be in the here and now and experience true meaning, we need to do what we are doing right now, but do it with awareness. In other words, be who you are, but *be* it intensely. As sages have said, "The past is dead, the future is imaginary; happiness can only be in the eternal now moment."

The "here and nowness" of the moment is richly illustrated by the Zen story of a monk who was being chased by several tigers. He came to a halt at the edge of a cliff and looked back to see the tigers still in close pursuit. He saw a vine hanging over the cliff, and quickly eased himself over the edge and began crawling down the vine. He looked below and saw sharp and jagged rocks many feet beneath him. He looked up and saw the two tigers looking hungrily down at him *and* two mice that were gnawing away at the vine. At that moment, the monk saw a beautiful, red, juicy strawberry within his reach. He picked it and enjoyed the most splendid strawberry in his entire life. Although the monk was only minutes away from his death, he could enjoy the moment fully. Life continues to send us tigers *and* strawberries. We have a choice. We can enjoy the strawberries or we can paralyze our consciousness with fear over the tigers.

The poet Kahil Gibran writes that we are dying every moment, and in dying we are preparing the way for new life—that life and death are one. We experience dying at every point in our lives in small ways. Old cells die and are sloughed off and new cells replace them in order for the body to remain healthy. Old habits and beliefs must die before others can take their place if one's consciousness is to grow. Whenever there is a death, there is a rebirth, since death and life are one. (This is a good time to process this hypothesis with the group.)

As we become increasingly aware that death and birth reside in every situation, the experience of death becomes a more familiar transformation, one to be embraced and accepted. If each small death has within it a new life, why should the Big Death be any different? Abraham Lincoln once wrote, "Life is eternal, love is immortal, death is but a horizon, and a horizon is only the limit of our sight."

Our fears of death and the unknown frequently reveal quite a bit about how we hold back on living life to its fullest. At this point, it is helpful to ask participants to write down what they fear about death. We then take the time to look over these fears (incompleteness, hardship on family and friends, sense that a purpose in life has not been found, pain, etc.), and ask participants how these fears reflect the ways in which they are failing to live their life right now. In essence, we are looking for ways in which fears of death reflect one's real fear of life.

We then have an exercise in which participants list the 10 things they would take with them if they had to evacuate for a hurricane. After completing this list, we ask them to write down what will be important to them at the moment of their deaths. In other words, what would it take to allow them to die satisfied? And finally, we ask them to write their epitaphs — one sentence that sums up their lives, its meaning and purpose. After they are finished, we process what they have written.

Depending on the group, we may continue on with a "death rehearsal." Some group members may be so terrified of death at this time that the exercise is put off until later; nevertheless, it is important for each participant to experience it sometime during his or her tenure at GETTING WELL. Dr. Alexander Levitan, an oncologist in Minnesota who demonstrated this technique at the Fourth World Conference on Imagery in Minneapolis in 1991, has found it of immense comfort to "terminal" cancer patients. In turn, we have found the exercise to be a wonderful desensitization technique for those fearful of death and for those who wish to stop "trying not to die" and instead to start living.

The purpose of this imagery is not only to rehearse one's death, but also and more importantly, to stimulate a review of one's life and one's values. In a certain sense it is a metaphor for the death of old values, beliefs, and responses to life. Levitan used a light trance on the cancer patient with whom he demonstrated this technique; however, simple relaxation is quite adequate. Here is the exercise we use at GETTING WELL:

Sit comfortably and let your body and mind relax. . . . At some point in the distant future when your own death is inevitable . . . you may realize that death is close at hand. . . . You are not in pain; . . . however, you realize that you are moving toward death. . . . See this scene as clearly as you can and in as much detail as is possible. . . . You may wish to experience whatever physical deterioration has occurred . . . and how you feel about dying. . . . What will you lose by dying? . . . Explore this scene and all the feelings you have about dying (*long pause*). Now see yourself on the day of your death. . . . What is the day like? . . . What do you do? (*long pause*) And as you lie on your death bed, who is there? . . . Who do you wish to be there? . . . How do they feel about your dying? . . . What do you say to each other? . . . Is there someone special with whom you have a long conversation? . . . Explore this scene thoroughly (*three- to four-minute pause*).

Now see yourself going through the death process and see the moment of your death. . . . What is it like? . . . What happens? (*three- to four-minute pause*) Imagine your wake and your funeral or memorial service. . . . Who is there? . . . What are they feeling? . . . What are they saying?

See what happened to your consciousness at the point of death. . . . Where does it go? . . . If it is appropriate, follow your energy out into the universe where it has its source . . . review your life in detail with the "Karmic Board of Review." What were you pleased with about your life? . . . What would you have chosen to do differently? . . . What emotional baggage or impaired relationships do you still have? (*four-minute pause*)

Now, imagine you have the opportunity to come back to a new life. . . . What would you like it to be like? . . . What changes would you make? . . . What do you want to accomplish in your new life? . . . What would be important to you? (*long pause*)

When you get ready to come back, do so—feeling alert, relaxed, and at peace.

The exercise is then processed with the group.

The Transformative Power of Grief

John Schneider has said,

> We can experience transformation in many ways. Some choose to undertake the transformative journey, while others are thrust into transformation by events which challenge, even threaten their very lives. It is my belief that all of us are frequently presented with opportunities for growth, by choice or not, and that one of the most universal is the process of loss and grief. How this can be seen as an opportunity for growth, rather than a tragedy of living, comes from understanding the role of loss throughout life, the transformative potential of grief, and the nature of the grieving process. (1989a)

Not only has Schneider been active in research on the effect of imagery on components of the immune system, but his psychotherapy practice has also involved people with various grief issues. His idea that the grieving process can be transformative has brought new meaning to those faced with the loss of a spouse, a life-challenging diagnosis, or the death of a dream. It is important that participants understand that life is full of losses, both natural losses such as losing the comforts of the womb, growing up, aging, and dying, and developmentally disruptive losses such as life-threatening illness, divorce, rape, and abuse as a child. They must also understand that we have a choice in how we handle these losses, after the initial grief is over. We can plunge ourselves into grief or we can reassess our loss and discover an inner richness we never appreciated before. The latter course means we must totally rethink our ways of being; it means being empowered by our roles and rules rather than being *locked in* by them. As Schneider says, "We can transform by finding strength in acknowledging our weaknesses instead of denying them, discovering new realms of consciousness, and rediscovering innocence through renewal and forgiveness." (1989a, p. 28)

Schneider describes the first phase of grief as discovering what is lost and how bad that loss is. As we explain to our participants, at this point in the process, we need to honor our defenses' protection. However, we may wish to be more open to those defenses which conserve our energy, such as standing apart from everyday life, engaging in pastimes, or escaping through dreams. Defenses that prevent one from going inward, such as trying harder, being optimistic, and keeping busy, may be ways of coping that deplete energy. Despite the use of such defenses, the reality of the loss eventually catches up and one is faced with the choice of giving up or going on to the next phase. (At this point we may ask for examples from people's lives of how they have handled the initial stage of loss.)

The second phase is comprised of discovering what is left, allowing the meaningful aspects of what remains in one's own life to be recognized, remembered, and validated. This is a time of finding ways to contain the loss rather than limiting one's awareness of it. Phase two may involve remembering the way things were and finding ways to rebuild what was destroyed. And it may be the time during which one makes the choice of seeking to discover ways to grow from one's losses or of simply accepting and adjusting to them.

In the third phase, there is a shift from a focus on limits to an exploration of opportunities. Included in this phase is discovering life's potential after accepting the reality of the loss and the limits on what one has left. There may be some rites of passage to undergo—such as saying goodbye or relinquishing the security of old beliefs—as tokens of a commitment to growth. This may be a point at which, as Schneider states, "Grief can help us shift from seeing ourselves as the center of the universe to seeing the universe as the center of who and where we are" (1989a, p. 31).

As we process these ideas with the group, participants often ask us how people find the strength and courage to go through their grief and eventually transform loss into creative life experiences. Our answer is they learn to accept every consequence of living and dying, including birth, change, and death, as universals of our earthly existence. We explain that those in the grieving process need to acknowledge all aspects of what living fully means: loss, joy, change, laughter, success, failure, love, anger, guilt, betrayal, and good health, as well as periods of pain and illness. Living means having *all* the resources of our minds, bodies, and spirits working together to strengthen our being. After these discussions, we ask participants to write in their journals about how they can use the losses that brought them to GETTING WELL to transform their lives.

Trusting the Universe, the Principle of Abundance

The didactic portion of this session presents the idea that the universe is a concept of abundance, yet most of us are trained in the principles of scarcity: There's not enough of everything to go around, whether it's money, land, men, women, jobs, love, esteem, praise, or time. When we live with this idea of scarcity, we constantly struggle to get "our share" of whatever it is. When we feel we don't have enough, we usually find it to be true that we do not get our share. And when the glass of water appears to be "half empty," we put our energy and power into filling it up rather than appreciating the abundance and prosperity that are already there.

As participants make shifts to seeing the world from the perspective of eternity and to being within themselves rather than being in the world, one of their main tasks is to release their attachments to scarcity and transcend the consciousness of lack. In other words, they have to learn that a scarcity consciousness represents a lack of trust in the universe and a lack of belief in oneself as deserving. Not surprisingly, there is a great deal of resistance to this principle, since it requires one to risk trusting the universe, to let go of limitations or lacks which may represent a certain comfort, and to think of the universe as endlessly abundant and perfect. Resistance to this abundance principle may represent the fear of becoming a homeless itinerant if we allow the line between work and play to dissolve and follow happiness without guilt.

Our homily continues with the idea that abundance is not something fabricated or manufactured, but rather something one connects with or tunes into. This may seem paradoxical to most participants. We explain this by saying that the acceptance of the universe (abundance) harks back to one's self-image and self-worth, as well as to what one believes he or she deserves and thinks is available. Our enculturation puts limits on what we're "allowed" to think is available, particularly if we were deprived in childhood. Most of us have been "culturally abused" by a society that teaches us not to be demanding or want more than our "share" and to do what we *should* do rather than what we want to do. (This may be a good time to process the hypothesis just presented with the group.)

As we so often hear from participants, the concept of trusting the universe and accepting abundance means going against all our beliefs in our limitations. Accepting the concept means accepting oneself as worthy and deserving of all the good that is out there. It means loving what you are doing and doing what you love—across the board—with the faith that in doing so you are only empowering yourself rather than depriving someone else. Only our sense of limitation and fears of scarcity keep us from actually choosing as our life's work what we want to do. We try to impress upon participants that, as they simplify their lives and focus on what they truly love to do, their obligations and expenditures will lessen dramatically, and they will move into a new consciousness of needs.

Rick was a successful 33-year-old salesman for a large corporation when he entered GETTING WELL because his physicians were unable to control his life-threatening cryptococcal meningitis. Although his job was extremely stressful and not satisfying at deeper levels, Rick was a good company man and even worried about the time he was taking from his work to be in the program. However, we saw profound changes in him as he began his inner journey.

As his trust in himself and the universe increased with meditation and other commitments to letting go, his obsession with material comforts began to dissolve, his blood work showed dramatic changes, and his direction in life began to shift. A sense of peace and connectedness seemed to surround him. A few weeks after the program he announced in the graduate group that he was preparing to quit his job—training someone to take his place and working through loose ends with his employers—and planning to go back to school (in counseling) in the fall.

"I have to live my life for what is important to me," he told the group. "I've sometimes betrayed myself just to have money coming in, and I guess I've given up a lot of me just out of fear of there not being enough money. My brush with death made me realize how important doing what I really want to do is. There's a part of me that's really scared about what I'm doing, but another big part that is yelling 'right on!' I am trusting the universe to provide what I truly need." Rick has since eased out of his job, married a woman supportive of his direction, enrolled in school, and worked part-time with GETTING WELL seeking foundation funding and teaching a class in meditation. He's doing what he really wants to, and he hasn't missed a meal yet!

Of course, we don't have to change whatever we are doing as our job or work; instead we can learn to love whatever we are doing. A Zen adage states, "Before enlightenment, chopping wood, carrying water. After enlightenment, chopping wood, carrying water." Being enlightened has little to do with what your behavior is or what you are doing, but everything to do with how you view those activities. Frequently, one may decide to continue with a less-than-perfect job in order to fund his or her "real" life work. I believe it is quite important to restate or relabel that job in terms of abundance: "I love my work because it allows me to do what I wish in life," or "My present job gives me an arena in which I can help people."

We want our participants to understand that the sense of abundance comes from remembering that when we're tempted to be stingy and give less is actually the time to give more. It involves seeing what we like and value in others rather than seeing their limitations or what we don't like about them. Opening ourselves to abundance means seeing everything in our lives in positive terms—even translating those things we abhor into positive statements. And, above all, bringing abundance into our lives means trusting the universe and its ability to provide all things for all of us if we only let go and flow with it. When one can love what the universe presents rather than demand that the universe present what one loves, one taps into the abundance available to everyone. (Although the session in which we present this material is heavily didactic, there is usually a great deal of discussion of these hypotheses.)

To conclude this session, we ask the participants to devise an affirmation involving abundance, using as many of the senses as possible and colorful, vivid words to describe their desired result. After participants assertively state their individual affirmations, we suggest they repeat the affirmation 10 times before they go to sleep, every night for a week.

Towards Unity in Diversity

In this lesson, we explain to participants the ways in which all good Americans are trained in individualism, and how we are taught that our uniqueness is the essence of our humanity. We discuss how the labels we give ourselves—male, female, black, white, fat, skinny—become the ways in which we define ourselves *and* the ways in which we limit ourselves.

The "syllabus" for this lesson (as is true for most high-level awareness sessions) provides much more information than one could include in an hour's time. I typically use the prepared material until a really good interactive discussion takes hold, then let the group take it from there.

Modern science states that there are microcosms within microcosms within macrocosms—that the structure of the atom reflects the structure of the celestial universe, that each of us as individuals is a mere cell in the body of the planet, and that within each of us are universes as vast as the heavens. I am intrigued by the analogy of our being like flies on the ceiling of the Sistine Chapel, living out our lives in the dun-colored "ugliness" of a background that highlights a toenail. It is not until we let go of our ego territory and view the ceiling, as Spinoza exhorts us, *sub specie aeternitas* (under the aspect of eternity), that we are able to see the angels, the gods, the full creation.

We resist seeing the unity of our existence because we have been trained otherwise, because it's easier to think in terms of boundaries where others have drawn the lines, and because defending our separateness gives us the opportunity to blame others or circumstances for what is not in our lives. Many of our culture's institutions, such as the military-industrial complex, churches, and businesses that separate us into superior/inferior categories, have a profitable stake in our keeping our "individuality" or separateness. But the fact is that anything that promotes our separateness diminishes our healing. For example, if I were a kidney cell in this body of humanity and decided I wanted to be on my own and not have anything to do with blood cells, liver cells, or epithelial cells, I wouldn't last very long. My full healthy function exists in the context of the wholeness of the body in which I am a kidney cell. (Let the group discuss these concepts before continuing.)

A *Course in Miracles* purports that this is a perfect universe. Just as the atom is perfection in its structure and functioning, the macrocosm is perfection in its unfolding. When we are able to experience the universe in its fullness, it is like viewing the Sistine Chapel from a distance — the dun-colored space that highlights the toenail becomes a part of the perfection. (This is a really tough concept to understand, much less accept, for most participants. As a result, there is usually a long group discussion at this point. This may be a time for the facilitator to reiterate that these hypotheses are not necessarily advocated by the program but are interesting dishes on our conceptual smorgasbord. The ideas may be tried on for size as possible helpful ways of reinterpreting one's existence and meaning. We encourage participants to discard concepts if they do not work.)

A corollary of the concept of a perfect universe is that we are already masterpieces, and we are just clearing away the garbage that obscures our perfection. The "garbage" is the blocks we have invented to avoid unity, peace, love, and joy. Carol Howe (1993), a gifted teacher of the *Course*, suggests that if we truly wanted peace and joy, we would have them. But we are faced with a dilemma: All the attributes we want, such as peace and joy, are a part of the unified state. And although we say we want the attributes of oneness, we still want to remain individuals. We have set up our agendas so that unity and individualism are mutually exclusive rather than a beautifully cooked stew where each ingredient maintains a certain distinction within the unity of the stew. Carol maintains that this agenda of separate identity, the ego, separates us not only from others, but also from ourselves and from the forces of creation.

We maintain this separation out of fear of oneness and love, and we perpetuate the conflict necessary to maintain our personal agenda of separateness. We invent fear to avoid being the person we were created, and we work hard to convince ourselves that the invention is better than the creation. But perhaps the greatest illusion that keeps us from unity is the idea that the outside world creates our inner experience. With this in mind, we ask participants to consider the possibility that it is our inner experience that "creates" the outside world. Experiencing unity involves the outer world's coming into sync with the inner experience, which means letting go of our "ego entanglements." This in turn elicits the fear of no longer being an "individual," the fear of death, and the fear of being absorbed. The lesson here is that we should not be afraid of the terror, for fear and loss are artifacts that we have invented, and the thing we have invented is not a real part of us. (Process this with the group.)

Many of the teachings of the *Course* may seem esoteric, and some controversial (e.g.,"There are no accidents"), yet a number of participants have found them helpful in dealing with the misery they are experiencing and in making a 180-degree turn in how they view their lives. We strongly urge members to take several days to look at the universe through these new "glasses" before discarding the somewhat strange and difficult hypotheses we have presented.

To assist them we suggest a number of exercises. For example, we propose that participants suspend all thoughts of separateness for an hour; during that time, they should regard everyone they meet as connected to them in an invisible way. At the same time, they are to see themselves sharing something with everyone they meet or even read about in the newspaper. Another exercise involves making a concerted effort to send out love in response to hate (following the teachings of Christ, Gandhi, and other great spiritual leaders), with the idea that the more one sends out harmony, forgiveness, and love to others, regardless of their behavior, the more one exists in unity. In yet another exercise, the participant spends some time fully experiencing the perfection of all things even (*especially*) in moments of anger or suffering, remembering that the moment of suffering is often the moment of awakening.

It is also challenging for participants to come up with situations in which they feel that the *Course* or the principle of unity does *not* work. This usually provides a thought-provoking ending to a stimulating hour, and additionally, leads to further foment of ideas. And that is really what high-level awareness is all about.

Lessons for the Author/Clinician

I have found many of the concepts in A *Course in Miracles* to be not only intriguing but also quite pragmatic. Whenever situations and people become difficult in my "illusions," I like to run the idea of the perfection of the universe and all of its beings through my "computer." Of course, it is sometimes difficult to see perfection in the vagaries of an insurance company, the rigidity of a physician, or the truculence of a hospital administrator; nonetheless, seeing the situation under the aspect of eternity usually gives me a good laugh if not the insight needed to let go of the need to control the situation. I also seem to be developing the *habit* of seeing myself and others as perfect just the way we are, rather than seeing us with just the occasional glimpse of that perfection. I am certainly no paragon, and this is not about perfection; but this shift in my perceptions has decidedly reduced my struggles with the world and increased my peace of mind, inner locus of control, and effectiveness for GW's causes.

The concomitant idea of the choice of love or fear as one's reaction to any situation is a fascinating one for me. What a powerful choice that gives me in circumstances that before seemed impossible to handle or gave me no choice but fear in processing them. Of course, I don't always choose love—sometimes anger or fear is how I want to feel—but I *do* have the choice.

15

Therapeutic Touch: Transpersonal Imagery and Energy

We could imagine a science based on the assumption that we contact reality in two ways: First is through physical sense data which form the basis of normal science. Second is through a deep "inner knowing" in an intuitive, aesthetic, spiritual, noetic, and mystical sense. — *Willis W. Harmon*

The healer does not "do" or give something to the healee; instead he helps him come home to the All, to the One, to the way of "unity" with the universe, and in this "meeting" becomes more complete, and this in itself is healing. In Arthur Koestler's words: "There is no sharp dividing line between self-repair and self-realization." — *Lawrence LeShan*

Healing, once in progress, seems to take on a life of its own. The need to heal seems to well up from a depth little known to the healer and to progress with a surety of purpose that can elicit a sense of awe. The healer is as a spectator watching the patterning of vital energies taking place, forced to realize that there is an intelligent process at work. — *Dolores Krieger*

Therapeutic touch (TT) is a technique whereby energy is transmitted from one person to another for the purpose of healing. In a sense, it goes beyond merely relieving pain or helping lungs to clear. It brings everything together. Unlike laying-on-of-hands, therapeutic touch doesn't have a religious context, nor does it depend on the faith of a client for its effects (Krieger, 1987). In my mind, TT is tapping into the wholeness and unity of the universe and becoming attuned to the energies of the universe (or God or the One, as you please), in which lies true healing of the body, mind, and spirit.

As an undergraduate in philosophy, I was taken with Henri Bergson's concept of *élan vital*, the life force, consciousness or flow of the universe. When one tries to analyze the force, the very investigation cuts across the flow and in a certain sense blocks the flow of the *élan*. The "highest good"

251

is being a part of the flow and at one with the purpose and intention of the force—being centered and in the moment. Therapeutic touch creates that experience for me, and participants have described this felt sense in similar terms. Letting the universe flow through oneself while at the same time flowing through the universe with the intention of healing and oneness without the parameters of time or space epitomizes the TT encounter. With its focus on intention, therapeutic touch recognizes, as do many modern physicists, that consciousness is the most powerful force in the universe. And intention is but focused consciousness.

A more recent fascination of mine is Michael Talbot's stunning book, *The Holographic Universe* (1991), which sets forth the theories of David Bohm, Karl Pribram and other scientists who have expanded on Einstein's theory of the continuity of the space-time continuum. Bohm suggests the possibility that the universe is holographic in nature, meaning that *everything* in the universe is part of a continuum, everything is an extension of everything else, and we are not merely made of the same thing, we *are* the same thing. He further asserts that consciousness is present in all matter, and every cell in our body enfolds the entire cosmos, as does every leaf and every raindrop. With these assumptions of the new physics, therapeutic touch and other transpersonal phenomena assume a "normalcy" not possible under the premises of Newtonian-Cartesian physics, which has determined the world view of most of us in the Western world.

I bought Dr. Dolores Krieger's book, *The Therapeutic Touch* (1979), at a discount store a month or so before we admitted our first patient to GET-TING WELL in 1987. It lay around unread until several weeks after the program started, when I devoured it from cover to cover. In it I learned that, in essence, TT involves directing energy in a specific manner from the excess store of energies of a healthy person to someone who is having problems with the balance and flow of his or hers, and directing energies from one place to another within the body of the healee. By the statement, "We do not stop at our skin," Krieger means that people are energy fields. The energy field is the fundamental unit of a living system, and as Einstein indicates, the physical is just one manifestation of that energy. TT assumes (much as Qi Gong does) that sickness or pain is merely an imbalance or blockage in the energy field, and that people are open systems engaged in continuous interaction with the environment. Therefore, when one person utilizes his or her intent to heal another, the energy transfer takes place, stimulating healing in the other person.

I was most impressed by Dr. Krieger's credentials (including a Ph.D. in nursing and a professorship at New York University), and I felt the techniques to be intuitively compelling; however, I had no idea how to get started. As I turned the last page of the book, I received a call from a registered nurse with breast cancer who was interested in coming into the program. I suggested a time for a consultation, which did not suit her schedule since she would be assisting at a workshop on therapeutic touch! Twenty-four hours later, I was sitting in a "Light Touch" workshop presented by Judie Chiappone, a registered nurse, licensed massage therapist, gifted teacher, and student of Dolores Krieger's. Judie, who has since become a colleague, a trainer for my staff, and a good friend, said, "Dee, it was so much fun to watch you. You started the day with your arms crossed, a true skeptic. And as the day went on, you began to have a sense of your own energy and the energy of others. Then I saw you at the end of the day just really flowing with it! *That* was quite a transformation!" (And what synchronicity!)

Judie's workshop gave me the courage to present TT to our patients. Although I was rough around the edges, I remembered that it was intention, not technique, that made the difference. Even on that first day, wonderful things happened: pain disappeared, breathing became free, and everyone in the group experienced a mysterious connectedness that was healing in itself.

Although therapeutic touch is the specific technique the GETTING WELL program has employed, there are many body/energy techniques which are probably as effective as TT and have similar underlying philosophies (e.g., Reiki, polarity, Shiatsu, and massage). Given the idea that our intelligence and consciousness are in all parts of our bodies, I feel that some energy work needs to be included in a balanced program. What it is doesn't seem to matter.

Therapeutic Touch and Qi Gong

In 1988, I was a member of a delegation of behavioral medicine specialists who went to the People's Republic of China for the purpose of exchanging ideas and scientific information with their physicians. Pat Norris, the leader of our delegation, was particularly interested in energy medicine and made it possible for us to attend a number of meetings and demonstrations by Qi Gong masters. The masters we met were typically trained in traditional Chinese medicine and had another six years of training in Qi Gong, the art and practice of moving the Qi (life energy) throughout one's body (internal Qi Gong), emanating the energy from the body, and influencing beings or objects outside oneself (external Qi Gong). In my early morning walks, I saw thousands of Chinese in the parks and public squares practicing internal Qi Gong, which is analogous to meditation with movements. We heard numerous testimonies of patients for whom internal Qi Gong had effected cures from cancer, hypertension, heart disease, and even baldness; however, my real fascination was with the external Qi Gong of the masters.

Our first encounter with a Qi Gong master was at the Mental Hospital in Beijing. This gentle and gracious being brought forth what looked like a thick extension cord with a plug at one end and two loose wires where a receptacle would be. He inserted it into an electrical outlet (220-volt current), and put the ends of the wire to a light bulb, which cooperatively lit up. Then, taking the live wires in one hand, he used his fingers to light the bulb. He then motioned for one person to hold his other hand and to join hands with other people in the room. I was about the seventh "link" but could distinctly feel the electrical current coming through the human chain. The master was acting as a transformer or a rheostat for the powerful electrical current, which would have killed an untrained person.

The Qi Gong master had a number of us sit in a chair, one at a time, while he touched his fingertips (his own energy augmented by the electrical current) at various places on each person's body. It was a most peculiar sensation. When he touched my biceps my whole arm involuntarily jerked up, and when his fingers touched my forehead in the area of my "third eye," an immediate, very specific, color image appeared to me. Other volunteers experienced a similar "vision," and a couple of research-hungry clinical psychologists on our team had us document our experience with color drawings of our images, all of which were remarkably similar. I can still see the green and yellow grid which I experienced in such detail—a surprise to me since I do not consider myself a "good" visualizer.

That afternoon, we visited the College of Traditional Medicine in Beijing, where they are attempting to use Western research methodology to document the effectiveness of Qi Gong, acupuncture, medicinal herbs, and other ingredients of Chinese medicine. We saw Faraday chambers for measuring the energy of Qi, giant electron microscopes to examine herbs, and banks of lab rats with implanted cancerous tumors that the Qi Gong masters would dissolve with their powerful technique called "pointing," which involves intending energy through the index finger for the purpose of healing.

At a scientific exchange session later that afternoon at the Beijing College of Traditional Medicine, the *pièce de résistance* was a demonstration by a physician/Qi Gong master. The master first brought in and discussed the case of a boy with Cushing's syndrome whose hypertension (200/120) had been lowered to normal over a period of several weeks using external Qi Gong techniques such as pointing. His meticulously kept records were shown to the audience. Then the Qi Gong master held a 100-capsule bottle obtained by the college's chief physician, fresh from the pharmacy with a wax seal over its cork closure. The Qi Gong master held the bottle in his hand, did some breathing exercises, looked at the bottle, and gently tapped its bottom. I saw something that looked like an electrical flash, and the master pointed to a member of our delegation at the other end of the

25-foot conference table and (in translation) said, "Look in your pocket." She had no pocket in her clothes, but found in a pocket in her purse a capsule that had not been there earlier. Our leader, Dr. Norris, took the wax seal and cork from the original bottle of pills and counted out 99 capsules; the matching pill from the delegate's purse was number 100.

One might think this was an elaborate parlor trick; however, one must remember that this demonstration occurred within a community of elite Chinese physicians and scientists who would have everything to lose from perpetrating a hoax. (I remember my reaction that night: "How in the world can I believably tell people back home about this?" Because much of what we saw was so incredible, I feel glad that we have videotape documentation of the many exceptional events we experienced in China, although the tapes give only a pallid representation of the actual encounters.)

Even though their equipment was far from sophisticated, the Chinese scientists were rapidly realizing the need for control groups and for replication of results and other acknowledgment of scientific method in order to convince Western scientists and physicians of the power of energy medicine. For example, Dr. Feng of Beijing has published articles documenting replications of an experiment wherein Qi Gong masters have increased or decreased cell growth in a variety of bacteria, and the professor involved with the masters' decreasing the size of implanted tumors in rats assured us that the study had been replicated (with controls) several times.

In Nanjing, Pat Norris asked me to make one of the presentations to physicians and professors at the University Hospital. It was a rather excruciating experience (particularly with my problems in needing to be understood) to have every phrase of my talk translated with little recourse to "what I really meant." For example, I made a statement comparing Therapeutic Touch to Qi Gong, suggesting that both tapped into the human potential with which we are all born and which is a natural expression of our humanity. As this was translated, there was a buzz in the room, and I realized I had transgressed woefully into a sacrosanct area. Although Pat Norris helped pull things back together, I realized how reluctant the Chinese were to part with the "secrets" of Qi Gong or to have its miracles made a part of common humanhood. (Despite their feelings, however, a number of research studies support the hypothesis that the more experienced the healer, the more powerful the "healing" effect.)

My further experiences in China reinforced the sense of cabalistic mystery about the powers of Qi, and although the people we met were among the most gracious and generous I have ever encountered, the enigmas and the total truth of Qi Gong seem to be a precious possession that may be wasted on the Western mind. David Eisenberg, M.D., a physician invited to study the medicine of China in 1979, has written one of the few books,

Encounters With Qi, which explore and elucidate in a scholarly and human way the excitement of Chinese medicine.

I believe that the Qi Gong masters as infants were no different from the rest of us humans. For whatever reason, they broke the bottle of limits which our cultures put us in, and now represent the exceptional expansion of a certain area of our potential. I also believe that TT is an analogous — if not identical — process.

Australian Aborigines and Transpersonal Phenomena

My husband and I spent the first year of our marriage in Australia. While he was living up to the demands of his Fulbright scholarship, I became interested in the art and culture of the Aborigines. It was not until we came back home, however, that I discovered the book, *Living Magic* (1956), by Ronald Rose, which described his scientific exploration of the transpersonal activities of these native people. Of course, Rose's interpersonal sensitivity did not allow laboratory-type corroboration of his observations; however, they truly were made with objectivity and rigor. He describes bone pointing, the method by which an Aborigine kills his human victim by pointing a bone at him (often without the victim's knowing this is being done). The same type of technique, with an entirely different intention, is used for healing. Rose also tells of regular, specific communication among distant tribe members through telepathy, as well as cures effected by "clever-men" who remove stones and sharp sticks from their patients' bodies without breaking the skin. These and others of Rose's observations gave credence to the fascinating stories the Aussies had told us about their indigenous people.

More recently, Dr. Marlo Morgan's book, *Mutant Message Downunder* (1991), describes this American woman's four-month, barefoot "walkabout" across Australia with a nomad tribe of Aborigines. She shares their remarkable healing powers, their telepathic communication with tribe members, their intuitive knowledge of the earth and sky, and their unity with the environment and the universe. One of the most striking observations is that the Aborigines carried no food (or much else) with them across incredibly barren deserts. They trusted the universe, and the universe always provided abundantly when time came to drink or eat (particularly if one liked worms).

The wisdom of this community, who *were* the people they were born to be, was a part of the fabric of their existence. Here are some examples from Morgan:

Healing has absolutely nothing to do with time; both healing and disease take place in an instant. (p. 83)

Dreams are the shadow of reality. (p. 100)

When thinking became flexible, joints became flexible, no pain, no more. (p. 102)

To be one does not mean we are all the same. Each being is unique. No two occupy the same space. As the leaf needs all the parts for completion, so each spirit has its special place. People can try to maneuver, but in the end, each will return to the right place. Some of us seek a straight path, while others enjoy the weariness of making circles. (p. 109)

Be water. When you can be water you will find water. (p. 118)

I was particularly taken by the unmitigated love this tribe had for the earth and its creatures, as well as by the unqualified respect it had for the thoughts, ideas, and paths of other humans.

Despite a rigorous lifestyle, these people have a long lifespan, with heart disease, hypertension, cancer, diabetes, and other "diseases of civilization" unknown in their indigenous, at-one-with-nature setting. However, when the Aborigines move into the civilized world of the white man and take up the trappings of disconnectedness, these illnesses and conditions become rampant among them.

It is interesting to note the similarities in "energy work" across these vastly different cultures. Although "bone pointing" in the Aboriginal culture could be a deadly practice, similar pointing techniques were used for spectacular healing events. Chinese traditional medicine uses "pointing" (of fingers) for intensive healing effects very similar to therapeutic touch's use of "ultrasound" (focusing energy in the fingertips for intensive healing). In all of these techniques, the essential element seems to be the focusing of the consciousness or intention.

Research on Transpersonal Imagery and Intention for Healing

Dolores Krieger (1979) suggests that *prana* (vital energy) is overabundant in the healthy person, while the ill person has a deficit of prana. Prana can be activated by will and transferred to another person. Krieger saw a relationship between prana and the oxygen molecule, and used hemoglobin as a variable to measure the effects of TT. For example, in three studies she was able to demonstrate that the level of hemoglobin increased significantly in groups that were treated with therapeutic touch.

I was most impressed with the early use of therapeutic touch by Krieger trainees in New York City neonatal units. The nurses knew the babies needed touch to survive, yet the tubes and isolettes necessary to keep the infants alive militated against touch. So the nurses intended energy with their hands through the isolettes several times daily. Surprisingly, many of the infants who were not expected to survive not only survived but also thrived and grew into healthy adulthood.

In a videotape produced by the Hartley Film Foundation, *The Thera-peutic Touch: Healing in the New Age*, Krieger relates a study in which a healer, Oscar Estebany, energized water. This water was given to half of a group of plants while a control group received tap water. The plants that received the healer-encrgized water had a significant increase in chloro-phyll, suggesting an enhancement of their cellular metabolism — just as an increase in hemoglobin indicates the same process in animals. On the same tape Krieger shows yet another controlled experiment using another healer, who significantly increases the activity of enzymes through her intention in the beaker she holds, as compared to the beaker with no intervention. Krieger herself has studied the change in hematocrit ratio using therapeutic touch in controlled, replicated studies reported in *Living the Therapeutic Touch*. The hemoglobin values consistently increased with TT in the experimental group, and just as consistently showed no change in the control group.

The International Society for the Study of Subtle Energies and Energy Medicine, formed a few years ago by scientists such as Elmer Green, Ph.D., has begun to garner some interesting studies on TT, Qi Gong, and the measurable power of consciousness on the physical state.

Dr. Randolf Byrd (1988) has studied the effects of intercessory prayer on heart patients in San Francisco General Hospital's cardiac care unit. Byrd's research was a randomized, double-blind, controlled, prospective study involving nearly 400 patients over a six-month period. As patients entered the CCU, they were randomly allocated to one of two groups. One hundred ninety-two were assigned to the group being prayed for by prayer groups up to 300 miles away, and 201 patients were in the control group, which was not remembered in prayer. For each patient in the test group five to seven people in various locations were aware of his or her name and condition and praying. The prayed-for group turned out to be five times less likely to require antibiotics, and three and a half times less likely to develop pulmonary edema; its members required no artificial airways (while 12 of the unremembered group did), and although this is not statistically significant, fewer patients in the prayed-for group died.

I interpret this study as a paean to the power of intention, seeing prayer as positively intended "energy." To me this is analogous to the focused consciousness or positive intention we use in therapeutic touch in a "secu-lar" sense.

In *Recovering the Soul: A Scientific and Spiritual Search*, Larry Dossey, an internal medicine specialist, has explored the work of Spindrift, a unique research organization in Salem, Oregon. Their basic assumption is that all humans, as well as other living beings, have divine characteristics as a result of their unity with God. Spindrift has looked at the questions of the reality of spiritual healing and the effects of prayer — whether or not prayer "works." They have asked if there is an effect that can be measured, and whether that effect can be reproduced. One trial to test the effects of prayer involved the germination of rye seeds, which were divided into two groups equal in number. The seeds were placed in a shallow container, with a string dividing side A from side B. The seeds on one side were prayed for by a healer, while the seeds on the other side were not. Then the rye shoots (germinated seeds) were counted. Consistently, there were significantly more shoots in the prayed-for group than in the control group.

Another experiment involved rye seeds stressed by the addition of salt water, with the balance of the seeds receiving no salt water. The results of the prayer under these conditions were even more powerful, with the ratio of the prayed-for shoots to the control sprouts increasing sharply. As the stress (salt water) put upon the rye seeds increased in subsequent studies, the prayer became more effective. Actually, I am not surprised by this, for in working with people we have consistently seen the most prodigious effects of therapeutic touch when people are in the worst shape, with pain or other physical or *emotional* conditions. Although the person who is not dealing with profound stressors certainly benefits from the positive intention, across the board the effects are far less dramatic than those resulting from intervention in more stressful challenges.

Another interesting result of the Spindrift studies involves the effectiveness of directed prayer versus undirected prayer. Directed prayer is analogous to specific imagery; a specific outcome is intended, such as a tumor shrinking or pain disappearing. In the seed germination experiments, the direction was praying for the seeds to sprout. Undirected prayer involves an open-ended, "Thy will be done" approach that does not involve the image of any specific outcome. Dossey observes that the Spindrift experiments are unequivocal in that the undirected prayer appeared quantitatively much more efficacious — up to twice as effective as directed prayer. This certainly has powerful implications in terms of directed imagery or therapeutic touch. The physical processes involved are so complex that when imaging a specific healing process, it is difficult to know what kinds of cells to increase or which tissues need more or less blood. Sometimes imaging or praying for a certain result may even be counterproductive, based on rapidly changing medical knowledge. Perhaps directed images or prayers miss the whole point of "healing" — of becoming one with an intelligent, loving, aware universe. In other words, it is very easy to become so obsessed with some tiny piece of the puzzle that we miss the entirety of the picture.

In his keynote talk at the 1990 National Institute for the Clinical Application of Behavioral Medicine, Larry Dossey told of a study comparing the effects of a subject's using imagery on himself or herself to the effects of a healer imaging or intending the same outcomes for the subject (without the subject's knowledge). The results were equal, with the healer's intention being slightly more effective (but, statistically speaking, not significantly more so) than the subject's intention. This certainly has splendid implications for therapeutic touch and "white lighting," which is intending love or healing energy to someone at a distance with or without his or her knowledge. Not only does it prove our energy field extends beyond our skin, but it also shows that our thoughts and intentions extend powerfully beyond our brains.

Over a decade ago at a hospital inservice a Transcendental Meditation (TM) practitioner told us about a study from TM literature. A city in which over 1 percent of the inhabitants actively use meditation was compared to a town of equal size in which less than 1 percent of the population meditated (Borland & Landrith, 1973). As it turned out, people in the "meditation" city committed only half the violent crimes committed by those in the "non-meditating" city. These data reflect the thrust of the video, *The Hundredth Monkey*, which is based on the suppositions of Ken Keyes' book of the same name. A group of scientists observing a tribe of macaque monkeys on a remote island off Japan threw sweet potato slices on the ground for the monkeys to eat. The macaques disliked the dirt that stuck to the slices, and finally, one of them found it could wash the slices and make them more palatable. Monkeys observed and repeated the behavior of the model and taught others. When the approximately hundredth monkey caught on to this trick, *all* the many hundreds of monkeys on the island started practicing the new behavior before nightfall, *without having observed or learned from any of the original 100 monkeys*. At virtually the same moment, whole tribes of the same species of monkeys on islands hundreds of miles away started practicing the behavior without a teacher or model.

Dr. Rupert Sheldrake (1989) of Cambridge University conceptualizes the world as a great learning system. When the consciousness reaches a critical point within this invisible organizing force (whether it is the hundredth monkey or the person who breaks the 1-percent barrier in the crime-ridden city), the knowledge or consciousness becomes a part of everyone. For example, when rats learn a new trick, rats all over the world are more likely to learn the trick much more easily than the original student rats. The idea that the contents of our minds and consciousness are deposited in a giant information bank and have an impact far beyond our daily contacts is exciting and powerful to most participants. The thought that the ability to heal the world has its seed within each of us is a powerful antidote to the helplessness many feel in the face of the ponderous problems of the world. That one can be the hundredth monkey, that one may be the individual critical to shifting the consciousness of one's family, city, country, or planet, is a mighty epiphany.

Barbara Ann Brennan, at one time a physicist with the space program, has produced a magnificent volume, *Hands of Light* (1988), which explores all aspects of the human energy field, from its historical/scientific base and its relationship to psychodynamics to issues of increasing one's perceptual range and looking deeply into the process of spiritual healing. Brennan's strong background in physics and aeroscience gives credence to her examination and exegesis of some of the more esoteric healing paths. *Hands of Light* is essential reading for anyone wishing to do energy work of any sort and is a wonderful resource for facilitators and participants who wish to use therapeutic touch as a springboard for further study of energy fields and thought fields, or for exploration of other transpersonal phenomena.

Michael Talbot's book, *The Holographic Universe* (1991), is an excellent compendium of the research that has been done in the field of transpersonal/paranormal phenomena, from telepathy, psychokinesis, and ESP to near-death experiences, imagery, and PNI. Moreover, Talbot has placed transpersonal experiences within the context of a scientific image of the universe which validates and embraces them.

The fine work of Barbara Ann Brennan, Dolores Krieger, Karl Pribam, Larry Dossey, Michael Talbot, David Bohm, and others simply has not achieved acceptance in the scientific community commensurate with the quality of the research these people have done. As Talbot (1991) writes (concerning the suppression of data on the paranormal), "Science is not prejudice free . . . one reason is science is not always as objective as we would like to believe. We view scientists with a bit of awe, and when they tell us something, we are convinced it must be true. We forget they are only human and subject to the same religious, philosophical, and cultural prejudices as the rest of us" (p. 6). He indicates that many of civilization's greatest insights and advances have at first been greeted with passionate denial. "We are addicted to our beliefs and we *do* act like addicts when someone tries to wrest from us the powerful opium of our dogmas. And since Western science has devoted several centuries to not believing in the paranormal, it is not going to surrender its addiction lightly" (pp. 6–7).

Teaching Therapeutic Touch to Participants

Therapeutic touch seems frankly "weird" to many of our participants, and others are concerned that this technique, which has spiritual overtones, may not be consonant with the beliefs of their churches. To allay their fears, we try to present our weekly therapeutic touch workshop from a scientific point of view—as a technique that will bring relaxation, relief from pain, feelings of peace, and possibly some relief from physical and psychological energy blockages. I will usually talk about my experience with Qi Gong, the prayer research, and the encounters other participants have had with TT. I make it clear that, although the research is beginning to converge, we are only at the beginning of a new scientific consciousness and are stretching the limits of experience and belief. As pioneers, we must do much on faith in our inner truth—*creating* hypotheses to be tested by the scientific method. Brennan's *Hands of Light* is available to all participants (and we facilitators each have a copy). We also have available a two-hour video tape by Judie Chiappone called *The Light Touch*, which has a cogent 20-minute introduction to the concept that some therapists like to play for the participants at the beginning of the session.

The facilitators have different ways of introducing the techniques, but they all seem equally effective. One facilitator will have participants stretch their fingers and rub their hands together (to increase sensitivity), hold their hands about 10 inches apart, then slowly move their palms closer and notice when the energy from one hand is felt by the other. Other facilitators will have participants hold their hands a couple of inches apart, perceive energy on their right shoulder, move the energy with intention down their right arm to their hands, have the energy make the jump between their hands, and follow the energy up their left arm up to their left shoulder. It's interesting to process people's experiences because some will immediately have quite intense feelings and some will feel nothing initially. Those who feel nothing need reassurance that however they feel or don't feel is okay; it really makes no difference as far as whether TT is "working" or not. Chiappone admits that she is not a "feeler" herself, and frequently she just "declares" what is happening. *However* one perceives the experience is okay!

After the introduction, we bring a couple of chairs (depending on the number of therapists involved) to the center of the circle and invite people to be the healees. (It is important to emphasize that the therapist is *not* doing the healing, that the healee is actually his or her own healer—the therapist only facilitates the process.) We always wash our hands before TT and between subjects so that negative energies we may have picked up are not transferred. We usually allow at least 10 minutes for each individual, and have two or three facilitators working at once.

We ask that everyone in the room be involved in the process and intend their love and healing energies to the targeted "healees." We start the process with a "triple awareness breath": Participants take a deep breath; as they exhale, we say, "First, center yourself, second, put a protective 'shield' around yourself and anyone you may be working with, and third, intend only the highest good."

Dolores Krieger (1987) usually scans the individual after the triple awareness breath, picking up imbalances in energy that her hands may perceive. The scan involves going over the person's body with hands held two to four inches from the skin. This is an optional procedure which, for a variety of reasons, our staff rarely use. I do not recommend using scanning without training.

The next step is "unruffling the field." "Unruffling is done with a sweeping movement of the hands, a few inches away from the body, usually from head to foot. It involves faster, longer sweeps than in the scanning process. . . . You are merely clearing 'clutter' out of the energy field. Cleaning house, so to speak" (Chiappone, 1989, p. 37). Chiappone remarks that unruffling accelerates the effectiveness of the work one does by clearing the way to "let it in." Unruffling also helps to balance or redistribute the energy from areas of overload to areas where it is lacking. In "swampy" areas or areas of congestion, it tends to free up the healee's energy so that the energy flow is restored and balance can return. In Chiappone's workshops, she suggests that part of the power of unruffling has to do with ionization—brushing away positive ions (which cause confused, uncomfortable, off-center feelings), and replacing the energy field with healing-accelerating, negative ions (responsible for good, connected, vital feelings). We can't measure whether or not that happens, but the placebo effect is remarkable (*if* that's all it is).

After the unruffling is complete, I ask the healees softly if there are particular areas on which they would like me to work. They may mention a sore shoulder, a tumor in the lung, feelings of fear and confusion, or some other aspect of mind, body, or spirit which is bothering them. I may also have intuitively picked up areas where I feel tension, difference in temperature, or some other imbalance in the subject to which I may also attend. I'd like to point out that this is my particular style of doing therapeutic touch, and not a paradigm for everyone. As long as the intention is present, the actual techniques do not matter.

I do not have Dolores Krieger's gift for sensing problem areas, and I tend just to let the intelligence of the healing energy go in and heal in the knowing way it does. Perhaps because of my "deficit," I intend the energy itself to do the work rather than trying to manipulate the process too much. As Judie Chiappone says, "The divine energy has a 'knowingness' all its own and can be intentionally released to do the highest good in the process" (1989, p. 39). However, if your intuitive style is different, be yourself and go for it! For example, I tend to be a talker during the process, and in the course of a session, I may initiate dialogue with the subject. However, it is not necessary to talk or to explain anything for the process to work. Case in point: the process worked on rats for the Qi Gong masters without the rats being conscious of what transpired. The process works! And although we humans have the ability to block the process, if one remains open to letting the energy work, it will. In offering a "script" for TT, I am merely offering my spiel, my style, to use as you wish.

The basic goal of TT is to reestablish flow where there are blockages and then to get out of the way and let the process happen. I usually start by putting a hand on each side of the person's head and resonating energy into the immune system control center, the pain control center, or whatever control center is appropriate. I suggest that this powerful energy is going into the center, evaluating the situation, pulling the levers, pushing the buttons, and turning the knobs that will put the control center in perfect balance for the needs of the body at that time. I imply that the energy is very intelligent and knows what to do without our guiding it or even understanding what it is doing.

After completing this generalized balancing of the control centers, I usually focus on areas the person says are problematic and areas where I sense tension or imbalance. Intention always supersedes technique in TT; however, I find that techniques (such as Chiappone's "double hand boost" and "ultrasound" and my own "sloshing the energy") seem to concentrate my intention. The most important focus is to intend that the energy flows, and it will!

The double hand boost involves putting one hand over the other on the problem area and intending light, love, and energy into the area. Remember that the energy is equally effective whether you are actually touching the person or holding your hands several inches away (or even many hundreds of miles away). The energy also goes through clothing, through the back of a chair, or through one's body (sometimes it is more convenient to work on a problem in the spine from the front of the body). As I am doing the double hand boost, moving both hands around the area if it is large, I put my intention into words. I may say for example, "I am intending energy and love into the area of your pancreas. You may wish to see that intelligent, light energy knowing exactly what to do, healing, soothing, and cleansing any problem area." I prefer to let that powerful, divine energy "do its own thing"; however, for those so inclined it may be useful to use some of the "seeds for imagery" found in the next section and make a guided imagery of the process.

Ultrasound uses the energy that extends from your fingertips as tools. This is a little like putting nozzles on the energy, causing it to become much more focused and intensified. I begin to move the hand with the fingers converging in a circular motion over the targeted area. As I move it, I usually tell the person what I am doing: "I am using a technique called ultrasound in which I put little nozzles on my fingertips so that the energy is much more powerful than usual. You may find it is stirring up a lot of debris and gunk and perhaps making the area muddier than usual for the moment. You may even feel the pain become more intense, but when the powerful energies of your body clean away the debris and the waters settle, you may find a clarity and healing that you have not experienced for a long time." Ultrasound is a powerful technique to use with joint pain, sore spots, or even with a painful spine.

"Sloshing the energy" involves finding chakras (energy centers) both above and below the problem area. For instance, if the problem area is in the lungs, I might put one hand above the throat chakra and the other above the energy center just below the navel. I then move my hands up and down as if I were sloshing water back and forth in a pan—greatly increasing the power of the water flow. I say, "Now we are sloshing the energy back and forth and it is breaking down any blockages just as if they were mud pies in a pan of moving water. It's like bringing a fresh stream into a swampy area. The power of that clear river dissipates the swamp and it becomes clean, fresh, vital energy as all the dirt and mud and disease are carried away by the powerful forces of the body. . . . " I don't worry too much about mixing my metaphors or having a perfectly calculated script. I don't want to get in the way of the person's own imagery; however, I do wish to give him or her a slight structure for creating the shifts—body, mind, and spirit. The important point is to be yourself and to let your light, love, and energy flow.

Chiappone points out the importance of breathing through the whole process. She suggests breathing in energy from your higher source through the crown of the head and becoming a channel for that energy as you breathe out the energy through your hands. If one stops breathing energy from the Source, one's own energy will be dissipated; however, as long as one keeps breathing, there will always be more than enough.

After the "treatment" is completed, one facilitator (with long arms) usually reinforces the subject's energy flow by placing one hand on the top of his or her head and the other hand on the feet, and intends a powerful energy flow from "crown to ground." After a final unruffling of fields, we "ground" healees by pressing our hands on their shoulders and then disconnect by running a hand down the space between the subject and ourselves. Then we wash our hands.

One facilitator usually has participants pair up and teaches them to use TT on each other, essentially the previous process I have described. I like to give members guidelines for using therapeutic touch on themselves. One method is to ask them to intend the healthy energy in their bodies into the palms of their hands. When their hands become quite hot, I suggest that they place them on some area on their bodies where their energy is blocked or turgid or where pain or other issues prevail. Then I propose that they beam the energy into the targeted area, possibly seeing it as a warm, melting sun dissolving anything that is not right and totally clearing the area of pain or disease. A similar self-healing process involves placing hands over the problem area, breathing in from one's Source through the crown of the head, and exhaling the healing, light energy through the palms directly into the problem area. Dr. Krieger states, "We must empower our patients in the interest of their own well-being. The more thoroughly and consciously healing becomes part of one's lifestyle, the more clearly it is perceived that in the last analysis, it is the patient who heals himself or herself" (1987, p. 122).

One of the beautiful side effects of therapeutic touch is seeing its energy bring the whole group together into a higher connectedness. Frequently group members begin to use the technique on each other daily, with the exchange of energy and love which that entails. Even when that does not happen, the TT session brings disparate members into a wholeness as a group. It is almost as if individual differences are transcended and members are transformed into a unity with themselves, others, and beyond.

Lola, the woman with lung cancer and emphysema, came to group in a wheelchair one Thursday (TT day). She had spent a bad night, and her lungs were so congested that she needed intermittent oxygen. Although she was like a rag all morning, she figured she might as well be miserable in group (where something positive *might* happen) as in her hospital room. I happened to be the one to use therapeutic touch on her that morning, and even I, non-feeler that I am, could feel the palpable blockage and imbalance of energies in her chest. I used my whole bag of tricks, such as double hand boosts, ultrasound, and resonating energy from palms placed on the front and back of her chest. When I "sloshed the energy," she suddenly broke into tears and then deep sobs as she "got her feelings off her chest." As the ice floe of her emotions cracked, so did the congestion in her chest. "I just can't believe what is happening," she sobbed. "It's all breaking up! I can't tell you how long it has been since I last cried. It's such a relief." Lola's session took longer than the usual 10 minutes, and deeply affected all of us in the room. It was a turning point in her psychotherapy, and I believe that it may have been a critical physical point for her, too. She returned from lunch without her wheelchair and breathing normally, and over the next two weeks made progress her physicians and nurses could not believe.

Sometimes the most doubting participants have the most dramatic results with TT. Joel, a 35-year-old man with cancer which had metastasized to his spine, was dependent on pain killers which did not even begin to keep his pain under control. He entered the program because his sister, a gentle and enlightened individual, had practically strong-armed him into coming. Joel happened to enter the psychiatric hospital (in which we were housed at the time) on a Thursday, so one of his first sessions was therapeutic touch. The facilitator gave him the usual treatment, reminding him, as we all usually do, that results may not be immediately effective— that they may manifest themselves up to 24 hours later. After the touch, he grudgingly admitted he felt a little better, but not great. I saw him again about three hours later and he was exhilarated. "I have just had the first pain-free hours in six months. I can't believe it!" he exclaimed. (An added note: one of the reasons he had entered the hospital was to become free of drugs, including nicotine; therefore, he had taken no pain medication for nearly 18 hours.) With the knowledge that he had some power over the pain, Joel began to release more of his resistance to the program and went on to make significant changes in his life.

"White Lighting" and Interpersonal Connectedness

"White lighting" is using one's thought as energy for healing at a distance—intending that white, healing light surround someone or something. Some people see it as being related to prayer, which it undoubtedly is; however, many people like the directness and lack of religious trappings that white lighting offers.

Participants (and facilitators) most frequently use white lighting for people having a physical crisis, loved ones going in for tests, or fellow participants facing surgery. This is a powerful process in several ways. First, all evidence points to the palpable power of focused thought or consciousness. Second, the very act of sending light and love to someone gives the sender a feeling that he or she is not helpless and is involved in the process; thus, it is healing for the sender, too. Third, the power of the act is increased several fold when the healee is aware that the white light is being sent to him or her. Of course, what is being transmitted is love and a sense of caring in the deepest sense.

Sending white light involves connecting with the individual or process to which one is sending. For example, before a difficult meeting one might send white light to each of the participants in the meeting—sending love and positive intentions. The very opening of one's heart to love, which is a prerequisite to sending the white light, creates significant shifts within the sender and possibly melts the defenses of the receiver. The shifts within the sender establish a new psychological ambience, which will probably be followed with behavior that is more open and "negotiating." My own and participants' experiences with white lighting "adversaries" has been astonishing. We have seen interpersonal Berlin Walls crumble through the power of positive intention—just as many of us believe that the actual Wall itself fell due in no small part to global white lighting.

Lessons for the Author/Clinician

My encounters with the healing of the Aborigines, therapeutic touch, and Qi Gong changed my whole approach to and beliefs about the world.

Things will never be the same for me—in a most wonderful way. This splendid shift opened my mind to vast possibilities which I had always rather suspected, and which I can, in a certain sense, now trust. One of the lessons I learned from this enlightenment is that I don't have to practice or be an expert on everything noetic or paranormal to respect and believe others' experiences therein. I can just intuitively enjoy my belief that all sorts of possibilities exist and that they will be available to me when I need them.

Another lesson of therapeutic touch and transpersonal imagery is that healing takes place within each individual. The therapist holds no special powers (except as a loving human) and needs no special "anointing." The facilitator does merely that: facilitates and helps awaken the healing within the "healee" through intending love. The very act of opening one's heart to send that love and light is every bit as healing to the sender as to the receiver. I usually thank the person I have been working with, for the healing experience is a reciprocal one.

I've found white lighting to be a practical tool, which I use frequently. Intending love or white light has served to untangle the many interpersonal webs in which I have found myself—rarely in the manner I expected, yet always in wondrous and curious ways. For example, a meeting with a group of oncologists who were rather hostile to the concept of PNI was scheduled and rescheduled several times. Initially I felt angry, resistant, and fearful about the meeting; however, just about every evening I sent white light to each member scheduled to be there, in addition to doing my homework and getting a professional presentation ready. Nearly three months later, when the meeting finally came to pass, I was ready. Ready, not in the sense of having my weapons and defenses honed, but in the sense of feeling at peace and of having feelings of acceptance, and even love, for those present. It turned out to be a meeting of negotiation rather than a debate. Several of the physicians had shifts in their feelings and seemed to gain a new perception and understanding of me and of GETTING WELL (and it wasn't just because I was prepared for the meeting!). Afterward, a member of our "camp" observed, "I think I just saw a miracle happen." And I know a miracle had happened within me.

I regularly send white light not only to friends, "enemies," and participants in the program, but also to people I've only talked to on the phone or may have seen only once in a consult. A number of years ago, I saw a young couple, Harry and his wife, who were interested in the program. However, his medical treatment took him to the state university medical center for extensive treatment before he could even consider the program. Although he did not enroll in GW, Harry, with his seemingly hopeless condition, had struck a chord in me, and I white lighted him off and on for several weeks. After that, I somewhat forgot about him, and then for some reason remembered him in my thoughts very vividly and strongly one night a couple of months later.

The next morning I got a call from Harry from his bed in the university hospital. "Dee, I'm not sure why I'm calling you, but I felt I needed to," he said. "I've been having a really rough time, but in the middle of the night last night something changed. I feel like I have a shot at it now. Somehow, I knew that you would want to know that." I told him of my thoughts about him the night before, he told me the time of his epiphany, and I realized that it was exactly the time I had been doing my white lighting. My next call from him came several months later after he had found a job teaching in a private school in Boston. Although Harry never came into the program, I felt he was a major step in my awakening, in my own awareness that I extend beyond my skin and that my thoughts and intentions emanate far beyond my brain. It is also exciting to think that somewhere along the way, I may be touching the "hundredth monkey" in the awakening beginning to take place.

16
Expressive Therapies

The making of art can be an instrument by which we may reacquaint our current self with our original self . . . to help *us* realize that our original self is still alive and recoverable. Once reacquainted, we are likely to find a wise, powerful, and remarkably witty companion has been restored to us, to accompany us through life. — *Peter London*

The therapeutic process is therapeutic in itself because it allows us to express and examine the content and dimensions of our internal lives. We live full lives to the degree to which we find a full range of vehicles which concretize, symbolize, and otherwise give expression to our experiences. — *Joseph Zinker*

Creativity is the real magic of our universe. It is the shape of our courage and the force of our souls. — *Adriana Diaz*

Expressive therapy elicits outward and palpable manifestations of the inward, frequently unconscious processes of mental imagery. Vija Lusebrink describes it as "imagelike representation created in an external medium with its own qualities influencing these representations" (1990, p. 35). Expressive therapy is a vehicle for tapping into the essential self, of peeling away the many layers of the onion of societal conditioning, the consensus trance, and the "cultural abuse" endemic to our "civilized" social organization. Self-expression in the true sense returns the source of imagery from external expectations or aesthetic values to the fountainhead of creativity—the true self. In his splendid book, *No More Secondhand Art*, Peter London writes, "Every gesture and utterance emanates from within. By examining these external gestures and utterances we can infer what must lie below. . . . [It is] creating on the physical plane what is on the plane of consciousness" (p. 35). "The artwork is after all," writes Valerie Hookham (1991), "a two or three dimensional representation of the client's image. . . . If someone is 'stuck' in treatment (especially if it is an intellectual person), art can be a way around the intellect into emotion" (p. 267).

Expressive therapy lays open the unconscious process for both self-knowledge and for change or re-creation. The expressive realms of drawing, making music, movement, journaling, etc., tap into the right brain, which, in turn, is a rich terminal of innervation for bodily functions. In other words, connecting with the images of the right brain allows us to unite consciousness and body and gives us the opportunity to design our own blueprint and co-create our own being.

This session provides an excellent means of expressing feelings, such as rage, fear, sorrow, and joy, in a variety of meaningful ways. The literature is replete with evidence that repressing feelings is harmful not only to the psyche, but also to the body; when one can identify, expand, and express those "secret" feelings, it aids in the healing process. Time after time, we have had unacknowledged feelings "jump off the page" at an individual and have seen that experience provide the crack in the door needed for the person to start responding to those feelings.

Schwartz (1990) has suggested that specific psychobiological mechanisms create a repression of feelings, which can lead to a disconnection between one's report of conscious experience and physiological responses of anxiety, anger, or depression. In addition, he has presented data linking this repression with compromised immune functioning and physical illness. Pennebaker (1990) has found a clear correlation in the data between confessional writing, a stronger immune system (increase in T-lymphocyte response), and better general health, judged by the number of visits students made to his university's health center. The writing that was effective in changing health parameters included not only the facts but also the feelings involved in a traumatic experience. Writing down just the facts of a traumatic event or only venting feelings about the event gave results no better than those elicited from a control group writing about superficial topics.

Frequently, drawings or journal entries provide an insight into an individual's blockages in the healing process. I particularly recommend Greg Furth's book, *The Secret World of Drawings*, to aid facilitators in recognizing the metaphor and meaning in participants' (and their own) drawings and other expressive work. (As a matter of fact, the leaders of our expressive sessions have been trained by Greg Furth.) It goes without saying that we, as facilitators, do *not* interpret patients' work for them! However, we do need to be able to ask questions that can lead the individual to his or her own insight. I remember one drawing in which a participant had placed himself on one side of a house with the rest of his family on the other side of the house. He reflected on his drawing in response to some nonthreatening questions by the therapist: "I've let the house come between me and the rest of the family, and I'm constantly upset by the whole situation." His awareness of this conflict in his values created a shift in his therapy's direction and allowed major progress to be made in a short time.

Drawings and other expressive media are useful in creating palpable reflections of healing images or epiphanies. A drawing of one's "special place" or of a particularly moving experience in transformational fantasy is a wonderful cue to recreating the image that spontaneously arose within. After a transformative experience in the guided imagery session, participants will frequently run for crayons or felt pens and commit their images to paper — a powerful reinforcement of the experience. I also like to believe (although it is not yet proven) that, if one changes one's drawings in a healthy direction, the inner image can be changed to reflect those positive changes in the body.

Sometimes the major block to successful expressive work with participants is the therapist's own resistance. Valerie Hookham writes,

> It has been my experience that once the therapist gets over his or her reluctance to use expressive therapy, the client is quite willing to comply, even clients who claim that they are not artistic. I have experienced many stunning examples of creativity from "nonartistic" people. Human beings are capable of much more creative expression than they may believe, in my experience. (1991, pp. 269–70)

Of course, we do not expect participants to implement *all* modes of expressive work in their lives *every* day; however, we are pleased to see the ease with which individuals metaphorically create their own dances, sing their own songs, and paint their own portraits. Having a variety of channels of expression means that one always has a companion to share the pain and to participate in the joys of life.

Mirabella, an artist in her mid-thirties, had been given three months to a year to live when she entered GETTING WELL. A rare thymus tumor was strangling one of the main vessels returning blood to the heart and had also spread to her lungs and her heart lining. Her physicians had decided that it was too risky to operate, so she opted for a bold course of chemotherapy, radiation, and self-expression through her art. Where before she had been reluctant to express her feelings openly in her art, Mirabella became deeply personal in her expressions on canvas.

Shortly after completing the GETTING WELL program, she had a show that included paintings she had done before her cancer (which were nice) and ones that represented her healing process (which were incredibly powerful and moving). She spoke about the latter in an interview (Sandich, 1993), " . . . the images just flowed through me, and they were very personal. Before I was always a little shy about revealing myself. Even if I had something personal, I would pretend that it really didn't mean anything because I didn't want to discuss it." As it turned out, her tumor shrank, and subsequent surgery was successful. I have since considered Mirabella's story as the the epitome of the healing of medicine, meaning, and expression.

Expressive therapy is designed to follow high-level awareness and is frequently a key in carrying the search for self and the work on connectedness and meaning into new dimensions.

House-Tree-Person and Image-CA

House-Tree-Person (HTP) has always been a staple in my standard battery of psychological tests; however, at GW it has served not only as an evaluation instrument but also as a therapeutic tool. Even when we were using it in the hospital setting as part of testing to support a psychiatric diagnosis, we administered it in expressive groups as a therapeutic activity. Rather than using pencil only for the drawings (as is conventional), we have people use colored pencils or crayons. Felt-tip pens do not show subtleties of pressure, and for that reason we avoid them for this exercise.

Although, traditionally, separate pieces of paper are used for each item of the HTP, we give participants the choice of drawing on separate sheets or on one large sheet. Typically, we say, "I am going to ask you to draw a picture of a house, a picture of a tree, and a picture of a person (or family). You can do it either on several sheets of paper or you can use one sheet for everything. We ask you not to draw stick figures, but other than that, you can do it any way you wish, and take as long as you wish" (hoping there are no obsessive-compulsives in the group). When the participants are finished, we ask them to tell the story of their pictures and sometimes ask them to tell the story from the stance of an element in their picture, say, their house. Following Greg Furth's lead, we ask questions about unusual parts of the picture in addition to the prescribed HTP questions. Some examples are: "Tell me about this knothole on the tree," "What's happening over here?" or "What's that person doing?" Frequently, the participant will get into material surprising to him or her, and the way is paved for some deep, future work. We use the HTP on alternate Mondays so we can get a feel for progress being made over the four-week period.

On the Mondays in between, we use the Image-CA (Achterberg & Lawlis, 1984) which is specifically for cancer patients, or a generic rendering of this powerful instrument (playfully called the Image-GW) for those with a variety of life-challenging conditions. The Image-CA starts with an imagery experience involving relaxation, imaging the tumor or cancer site, seeing the immune cells searching out any problem cells and destroying the cancer, and picturing chemotherapy or radiation effectively killing the cancer while protecting healthy cells. After this imaging, patients are requested to draw a picture that shows their tumor or disease, the body's defense against the disease, and their treatment for the disease if they are receiving any. These elements then can be scored on a variety of dimensions, such as vividness of the disease, strength of the body's defenses, and vividness and effectiveness of the medical treatment. (See Achterberg & Lawlis, 1984, for specific questioning and scoring.)

The predictive value of the Image-CA (properly done) is quite astonishing. In looking at what the next six months hold health-wise, Image-CAs with scores reflecting a positive change were 97 percent predictive of improved physical health. Those with scores indicating a decline in health were 100 percent predictive! Our experience (using the generic Image-GW) has been similar over a wide variety of diseases, despite a more intuitive, nonquantitative scoring system. The Image-GW exercise is particularly beneficial in helping participants make their own imagery more powerful. For example, a person who sees his or her cancer as a vicious, large black crab that is impervious to the immune system and medical treatment, or an individual with lupus seeing it as an untamable fire, may be encouraged to change some of the symbols in his or her imagery, in order to create a more salubrious environment for healing to take place. A repeat of the Image-GW done two weeks later usually reflects powerful, creative changes.

It is a good idea to tape the imagery you plan to use for this exercise in order to maintain reliability, whether you are using the Image-CA or a more generic imagery. In my generic imagery I usually implement a couple of minutes of relaxation and then ask the participant to be where his or her physical problem is. I say something like this:

> Remember that whatever your condition is, your body has powerful resources to regain balance. See your problem now, either symbolically or anatomically, be aware of the shape, colors, textures, and activity of that problem or condition.... What's it like?... How does it behave? (*pause*) When that picture is clear in your mind, see in your mind's eye the powerful forces of your body's healing system ... see what it is that your body is doing to restore perfect balance to your being ... and you may see it in a symbolic or anatomical way (*pause*). And now see your treatment or other strategies that you are doing medically, nutritionally, or otherwise ... see that treatment working powerfully in league with your body's splendid healing resources to bring your body, mind, and spirit into perfect balance.... See that healing process in living color — right now. (*pause*) And now see those things you want most in life ... that have deep meaning for you ... happening in your life.... Now, thank all parts of you for taking part in this healing, relaxing experience. Soon, I'll ask you to come back to the room and draw a picture of your condition, the resources of your body healing your condition, and the powerful part your treatment is playing in your healing.

Paper, crayons, and pens should be ready for participants to draw their images. It is also important for patients not to be hurried in their drawings or in their explanations, even if this involves extending the session or letting them finish in the evening.

Ellen, an emergency room nurse in her forties, was so in touch with her body's "felt sense" that she had diagnosed her own pancreatic cancer and actually told her skeptical physician its shape, color, and location. When an MRI confirmed her suspicions, her physician was pessimistic about her future. He indicated that the radiation, which was her only hope, would certainly destroy one kidney, and probably the other as well.

Ellen entered GW two weeks before her first radiation treatment, and her Image-CA indicated strong work on the part of her immune system. Even though she had not yet had her first radiation treatment, she drew the radiation powerfully eradicating the tumor. "I just can't afford to lose a kidney, much less both," she said thoughtfully, "but the radiation needs to be this powerful to get the tumor." For the next two weeks she worked on changes in her imagery as well as in her life. We asked her about the rather strange drawing she did before she left.

"The immune system is still doing its work," she explained, "and the radiation is still strong, but before the radiation equipment is turned on, I am rolling up both my kidneys, just like window shades. While the machine is on, they're out of the way of danger. Then I unroll them, and they're not hurt one bit." Ellen went on to successful treatment for her tumor, kept both of her kidneys, eventually went back to work, and continues to amaze her physicians over three years later. I find Ellen an excellent example of the joining of the powers of modern medicine with those of mental imagery.

Obviously, if one is using these tools for research or a formal evaluation, the standard protocol for HTP or Image-CA should be used. Our relaxed renditions, however, seem to serve us and our participants quite satisfactorily.

Exercises Using Drawing, Collage, and Painting

Drawing, painting, and collage form the backbone of the expressive therapies at GETTING WELL, and we have seen these sessions evolve with the facilitators. At GW's inception I relied on exercises that were comfortable for me: "Rosebush," Image-CA, Image-GW, HTP, "Spiritual Journey," painting emotions, and other exercises I had used with individual clients. Kathy Ellis brought right-brain workshops, collages of the person one was born to be, and a number of other creative activities to the program. Brenda Stockdale Mulligan helped get our creative expression program written down and organized, and also left her very special mark on GETTING WELL. And now Gayla Bacon, M.A., brings her special love of Jung, myth, and metaphor to participants.

In recent years some splendid books on healing through self-expression have been published: *Drawing the Light From Within* by Judith Cornell,

Source Imagery by Sandra Shuman, *No More Secondhand Art* by Peter London, *Freeing the Creative Spirit* by Adriana Diaz, and *The Creative Journal* by Lucia Capacchione. I strongly recommend that facilitators begin work on their own images and meaning before guiding participants through the exciting labyrinths of expressive therapy. Any and all of the books mentioned are wonderful guides for the leader as well as the participant.

Source Imagery

Sandra Shuman's book (1989) explores the unconscious mind and facilitates discovering one's source and releasing the power of one's creativity. There are numerous exercises which stimulate deep levels of creative imagination. "The Magical Beast," for example, suggests that the participant think about his or her favorite animal. As the image of an animal admired for its beauty and particular kind of power is conjured, each person is asked to meditate and begin to picture the animal in his or her mind's eye. It can be any size, shape, or color and may have rather chimerical characteristics. The individual should not only image how the animal looks but also notice that it is endowed with certain magical qualities. Let the individual's child-within touch and become friends with it. The child notices, fascinated, that the animal is strong and awesome, but also quite amiable and approachable. Allow some time to let the image develop, and then have participants draw a picture with the coloring/cutting materials available.

This exercise allows participants to explore fanciful, imaginative aspects of themselves. It is particularly pleasant to have some unusual materials, such as sequins, gilt paint, silky fabrics, and other trims available, in addition to magazine cut-outs to embellish the images. Participants tend to become deeply involved with this project and may continue to add details over several days. Curiously, many times a person's magical beast is the "monster" in the back corridors of his or her mind, and this exercise allows the person to see the engaging side of fearsome obstacles. At the very least, it is fun, and it taps into surprising creative gifts people had not realized they had.

"Seed, tree, star" is an evocative exercise in which, after a preliminary relaxation procedure, participants are asked first to imagine a tree of any size shape or color, then to imagine a seed, and finally to imagine a star (allowing the image of one object to fade before the next is invoked). Individuals are then asked to relax again once more and, using their imaginations, to recall their images and see them joining or touching each other, creating a picture together. When they come out of the meditation, members are asked to draw their pictures. When the pictures are completed, each individual processes his or her picture with the rest of the group.

Drawing the Light from Within

Judith Cornell's book (1990) is a rich treasury of enchanting visualizations and tools for exploring one's consciousness and creativity—allowing one to represent more meaningfully and accurately the images within. Although we don't have the time or expertise available to teach technical skills while the individual is at GW, I recommend this book to those who wish to carry the work further. I have found it immensely helpful in my own personal quest to put imagery on paper. We use a number of Cornell's guided imageries, each of which is an hour's session. It is important that the facilitator read the book and have the pleasure of experiencing the context from which these healing visualizations are drawn; thus, here I give only sketches of some of our favorites.

"The Hall of Illuminated Arts and Design" (pp. 34–35) is a visualization that carries one on a journey out into the universe and back to earth through beautiful forests and by sparkling streams into the center of a highly evolved culture of artisans whose hall of illuminated arts and design is inspiration for a project.

"Vision of a Peaceful Planet" (pp. 166–167) takes one on a journey which resonates with the abundance of love and peace on the planet. Visits to one's power animals bring forth a feeling of harmony in the universe and in oneself.

"Journey to the Hall of Wisdom" (pp. 187–189) stretches the imagination to reach the wisdom contained in other parts of the universe and includes a spiritual guide who leads one to a hall of wisdom on another planet.

These tantalizing journeys are evocative of splendid and meaningful images, so that extra time may be required to complete the art work. People are frequently transported to such deep parts of their beings that processing is best left for another time—possibly during an individual session.

Freeing the Creative Spirit

Adriana Diaz's book (1992) is an enchanting exploration of the creative, spiritual essence of the human experience. Although some of her exercises may seem too esoteric for some groups of participants, I find her volume to be invaluable and her practices wonderfully mysterious and evocative for my own work.

I particularly like her exercise, "The Breath of God," in which one uses music, breath work, and a straw to blow brilliant watercolors or colored inks around a large piece of paper. Blowing the watercolors with a straw gives a great sense of freedom, which in turn relieves the participant of expectations he or she may have.

Gayla Bacon, one of our facilitators, finds the Diaz exercise, "Self Portrait," to be extremely powerful. For this experience, a piece of butcher paper a couple of feet longer than the height of the participant is needed. Tape the paper lightly at the four corners, then have the participant lie down on it and move around for a while. When he or she decides on a position in which to be outlined, a partner completes the project with a soft-lead pencil, then tapes the outline to a wall.

Gayla has participants study their outlines for a few days and reflect on questions such as the blessings in their lives, their dark sides, their relationship to work, descriptive songs, their dreams, etc. Then, following Diaz's instructions, she asks them to reflect the answers through paint and collage on their butcher paper "mirrors." When the self-portraits are finished, there are further exercises, such as establishing a new name for the portrait (in the tradition of Native American naming), creating a brief statement about this person, and designing a small ritual for the participant to celebrate himself or herself. Participants find this to be an experience evocative of powerful healing.

The Creative Journal

I used Lucia Capacchione's book (1979) as a model for my own "painting" journal, and I highly recommend it to participants wishing to continue expressive work after leaving the program. It is a wonderful adjunct to "regular" journaling with the main expression being drawings. Her exercises are in the form of questions: "What do my inner and outer selves feel like at this time in my life?" "What have been the key events and experiences in my life?" "Where am I in my life right now?" "What is the theme of my personal growth at this particular time—what does the current challenge I'm dealing with right now look like?" "How do I see myself?" "What is the side of me I like about myself—and what does the shadow side look like?" and "What is meaningful in my life?" Her section on drawing/painting dreams is helpful in the dream work (both waking and sleeping) we do at GW.

Right-Brain Workshops

For several years we have used Marilee Zdenek's tapes and book, *The Right-Brain Experience*, for Sunday afternoon "workshops" for participants. Initially, we used her tapes as the basis for the two-hour sessions because the weekend therapists didn't feel comfortable facilitating expressive sessions by themselves. The right-brain workshops became an immediate success with both participants and therapists, and we have continued them with basically the same format.

The sessions begin with Zdenek's taped introduction to the right-brain experience, which includes split-brain research, examples of properties of the left brain and the right brain, and benefits of the more intuitive, emotional right-brain experience. The tape has the advantage of moving the "novice" methodically through the basic steps in the shift from the logical, sequential, analytical, verbal thinking of the left brain into the sensory, in-the-moment, metaphoric knowledge of the right brain. She gives instructions for making mandalas which will help "outsmart the left brain," numerous images based on youthful memories (e.g., remembering a "secret" from childhood) and sensory experiences (e.g., "experiencing" an orange), non-dominant-hand exercises, drawing upside down, fantasy, and dream work. In her book, Zdenek has a number of guided visualizations which can in themselves form the basis for sessions in drawing or journaling or both.

"Child with a Gift Imagery"

Valerie Hookham, M.S.W, A.C.S.W., an extraordinary friend and gifted therapist, has combined imagery and expressive work with psychotherapy with dysfunctional families and people with chemical and other dependencies. She has trained our staff and has generously shared her ideas and awareness. One of our most richly evocative sessions is based on her "Child with a Gift Imagery," which she has graciously given me permission to use. Here is the session:

> Sit in a comfortable position. Loosen any tight clothing. See if you are willing to make an agreement with yourself that for the next 45 minutes you'll let all your troubles, issues or problems go. You might even picture yourself piling them off to one side of you. They'll be there waiting for you if you want to pick them up again. As you sit, begin to pay attention to your breathing. Allow yourself to breathe deeply and fully.
>
> Imagine that your mind is like a movie screen or a slide projector screen with different images flashing across it. Allow the images to come and go at random, knowing that you don't need to hold onto any image or to push it away.
>
> As you view the images on that movie screen, that slide projector screen, begin to allow images of you as a child to emerge. You might see images of you as a toddler, preschooler, in grade school or as a teenager. The images might come from pictures, from stories that you've heard about yourself, from memories of favourite clothes or toys that you had.
>
> Allow all the images of you to flash across the screen.
>
> Then, see which image comes up most frequently or that you feel most drawn to. . . . Allow that image to come into as sharp a focus as you can. See if you can see how you wore your hair. What kind of look you had on your

face, what kind of shirt or dress you wore. What did you have on your feet? Were your knees skinned? See that image of you as clearly as you can.

You notice this child, this *you*, coming towards you. It has something for you. It could be something that's heretofore been lost to you or maybe it's something you never had before that you now need. Allow yourself to accept the gift. Experience it.

Then I'd like you to come back into the room. Open your eyes and draw (or paint) the gift you received.

Then paint a picture of the child who brought it to you.

The processing of these pictures is usually quite dramatic and emotional and opens significant issues for therapeutic work.

"Rosebush"

I have used this imagery/drawing exercise for many years, but I am unsure of its origins. I've found it useful in therapy for pulling forth a metaphoric rendering of a client's view of himself or herself, and as a rich source of analogies and metaphors with which to further the therapeutic process.

Asking participants to close their eyes, the facilitator uses a brief centering or relaxation exercise and then asks them to imagine themselves as a rosebush.

> Be that rosebush: What is it like? Let your imagination flow as you feel as a rosebush within every cell of yourself. Where are you planted? How do your roots feel? What are they like? What are your stems and branches like? Explore all aspects of your "rosebushness." What is your environment like? What is your day-to-day life like as a rosebush? What happens to you as the seasons change? What does this rosebush need in order to flourish? What causes it to wilt? Continue to explore your existence as a rosebush. Look at how you feel about your life, where you are planted, and what happens to you. Let your fantasy continue for a while. (*long pause*) When you come back to the room you can express your experience of being a rosebush in a drawing.

When participants have completed their rosebush drawings (approximately 20 minutes), ask each person to tell about his or her picture in the *first* person, *present* tense. For example, "I am a rosebush in full bloom planted in rich soil; however, my thorns are so long and sharp that they scare some people away." We suggest they put their drawings in their journals and recall their fantasies in prose on the opposite page as homework for the evening.

The facilitator may wish to notice support (fences, etc.), colors, where the bush is growing, whether the root system is deep or shallow, the health of the bush, how many blooms are on the bush, and the "feel" of the whole picture. As can be expected, the drawings are quite revealing.

Jetta (the young woman who had over 50 tumors in her abdomen when she came to GW) was presented with this exercise on her first day in the program. Her rosebush revealed the extreme depth of her depression, hopelessness, and despair, in its small size and in the predominant blacks, greys and browns in her picture. Leaves and petals were falling from the sagging, bare plant, and a broken-down mailbox showed in the foreground. Barely discernible behind the rosebush was the outline of a tombstone. Truly a bleak prognosis!

After 28 days in the program, Jetta was a different woman. She had developed her powerful imagery of her immune system "housekeeping" services cleaning the "hotel rooms" in which her tumors hid themselves, and she felt more validated, hopeful, and powerful in every way. On the last day she was in the program, the expressive therapy session was "Spiritual Pilgrimage." Jetta chose to render her spiritual path in a metaphoric manner—the drawing of a hot-air balloon. The balloon had a thin, rather confused base which represented the first 28 years of her life. However, the rest of it burst forth in brilliant color, and continued to expand to twice its width and length in her depiction of her future—in fact she had to tape three sheets of paper together to complete the drawing. Her spiritual pilgrimage was, indeed, testimony to the hope and meaning which had returned to her life—and to the future that she continues to celebrate.

"Spiritual Pilgrimage"

This exercise, adapted from Tubesing and Tubesing's *Structured Exercises in Wellness Promotion*, gives participants an opportunity to image and express their spiritual journeys through life. Preceding the drawing/collage/painting exercise, the facilitator explains that as humans we are by nature spiritual; we search for meaning, ultimate truths, and connectedness with the process of creation. We search for values, for meaning in the face of disease, suffering, and death. We search for faith and trust in the supportiveness of the universe, and for hope in the midst of "whys." The human spirit is a powerful healing force, not only when our lives are challenged, but also in the more mundane challenges of boredom, day-to-day conflicts, and alienation from oneself and others. We all have a spiritual history that contributes to our feelings of well-being and to our sense of self.

After the explanation, we ask participants to use the paper, crayons, paints, magazines, etc., in front of them to depict their past and present spiritual issues. These issues may include one's first encounter with death, times when life did not seem worth living, epiphanies, moments of doubt, conflicts of value or purpose, changes in religious beliefs, times of sorrow, and times of joy and celebration. We encourage them to be abstract or nonrepresentational if they wish. After the past and present have been drawn, we suggest that they depict what they see to be their spiritual evolution in the future. Then the participants process what they have drawn and write a narrative in their journals as homework.

Image Book

The image book is a part of one's creative journal that consists of pictures and images which define one's higher self and the direction of one's life. Participants frequently find it useful in implementing cognitive or behavioral changes; it is also a way to reflect their strengths, goals, and aspirations.

Participants are asked to cut from magazines words and pictures that reflect their higher self. We suggest that, rather than deliberately looking for specific pictures and words, individuals go through magazines with the theme of their pages in mind and see what words or pictures jump out at them. The images should reach far beyond the person's current concepts to reflect the person that individual was born to be. The pictures and accompanying cut-out words or affirmations may concern prosperity, health, body-image, self-esteem, spiritual growth, or other aspects of one's existence. It is suggested that any faces be cut out of the pictures so that the image book's designer can place his or her own face in the picture as the subject.

We suggest that participants review the pages of their image books daily, placing themselves on the pages, and that they work to make their represented goals become accomplished facts.

The use of collage techniques bypasses the frustrations that many feel in not being able to draw or paint. A collage is also uncannily revealing about the images and the emotions of its creator, and is a potent representation of what is going on in the creator's unconscious mind. Both choice and placement of pictures are no more accidental than one's dreams and other images. We usually find that the process of interpreting one's image book or other collages is healing and frequently inspiring to participants.

Mandalas

Carl Jung recognized archetypal images in the healing mandalas to be found in all the great religions. These archetypical images are also to be found in our dreams and creative acts. Specifically, [the mandala created by the Chartres Labyrinth] represents the spiritual journey of humanity, which does not proceed in a straight line but meanders in seemingly repetitive circles which nevertheless lead to a healing center. (Jones, 1992)

Several months ago we received a call from a woman visiting Orlando from Rotterdam. Kiria (her professional name) had heard about us in a number of places and she wished to share her work with mandalas with our participants. A student of Jungian psychology, Kiria had precipitated her own healing from "terminal" cancer a number of years earlier through mandalas. She brought with her a wonderful manuscript on mandala construction in which she hoped to interest a publisher. Unfortunately, she gave us no permanent address, and slipped from our grasp just as quickly as she had slipped in. However, Kiria left a wonderful legacy to our patients and facilitators—a shimmering afternoon of mandalas, enlightenment, and self-realization.

Kiria always has people work within a circle which she calls "a symbol of wholeness, a sacred space." She had us use a plate to draw a circle on a piece of paper. For our first mandala (which means "circle" in Hindu), she had us start at the edge of the circle with a curved line which was to be repeated four times. Then we were to draw another set of five lines until the circle was filled or was finished for us. She emphasized that the mandalas have nothing to do with artistic ability; they are expressions of one's inner life at that moment. We worked with crayons; however, she suggests paints or colored pencils (never felt markers) as the medium. She was very insistent that we not turn the paper when we drew. ("It strangles the soul, and you will feel very uncomfortable with the reflection of your self-within if you turn the paper!") Our next mandala started from the center of the circle and worked out to the edges, again using the curved lines. ("No angles, please!") We were all amazed by the wondrous works we created.

Then Kiria suggested we start from the center with our "stream of consciousness" designs, and go from there. Adriana Diaz (1992) further proposes we divide the circle into four or six sections and use a theme such as how we relate to others, power animals in our lives, or mystic perceptions.

The circle does, indeed, give a transcendent organization to the gifts of the unconscious. And more than one of us, participant and facilitator alike, has become addicted to the mystery of the circle—the labyrinthine mysteries of the mandala.

Myth, Legend, and Poetry

Although at GETTING WELL we focus on participants creating their own stories and poetry, we have had powerful results using prose or poetry as an inspiration for beautiful mixed-media expressions.

Poetry and stories are ways of using left-brain materials (words) to elicit right-brain responses (sensory images). Some of these responses are on the conscious level; however, the greater impact may be at the "unconscious," cellular level, which determines the integrity of the body. Poetry, myth, and legend are powerful tools for shaping core beliefs and perceptions. For example, my father's morning wake-up call of "Let us then be up and doing with a heart for any fate, still achieving, still pursuing, learn to labor and to wait" ensured my internalizing the work ethic. Contrast the putative psychological effect of Longfellow with Whitman's "To me every hour of the light and dark is a miracle, Every cubic inch of space is a miracle. . . . All these to me are unspeakable perfect miracles. . . . " One cross-grains our essential being while the other allows us to flow with nature and the universe—to transcend the barriers to healing our culture presents.

One particularly moving expressive session uses the compact disc, "Skeleton Woman," in which the group, Flesh and Bone, have set to music Clarissa Pinkola Estes' legend by the same name from *Women Who Run With the Wolves* (1992). We start the music, read the tale of the Skeleton Woman, and while the eerily beautiful music continues, ask participants to create some aspect of this legend from paint, found objects, collage, etc. There is always a sense of passion and reverence as people gather their objects and create their symbolic representations. This exercise generally requires more than the usual hour.

Although a number of good sources of poetry to encourage imagery exist, *Leaves of Grass* by Walt Whitman is a favorite of mine. Whitman sees the beauty and mystery in the commonplace things in life, and his poem "Miracles" evokes especially wonderful images and shifts of consciousness for participants. We usually use slow "imagery" music for the reading of the poem and have paper, crayons, magazines, and paints available for participants to express their interpretation of the poem. I am always surprised at how deeply the words of poetry and stories penetrate and how profoundly the nonverbal expressions are articulated by participants both on paper and in their lives.

Other Exercises

We use a number of expressive exercises which require no guided visualizations or other preliminaries—just a statement of the task and provision of materials to explore the task. Some of these include:

- Draw your family as anything but humans.
- Make a representation of your guilt (anxiety, fear, shame, depression, joy, love).
- Paint/draw a picture of the next issue you need to address in therapy (Hookham, 1991).
- What would you paint on your sweatshirt so people would know it was you coming? What would you paint on the back? (Hookham, 1991).
- Paint a picture of a nightmare you have had.

- Draw/paint a picture of who will be at your deathbed. Paint a picture of what you will leave behind (Hookham, 1991).
- Make a collage of how you felt as a child on one side of a posterboard and of how you would like to have felt on the other side (Hookham, 1991).
- When dealing with unresolved grief and loss, have the client construct a memorial to the deceased along with a eulogy (Hookham, 1991).

Journaling

In journaling, one carries expressing the image a step further. James Pennebaker says that we think first in sensory images which are stored in the right hemisphere of the brain. Then our left hemisphere clothes the images in concrete language, allowing those elusive, amorphous images to be analyzed, processed, identified, and integrated into experience. Thus, the process of putting images into words and giving expression to those words enables us to analyze and transform an experience that was previously inaccessible. Journaling gets the images outside oneself where they can be manipulated—otherwise, they run around inside one's head creating chaos and confusion in the mind-body. Pennebaker insists that the essential element in journaling is not catharsis; rather, there is something deeper going on—processing of the event and gaining insight into the experience. Writing brings structure to the experience, encapsulates the situation in words, and seems to allow people to get beyond the circumstances. Dr. Pennebaker observes that writing does not necessarily help the person feel better right away. In fact, the individual may feel much more anxiety or depression for a while; however, as insights are reached, the bad feelings lift dramatically. It may be good to warn participants that it will get worse before it gets better—but it always gets better if they persist.

Journaling is an integral part of the GETTING WELL experience. Homework for didactic sessions frequently involves writing in one's journal (everyone is given a notebook) about a problem area. We have at least one expressive session a week specifically on journal writing, and usually a couple more (right-brain workshop, creative journaling, etc.) which reinforce the writing sessions.

Chick Wallace, a friend, mentor, and poet, has co-authored a book, *The The Healing "I"* (Block et al., 1992), which includes a number of ideas on structuring journal writing sessions. *The Healing "I"* chronicles the writing careers of the four poet/writer/authors—careers which began for each with an ineffable tragedy in life. They know firsthand the healing powers of writing, and give powerful examples of the writing/poetry which started their healing process, as well as splendid exercises to get one started and to dissolve blockages in the process. Their chapter on grief work is particularly moving and well done. The authors say about writing as therapy, "Remember that you may not always find *answers*. You may not always find solutions. There may not *be* ready answers or pat solutions. What you need may be simply a fresh way of looking at things. *But you will grow!*" (p. 18)

Journaling seems hard for most participants to initiate. For that reason, for at least two of the journaling sessions we use journaling tapes, *Writing the Natural Way* by Gabriele Rico and *The Journal Tape* by Kathleen Adams. These tapes present a succinct, motivating approach to writing and make up the great gaps in our expertise while giving participants concepts and techniques to make journaling less threatening.

A couple of journaling techniques which we find to be useful to dissolve blocks in written self-expression are "clustering" and "lists of 100." Clustering (Rico, 1983) is an easy writing technique which helps one access a great deal of information in a short period of time. To begin, write a key word or phrase in the middle of a page, circle it, then begin to free associate, circling and attaching each new concept or word to the one preceding it. When the end of a conceptual line is reached, go back to the original word and go off in another direction. Although one may spend no more than five minutes clustering, there is usually an incredible wealth of material. Prose or poetry created from the cluster always surprises the writer with its depth and insight. A result of clustering is Betty Coward's 1988 poem, which she has given me permission to quote:

> *We Are Together*
>
> Hope lined faces
>
> Voices with spirit
>
> Weary bodies taking yet one more step
>
> Hands joined in friendship
>
> Hearts joined in love
>
> New lives beginning
>
> Today is our dawn.

Journal lists of 100 (Adams, 1990) are wonderful for clarifying thoughts, getting below the surface, and focusing attention on what is *really* going on. The main rules for lists of 100 are to write as fast as one can, don't worry about repeating, and don't worry about making sense. Anything that is a current issue for a person is a good candidate for the lists. The list is not so important for the information one gathers, as for the inner state this process allows. The very fact of having to write 100 of anything breaks down many of the barriers between conscious and unconscious, and between left-brain and right-brain thinking. Almost anything is fodder for a list of 100; however, some particularly therapeutic results have occurred for "100 Things — I Miss, I Want To Do Before I Die, I Am Fearing Right Now, I Value in Life, I'm Angry About, I Want to Tell My Mother (Father), People I want to Forgive, Possessions I'm Tired of Owning, I've Never Mourned or Grieved, I Find Hard to Share." After the list of 100 is completed, the person writes reflections on the list.

"Letters that never will be sent" make wonderful journal entries. This exercise works well as homework for both group and individual sessions in which the clients have issues and baggage about some individual in their lives — a husband, mother, father, friend, child, etc. A letter to the person's disease, which is answered by the disease — essentially a dialogue with the person and his or her symptoms — is usually very revealing and not infrequently leads to new insights. Writing out a dialogue between the client and his or her parent(s) is another variation on these powerful "letter writing" techniques. Also, many of the exercises for drawing/painting are quite appropriate for journaling or a combination of the two.

Mask Making

Plaster Masks

Mask making is one of the most exciting sessions at GETTING WELL. As the masks are being made with plaster gauze, we talk about the symbolism of the layers upon layers that we put upon ourselves or that are put upon us by cultural pressures, how those layers smother our real selves, and how they immobilize the most important part of us. After the plaster has been put on the participant's face and the mask is fully hardened, all it takes is a smile to loosen the mask (assuming we haven't forgotten to put petroleum jelly on first!). Then, at another session, we paint the masks to be the persons we were born to be — our essential selves.

Probably the most useful (as well as the most beautiful) book on the subject is *Maskmaking* by Carole Sivin. Because GW was in a hospital setting when we initiated mask making, we had access to rolls of plaster gauze, so were able to make plaster masks, which have a special quality of their own. With plaster, it is important to have all materials ready, since the process involves quick work. Materials include: rolls of plaster gauze (the type from which casts are made), petroleum jelly, shower caps or scarves to hold hair out of the way, old scissors, cloths and newspapers to protect the person and the floor, paper towels or rags for cleanup, and warm water in a container. (Be sure not to pour the water down a drain or in a toilet after the session because the plaster will stop up the pipes.)

To begin the mask making, first, with hair held back by shower cap or scarf, cover the person's face with a thick, protective layer of petroleum jelly, paying particular attention to eyebrows, mustaches, and beards. The participants and facilitator usually cut strips of the plaster into a variety of lengths and widths ahead of time and have them on a cafeteria tray close by. Saturate the gauze strips one at a time by dipping them into the warm water and draining excess water from them. Press a strip onto the subject's forehead and rub lightly to be sure there are no air holes. Then place another strip overlapping the first one and so on, until the subject's face is covered with at least two layers of plaster gauze. If the eyes are to be open, be sure that the holes are the same size. If they are to be closed, press a square of wet gauze over each eye and press gently to capture the shape. Similarly, when doing the mouth, press a square of gauze between the lips and around the contour of the mouth. When everything else is finished, put an extra layer around the entire edge of the mask for added strength, remembering to have the mold extend slightly under the jaw and chin.

When the mask is dry enough to be removed (approximately five minutes), the subject can loosen it by smiling and moving facial muscles, so the mask can be removed gently from the face. It is usually best to have two people applying the mask material, one "expert" and one "apprentice." When masks are made again two weeks later, the apprentice (usually a participant) moves up to expert; thus, we are able to make more masks during an hour's time than the rather complex process would suggest.

Painting day is always a magical time during which participants create through their masks the persons they were born to be. Remember that a mask will need to dry for a day or so before being painted. Poster paints, acrylics, feathers, shells, glitter, pearlized paint, gilt, ribbons, and whatever else seems to be "right" go into the decoration of the masks. After the masks are complete, psychodramatic work may be done in dialogues in which the masks or other work that comes forth is processed. Steven Larsen says in his splendid book, *The Mythic Imagination*:

> Masks are best treated among us, as among our ancient ancestors, as power objects. They act "as-if" they were persons, or entities. If they can heal, they

can harm. They can, it seems, "act up" when ignored or treated carelessly. For these reasons, we recommend storing the masks in a safe (and even ceremonial) manner or, if it seems indicated, burn them or bury them in a natural place to dispose of them. Some masks like to be displayed; let them, by all means. But ask the mask! (pp. 324–325)

Our masks seem to like to be displayed, and they watch over us and join us with the energies of those whose visages they represent, long after their people have left and returned to their homes.

Drawing Masks

This is a nice little exercise which can be used instead of or in addition to creating plaster or other three-dimensional masks. Participants are asked to draw the different masks they wear. We encourage them to do as many as they can think of, and to label them. Then participants are asked to draw what they think they would really be like if the masks were stripped off—to draw themselves as vulnerable and exposed. Many times a "shell of a person" is revealed, someone not capable or assertive, someone who may feel he or she needs masks in order to function. Finally, group members are asked to draw what they think a self-assured, capable, assertive person is like. The facilitator then shows each one in turn that this capable person is really himself or herself, but that due to conditioning many believe they are *really* the vulnerable and exposed image. The lessons here are that it is safe to take off masks, and that if you wear one, be cognizant of wearing it as a *choice*.

Music

Hal Lingerman writes in *The Healing Energies of Music*:

The universe is a tonal harmony of many sounds—many lives interacting and vibrating together as they fill the great silence. [Music's] rhythms and melodies echo the eternal harmonies of the heavens. In this way music is a mirror of holy resonance: it opens transparencies in us, enlarging our horizons and helping us to feel what is beautiful and inspiring . . . it attunes us to powerful waves of life energy and to the unfathomable Source of all Good.

Just as color and light have a direct impact upon our psyche and physiology, music weaves a spell that energizes or soothes body and soul.

We use music with imagery and transformational fantasy, and during expressive projects as a royal path to the right brain. For example, we occasionally use it as a stimulus for expressive projects such as "paint the first movement of Beethoven's Sixth Symphony" or "put Handel's Water Music into color." Music has the amazing power to shift one's consciousness immediately and allow one to reflect on the world with new eyes.

In a keynote address at the Fourth World Conference of Imagery in Minneapolis in 1991, Don Campbell indicated there is a rhythm and energy that music allows us to explore in ourselves. He points out that rhythmic sound in the background changes pulse, heart rate, breathing, skin temperature, and brain wave patterns in 40–50 seconds. Campbell, who is one of the world's foremost researchers on the physical/emotional effects of sound waves, tells of the work of his mentor, Dr. Tomatis, who was asked to consult with the Benedictine monks. For hundreds of years, this order marked the canonical hours with lengthy chants interspersed with their arduous work during the day. With the modernization of the Church, the order dispensed with most of the chanting, as they became more active in the outside world. As a result, the order fell apart. Members did far less work, but were exhausted and constantly ill. When Tomatis was called in, he determined that the removal of the chanting was the source of the problem. He had the chants reinstated, and the Benedictines returned to their former high level of productivity and sense of connection.

Toning is essentially resonating one's own sound throughout one's being. It is very similar to chanting. "By releasing tensions and stimulating circulation and nerve energy in the body, Toning is a natural method of healing," says Laurel Keyes in her fascinating little volume, *Toning* (1973, p. 23). She has suggested that the colloidal field of our bodies (or the glue that keeps our cells connected) needs the vibrations of our voice literally to keep us from falling apart (as the religious order did). "Sound is the meeting place of the abstract and manifested idea," Keyes asserts.

Toning involves sitting quietly and watching one's breath for a few minutes, then inhaling healing white light through one's crown. When exhaling, one emits a soft humming sound and feels all "imperfections" leaving the body. This should be done for 10 minutes daily. Alice Cash, Ph.D., of the University of Louisville Arts in Medicine program, combines work with drums and other rhythm instruments with toning, yielding wonderful expressive and stress management effects.

The participants and some therapists at GW seem somewhat uncomfortable with using toning, probably because toning goes against the cultural proscription against making "unmeaningful" sounds, yet we all seem pretty comfortable with "singalongs" done to recorded chants. Speaking of which, most of us at GW are "en-chanted" by *Many Blessings*, a glorious tape of healing hymns to the spirit and human connectedness. The energy is palpable as the group forms a "healing circle" and spends several minutes singing and repeating the simple sounds of a Native American chant or a simple song about giving and receiving from each other.

Making one's own music is immensely healing. GETTING WELL has a full range of guitars (acoustic and electric), as well as keyboards, organs, drums, kazoos, tambourines, an auto harp, and some rhythm band instruments which are brought into play on Saturday afternoons. (We still don't know whether to call this workshop "Expressive Therapy" or "Laughter and Play"!) It is fun, however, and sometimes we even sound pretty decent. Our songbooks have easy guitar and organ chords, and having the instruments accessible invites participants to regain a forgotten pleasure in making music or even learn a new source of musical expression.

Jerri, a nurse whose MS precipitated a fall which injured her back and led her to confinement a wheelchair, described herself as feeling dead inside. A week after she arrived from North Carolina, the family of a participant who had died donated an antique electric organ to GETTING WELL. Jerri's eyes lit up as she watched the beautiful instrument being moved into the expressive therapy room, and we all rejoiced as she wheeled her chair to the console and began timidly to touch the keys. The next morning, the house was ringing with sound when we came in; each morning thereafter, Jerri came in nearly an hour early to unleash her creative fires on the organ. At the same time, we noticed a shift in her therapeutic direction, and many doors began to open for her.

Movement, Bonsai, Sandplay, and TinkerToy® Therapies

Presently, the work we do with movement is quite simple. We play tapes of a variety of music and propose that participants move to the music in whatever ways they wish. At first the movements are tentative; however, people are soon moving freely, with an amazing variety of expressive motions. Even people in wheelchairs or with low energy can fully participate. We may suggest that they breath in healing light energy from their crown centers and express it in their movement. This is an excellent therapy, and I would like for us to do more in this area in the future.

"Bonsai therapy" had its inception when a participant brought in seven or eight bushy junipers in pots and gave his cohorts lessons in Bonsai. This activity made a deep impact on participants. GW therapist Gayla Bacon sees trimming the trees as "a metaphor for our lives." And she adds, "We need to clean out some of the density in order to get to the essence of who we are."

Jeannie Bagdhadi, a 38-year-old chronic fatigue syndrome patient who calls herself a walking GETTING WELL miracle, says about Bonsai therapy: "In clipping away at my tree, I realize that I have to get my old stuff out. There's no room for new experiences and ideas unless I do." As participants observe their trees, they are reminded that they must continue to get rid of the dross in order to create harmony and balance in their trees and in their lives.

Sandplay is a recent addition to GETTING WELL; however, our made-to-order sandboxes (19 inches by 28½ inches by 3 inches deep) are already a favorite with participants and therapists alike. Our collection of small figures, objects, shells, etc., to use in the boxes is still modest, yet the materials continually evoke deep meaning and are a source of important shifts in participants' conceptual landscapes. We use sandplay as another medium in which individuals can symbolically play out a problem they are experiencing, express feelings, or explore the geography of their souls. Stephen Larsen writes:

> The sandtray becomes not just a little, circumscribed world, but a border realm, through which an adventurer may cross over into worlds beyond. In a sense, it becomes itself the portal that permits our passage, or it can become a window through which we can safely look without passing, a window through which we ourselves can be seen, or it can become a magic mirror . . . The sandplay creates a way to see. . . . This seeing . . . has to do with consciousness, and with opening awareness. (1990, p. 279)

Of course, we let participants interpret their own symbols rather than putting our own interpretations on their work. I strongly recommend familiarizing oneself with the techniques and caveats by reading *Sandplay* (Kalff, 1980) or *Jungian Sandplay* (Ryce-Menuhin, 1992) before introducing this powerful therapy to patients.

Rosalind Brigham has a gift for making almost any activity into a therapeutic endeavor. TinkerToy® therapy is her creation. In this session, she pours the can (or cans) of TinkerToys® out onto the table. Each person in the circle then puts a piece on the structure until all pieces are used up, remembering that symmetry is not well accepted. Next, everyone is asked to contribute a letter, and all the letters together create a name for the concoction. Finally, each person describes the function of a part or whole of the object. Roz says that participants usually start out rather leery of the project, but end up with great ideas and high enthusiasm. After being introduced to this creative endeavor, many members buy their own sets of TinkerToys® or Leggo® and have a wonderful time with individual or joint designs. This activity can be adapted for use with a large piece of butcher's paper with each participant contributing crayon, felt pen, or paint strokes to the community "painting."

Lessons for the Author/Clinician

I grew up in a home filled with music, with parents who had a love of beauty and creativity and doted on the expressive efforts of their daughters. Although I had a fine musical education, I definitely did not appreciate it until I was an adult—as a child, I always wanted to draw and paint rather than play the violin. As a grammar school teacher fresh out of college, I delighted in doing art projects along with my students. And when Bob's Fulbright grant took us to Australia, my paint box kept me occupied while he contemplated math and computers. Thus painting became an integral part of my life for many years, and I was even able to earn my tuition for my master's degree in clinical psychology by selling my watercolors and winning prizes (although, admittedly, it was not really a very expensive program at the time). However, my art went out the window when I began my first job as a psychotherapist. For years, I drew psychological portraits of people in words rather than with watercolors. And although I tried to make time to include art in therapy, there was barely time for House-Tree-Persons.

GETTING WELL was a wonderful excuse to include self-expression not only in the lives of clients, but also in my own. I rejoiced in helping people learn to play simple chords on the guitar and sound good in just a few minutes. I fell in love with the auto harp that I bought for GW, and I even got my violin out to play in family groups. It was as if a dormant part of me was awakened with the music, and I felt more deeply connected with myself and with my feelings through their expression.

Several years ago, inspired by Lucia Capacchione's *Creative Journal* and Sandra Shuman's *Source Imagery*, I started a "painting journal." I found a large spiral-bound 8½" by 11" sketchbook with paper that (if taped) can handle watercolor, and began experimenting with the exercises in these two books. I found it particularly nice just to paint with no thought of sale or anyone's critique in mind. I tend first to paint my emotions and then to write about the experience of both the feelings and their exegesis, later pasting that sheet of paper on the page opposite the drawing or painting. It's a great ongoing project to stay in tune with where I am, to express feelings of joy, or to get a sense of how a particular expressive therapy lesson will connect. It is also a veritable life-saver when I have really tough times personally or with the program.

The journal not only offers a vehicle for me to paint and write about my feelings of despair, terror, disappointment, grief, and panic—to get them "out there" where they can be dealt with—but also serves as a reminder of what I have been through and how resilient I actually am. Participants seem to appreciate that I have done the exercises myself, from clustering to painting anger and all the others in between. They also like to see other options for their creative journaling (but I make it clear that it is only *my* way, not *the* way).

I once read that the best way to get out of a funk is to pull forth a memory, not of the better times of joy and peace, but from a period that was *really* terrible. I created a "favorite" entry for that purpose soon after the psychiatric hospital in which we were situated chose not to renew our contract because we had not produced enough profit. As a result my associate director of five years gave me less than two weeks' notice because he couldn't take "starting over again," and I was feeling totally alone and vulnerable in a voracious world. Just before an appointment during which (I thought) GETTING WELL's future would be decided, I got out my crayons and felt-tipped pens, drew my fear on one page and wrote about it on the opposite page with my left hand. The terror is palpable in that entry, and even as I am writing this, I am reliving that time. *However,* rather than being terrorized, I'm thinking to myself, "Wow, I made it through all that!" During this transition period from inpatient/for-profit to outpatient/not-for-profit, there were incredible financial and other pressures on me, but they pale when I look at that journal entry, and I feel almost lucky to have only those problems which exist now.

Another use I find for my journal is illustrating concepts which I find difficult to grasp. For example, *A Course in Miracles* and *Emmanuel's Book* present ideas that require me to look at the world in totally new ways. Drawing my image of those ideas allows them to be more lucid and, strangely, to become concrete.

More than anything else, GETTING WELL has given me license to express myself for pleasure and healing rather than for critical approval or monetary reward. It allows me to enjoy "doing it myself"—whether it's singing, beating a drum, or painting a feeling—rather than receiving my gratification *only* from "spectator art" such as *listening* to music, *watching* a play, or *viewing* an intriguing painting. In my life, there will be, as Peter London's book title vividly states, "No more secondhand art!"

17

Individual Therapy, Family Therapy, and Follow-up

There's a story underlying every pain. Once you get to the story, you get to the pain. —*Steven Vasquez*

When an individual has cancer, the family has cancer. To the degree which an individual is affected by the "idea" of cancer, it can be argued that every member of the cancer family contracts the disease. —*Brian L. Lewis*

One cannot truly accept others unless one also accepts oneself, and self acceptance at any level is essential for satisfying relationships. In the absence of self acceptance, relationships with our intimate other, with family, community, the world, nature, and the universe may be confined to fulfillment of social role expectations. If every encounter with another is viewed as an opportunity to heal and be healed and extend love, one may learn to heal and be healed in a relationship. —*Frances Vaughan*

Combining individual therapy, family counseling, and follow-up into a single chapter is in no way meant to diminish the importance of any of these elements of the GETTING WELL program, for each is essential to the whole. In these areas changing one's consciousness or imagery continues to be the major focus for intervention.

Individual Therapy

Although a number of mind-body programs employ individual therapy exclusively (such as Pat Norris' program at Menninger's), at GETTING WELL individual therapy is basically an adjunct to group therapy. This is partly due to time considerations. With six hours of group sessions daily, there simply is neither the program time available nor the staff required to make individual sessions a major focus. More important than the practicalities, however, are the philosophical considerations. We believe that the power of group can be vitiated by poor use of individual therapy. People generally are more comfortable telling their secrets and their stories to professionals and may save material salient to the group process for the "safer" individual session. Although we professionals have a great deal to offer patients, I still believe that the most powerful healing takes place in the relationship with their peers.

Shirley (whom you met in Chapter 6) formed a strong attachment to one of our therapists, managed to wangle a daily session with that counselor while she was in the program, and initiated long phone calls to her later, instead of coming in for follow-up sessions. Shirley's complex incest issues certainly required more attention than usual, and the situation would not have been a particular problem if Shirley had been making progress. But she felt she was stuck and sometimes even thought the program was only making her worse. We are not equipped to offer individual counseling as an independent treatment modality, so we finally had to suggest that, if she could not bring up her issues in group, we would have to refer her outside the program for treatment. Shirley finally "came out" in group (with a facilitator she had previously disliked intensely), and with that disclosure she shifted her life. We all realized how difficult this was for her and gave her support both in group and individually. Shirley now asks for hugs and has opened her heart for both giving and receiving love. I feel sure that if we had allowed the real "work" to be done in individual sessions, Shirley's outcome would have been similar to that of her three years of weekly sessions with a psychiatrist—virtually no progress, combined with the loss of hope that *anything* could change.

We make it clear that the main work is to be done in the group sessions, and that individual sessions are for additional work on one's idiosyncratic imagery, thorny relationship problems, difficult emotional blockages, and any other issues we cannot deal with adequately in the group sessions. Individual sessions are also an appropriate venue in which to uncover crucial sensitive issues with the participant and to prepare him or her to talk about those feelings in group.

More than a decade ago I realized that in an hour's therapy session the core was about 20 minutes, with the rest of the time taken up with banalities. Having shorter sessions allows both therapist and client to focus intensely on the issues at hand. Thus, standard length for individual sessions at GETTING WELL is 30 minutes, which allows everyone to have a session (if desired) nearly every day. The therapists who facilitate the group sessions are also the individual counselors, so much of the necessary "relationship" work has already been done in group. Participants average four to five individual sessions a week, usually with different therapists. Although counselors sometimes feel that I am clipping their wings with my insistence on half-hour therapy, I believe it emphasizes our team approach and reduces the participant's dependency on a single therapist. In addition, it is useful for therapists to hone and intensify their skills rather than relax in the often wasteful comfort of the 50- to 60-minute session. (Certainly, what we are doing at GW will not apply to every program. I am merely setting forth what seems to work for us.)

Talley, a beautiful 34-year-old-woman, came to GETTING WELL to deal with rage and depression. In her first 10 days in the program, she had opted for individual therapy only a few times and seemed to be just floating on the surface. During a group visit to the "room of secrets," she found very little beyond a number of boxes, and said, "But I don't seem to be able to image like others." After a high-level awareness session on guilt, Talley told me that she wanted an individual session later, then went on an hour-long walk. When she returned, we sat down and she said, "You know, you said that most of us don't feel guilty about things we *should* feel guilty about, like killing someone. Well, I did kill someone, and I don't think I can get over the guilt." As she talked about her prison experience, her deep regret, and her concern for the family of the child she had hit with her car, a big boulder of jammed-up emotions began to crumble. I asked her if she had spoken about this in group, and she had not. We talked about the possibility of her bringing up her secret in group the next morning, and she agreed that she was ready.

Talley did not wait until group the next morning. That evening, a number of the participants from out of town stayed around the house until midnight, watching videotapes and listening to Talley pour out her secret. The next morning she shared with the "formal" group the anguish that had consumed her life for the last five years. The support from the group, as you might have guessed, was powerful and healing. And the support that I, as the facilitator, gave Talley in the group session was received in an even more effective way than it had been on an individual basis.

Individual therapy is exactly that at GETTING WELL. Many of us gravitate to transformational, interactive imagery in individual sessions, while others use approaches which feel "right" and fit the individual needs of the participants. A number of our therapists find that the individual therapy we do at GETTING WELL is different from traditional psychotherapy. Primarily, we do not have the luxury of time, and so we must create the expectation (image) that powerful, permanent change is possible in days and weeks rather than months and years. Rather than focusing on changing discrete behaviors (hoping for a shift in consciousness), we tend to go directly for the epiphanies, which in turn change the behaviors.

Larry LeShan (1992) has made the point that traditional psychotherapy does not meet the needs of the patient with a life-challenging illness. He likened traditional methods to a Rolls Royce, a luxurious car that runs wonderfully well. We drive the Rolls to New York; then, because it is so comfortable and runs so beautifully, we decide to drive it the rest of the way on our trip to London. Obviously, that's not going to work—we need to make a total shift of modalities, which is what we at GETTING WELL have done in our approach to therapy.

For example, we find that keeping our eye on the question, "Why does *this* person have *this* disease at *this* particular time?" is a helpful way of keeping ourselves focused in individual sessions. There is usually loss of a major emotional focus, which has precipitated in the individual with a life-threatening disease what LeShan calls a "hopeless, passionless grief and despair." The loss is rarely available consciously, so it is quite important to really hear the person's story and for that person to feel that he or she has been heard.

Although I have presented a number of generalizations about participants, we must remember that no two patients are the same; we must have faith in persons' individuality in order to treat them successfully. Some of the main work of the individual session (if it has not been completed in group) is finding what it means to the patient to be this particular person, that is, "What does it mean to be you?"

Arthur W. Frank, Ph.D. (1992), has offered guidelines for dealing with the seriously ill patient which our staff has found to be valuable in "being present" for participants:

- *Witness* the experience of suffering and help the person order this experience.
- Recognize that, although you as a professional do *not* know what the person is experiencing, this doesn't mean that you can't help.
- Resist the temptation to bring too much order to patients' stories. Listen without putting the person into a theoretical cubbyhole.
- Remember that your role is to help the ill person discover his or her *own* meaning in what is happening.

Family Group, Family Participation, and Family Therapy

Family members and significant others are a crucial part of the healing process. The diagnosis of a life-threatening illness throws a monkey wrench into the dynamics of a family system, which in turn has a profound effect on the individual. While the identified patient may be extremely fearful, family members may be even more disabled with anger, helplessness, and hopelessness. In many families a wall is erected around the patient—a protective yet nonetheless sometimes impenetrable wall. The patient doesn't want the family to know how upset he or she is, and family members do not want to admit to terror or hopelessness for fear that it will bring the patient down. All too frequently isolation occurs in the family system just when the patient and family members need each other most.

The interpersonal environment of the family is a crucial factor in the patient's healing. In all the modalities in which family is included, the focus is on establishing or enhancing the ability to discuss feelings. Sometimes the main thrust of the family group is teaching family members basic communication skills. One must expect to see denial, anger, fear, grief, depression, and bargaining in family members. Frequently, with participants facing death and the family facing the loss of a member, old and hidden issues burst forth (e.g., mother issues projected onto a wife) and need to be resolved. All too often families are terribly distressed that the homeostasis of the family is disrupted so violently at such an emotional time. Our staff looks at the family's being thrown into turmoil as a gift— an unprecedented opportunity for family members to regroup in ways beneficial to the system and the chance to learn to give and receive love meaningfully.

The area of therapy and support for the life-challenged family is a subject for a whole book in itself. I believe that unless therapists dealing with the family are well trained in family dynamics, serious damage can be done. Although that training is beyond the intent of this volume, I would like to give a feel for the variety of ways in which we deal with the families of patients. (For a fuller treatment, see Sotile, 1992.)

Family Support Group

At GETTING WELL we have a weekly support group available to family members and significant others of people presently in the program. We specifically exclude the identified patient so that members of the family can express themselves freely without having to worry about "hurting" the participant. One never knows what issues will come up in the family group, so I feel it is particularly important to have a trained clinician present. Brian Lewis, Ph.D. (1989), points out that families are autonomous, and change can be neither predicted nor forced. In the case of the family group, the therapist is usually dealing with members of more than one family, which makes the group potentially more unpredictable, but also more powerful.

Trent was 11 years old when he chose to enter the GETTING WELL program. He had successfully battled leukemia from the age of three to the age of six; then, at age eight, he developed a brain tumor. He had received most of his treatment in Boston at the Harvard complex of hospitals; however, after numerous surgeries and radiation, the tumor continued to grow back larger than before. His surgeries had left him neurologically impaired on his left side, unable to see out of his left eye and at one stage unable to walk unassisted. A few months before he entered GW, his physicians in Boston had sent him home to Florida with instructions to his parents, "Make this a good Christmas for him, for it will undoubtedly be his last."

Trent's mother never left his side, and despite his numerous hospitalizations, he had never spent a night away from her. At the time, GW was housed in a general hospital and participants were expected to reside in the hospital. We decided this would be a good opportunity to start the mother-son separation process, with Trent staying in the hospital, his mother coming with decreasing frequency to the program during the day, and the family (father, mother, and teenage sister) coming for the family group and later family therapy.

One can imagine how skewed the family dynamics had become, with Trent being at death's door most of his life. The family group quickly brought forth the fears of the family as well as the anger and resentment of Trent's sister, 14-year-old Liza, who felt she had been forgotten by the family. The family began to realize how they cast Trent in a sick/helpless role, which was not fostering his recovery. In many ways they had lost hope for him and did not see him as entering the normal world ever again.

Meanwhile, although the first couple of nights without his mom were somewhat difficult, Trent created a new family of GETTING WELL participants, who, while loving and accepting, didn't put up with his victim role. Although I was sometimes concerned that the program's material was over his head, he invariably showed wisdom far beyond his years and brain functioning. He developed powerful imagery of the immune system as Ghost Busters beaming God's loving light at his tumor. And he was a joy/ terror during laughter and play and expressive therapies—really showing everyone "where it should be at," as he often said.

We dealt with the family for several months after Trent completed the program, working on marital therapy with the parents, individual and family therapy with his sister Liza, and of course, follow-up with him. It became important to include him eventually in the family therapy since he had been the "very sick kid" and had been left out of important decisions by physicians and sometimes by his family. Soon he began assuming the role in the family of "normal 12-year-old kid." An X-ray during this time showed only a calcium deposit where the tumor had once been, and Trent reported to us that it was "dead as a duck, flat as a pancake." Additionally, his neurological complications began to fade. He no longer walked with a marked limp and his vision began to return. The next school year, he spent the first *full* year in public school in his whole life and had even earned a place in the marching band.

A week after his sixteenth birthday, I asked Trent to be my partner on a television program that was to be taped in Daytona Beach. Although Trent had just earned his driver's license, Liza drove him to our hospital, and we made the hour's drive to Daytona together. Trent had just received reports on an MRI in which the physician stated that he could find no evidence that there had ever been a tumor at that site! An equally important miracle was the deepening relationship between Liza and Trent and the normalization of the family. Although there were undoubtedly many factors in Trent's healing, I cannot help but believe that the changes made by his wise and wonderful family contributed mightily to his new consciousness — his new blueprint as a healthy family member.

The weekly family group reflects the whole panorama of problems that visit a family in which a member is at risk. One can expect older children acting out from fear of their parents' dying, wives distraught with fear yet furious at their husbands for having cancer or heart disease, and husbands feeling enormously guilty for having been abusive in the past to their now-ill wives. Family reactions absolutely run the gamut; therefore, it is important to have flexible, nonjudgmental, well-trained therapists to run this group and make decisions about the need for family therapy. As in the case of Trent, the family group is often the jumping-off point for more intensive family therapy down the road.

Family Participation in the Program

GETTING WELL invites family members to participate in the program along with the identified patient at no extra cost. Although it is preferable to have family members participate one at a time, we are flexible about these arrangements. This is very powerful family involvement, since the significant other is learning along with the participant and the two of them provide reinforcement for each other both during the process and after they leave the program. Learning together provides the milieu for what most people consider to be a peak experience in their relationship. When significant others attend the program, we ask that they excuse themselves during group therapy so the designated patient can speak freely (as the family member has in the family group).

Belle and Bart had been a team for nearly 35 years, and they considered the fight against his metastatic liver cancer a team effort. There was no question in their minds that Belle would be his partner in the program, one of the main reasons being that his physicians had given Bart only a couple of months to live. "I don't think I can go on if this doesn't work," Belle confided in us one of her first days in the program. "I'm really scared."

Bart, a successful lawyer in Virginia, had been used to having paralegals and skilled secretaries carry through his ideas, and Belle, a writer and poet, seemed to slip naturally into that role. She took notes in sessions, checked on Bart to see if he had done his imagery, and listened to tapes — the meat of which she conveyed to Bart. We quickly realized that Belle (with very loving intention) was taking the responsibility of healing from Bart, so in a family session we took a look at their situation, and they gained some insight concerning personal responsibility. Bart became an active participant in the program rather than merely half of a couple, and Belle began to work on her own consciousness shifts.

By the end of the four weeks, they were both different people, yet they were more in love than ever. Belle, having achieved serenity and peace of mind, felt empowered to handle whatever the future held. Bart had taken active responsibility for his health through imaging, journaling, and otherwise taking back his power. They had begun savoring life rather than dancing to the tune of Bart's tumors. Although Bart's physical situation improved greatly, he died several months later from post-surgical complications. A few months after his death, Belle wrote,

> I think you realized that [Bart] and I had a very special relationship and it is a constant learning experience for me to think in terms of life without him. Being able to participate in the GETTING WELL program has been a vital key in my adjustment. There have been countless times when something I learned with you has given me courage or has made me stop to evaluate my attitude in a new light. . . . I'm so glad [Bart] and I had the time together in Florida. We developed a bond that we could not have formed here. . . . Your program gave him the confidence that he could participate in his healing, and though he was not cured, he lived out his days feeling he still had some control — and he *did* have control how he greeted each day. . . . I am trying to cherish the past and preserve it, but not live in it.

When I spoke to Belle on the phone to ask permission to use her letter, she reiterated the gratitude she feels at having had the month together with Bart without having to deal with business or well-meaning friends. Nearly four years after his death, she says it is difficult sometimes but that the program has allowed her to evince a strength she would not otherwise have had.

A different story is that of Tate, a woman in her mid-twenties who entered the program soon after a hysterectomy precipitated by uterine cancer. She and her husband Ben had been trying to have a baby for several years; however, now the only option was adoption. Because of his duties at a distant university, Ben could be in the program only a couple of weeks, so Tate stayed on without him.

During Tate's first few days in the program, I assumed that she was grieving the loss of the dream of having a biological child, and we all went overboard to help with the process and open the door to other options that would fill their lives with children. How wrong we were! Tate did *not* want children, and was somewhat dismayed that her hysterectomy had not ended the discussion. However, children were very much a part of what Ben believed the good life included. Although Tate had spent most of her life being what she thought everyone else wanted her to be, she was actively exploring who *she* really wanted to be. This involved being her own person in the marriage, which was not a part of the original silent agenda. As a result of the program, Tate and Ben's relationship has changed greatly. Tate is more assertively living her life the way she wishes, and although Ben is dismayed at some of the changes, they actually seem closer than before. Tate has blossomed and has taken several risks with her job and her life (which previously would have been inconceivable to her).

Tate and Ben's story illustrates the power of having a significant other go through the program (and to show how far off base my initial assumptions were). If we had continued in the track of keeping this "adorable couple" together we would have missed the boat concerning the dynamics of the disease process, and, more importantly, never realized what Tate needed to do with her life. Of course, Ben's life is important, too. Tate's needs were being expressed in a passive-aggressive manner to Ben, frequently in ways that undermined his tenuous self-esteem. Tate and Ben are planning another visit to the program in the near future, and it will be exciting to deal with two whole people rather than a couple living a bad dream.

Marital and Family Therapy

Family therapy takes many forms at GETTING WELL. Couples therapy may take the place of individual therapy time several times a week, or the participant may join family members who have come in for the family group for a session afterward. Sometimes we schedule special sessions for spouses or parents who have been reluctant to come in. Frequently, the patient requests that we be present at a "declaration of independence" with family members, or we may almost *insist* that he or she bring in a significant other who presents a major problem. We learned years ago that we could not afford the rigid "rules" under which many family therapists work. Being a trained and licensed marriage and family therapist, I respect the guidelines that many practitioners have (e.g., the whole family must be present at sessions), yet we take what we can get.

Follow-up on couple/family issues is important. If a clinician has referred the patient, we, of course, refer the participant back to him or her.
However, since so many of our participants are from out of state, we are
trying to develop referral sources for GETTING WELL families in all parts of
the country. We feel it is imperative that the marital/family therapist
share GETTING WELL's theoretical outlook, because *dealing with the life-
challenging illness is different from dealing with usual family disruptions.*

Alba, a beautiful 28-year-old insurance executive with her second recurrence of metastatic breast cancer, felt reluctant to enter the program because she would have to leave her four-year-old son at home with her
emotionally abusive husband, Blackie. However, she was consumed with
fear about dying before instilling a core of love and gentleness in her son
which could survive Blackie's macho training. Although Alba was capable,
even brilliant, in her demanding job, she was like jello with her husband,
and it was painful to hear the stories of his domination and emotional
cruelty. For example, he chided her for sounding so cheerful and healthy
when she spoke on the phone with one of their friends: "I've told them
you're going to die soon. You're really making me out to be a fool when
you act so cheerful." This seemed to be the tenor of their relationship,
and sadly, Alba, the product of a dysfunctional family, appeared to accept
it as her legacy.
      While in the program, Alba developed a strong sense of herself and
decided that she would separate from Blackie as amicably as possible, as
soon as possible, if things did not change. However, in the hope that the
marriage could be saved, she finally was able to persuade him to come in
for marital sessions shortly before she graduated from GETTING WELL.
During the first session, I saw real hope that the relationship could work,
and so did Alba. However, Blackie did not show up for the next scheduled
session.
      Shortly after Alba had completed the program, a visit to her physician
showed her tumor markers were dramatically reduced, and a nagging infection at the site of her mastectomy had healed. Additionally, Alba felt better
than she had in years. A number of weeks later in the follow-up group,
however, she looked as if the burdens of the world were back on her
shoulders. "He really hasn't changed," she told us. "He's so proud of himself
for pulling the wool over your eyes at our counseling session. And I'm
really scared about leaving him—afraid of what he might do to our son."
Another few weeks later, Alba announced in group that her tumor markers
were up and that her doctor had found evidence that the cancer was
active again. Her oncologist thought the only thing that would save her
was a bone marrow transplant. Arrangements were made for her and her

son to stay with her mother and sister in North Carolina while she went through the procedure at Duke. Later she described the couple of months she was away as some of the happiest in her life. "I felt I was around people who really cherished me. I really felt at peace, although the transplant was certainly no piece of cake." Her transplant was deemed a complete success, and the next time we saw her she was thin and hairless — but glowing. She came regularly to follow-up sessions and was an inspiration to several "generations" of GETTING WELL participants.

She stopped coming for a while, and the next time we saw her was at a memorial luncheon for a man whom Alba inspired and by whom she was uplifted. She was gaunt, and she whispered to us, "It's not worth it to go on. Things aren't going to change. I think I'm giving up." In a couple of months she was dead. This is not a pretty story, but I believe it illustrates the crucial influence of the family environment and the necessity for family therapy in the healing process. I rather doubt that therapy would have facilitated Blackie's giving up sufficient control to allow Alba to be herself; however, it might have effected an amicable dissolution of a dysfunctional relationship. We can't know, but we can learn from the story.

Follow-up Program

Follow-up sessions are critical for participants' reentry into the "real" world. Although shifts of consciousness are more permanent than changes made only at the behavioral level, regular reinforcement of changes of both kinds is essential for their solid incorporation into the participants' lifestyles and mindstyles.

At GETTING WELL we have two regular weekly follow-up groups, one during the day at the program and one that meets in the early evening at a nearby hospital. The groups are different from each other and give participants a choice of times and focus (we ask that they attend one *or* the other). Presently there is no charge for the groups; however, we may need to take a close look at that, since people sometimes feel they get what they pay for.

The Wednesday morning (10 a.m. until noon) group has been in operation since the inception of GW. It has had a variety of formats, and frankly, I'm not sure one is better than another. An important part of the follow-up program is the networking the participants create with other members wherever they may be. They exchange letters and phone calls, and follow-up group is a place they and we can share those contacts.

We have generally combined the follow-up group with a meeting of the active participants. The participants seem to gain strength from the graduates, and the graduates gain strength from teaching their lessons.

The drawback is that the issues of participants and graduates are frequently different. We have successfully separated the two groups, but then a certain vitality seems to be missing. With this group (which is constantly changing), we have tried a number of approaches. We used the seven-week structured program of Cunningham et al. (1991) quite successfully, yet a couple of months later the members rebelled at going on to the next stage. I particularly like a format I call "I want to hear a success story," but sometimes that does not allow for discussion of serious issues. On the other hand, if we do focus on serious issues, it becomes more like a therapy group than an upbeat support group. Perhaps the most important factor in the success of this group is having a flexible and imaginative leader who can respond to the ever-changing needs of the members.

The Tuesday evening group is run by therapists trained at Bernie Siegel's ECaP (Exceptional Cancer Patients) in New Haven, Connecticut. This group is open both to GETTING WELL graduates and to others with life-challenging conditions who have not necessarily been through the program, both as a public service and to let people know about GW. It is a wonderful group which combines singing, drawing, laughter, and emotional support. Unfortunately, some people use the group as a safe substitute for committing to a stay at GETTING WELL, where their issues would be dealt with in considerably more depth. However, although we may be inappropriately allaying anxiety for prospective participants, it is an excellent follow-up group for graduates.

Since GETTING WELL attracts individuals from all over the country, follow-up for out-of-towners is a concern. Although we keep in touch by phone, this is not as effective for the graduate as a good support group or a therapist who is in tune with his or her special needs. As we pointed out earlier, the life-challenged individual needs a therapist who transcends traditional psychotherapy agendas and is able to meet the graduate's particular needs. We have been instrumental in organizing support groups in cities in which a number of graduates live (e.g., Atlanta); however, in general follow-up has been a continuing problem. We have a number of practitioners and support groups to which we feel confident referring graduates; however, we would like to build our referral sources. Unfortunately, many support groups for specific diseases are (according to our participants) quite negative and focus on how one will cope with the next stage of the disease rather than on learning to live with grace, passion, and peace. I have found the ECaP directory as well as the directory for Attitudinal Healing Centers useful; however, I invite individual therapists, support groups, and behavioral medicine programs in tune with the philosophy of GETTING WELL to get in touch with us to further develop our referral network.

Lessons for the Author/Clinician

As I was writing this chapter, I replayed the story of Alba many times in my mind, wondering if I should have made a bigger push for marital therapy before she was ready to embrace it. I have lost some sleep reviewing the "what ifs" and "shoulds" of my part of her story. I remember not going to the funeral because of my anger at Blackie, yet my associate who attended reported that he appeared to be dissolved in grief at the service and genuinely grateful to the GETTING WELL staff.

These mental peregrinations led me to a file that contained a four-page letter from Alba, written as she completed the program. She wrote:

> I portrayed confidence, positive attitude, and a continual battle for life. Deep inside I was overwhelmed by fear, anger, and a strong desire to crawl into a corner and just give up. The opposite emotions left me numb and depressed. I was physically and mentally exhausted. Constantly plagued by resentment and guilt, I wondered what horrible thing I had done in my life to deserve cancer and particularly for the third time. I felt alone and unable to cope — totally out of control of my life and emotions.
>
> The mind is a powerful force. It can be destructive, as it was for me, or it can be a strength with no limits, as it is becoming for me. The depression that was steadily increasing is now steadily decreasing. I'm finding happiness in harmony of mind, body, and soul. I honestly believe that the new me will survive cancer. I know that my work does not end in 28 days, it is a continual growing, and there will be difficult days. I now feel that I have the emotional strength to face those days as a challenge.

As I read these words, I realize that Alba has, indeed, survived cancer. She lived her life the way she needed to live it, and I feel honored to have been a part of it. I'm learning that all stories don't necessarily have the neat ending that I would wish; however, their ending may be the right one for those involved.

18

Synergy, Epiphanies, and Miracles

Miracles happen at the unconscious, archetypal level; they don't come from the cold intellect. That is one reason why doctors have trouble "seeing" miracles. To see, you have to believe. —*Bernie Siegel*

Miracles happen, not in opposition to Nature, but in opposition to what we know of Nature. —*St. Augustine*

The universe is a billion times more beautiful, abundant and malleable than humans ever dreamed it to be. We shape our "reality" from the miniscule amount of information our sensory mechanisms gather and organize from experience into our "map" of reality.... Reality is not an immutable absolute as has been long believed in Western culture but is the reflection of our conditioning and beliefs based upon an infinitesimal sampling of the information available to us. Whatever the nature of the ultimate reality, humans can only consciously discern it through the lens of our sensors and as shaped by belief. Thus far in human history we have been perceiving the universe and ourselves in a very limiting fashion. —*Edgar D. Mitchell*

Synergy—the combination of strategies or viewpoints—represents the creative process in action. The ideas or materials from which synergy evolves are frequently quite commonplace. For example, most of the concepts we present at GETTING WELL have been around for a long time; yet when an individual puts them together in his or her own idiosyncratic way, a larger whole is created. To look at synergy another way, perhaps the larger whole was already in place and synergy is the letting go of the fragmentation of consciousness which kept one from embracing the wholeness in the beginning. Nonetheless, the consciousness shifts, an epiphany takes place, and the world will never be quite the same for that person again.

I see synergy as the process underlying shifts of consciousness (or epiphanies), and miracles as physical manifestations of this mental/spiritual process. Bernie Siegel has said that miracles and epiphanies don't happen in the intellect; rather, they occur at the synergistic, right-brain, unconscious level. Although these concepts are almost by definition beyond analysis, I believe it is important both from a research and a clinical point of view to take a look at the components of emotional and physical healing to see what it is that creates synergy and to provide fertile soil for epiphanies and miracles.

Predisposing Qualities for Miracles and Spontaneous Remissions

As we have seen, a shift of consciousness, a sudden change in attitude—an epiphany—was a common thread that researchers identified as preceding each of the hundreds of "miracles" and spontaneous remissions studied (Green & Green, 1977). Similarly, Roud (1990) reports that Japanese doctors from Kyushu University studying five spontaneous cancer remissions found that all five people developed a dramatically different outlook on life as they released worldly attachments and became closer to their true natures. Weinstock (1977) reviewed 12 cases of spontaneous remission and found that all shared a deep sense of hope. Kennedy et al. (1972) found the common factors in the 22 "cures" of patients with advanced cancer were hope, a better self-image, and a deeper appreciation of life.

One problem with discussing the conditions necessary for spontaneous remission is that many people become determined to create their own miracles, and pursuit of this goal becomes their singular focus. They attack rationally and intellectually, as though they were writing an important paper or studying for a final exam. It is this rational approach which causes them to miss the point—and the boat.

Larry Dossey (1993) makes an important distinction between "rational healing" and "paradoxical healing," noting that rational healing is involved with *doing*, and paradoxical healing is involved with *being*. A continuum exists from rational techniques, such as surgery, radiation, and medication, through lifestyle changes, coping skills, psychological counseling, biofeedback/imagery, and the placebo effect. At the far end of the spectrum are prayer, shifts of consciousness, and miracles—paradoxical healing.

Formulas, prescriptions, strategies, coping skills training, and goals work quite well at the rational edge but become ineffective and even counterproductive as one approaches paradoxical healing. For example, the best way to fail at biofeedback and imagery is to put too much effort into them. Achieving success in these and other areas of paradoxical healing requires states of mind or qualities such as letting go, surrender, "thy will be done," or "whatever happens I'll find meaning in it" (not from the position of victim but from empowerment or choice).

Dossey rebukes the New Age fantasy of a linear, one-on-one correlation between spiritual enlightenment and physical health, citing examples of saints who have died terrible deaths and, on the other hand, curmudgeons who smoke three packs of cigarettes a day and live to a ripe old age. True enough, but I believe rational healing and paradoxical healing are interactive, that surgery, medication, and healthy lifestyles make it easier for healing to take place. Certainly, an enlightened attitude appears to increase the probability that rational modes are successful. Above all, it does seem clear that there are no guarantees—and if one tries too hard, *nothing* works.

Brendan O'Regan (1986) spearheaded the Institute of Noetic Science's search of over 3,000 articles found in journals from all over the world which documented spontaneous remissions from all kinds of ailments, and first determined that they were not merely "misdiagnoses." He found several remissions were preceded by an infection or non-pertinent surgery; however, *most* involved a shift of consciousness, an emotional change—an epiphany. The epiphany, whether it be falling in love, a near-death experience, changing one's personal mythology, seeing oneself as good and lovable, finding hope, glimpsing the wholeness/unity of the universe/nature, a strong faith/belief, or becoming united with a "higher power," seems to be a necessary (but possibly not sufficient) condition for a physical miracle to take place.

O'Regan tells of a priest he met at the shrine of Mejegorde who is known to predict who will experience a miracle. Those most likely are individuals for whom a miracle is not uppermost in their minds. "They have an open mind and have asked for healing, but they have not come with this as the single-minded purpose of their trip" (p. 9). In addition, the affected ones come in a state of "psychological void," indicating an openness to paradox, mystery, cosmic laws, and the fullness of life.

Caryle Hirshberg (1993), O'Regan's research associate in the IONS remission project and now project manager, observed the following qualities (of *being* rather than *doing*) in those people to whom a spontaneous remission occurred:

- A shift from dependency to autonomy. There was a change in the belief system from feeling out of control to feeling that the process of healing came from within rather than without.
- A change (upgrade) in the quality of interpersonal relationships.
- Acceptance of the diagnosis. Survivors faced the crisis and went through it.
- Strong mood fluctuations. Survivors tended to express all feelings and were as passionate about their grief as they were about their joy. Being expressive about the disease was a key aspect.
- A change in diet. (Hirschberg saw this shift more as a result of the

change in beliefs about oneself than of being responsible for the change in consciousness or the spontaneous remission.)
- A confrontation with the disease and an active decision on what to do about the diagnosis.
- Less anxiety and depression.
- A change in attitude toward life; becoming more actively involved with others.
- Spiritual changes involving the connection of mind, body, and spirit.

For nearly 20 years, Paul Pearsall, Ph.D., a neuropsychologist, researcher, and writer working in a Detroit hospital clinic, studied 17 patients with terminal diagnoses who had "created miracles" in their lives. In 1988 he was diagnosed with two different "terminal" cancers and had several near-death experiences, a bone-marrow transplant, and a complete recovery in less than a year. In his book, *Making Miracles* (1991), he suggests there are seven characteristics of those who are "miracle prone":

- A confidence and awareness beyond the rational, logical, simplistic knowing of everyday life.
- Experience with several crises and the development of a psychic toughness and an awareness of a complementary side to all feelings. Recognition of the dualistic nature that is natural to everything, even the most apparently hopeless situation.
- A yearning for much more from life than mere coping, survival, success and security. A desire to transcend the here and now. Active involvement in the search for the meaning of life.
- A simplicity of lifestyle free of the need to acquire goods and possess expensive things.
- Expression of creativity and avoidance of becoming "well adjusted" to a stressful, see-and-touch world.
- A tendency to be a psychic gambler, a willingness to take risks for the fulfillment of dreams, and a predilection to thinking in a freewheeling style that reflects the uncertainty of all of life.
- Exhibition of a patience, forgiveness, generosity, truthfulness, and equanimity that Pearsall calls "loving kindness."

Pearsall agrees with O'Regan that those who experience miracles "are in a very different place psychologically, emotionally, and indeed psychophysiologically" (1986, p. 9). However, he indicates that these characteristics of his 17 miracle-prone patients are not representative of a "type" of person, but do represent typical choices these people of uncommon consciousness made in the face of a serious diagnosis.

In his studies of survivors, Al Siebert (1993) found that the biggest challenge to survival was breaking free of prohibitions that act as invisible emotional handicaps. He went so far as to state: "The biggest barrier to developing a survivor personality comes from having been raised to be a 'good' person" (p. 65). (Similarly, Pearsall names "guilt" as the number one block to making miracles.) He hesitates to give a list of characteristics which people might see as "rules" for survival since "people who follow instructions on how to be successful are seldom as successful as they could be" (p. 18). Nonetheless, guidelines such as the following may serve as license to allow some people to experience themselves in ways they may never have allowed themselves to:

- Being playfully curious: asking questions, wondering, experimenting, having fun, laughing.
- Possessing synergism and a need to have things working well—together they create serendipity.
- Becoming empathic, intuitive, creative, and imaginative.
- Having an inner locus of control. ("Those that prayed to God to rescue them, and waited passively for help didn't make it. Those that survived the prison camp experienced 'a life force from within'" (p. 207).)
- Having strong self-esteem, solid self-confidence, and a positive self-concept.
- Flexibility and adaptability. Emotionally biphasic and paradoxical.

Siebert's survivors consider flexibility an absolutely essential quality. A part of their flexibility was having biphasic emotional and personality styles. "Survivors puzzled me at first," he notes. "They are serious *and* humorous, hard-working *and* lazy, self-confident *and* self-critical. They are not one way *or* the other, they are *both* one way *and* the other" (p. 25). His findings are consistent with those of Hirshberg (strong mood fluctuations) and Pearsall (coexistence of complementary emotions). Survivors are proud *and* humble, logical *and* intuitive, selfish *and* unselfish, self-confident *and* self-critical, cooperative *and* rebellious, spiritual *and* irreverent, optimistic *and* pessimistic, consistent *and* unpredictable. They express hope *and* despair, anger *and* love, fear *and* peace, a positive attitude *and* a negative attitude. (Pearsall says, "Tell people they do not have to have 'a positive attitude' to resolve their problems" (p. 31).) Survivors are complex and paradoxical, which in turn gives them flexibility in how they choose to react in tough situations.

Perhaps the connecting thread in the biphasic, emotionally expressive aspect of survivors is that they acknowledge the contradictory parts of themselves, are comfortable with who they are, and find their own songs to sing rather than imitating the songs of others who have been healed.

New Physics, New Realms of Reality, and New Possibilities

A miracle is when something that cannot happen does anyway. It is not a question of the manifestation of hitherto unknown natural laws, if there are such that multiply loaves and permit walking on water, but rather a temporary suspension of nature itself by some outside supernatural action. If this can happen, there is a problem. In science, exceptions do not prove the rule. Doing research at all means making at least a few basic assumptions: that nature is knowable, and that it is constant. Experiments can be done, and most important, repeated. The genuine possibility of divine intervention as an unknown variable knocks the whole house of cards to pieces. (James Hansen, 1982, p. 51)

The mystic in me likes to believe that miracles are some kind of supernatural divine intervention, yet an even more deeply mystical part of me does not believe that miracles are supernatural. The proponents of the new physics feel we live in a universe we are only beginning to fathom and that perhaps the natural and the divine are the same, yet of such infinitude that we only occasionally have a glimpse (an epiphany) of the grandeur of it all. It is possible that only in death and the final rejoining do we fully know and fully flow with the universal intelligence or the cosmic consciousness.

I see miracles as the playing out of natural or divine law with which we were not formerly acquainted. For example, though some considered the fact that Columbus did not fall off the edge of a "flat" earth to be a miracle, the real miracle was the opening of the layer of consciousness that allowed Columbus to perceive the earth as being round before he set sail.

I sometimes think of us as being in the center of nesting Russian eggs. Our reality is limited by the wooden shell of the particular egg in which we find ourselves. As we drill conceptual holes in the immediate shell and glimpse a new layer of possibilities, that shell begins to crack and we have a new realm of "reality." It is in the nature of scientific inquiry (and human consciousness) that major advances come from people who look at things in a different way — who break through the shell of their immediate nesting egg.

Talbot (1991) asserts that if we assume consciousness can mediate directly in the implicate order, then such "miracles" as walking on burning coals and handling red-hot irons with impunity become explainable problems or events. He suggests that what we consider to be the laws of physics are actually just cosmic habits. Thus, the ability of consciousness to shift from one entire reality to another indicates that, while the usually inviolate rule of fire burning flesh may be only a single program in the entire cosmic computer, it is "a pattern that has been repeated so often it has become one of nature's habits" (p. 137). Matter is also a habit, and the objects we see "out there" are merely habits in the flux and flow of the cosmic ocean. The flux is the reality, even if we consistently see only the habit.

Talbot also states that since the universe and the laws of physics that govern it are products of this flux, they too must be viewed as habits, deeply ingrained, but habits nonetheless. And despite the apparent constancy of the laws of physics, extraordinary characteristics such as immunity to fire suggest that at least some of the rules that govern what we know as reality can be suspended. "This means that the laws of physics are not set in stone, but are more like Shainberg's vortices, whirlpools of such vast inertial power that they are as fixed in the holomovement as our own habits and deeply held convictions are fixed in our thoughts" (1991, p. 137).

In *Cosmic Joy and Local Pain* (1987), biophysicist Harold Morowitz suggests "the cosmic grandeur of the universe does not spare us from local pain" (p. 300); however, the workings of the universe as revealed by the new science may explain the miracles of our daily lives. Accordingly, Pearsall (1991) has listed 10 findings of science which lead to uncommon ways of looking at the world:

- *Theory of non-locality.* People and events can "happen" instantaneously everywhere, anywhere, and at any time. We are all everywhere and a part of everything. "We are each a manifestation of God's presence in everything. This means we lead a divine life even as we live our daily life" (p. 6). This theory that people and things are affected by events that are not just in the here and now provides a framework for understanding synchronicity and "coincidences."
- *Theory of "observer participancy."* What we discover is profoundly affected by what we are looking for and how, when, and with what we are doing the looking. "Whether we see limited and local order in a universe of total chaos or an infinite order revealed through what appears to be chaos is, therefore, one of the key choices of our lives, because in choosing a world view we actually create the world that we experience" (p. 27).
- *The uncertainty principle.* The chaos we see daily is evidence of the constant state of flux that characterizes the universe. "It is this very indeterminism and openness of the quantum world that gives our universe its potential for the unexpected, the new, the creative, the miraculous . . . in our uncertainty there is always hope" (pp. 34–35).

- *The complementarity principle.* All being can be described equally well either as particle or wave (mass or energy, body or spirit). "We are not just 'things' that eventually burn out or break. We have life on an energy or 'wave' level in addition to our 'particle' level" (p. 27). All reality can be seen in a dual way. A tumor can be seen as mass *or* energy. "This freedom makes any miracle possible" (p. 9).
- *Concept of oneness.* Everything in the cosmos is inseparable. "The closely related principle of non-locality defines our shared and timeless omnipresence within the universe, and the oneness concept emphasizes our connection with one another" (p. 10).
- *Levels of reality.* There are several levels of reality that include but transcend our finite, local, see-and-touch world. Ancient spiritual healers of Maui "defined illness and personal crisis as becoming trapped in one level of reality and saw ultimate healing as restoring a person's ability to know and experience all levels of the reality of their spirit" (p. 10).
- *The principle of relative timelessness.* "Our most creative scientists typically describe their miracle discoveries as taking place when they freed themselves from the mechanical measures of directional time. Creative people characterize their work as spontaneous, coincidental, sudden, and even surprising. . . . Miracles are made when we learn to be free of a linear time line and understand that past, present, and future are not separate" (p. 11).
- *The existence of growth energy fields.* These fields influence the development of all living things and include the concept of life energy (Qi, prana, holy spirit, etc.). "Sudden coincidences are the pulls and pushes from these growth energy templates" (p. 12).
- *The principle of entropy.* Everything and everyone is in the process of falling apart and burning up. This is a positive and necessary force, for "we are only falling apart so we can fall together again in a different and higher order" (p. 13).
- *The principle of chaos.* Science has discovered a remarkable order within chaos. "Making miracles requires the skill of seeking and appreciating the 'chaotic order' that is a natural part of our universe. . . . Scientists are learning to celebrate rather than fear chaos and to look within it rather than away from it for clues to the meaning of our living" (pp. 12–13).

Gary Zukov presents a fascinating, in-depth history and exploration of these principles of quantum mechanics in *The Dancing Wu Li Masters*, which is written for non-physicists but has substantiation by some of the world's finest physicists. He writes that these theories are

... not only different from the way we have looked at the world for three hundred years, [but] *opposite*. The distinction between the "in here" and the "out there" upon which science was founded is becoming blurred. . . . [This] distinction may not exist! What is "out there" apparently depends, in a rigorous mathematical sense as well as a philosophical one, upon what we decide "in here." Observer and observed are interrelated in a real and fundamental sense. . . . There is a growing body of evidence that the distinction between the "in here" and the "out there" is illusion. (1979, p. 115)

Grof (1988) proposes that altered states of consciousness may be necessary to make such changes in the laws of physics, and suggests that the deeper and more emotionally powerful the beliefs, the more dramatic the shift of consciousness and the more profound the changes one can make in one's body and in reality itself. Physicist David Bohm (1980) believes that the entire universe consists of thought or consciousness and that reality exists only in what we think. Talbot (1991) quotes from a personal communication with biologist Lyal Watson, who has studied paranormal events all over the world: "I have no doubt that reality is in a very large part a construct of the imagination. I am not speaking as a particle physicist or even as someone who is totally aware of what's going on in the frontier of that discipline, but I think we have the capacity to change the world around us in quite fundamental ways" (p. 138).

Drs. Robert Jahn and Brenda Dunne (1987), who have done numerous well-designed experiments on the paranormal at the Princeton Engineering Anomalies Research Lab, believe that subatomic articles do not possess a distinctive reality until consciousness becomes a part of the picture. From a personal communication, Michael Talbot (1991) quotes Jahn: " . . . we have long since passed the place in high energy physics where we're examining the structure of a passive universe. I think we're into the domain where the interplay of consciousness in the environment is taking place on such a primary scale that we are indeed creating reality by any reasonable definition of the term." Similarly, Zukav states, "If the new physics has led us anywhere, it is back to ourselves, which is, of course, the only place that we could go" (p. 136).

In *The Holographic Universe* Talbot presents an excellent review of the literature on miracles and observes that most miracles seem to involve only *parts* of the unbroken whole. He surmises that if, hypothetically, miracles were examples of the mind's own latent abilities, they would understandably be partial in nature, since we so habitually think in terms of parts. He also states that if we begin to see the world differently, miracles would be different, and we would discover more miracles in which the whole of reality had been transformed. He then concludes: "There is *no* reality above and beyond that created by the integration of all consciousnesses, and the holographic universe can potentially be sculpted in virtually limitless ways by the mind" (p. 160).

The concept that our bodies are in a state of constant flux reminds us that with every breath we take and everything we eat or drink we bring in billions of "new" molecules to replace the billions of "old" molecules that are eliminated by our bodies. For example, most of the atoms current-ly in our bodies were not there six months ago. Yet, except in unusual circumstances, we have the same physical appearance. We also have the same arthritic joints, the same back pain, or the same tumor that we had six months ago—even though virtually all the cells in our skin, joints, spine, or tumor have been replaced. Why is this so? One substan-tiated theory is that the intelligence/image/consciousness/blueprint of our organisms remains essentially the same from day to day—so if there is to be a change, the consciousness itself needs to shift. We have seen in multiple personalities, those walking laboratories, that when the image shifts, an entirely different body, mind, and spirit appears—a new "whole" emerges.

This idea that consciousness or intelligence underlies reality is put forth in the Bible, which seems to make it more acceptable for some people to shift their belief to a more encompassing idea of God, the Source, and even to the nature of reality as expanded by Einstein's theories. For exam-ple, the Gospel according to St. John states, "In the beginning was the word, and the word was God . . . and the word became flesh." In the Bible, "word" is a translation of the Greek *logos*, which has a number of meanings including mind, intelligence, image, spirit, logic, plan, and cosmic reason. Simply throwing new light on the legitimate nuances of the meaning of *logos* gives us considerable new conceptual latitude in how we view consciousness, imagery, and the nature of matter.

In helping to create epiphanies that enable miracles, we seek powerful "holoshifts," one of the most empowering being an image of a universe manifesting endless possibilities for shapeshifting—a universe of which we are co-creators.

Shifting Consciousness, Empowering Synergy, Creating Epiphanies, and Enabling Miracles at GETTING WELL

Although teaching a variety of coping strategies is one aspect of a compre-hensive behavioral medicine program, the main thrust is helping individu-als change core beliefs, shift their world views, and see their lives, diseases, and life purposes in new ways. And while some may think we go too far by exploring the nature of miracles, I disagree. Rather, I believe that it is our obligation as healers to see "what works," to share this knowledge with others, and to find "techniques" to empower the process.

We do not push one certain ideology at GETTING WELL. Rather, like a well-conceived philosophy course, we immerse participants in a variety of views of the nature of being, of knowledge, of meaning, of the universe, etc., against which they can test their images, beliefs, and values. The ideas presented are, more often than not, biphasic, contradictory, and paradoxical. We do admit to a therapeutic thrust of cognitive flexibility and encourage consciousness shifts which lead to openness to, embracing of, flowing with, and finding meaning in flux, chaos, mystery, uncertainty, and paradox. And we consistently emphasize that each individual's healing path is different and that GETTING WELL staff members are merely facilitators. Following this dictum, we focus on small consciousness shifts in a variety of areas intended to culminate in synergistic, epiphanic "ahas," which in turn create powerful waves, ripples, and eddies in the ocean of one's life. Our program is designed to contribute pieces of the reality puzzle that participants synthesize, recognizing the complete picture with only a few pieces of the puzzle in place.

Of course, it *is* possible to experience major transformations by deeply experiencing only one or two aspects of the healing process (e.g., meditation or exercise), just as we can putatively know the nature of the universe by studying the nature of the atom. However, each person's path to enlightenment is unique, and no one course will be right for everyone. Moreover, I intuitively feel that the more pieces of the whole picture (or, better yet, the more ways of seeing the whole) which are experienced, the more powerful the synergy and the more enlightening the epiphany will be.

The daily "curriculum" of GETTING WELL provides a gamut of experiences on the rational to paradoxical healing continuum. Most people already have embarked on the most rational component of their healing process, medical treatment, and generally participants seem culturally more drawn to the rational end of the continuum. Thus, they find themselves fairly comfortable with the concept of stress management, coping skills training, relaxation training, and lifestyle changes (nutrition, exercise, smoking cessation, etc.). Then participants find themselves moving toward the less logical end of the spectrum with social support, emotional expression, laughter and noncompetitive play, and imagery. Finally, they move into the paradoxical end, which includes high-level awareness, expressive therapies, transformational fantasy, therapeutic touch, meditation, consciousness shifts, epiphanies, and frequently miracles.

As we have monitored our participants it has become apparent that rational skills such as imaging a tumor growing smaller, relaxing away one's tension, or handling conflict cannot by themselves explain the massive shifts we see in people's lives and frequently in their bodies. The shifts seem to have less to do with the specifics of various lessons than with the synergistic reaction taking place within the individual.

Furthermore, we have noticed that in the period between days nine and 12 of the program, participants begin to "fall apart at the seams," feel "nothing is working," and seem disinclined to continue. Amazingly, however, within 48 hours of this predictable crisis, nearly every participant experiences major shifts of consciousness—and once the synergy is in gear, the puzzle is solved, and the epiphanies begin.

Even as one goes through a day at GW, the groups touch on all points of the continuum. The stress management segment of GETTING WELL presents logical evidence that changing perceptions may be infinitely more powerful than trying to change events. The group therapy segment focuses on accepting and loving one's essential self, which enables us to give and receive healing support. In addition, group facilitates the image of hope in the powerful, internal sense. The nutrition and exercise portion not only promotes being good to oneself, but also may be instrumental in shifting one's consciousness about one's participation in the planetary (and possibly cosmic) schema.

Laughter and play sessions allow participants to practice shifting perceptions and to create the mini-epiphanies that result from seeing situations from a new perspective. High-level awareness presents many philosophical possibilities, including ones that expand human potential far beyond traditional Western thinking. These include the transpersonal possibilities enabled by Einstein's and Bohm's new physics and the work of Pert and Rossi, themes from *A Course in Miracles* theorizing the illusory nature of the outside world and the integrating power of love/forgiveness, and freeing oneself from the prison of rigid assumptions and strangling attachments. Therapeutic touch or other energy work provides "hands on" encounters with the rhythm, flow, and unity of the universe and furnishes participants with an expanded apprehending of reality.

Daily expressive therapy synthesizes the inner experience, providing a window through which one's unconscious can be brought to light and supplying a springboard to transformative experiences. Imagery (which we see as the illumination of consciousness) is the integrative, synthesizing force uniting the various aspects of the program. Even in quite specific imagery, we catch a glimpse of the power of changing consciousness, which is the fabric of epiphanies. The more expansive reaches of transformational fantasy/imagery/meditation provide participants with a vehicle for apprehending the Whole and becoming one with the infinite sea of the universe and being.

Caitlin, an attractive woman in her late forties, had been treated extensively for cancer of the parotid gland by the best practitioners in the country, from the Cleveland Clinic to the Orlando area. Her checkup in 1987 indicated that the cancer was still active, and she was told that if she wished to live she should undergo surgery and radiation that would permanently disfigure her and undoubtedly paralyze part of her face. She elected not to have the aggressive treatment.

On Christmas Day of that year, Caitlin got in her car, started driving, and just continued to drive for days. "I couldn't stand it anymore and I just kept running and running," she explained later. "I heard a radio program about GETTING WELL, and I was so struck by what was being said that I pulled off the road in case a phone number was given." After getting in touch with us, Caitlin stopped running and immersed herself in the program.

She was like a walking "teachable moment," and virtually everything we threw at her, from the mundane to the esoteric, triggered new insights, synchronicity, and serendipitous events in her life. Moreover, Caitlin's shifts of consciousness spread to her co-participants and created an incredible potentiating energy that permeated the program's atmosphere. She also displayed the gift of being able to help others gently destroy physical, emotional, and spiritual boundaries that were keeping them imprisoned. And Caitlin also worked hard on her personal issues, including those in her stressful marriage. As she put her life back together, it seemed to fall into place in a greatly expanded whole, and she started saying, "The cancer just doesn't have a place in my life anymore. The cancer is gone!" And, indeed, a checkup with her oncologist revealed that the cancer was gone; there was absolutely no sign of it.

From time to time during the nearly six years I've known Caitlin, I've had apprehensive moments about her physical condition, such as the time her jaw swelled unexplainably or when a large lump appeared on her leg. However, Caitlin just gathers her "white lighting" troops, works on any life problems that are getting out of hand, and astonishes her concerned physicians with clear diagnostic tests. Her experience brought home to our staff that believing in the possibility and actuality of "miracles" was extremely important in creating an atmosphere in which they can occur with great regularity. (There is, however, a delicate balance between providing fertile ground for miracles and having physical miracles become the focus of the program.) I was certain Caitlin had found that balance when she stated at her graduation from the program: "If I could be assured that my cancer was totally gone and would never come back, but in order to have that assurance, I would have to erase GETTING WELL from my experience, I'm not sure I could make that choice."

Facilitating Imagery for Epiphanies

Jean Houston is one of the founders of the human potential movement. She and her husband, Robert Masters, have studied ancient and contem-

porary cultures, investigated both orthodox and esoteric methods of altering consciousness, and discovered procedures used by different cultures
to expand their awareness beyond the circumscribed range of possibilities
acceptable to the left-brain Western mind (Bankier, 1986).

Houston's book, *The Possible Human*, contains a wealth of exercises
and guided imageries to expand consciousness and induce creative and
conceptual leaps by reintegrating the body and mind. Although some of
her assumptions are esoteric and even alien to some of our participants, I
am using her work more and more as a vehicle for creating the ambience
for epiphanies. Pir Vilyat Inayat Khan (1986) offers a number of superb
meditations for increasing the magnitude of the consciousness. With these
meditations, as with Jean Houston's work, I find that I must be sensitive
to going against the beliefs of the participants in the group. However,
whenever I use these engaging meditations with more intellectually open
and "enlightened" groups, the results are wonderful.

More frequently, however, I use lightly structured imagery that not
only includes specific issues upon which participants are working but also
incorporates an expanded world view and connection with the ebb and
flow of the universe. Les Fehmi's "Open Focus" exercise (see Chapter 8) is
excellent for this purpose, as is a more introspective "finding the universe
within" type of exercise. I encourage professionals to create their own
idiosyncratic "scripts"; however, I offer here an example of what I use and
have found to be evocative of epiphanies:

> Let yourself relax deeply in ways that only you know how. . . . Take several
> slow, deep breaths, letting healing light and life come into every thought,
> tissue, and cell when you inhale, and releasing negativity, dis-ease, and dis-
> comfort as you breathe out (*pause*). Let feelings of relaxation cascade over
> your being . . . over your head . . . down your shoulders . . . over your arms
> and chest . . . down through your abdomen and hips . . . and over your legs
> . . . and let your body, mind, and spirit relax completely. (*The initial relax-
> ation can be extended, depending on the needs of participants or the philosophy
> of the facilitator.*)
>   Now, be in your head center — your home base — your center of comfort
> and security, and as you relax even further, mentally scan your whole be-
> ing — mind, body, and spirit — and let yourself focus on what seems like a
> problem area for you. . . . This may be a physical problem, such as pain,
> disease, or some other physical dysfunction, or it may be an emotional
> problem such as fear, depression or resentment, or it could be a spiritual
> problem such as isolation, lack of forgiveness or guilt. . . . And allow an image
> of that problem to arise, a symbolic representation of the problem. (*Continue
> with the examination of all aspects of the eidetic representation of the problem
> area, asking the problem what purpose it is serving for the organism and what
> needs to be done in order for the problem to leave. Then have the subject allow
> a healing symbol to arise; this may be completely metaphorical or may combine
> the natural healing mechanisms of the bodymind, efficacious medical treat-
> ment, and other interventions such as nutrition. Then let the healing take place
> in whatever way the subject feels is appropriate and effective, remembering to*

322 IMAGERY FOR GETTING WELL

let the healing be complete and to clean up any debris left by the healing process.)

Now focus on the site of the healing, noticing that the healing has been complete. See the healthy tissue . . . the healthy feelings . . . the wholeness and health of the spirit. As you focus on the wholeness and healing light and energy of the healing site, watch it begin to grow and expand . . . until it fills your whole being—mind, body, and spirit (*pause*) and now feel your healing light energy expanding beyond your being as you know it and extending out into this room, filling the room, touching, combining, and becoming one with the energies of everyone else in the room (*long pause*) and experience your light and love filling and extending beyond this building out into the world until it engulfs this city, and you join the energies of everyone in the area (*pause*) and feel your energy and love extending further until it covers the planet and becomes one with every other living being— every human, every animal, every plant—on the earth . . . a cell in the body of mankind, yet containing and experiencing the consciousness of all living beings (*long pause*). Now, feel your love, healing energy, and wholeness expanding beyond the planet out into the atmosphere (*pause*) and beyond the atmosphere of the earth, out into the solar system (*long pause*) and out beyond the solar system until your energy is one with the galaxies (*long pause*) and beyond the galaxies to encompass the totality of infinity . . . and eternity . . . and the wholeness of the universe . . . where space and time do not exist (*long pause*). As you are experiencing being not just a *part* of the universe, but being the whole universe itself . . . realizing that the universe is within you . . . and you *are* the universe . . . allow the cosmic consciousness to flow through you (*long pause*). Take a moment to look back at the problem you were focusing on earlier . . . and see that problem under the aspect of eternity (*long pause*). How does it seem now . . . seeing it in the scheme of things . . . and what else are you experiencing? (*long pause*)

Now, after experiencing yourself as the vast ocean of the universe, feeling the ebb and flow . . . in touch with infinity and eternity . . . timeless . . . without boundaries . . . without space . . . transcendent . . . see if you can see things another way . . . as the universe being telescoped within you (*long pause*) and now, become the vastness of the universe without again (*long pause*). Now spend a few moments shifting back and forth between these two aspects of wholeness until they become one (*long pause*) and when you get ready, return to your head center . . . where you continue to experience the wholeness of your self and the fullness of the universe (*long pause*) and after you have contemplated your experience, come back to where you started.

Brad, a young man with HIV disease, appeared to be a broken victim of his condition when he came in for an initial interview. Formerly a Navy air traffic controller, he had been awarded full disability for brain damage from a neurological disease which occasionally caused seizures, as well as for continuing liver dysfunction due to Type B hepatitis. Not surprisingly, Brad was depressed, anxious, and so listless that he spent much of his time in bed. Nonetheless, he was motivated to make changes in his life and really plugged away at all segments of the program.

Near the end of his second week, I used this imagery in a session, and when he came back to the present, Brad was absolutely glowing. "You won't believe this," he said, "but when I was looking back at my problem, I heard a magnificent voice saying, 'This is a gift, and you have been specially *chosen* to be the recipient of this gift!' I had never looked at it that way. The HIV had always seemed like a punishment for screwing up my life. But it's a gift!"

The ripples of this epiphany immediately touched all aspects of Brad's life. He stopped merely "plodding" through the program, as new insights became part of the fabric of his life. He no longer perceived himself as a victim, but, rather, as *chosen* to receive a divine gift. And how this epiphany has changed his life! Brad now actively volunteers (painting, refinishing, decorating, cleaning, and assisting with publicity and marketing) at GETTING WELL, his cognitive functions have returned to premorbid sharpness and creativity, and he is vitally living each moment of his life.

He is also doing well physically. During Brad's last trip to San Diego for his yearly round of extensive neurophysical testing, he called me to tell me that not only had his liver functions returned to normal, but his T cell count had doubled. "They can't believe what is happening to me," he said excitedly. "I'm a miracle to the Navy!" Thrilled as I am by the genuine medical miracle that has occurred, I am even more pleased that Brad sees it as only ancillary. The "real" miracle in his eyes is that he has been chosen to have the gift of living life fully.

Lessons for the Author/Clinician

Perhaps one of my greatest lessons during the GETTING WELL years has been allowing myself to be open to synchronicity—Jung's terminology for coincidences so unusual and so meaningful that they cannot be attributed to mere chance. Jung had noticed that these coincidences were usually associated with periods of transformation, profound changes in beliefs, and sudden insights—in other words, epiphanies. I have been no stranger to synchronicity throughout my life, although I have usually chalked it up to coincidence. However, as I have expanded my thoughts about "the way things are" over the last few years, synchronicity has increased manyfold, to the point that I have begun to *expect* it.

During the writing of this book, as I have been bringing into consciousness and translating into words my GETTING WELL experience, I have found that the frequency of synchronicity and the intensity of my epiphanies have increased immeasurably (as they do for those entering the program). For example, I had hit a major block in the introductory section of the chapter on therapeutic touch, and I felt hopelessly mired. In that day's mail, I received a totally unexpected gift from Diane Schovanec, a nurse at a distant hospital, who sent Marlo Morgan's book, *Mutant Message Downunder*, to thank me for a brief visit she had made to the program *several months earlier*. This self-published book not only reminded me of my interest in the magical ways of the Aborigines, but it also allowed me to see that experience in an entirely new way (which, of course, was most pertinent to the points I was trying to make). To complete the coincidence, only a week later, Diane showed up at a conference held in a totally different part of the country, where I was able to thank her for facilitating my epiphany. She revealed that she had sent me her personal autographed copy of the book, and added, "I just had a feeling that you would really get a lot out of it."

Last Christmas Eve I was again hopelessly stuck—on this chapter. In fact, I was beginning to wonder why I had included it and was even contemplating ways to excise it (although I realized it was crucial). The next day, one of my gifts from Bob was *The Holographic Universe*, a book by Michael Talbot. This might not seem strange; however, Bob *never* gives me books unless they are ones I have specifically asked for, and he knows that I am allergic to any science that uses symbols and formulae (such as math or physics). "Several weeks ago I was wandering through the math section and this book just jumped out at me," he explained. "You may not like it, but I got it for you anyway." Needless to say, I was reading it between opening gifts and attending parties on Christmas Day and the day after. I did find "swimming among quantum physics' strange and fascinating ideas easier than [I] thought" (p. 8), and, indeed, pondering these ideas *did* change the way I looked at the world. Interestingly, one of the principal ways it effected that change was by tapping into and allowing me a new way to synthesize experiences and intuitions I have had since my earliest years. Synergy, epiphany, and miracle!

Talbot triggered memories of the beginnings of my conscious thought processes about the nature of God and the universe. Since high school biology, I have been fascinated by the dictum, "ontogeny recapitulates phylogeny"—that the development of the individual organism parallels the evolutionary development of the species. I believe this concept is also true of thought—that the development of thought in a person or a human system recapitulates the history of human thought. In this case, Talbot triggered memories of the ontogeny of my own thought processes. I have a clear memory of myself at four years of age or younger questioning the church's idea that God was "out there." If he (yes, *he* at that age) is great, all-powerful, and found everywhere, I can't help but be a part of the process, too, I thought (although probably not in words at all). In fact, I believed that when I prayed I was really giving messages to myself *and* to whatever divine was running through me.

My thoughts were not a big hit in Sunday School, but few of my thoughts ever were. However, the idea that I was in some way a co-creator of my life was a heady one to me—although one that frequently would have to go underground. Even in those early days I did not see how an expanded, more integrally universal view of God in any way diminished the traditional concepts of the Deity. And the basic pragmatism that now suffuses my consciousness holds that whatever beliefs work to allow us to feel the best about ourselves and enable us to live our lives most fully are the beliefs we should foster.

My major epiphanies in the evolution of my belief system have come from enlarging my concept of the way things are and opening new "layers" of the universe that will accommodate not only the old beliefs but a whole echelon of new ones. I attribute this shift in consciousness to a poem I had to memorize as part of a presentation at Sunday School when I was nine or ten years of age. I don't remember the poem exactly or who wrote it, but it went something like this: "Hate drew a circle that left me out, heretic, rebel, a thing to flout. But Love and I had the wit to win. We drew a circle that took him in." The poem suggests truth and good are apprehended by enlarging our sphere of acceptance rather than narrowing it. When I studied Spinoza in college, I was struck by the elegance of the idea that opposites viewed *sub specie aeternitas*, under the aspect of eternity, ceased being opposites and became reconciled or unified with each other. This, in essence, is what GETTING WELL is all about.

I believe it is important for me, as a facilitator, to continue to allow the evolution of my consciousness and to continually open myself to epiphanies that expand the possibilities of the universe. Looking back, I realize that my own narrow views may have limited the ability of others to embrace their full beings and possibilities. I have also seen, as in the example of Caitlin, how openness to the extraordinary sensibilities of participants has allowed me footholds on new ways of seeing the nature of being.

Certainly, I don't see myself as some particularly highly evolved individual, and I frequently find myself on the narrowed path, as family, friends, and participants will attest. I am learning, however, that my cries of "Why can't that physician understand?" or "I just can't believe how unevolved or prejudiced that person is!" are beginning to remind me to "draw a circle to take them in" and to expand my realization of the situation to a more powerful accommodation. Each of us is a model for our clients—not by existing on a pedestal, but by living as an example of the exciting potential of being human. Just as Dolores Kreiger's investigations into the abilities of healers indicated that experience increased power, I believe that my staff and I have become more powerful enablers as the consciousness of each of us has expanded. And I believe we owe it to ourselves, our clients, our planet, and our universe to continue our spiritual evolution.

In a certain sense, GETTING WELL is the operational definition of my own evolution of consciousness, which continues to recapitulate the phylogeny of human thought or the collective unconscious. Within the program's microcosm we see the ontogeny of the participant's consciousness mirroring the program's evolution. Similarly, as GETTING WELL started as an epiphany, as a glimpse of wholeness, it continues to evolve, opening ever-widening circles of possibility and synergy and providing an atmosphere where discrepancies can be reconciled, consciousness can evolve, epiphanies can take place, and miracles can be expected.

SECTION III

Designing Imagery for Specific Conditions

with Adelaide Davis

The human mind is a slide projector with an infinite retrieval system, and an endlessly cross-referenced subject catalogue. The inner images we show ourselves form our lives, whether as memories, fantasies, dreams or visions. We can direct the mind's eye to our inner world to bring about the creative forces of spirituality and healing in our daily life. *—Mike and Nancy Samuels*

Synchronizing mind and body is not a concept or a random technique someone thought up for self improvement. Rather, it is a basic principle of how to be a human and how to use your sense perceptions, your mind, and your body together. *—Chogyam Trungpa, Buddhist scholar*

The power of the imagination is a great factor in medicine. It may produce diseases in man and in animals, and it may cure them. . . . Ills of the body may be cured by physical remedies or by the power of the spirit acting through the soul. *—Paracelsus*

19

Introduction to Designing Imagery for Specific Conditions

You must give birth to your images. They are the future waiting to be born ... fear not the strangeness you feel. The future must enter into you long before it happens. ... Just wait for the birth ... for the hour of new clarity. —*Ranier Maria Rilke*

We must learn imagery is everything. We create our world or it is created for us. We will be effects if we are not effectors, victims instead of masters of our destiny. —*Patricia Norris*

The natural healing force within each of us is the greatest force in getting well. —*Hippocrates*

Throughout the ages, there have been stories of individuals who died because they believed a fatal spell had been placed upon them or harbored an expectancy of death at a particular age. By the same token, there are examples of those who have defied the medical community's prognosis or held onto life through believing that they had more to do in this life.

Based on such information, it would appear that belief, rather than cognitive process, is the triggering process in wellness. Therefore, in order to facilitate the goal of improved medical response and enhanced life quality, we must access the belief system in the unconscious. Imagery is the process through which this access is gained.

Imagery is highly individual, and not dependent upon anatomical correctness. It relies on body wisdom and the perceptual proclivities of the imaginer. But as the patient experiences changes within the body through imagery, those changes are often reflected in succeeding medical tests.

In creating imagery for specific conditions, it is necessary to deal with all systems governing that condition. For example, in addressing immune-deficiency or autoimmune disorders, we need to tap into the pineal, the hypothalamus, and the pituitary glands, as well as into the lymphatic sys-

329

tem, thymus, spleen and bones. In systemic conditions, which are already recognized as stress-related, the stress-coping mechanisms of the left brain may be an excellent starting point. Shaffer (1986) suggests that stress occurs when we require the left brain to do right-brain functioning or the right brain to do left-brain functioning.

Rossman (1992) indicates that one of the traps of imagery is getting caught up in managing the body. For example, we certainly need to encourage our immune systems; however, even the most advanced immunologists really don't know exactly what's going on in the immune system. Even if we did know exactly what our immune or cardiovascular systems needed, keeping the action going would be virtually impossible. Our bodies are walking miracles with tens of thousands of enzyme changes occurring every second and billions of impulses, charges, and transformations occurring every hour. Even if one chose a relatively simple task, for example, keeping a gross movement such as one's heartbeat going, Rossman suggests that death would occur in five minutes or less, because the mind would wander away from the heartbeat image pretty quickly.

We also feel that "imagery for specific conditions" needs to be seen in the context of the person's whole life—his mental, spiritual, and emotional being, as well as his physical being. In our culture we go about imagery in the same way that we attack problems: find the problem, focus on the symptom, work hard, and mount an attack. However, at GETTING WELL we believe that healing in the deepest sense combines realigning our energies with universal energies, focusing on balance and harmony, and regaining our unity with the "divine order of things." It is not that we do not focus on the disease or the proliferation of T cells, the stickiness of neutrophils, or other biological aspects of the healing process. However, in the act of designing imagery for these and other specific conditions, we try to remember that true healing lies in reconnecting with oneself, with others, and with the flow of the universe.

GETTING WELL focuses not on the outcome but on the journey. In other words, our emphasis is not on physical healing but on living the most joyous, fulfilled life one can imagine. Physical healing may indeed be a side effect, but it is not a necessary outcome. The focus is on living life to the fullest and seeing any physiological change as a "lagniappe" or a delightful by-product. In our experience, the person who is focused only on the medical change is less likely to achieve that goal than the person who focuses on living well and making each day of his life a masterpiece. In fact, the person who persists in aiming only at the physical changes may receive little or no benefit from the program.

Although this section focuses on designing imagery for specific diseases, we need to re-emphasize that this is but one aspect of using imagery in a comprehensive behavioral medicine program. Certainly, directly attempting to reduce a tumor or to tame an autoimmune response is a natural desire of participants, as well as a legitimate component of such a program; however, we believe it is counterproductive to have such a specific action as the main focus. As important as using imagery to reduce physical symptoms is the use of imagery to deal with emotional, spiritual, and psychological issues which may underlie the development of the condition or which may have been stirred up by the diagnosis of the condition.

Before assisting patients in designing imagery for their conditions, it may be a good idea to review the section General Considerations in Designing Imagery in Chapter 8. They are listed here briefly:

1. It is necessary to explore the imagery already in place concerning disease, health, values, what is seen occurring in the body, and especially aspects of an individual's world view. Any guided imagery must be syntonic with the core beliefs of the individual. Imagery cannot be effective unless it is in line with one's deepest values and does not conflict with one's world views (e.g., beliefs about violence, religious views, the nature of man).

2. Similarly, guided imagery must be idiosyncratic and reflect deep personal meaning and metaphor. Ready-made visualizations by a therapist or those found on commercial tapes are of limited value and have a place only where they tap into the unique unconscious desires, preferences, and values of the individual. (For example, having a "slob" do a "neatnik" visualization just won't work at an effective level.)

3. Particularly with immune deficiency diseases, the disease symbol should be seen as weak, less intelligent, nonmenacing or not dangerous, smaller, less active, and less defined than the image of healing. With autoimmune diseases, the disease symbol may be seen in the beginning as wild, burning, and raging—but eminently tamable, reversible, or manageable.

4. The healing symbol needs to be seen as powerful, intelligent, active, vivid, focused, competent, and large. With autoimmune diseases, the healing symbol might involve the befriending and taming of the immune system without debasing its protective attributes for true "invaders." Healthy cells need to be seen as powerful, while unhealthy functions or cells need to be seen as weak and malleable. Images need to be anatomically correct, even though they may be metaphoric and deeply symbolic.

5. Medical treatment should be seen as eminently effective—with healthy cells being protected from the radiation, chemotherapy, or other treatment designed to destroy unhealthy cells. In autoimmune diseases, treatment to suppress the immune system can be seen as quite selective—suppressing only the components of the immune

system that need suppression, while allowing the immune system to protect the body from outside invaders.

6. The concept of restoring balance should be intimately entwined with all images. Imagery is both powerful and quite specific as to what is being imaged. Achterberg's findings that imagery worked on the function of the specific type of cells imaged and made no change in the immune cell types which were not targeted should give us pause. Frequently, medical science does not know exactly what is happening, and we could do damage by imaging an incorrect theory. The mind-body is incredibly intelligent, meaning that we may need to leave the exact process of what to do to up to our individual "control center." In the creation and use of imagery, we always need to include the concept of balance and wholeness.

7. For best results, the disease image needs to be seen as completely gone and the body as perfectly healthy at the end of the imagery session. In our experience, when an image of "mostly gone" remains, the message is picked up by the body. The idea of loving one's disease and not wanting to have it completely gone can allow the body to develop an acceptance of the disease and create a pleasant place for it to evolve. Remember, the image is a blueprint for what is to happen—so be sure the blueprint is what you want!

8. Trust the images that come, and don't make judgments about them, compare them unfavorably to someone else's, or feel that a meaning must be found for them. Have faith and trust that the image will be useful.

Images Which May Be Destructive or Counterproductive

In many situations imagery may actually become destructive rather than constructive. In addition, misunderstanding of the purpose and technique of imagery can sometimes interfere with the imagery process. Some of the most common pitfalls are listed below:

1. It may be a serious mistake when using imagery to concentrate too much on the effectiveness of the image and try to make it too scientific or biological. The harder the individual works on the image, the less effective it is (Schneider, 1989).

2. Concentrating too heavily on physical changes to the exclusion of mindstyle/lifestyle changes is usually counterproductive.

3. Imagery that makes the disease (virus, cancer cell, etc.) larger, stronger, or a greater force than the immune/health system is problematic, as is seeing the immune system or treatment as impotent.

4. Relying on imagery to the exclusion of sound medical treatment can be dangerous.
5. Be sure to be anatomically correct if you are doing an "anatomical" imagery, or the imagery could be counterproductive. We agree with Howard Hall that the innate wisdom of the body usually prevents too much damage—but why waste precious energy? If there are theoretical questions relating to the mechanisms of the condition, it may be advisable to use a more metaphoric, generalized healing image, keeping the end result in mind. Never forget that the body responds to the blueprint of the mind, so be sure the image is the one that is wanted.

Helping Participants Design Imagery

A frequent complaint of clients working on imagery is "I just can't image." When faced with that statement, Dr. Anees Sheikh asks the person how many windows there are in his house. Upon hearing the answer, Sheikh asks how he came up with that number. Invariably, the person says he had a picture of his house in his mind and he mentally walked around and counted the windows. A brief visualization using the image of a lemon being cut and juiced, with the person sloshing the juice around in his mouth and finally swallowing it, can dramatically demonstrate that anyone can image, and moreover that a particular image can produce a bodily response (salivation). Some participants are not good visualizers but can image powerfully through other sensory channels—kinesthetic, auditory, taste, smell, touch.

Before starting to work, we need to reassure the participant that he or she does image continuously, that imagery will become more powerful with practice, and that he or she will be able to develop meaningful, effective images. We have found it helpful to give some examples of effectively using imagery from the field of sports psychology. Another way to illustrate the presence and effectiveness of imagery is to have participants give examples of situations that have not turned out well, and then trace their expectations and images of the negative outcome back to their eidetic origins.

We believe that the participant has everything he needs to put deeply healing metaphors into place, and that we are merely facilitators. Following this line of thought, we find that getting a feel for the person's preferences, style, values, and desires is most helpful in assisting that person with crafting individual imagery. As mentioned earlier, it is important to explore any conscious and unconscious imagery the patient already has, and sometimes to modify or reinterpret those images that are fearful or inaccurate.

We have found it helpful to use Shaffer's "transformational fantasy" in bringing unconscious images and metaphors to light. The client's own image of his disease and the ways meaningful to him for healing this condition are so much more effective than any slick visualization provided by the therapist or by a commercial tape (even though commercial tapes or the therapist's images may provide a starting point for the imagery process). Using someone else's imagery also reinforces "outer locus of control," letting the patient believe that someone else can design something that is better for him than he can. It is, of course, important to let the client do the work. We are there merely to help release that deep intuitive knowledge and facilitate the journey!

We are frequently asked, "How many times a day should we do our imagery?" and our unsatisfying answer is, "Constantly." It is advisable to have two or three short "formal" sessions during the day; however, imagery needs to be reinforced repeatedly, even if only for a few seconds each time. Epstein (1989) makes an excellent case for brief (a few seconds to a minute), poignant images as being more effective than long, drawn-out ones. Imagery is not symptom relief; it is a whole new way of believing about your mind, body and spirit—and new mindstyles need constant reinforcement!

Frequently there are emotional and philosophical issues underlying the disease process. If "healing" is to be effective, it must take into account these bedrocks that affect our conscious and unconscious thought and functioning. We use cognitive restructuring and other standard therapy techniques to bring these issues to the surface so they can be dealt with; however, we are finding that eidetic techniques are quicker, more deeply effective, and longer lasting. Tapping into that idiosyncratic imagery process underlying feelings, such as anger, fear, bitterness, and lack of forgiveness, and using imagery resources within the individual to transform these conflicts into resolution and peace are an important part of the healing process.

One of the most powerful aspects of specific imagery is that it works! Changes *will* occur very specifically in the system imaged. This gives participants the knowledge that they really *can* make changes in their bodies and lives, and helps them realize they are not helpless. Specific imagery "hooks" the patient on the visualization process in a way that generalized imagery or "consciousness-raising" imagery cannot, especially for the "beginner." It is a wonderful introduction to the many, even more powerful, aspects of imagery.

In the chapters that follow, which expand upon a presentation made at the 1990 National Conference on the Psychology of Health, Immunity, and Disease, we first describe the condition and the physiological dysfunction involved. (We have used the *Professional Guide to Diseases, Third*

Edition as our principal medical resource.) We then describe a desired response for the condition and give "seeds" for imagery. This is meant to be a springboard for the clinician and the participant rather than a compendium of the nuances of physical conditions. It may be useful for many patients to understand their specific condition more thoroughly, and we encourage people to do so. Conversely, physicians, nurses, and other health professionals (as participants) may need to back away from specifics and see their disorders in a more metaphoric light. Epstein's *Healing Visualizations* gives "blueprints" for imagery for a large variety of physical conditions and intertwines the emotional concomitants of those conditions in the images. We consider it a superb companion piece to our work.

Seeds for imagery are meant to be just that—a help in germinating the participant's ideas for his or her own idiosyncratic imagery. Some participants find them useful as quick "in and out" images, as Epstein advocates; others use them as images to be expanded and intertwined in a more extended imagery session. We have found the "seeds" quite useful as a means to explore possibilities for the participants' own imagery creations. In using this method, we relax the person and ask him or her to allow the images to form as we read four or five of the seeds that may fit that individual's needs. We then suggest that bits and pieces of images that appealed to the person be pulled together into his or her own imagery creation.

20
Immune Deficiency Disorders

We are faced with the possibility that something of the mind is located in the entire body, not just the brain. — *Larry Dossey*

It is not a question of *believing* that the mind can effect healing, but of *knowing* from the inside that this is true. — *Patricia Norris*

The imagination should not be regarded as a panacea for all that ails the human species — unless, of course, we choose to believe there are no limits to consciousness and its inherent ability to alter the state of things. — *Jeanne Achterberg*

Immune deficiency diseases usually involve a breakdown in the effectiveness of the immune system to fight off foreign cells. In these situations, T killer cells and T helper cells may be lacking in number and effectiveness. Imagery for such conditions would focus on seeing the immune system increasing production of those cells and seeing the immune system as powerful and effective against foreign or malignant invaders.

Generalized Seeds for Imagery
for Immune Deficiency

- See the hypothalamus appearing depressed or shriveled, especially on the right side. The pituitary gland also may have a sense of being weakened. See yourself washing the hypothalamus, massaging it, talking encouragingly to it as it grows to a healthy size and color, firm and springy. The new energy will be fed into the pineal and pituitary glands, which will spread it to the thymus and lymphatic system.
- See the thymus gland appearing shrunken and discolored. To the touch, it may feel atrophied and granular. You are the supervisor of a "crew" of cleaners who pump up the thymus, then enter the factory to break down and clean out the hardened cells, clean the rust off

336

the "machinery," and repair it to produce healthy active T cells—in perfect balance.

Cancer

Description

Cancer is actually many conditions. Imagery will need to take into account the type of cancer being dealt with. For example, imagery for leukemia might be very different from imagery for a lung tumor. Cancer is a disease with a complex web of causality. One very significant factor in cancer is stress, with its destructive effect on the immune system. In the case of most cancers, high doses of stress chemicals destroy or inactivate immune cells, allowing cancer cells to develop into potentially life-threatening tumors.

Immune Dysfunction

Most cancers appear to be greatly, but not solely, influenced by the stress chemicals that in chronic or high doses help to inactivate the immune system. With the inactivation or destruction of immune cells, including macrophages, T cells, interleuken, and interferon, the immune system becomes unable to fight off cancer cells. In a compromised immune system, cancer cells can develop into a full-blown disease process. The reduction in white blood cells serves to reduce effectiveness of immune response.

Desired Immune Response

- Increased number of healthy white blood cells
- Increased number of natural T killer cells and T helper cells
- Increased power of appropriate immune components
- Increased activity of bone marrow-producing healthy cells
- Decreased tumors or number of cancer cells

Seeds for Imagery

- See the number of white blood cells increasing and see the cancer cells as the weak and disorganized cells that they, in truth, are. See your treatment working as it is supposed to in your body—your chemotherapy is killing cancer cells but not destroying healthy cells.
- See the chemotherapy as bullets made of ice which speed through

the system, between the cells. They are so cold that they suck any disengaged cancer cells from wherever they may be. The cancer cells crash into the bullets, are immediately freeze-dried and absorbed into the bullets as they speed through the system. The body is cooled and comforted by this process. The ice bullets converge on the clusters of cancer cells, where, fed by the cells they have collected during their journey, they are transformed to finish the work on the tumor.

- See the white blood cells as white tigers eating their prey—the cancer cells.
- The tumors are dirt in hotel rooms, and the white blood cells are the maids that clean the rooms. Unless the room is totally cleaned out, the door needs to be locked to avoid letting the germs out into the hallway. The maids are quite industrious and have powerful chemicals to combat the dirt and germs. The chief housekeeper is quite skilled and uses the maids well.
- See Ghost Busters with their laser swords—the white light of the laser sword is God's white light that cuts the tumor away.
- Imagine white blood cells as angels that fly through the body looking for cancer cells—and, with a tap of their magic wands, the cancer cells disappear.
- See the radiation as laser beams from a far-off star which stop when they encounter healthy tissue, selectively "zapping" tumors and any free-floating cancer cells.
- See the immune system as powerful, giant eagles feeding on kernels of corn (cancer cells). The cancer also serves as food for the healthy cells in the body.
- See powerful healing light energy breathed in through the crown of the head and acting like an electric fly trap whenever it meets up with a cancer cell. You can hear the "zap," and the fireworks display as the body is ridded of all the cells that don't belong.
- Wake up the bone marrow factories, seeing the assembly lines stamping out billions and billions of perfectly working cells to be made into specific immune system cells. Quality Control lets only perfectly crafted cells come off the line, sending any malfunctioning cells (e.g., leukemic) back to be refashioned. The factory produces exactly what your body needs, and can raise or lower production of certain cells such as platelets, red blood cells, and white blood cells.
- Imagine piranha coming up against a dark lump of undisciplined cells. The piranha work side by side, fin to fin, consuming the cells.
- See the sun shining on your back, reach up and grab the sunlight with your hands, holding onto the beam, which is so powerful that you cannot keep it steady. The beam eliminates cancer cells by a small explosion. The light has a vacuum that sucks up the cells, and

now the light shines over the whole body, destroying the free-floating cells.

- See white tigers (white blood cells) eating plums (cancer cells).
- See knights on white horses are destroying cancer cells with their powerful swords.
- See healing sunlight energy melting snowballs (cancer cells).
- Imagine fish (white blood cells) eating bits of bread (cancer cells).
- In your mind's eye, see ducks moving about in a marsh (the lungs), eating up grass seeds and sprouts (cancer cells and tumors), then drinking up the water and becoming very strong from the nourishment.
- "See yourself as *being* God's hands. . . . Seeing your hands as the Almighty's, touch the place on and in the diseased area, gently cleaning out all the dirt and contamination and then, *putting* in order what has been in disorder (for example, weaving together the fibers of the wall of the colon). Then, breathe out once and see your body in *perfect* condition" (Epstein, 1989, p. 75).
- "Breathe out three times and see the chemicals coming into your body as rivers of sunlight flowing throughout, flushing out the cancer cells and destroying them. Know that these chemicals are medicine that is helping you to heal as the tumor is weakened, shrunken, and destroyed. It is a friend that has come to help you" (Epstein, 1989, p. 83).

Human Immunodeficiency Virus (HIV) Disease

Description

Human immunodeficiency virus (HIV) disease is an illness which is (1) acquired; (2) occurs in those individuals whose immune systems were previously normal but have become severely deficient; (3) is characterized by a group of symptoms and signs that may differ from person to person, but result in opportunistic infections which produce no disease in healthy people. HIV is considered a retrovirus which invades healthy T4 cells within the body, transmuting them so that the virus is not recognized as alien. The disease is commonly thought to be the direct result of infection by HIV; however, there are a number of new theories appearing on the horizon.

Immune Dysfunction

The HIV virus destroys the T4 (T helper) cells, the loss of which eventually destroys immune function. As the normal T4 to T8 (T helper cell to T suppressor cell) ratio is upset, the body's natural immunity is disturbed.

Desired Immune Response

- Increased number of T4 (T helper cells).
- Restored T4 to T8 (helper to suppressor) ratio.
- Destruction and removal of infected T4 cells.

Seeds for Imagery

- Imagine the thymus gland producing T helper cells.
- See the thymus gland's T cell factory mass-producing T4 cells.
- See immune cells attacking and destroying the HIV virus.
- Imagine the clever spies of the immune system uncovering the disguises of the HIV virus and ferreting the virus out of its most hidden places.
- See sheep (white cells) eating grass (virus).
- Plug up the thymus and spleen and long bones (which are producing new healthy T cells). When storage capacity is reached, the healthy new cells burst forth into the body encased in a force field of light which protects them from the infected T helper cells. When infected T cells attempt to invade the shielded cells, the invaders are incinerated by the force field. The cinders drop to the bottom of the feet, leaving only healthy cells behind. Wiggle the toes to rid the body of the ashes.
- Put armor (or some other protective coating) on helper cells so that they cannot be penetrated by HIV virus.
- See a multitude of rabbits (three white ones to each brown one—T4 to T8) dressed in raincoats and wearing boots to protect them. With their powerful hind legs, they are kicking sea urchins (HIV cells) against a wall, smashing them to a powder. The powder falls into a stream which carries it out of the body.

Lyme Disease

Description

Lyme disease is the result of the introduction of spyrochetes into the system through tick bites or the depositing of tick fecal matter on the skin. The spyrochetes are transmitted through the body by way of the blood stream and lymphatic systems. They invade organs and joints, triggering inflammation, fatigue, malaise, achiness, fever, and other flu-like symptoms.

Desired Response

- Reduce number of spyrochetes
- Reduce inflammation and fatigue

Seeds for Imagery

- Breathe in an electric blue mist which pervades every cell in the body, circulating and sweeping the sanitized spyrochetes into the bladder, from which they are emptied from the system. The continuing flow of electric blue mist cleanses and disinfects the burrows in which the spyrochetes had lived. (Note: the electric blue mist is appropriate for any infectious condition.)
- See white badgers (immune cells) burrowing into the dens of fat grubs (spyrochetes) and gobbling them down. The badgers grow stronger with each grub they eat.

Infectious Diseases, Infections

Description

Infectious diseases occur when the system is invaded by viruses, micro-organisms or any foreign entity deemed incompatible with the homeostatic function of the body. They represent the multiplication of those organisms in or on the body tissue, producing signs, symptoms, and immunologic response. The host is injured by cellular damage from toxins produced by the micro-organisms, by intracellular multiplication, and/or by competition with the host's metabolism. The immune response of the host may compound the damage. Opportunistic infections are caused by pathogens that are ubiquitous but don't cause problems as long as the immune system keeps them under control. When immunocompetence is compromised, the pathogen takes advantage of the "opportunity" to proliferate. T cells are especially vulnerable to chronically elevated cortisol, and since T helper cells assist other cells within the immune system, there can be a chain reaction when this regulatory cell is compromised.

Immune Dysfunction

- Challenges cellular immunity (B cells)
- Challenges humoral immunity (T cells)

Desired Immune Response

- Increased number of natural killer T (NK) cells
- Increased helper T to supressor T cell ratio
- Increased production of antibodies (B-cells) and the ability of these antibodies to reproduce themselves
- Increased power of appropriate immune responses
- Restored balance in the immune system

Seeds for Imagery

- See electric blue mist throughout the body, cleansing and sanitizing the invading micro-organisms.
- See the thymus gland pumping out special soldiers to the site of the cold or infection. See those soldiers flooding into the area of the infection, confronting the invaders and reducing them to nonentities — to pulp. Now, see the body excreting the refuse.
- See yourself as an artist painting a clown face on the spleen. The clown begins to laugh and spews lymphocytes from his mouth. Those lymphocytes speed to all parts of the body through the blood stream as light, surrounding and consuming all foreign invaders. The thymus, looking like a closed lotus flower, begins, when massaged, to release T4 seeds which fly to all parts of the body, take root, grow, and begin to destroy the enemy invaders. The whole body is stimulated by the seeds. A thymus hormone flows from the open flower to the long bones, stimulating the marrow to produce T4 and T8 cells, which flow through the bones and into the blood to seek and destroy the enemy invaders (Epstein, 1989, p. 132).

21

Autoimmune and Allergic Disorders

Imagery is a language between the conscious self and the deeper levels of the body. —*David Feinstein*

If we wish to change some aspect of our life, we must first become aware of the images we hold and then create visualizations or the changes *we* wish to see come into being. —*Patricia Norris*

Recognize how that symptom intensity is actually a signal of just how strong another, deeper part of you needs to be recognized and understood right now. —*Ernest Rossi*

Autoimmunity can be defined as a failure of an organism to recognize its own tissue. The autoimmune reaction is the result of the disruption of the normal pathways of T and B cells by autoantigens. Such disruption may arise whenever there is a state of immunologic imbalance in which B cell activity is excessive and suppressor T cell activity is diminished.

In the design of imagery for autoimmune diseases, the concept of balance in the immune system is crucial. In general, a two to one ratio of T helper cells to T suppressor cells is considered optimal. Remember, the body has the intelligence to achieve whatever balance is needed, so it may be more effective to put that balance under the aegis of the control center in the brain than to try directly to manipulate it, unless you have an accurate biological view of what is happening.

The idea of the immune system as friendly, loving, and protective is essential. Frequently, symptomatic relief in the autoimmune dysfunction shuts the whole immune system down. Although resulting in relief for the aggrieved area, this process opens the rest of the organism to infection and immune diseases. For this reason, healing should involve balancing the operating immune system, rather than shutting-down a poorly functioning system.

Allergies are a result of the immune system's overreacting to substances not intrinsically harmful to the system. It is frequently interesting to return to the emotional milieu in which the allergy developed and assess the factor there.

General Seeds for Imagery
for Autoimmune Disorders

- See a balance scale in the control center of the brain. See the suppressor cell pan hanging high above the helper cell pan, showing the suppressor to helper cell ratio imbalance. See the suppressor cells becoming heavier and more numerous. The suppressor pan begins to drop, and the helper cell pan starts to rise. When the pans are exactly even, the immune system is balanced. Cells from each pan flow down a chute into a hopper to be distributed throughout the system.
- See yourself standing on the pituitary gland, leaning on the hypothalamus. One side of the hypothalamus is red and pulsating, and has a scowling face. The other side of the hypothalamus is shriveled and deflated, like an empty balloon, greyish-white and cold. The two sides of the hypothalamus negotiate a deal: The shriveled, cold side will send coolness to the swollen, hot side. Watch as the exchange takes place, as the hot side shrinks, and the cold side swells. Both sides become healthy pink, the same size, with smiling faces. A sense of peace fills the body.

Systemic Lupus Erythematosus
(SLE) and Scleroderma

Descriptions

SLE is a non-organ-specific, chronic autoimmune disease affecting connective tissue, cells, and many organ systems, either individually or in various combinations. Clinically, SLE has a bewildering array of acute and chronic manifestations. Nearly all patients have constitutional symptoms ranging from malaise and weight loss to prostration. Most will have muscle and joint inflammation and pain, as well as skin and mucous membrane lesions.

Scleroderma involves the skin, the joints, and the blood vessels. It is frequently misdiagnosed as SLE or arthritis. The skin gradually loses its elasticity and pigmentation and becomes thickened, tight, and shiny, mask-like, but unwrinkled. Bodily motion is greatly restricted by the inflexibility of the skin and the involvement of the muscles and soft tissues of the joints. The thickening and spreading fibrosis affect internal organs as well, creating, upon kidney involvement, malignant hypertension, which is a major cause of death.

Frequently, both SLE and scleroderma patients exhibit Reynaud's syndrome (cold, numb hands and feet). Medical treatment for these collagen diseases is usually limited to the administration of adrenocorticosteroids for the relief of symptoms. Unfortunately, steroid treatment has severe side effects, among which are depression, decalcification/osteoporosis, dowager's hump, weight gain, "moon face," impaired immunity, and cardiovascular problems. Although SLE may have periods of remission and exacerbation, scleroderma is generally regarded as incurable.

Immune Dysfunction

SLE patients have circulating antibodies to their own cells, cell constituents, and cell proteins (including DNA). Although it is believed that scleroderma patients do not have antibodies for DNA, the immune picture is similar.

Desired Immune Response

- Recognition of body's cells as "self"
- Increased suppressor cells
- Increased balance, gentle protectiveness, and "friendliness" of immune system

Seeds for Imagery

- See the immune system and the body as a rope all knotted up. See a magical spray covering the rope, see the knots unravel, and see the whole body relaxing.
- See the disease as a raging, angry wolf sending fiery lights into all parts of the body. See the wolf tamed by love, gentled by tender caressing, and gently stroked until he becomes the gentle, playful, and cuddly puppy that he is. He can protect you from intruders by his barks and growls, but when he is with his master all he can do is to gently lick, caress, and nuzzle. And you must nurture him and caress him in order to tame him.
- See the disease as wire, knotted and confused, burning everything. There is a light now going through the wire — it becomes loose and flowing, and then it turns into pixie dust. The immune system becomes a loving and nurturing light — friendly and protective — instead of damaging.
- See the kidneys with a nurturing rosy light being blown into them to protect them from infection or attack. See the kidneys packed in ice, reducing the swelling and cooling the burning you may feel.
- With lung infections, see the macrophages with long arms picking

out and consuming "icky" green things. See a heavenly spray calming all the body parts.

- See a slag heap made up of all the residues and wastes of the immune battle, and see plecostemus fish sucking away all the debris and becoming healthier and stronger. See the optimal two to one balance of helper cells to suppressor cells.
- See the disease as a raging stream, surging over rapids, knocking down rocks and trees. See magical or divine oil being poured on the water — calming the torrent into a gentle, nurturing brook.
- See the disease flashing red neon lights. See the body turn a rheostat, and see the lights becoming soft, pink, and calming.
- (For scleroderma): A sweet oil is gently massaged into the skin, working its way down into the deep tissues of the body. See the oil lubricating until the collagen and organs are smooth and flowing. See the collagen being regenerated, becoming smooth, supple, and moist.
- Reach into the muscles below the skin with hands that are glowing with an electric blue light, gently massaging the muscles; feel the atrophy releasing and breaking down and becoming pink, warm, and supple. Reach into the affected organ systems with the glowing hands, feeling the fibroids dissolving, and the organs throbbing with energy, gaining energy to become fully productive again. Hear the power-building whine of the machinery reaching full efficiency. See and feel yourself smiling and dancing with full range of motion.

Rheumatoid Arthritis (RA)

Description

RA is a chronic systemic disease characterized by inflammation of the connective tissue throughout the body; however, it is usually considered in terms of its local effects on the tissues — usually beginning in the synovial membrane within the joint. It usually attacks peripheral joints and surrounding muscles, tendons, ligaments, and blood vessels. It may have unexplained remissions, and exacerbations are often linked to stress. Immunosuppressants, analgesics, and anti-rheumatic agents are the usual medical therapy.

Immune Dysfunction

RA is thought to be an autoimmune disease in which the synovial membrane becomes inflamed from antigen antibody effects, particularly of the "rheumatoid factor" (a large immune globulin). Enlargement of the synovial membrane, scarring of the ligaments and tendons, cartilage degeneration, and bone spurs all develop as a result of the interaction with the inherited factor. Studies have linked certain personality traits to RA, including qualities such as self-restriction, detachment, compulsivity, repressed hostility and rebellion (especially against parental-type authority), and intrapunitiveness (Achterberg & Lawlis, 1980).

Desired Immune Response

- Recognition of synovial cells as "self"
- Increased suppressor immune cells to reduce effects of rheumatoid factor
- Reduced power and/or number of rheumatoid antigens

Seeds for Imagery

- See balm flowing over red, inflamed joints. The bones become pink as the balm flows over them, cooling them and putting a pearlized coating over jagged, damaged bone; see the pearlized coating build up into a smooth, protective shell. The joints now move smoothly and freely.
- Befriend the rheumatoid factors, loving them into being joyful and protective of the synovial membrane and other membranes. The synovial fluid changes from thick and viscous to clear and watery. See the whole immune system befriended and loved.
- See the RA as an angry tiger, but by gentle cosseting and caressing, tame it into a purring, cuddly pussy cat. See the anger within being expressed and tamed in the same way.
- See the immune system as a scale that is out of balance. And now, see the rheumatoid factor become smaller, less weighty, less powerful. See the suppressor cells grow in weight, power, and number, until the immune system scales achieve a perfect balance. When that balance occurs, a tiny bell will chime within.
- See the central control room for the body. Study the readouts on the computers, and let the body in its wisdom turn the proper knobs, push the appropriate buttons, and pull the right levers to bring its physical and emotional self back into perfect balance.
- See yourself lying on the beach on a beautiful day. Feel the waters flowing over, under, around, and through you. The water carries a fine golden sand that gently scours and cleanses every cell. See each joint smoothed and polished, each muscle, tendon and ligament stretched and limbered. As the wave recedes it carries away all debris, all swelling, and all deposits with it, leaving the body bright and shiny.
- Enter a room labeled "Arthritis." The room is dusty, dirty, and filled

with a jumble of large boxes. As the cleaning proceeds, it becomes apparent that the boxes are virtually empty—each containing only a small, friendly bug. See the boxes being carried out by helpers, and the room cleaned, scrubbed, and polished. The room is now bright and shiny as you close the door and leave.

- "See your arms (or legs, or fingers, or toes) as octopus tentacles, sinewy and undulating, elongating out in front of you for at least a mile. See and sense the flexibility of these members elongating freely, allowing you to bend them in all directions" (Epstein, 1989, p. 63).

Multiple Sclerosis (MS)

Description

MS is a disease of the central nervous system involving the breaking down and scarring of the myelin sheath by the immune system which no longer recognizes the myelin as "self." When this fatty insulation of the nerve fibers is disturbed, the messages that control bodily movements/functions are distorted or blocked or communicate to the wrong muscular destination. The condition tends to have an uneven course of exacerbations and remission; however, stress frequently precedes exacerbations. In general, medical treatment is focused on symptom relief.

Immune Dysfunction

Present theories concerning MS involve: (1) a viral etiology, (2) an autoimmune dysfunction, and (3) a combination of the two (the immune system attacking a virus sleeping deep within the cells of the myelin sheath).

Desired Immune Response

- Immune system recognition of myelin sheath as "self"
- Harmonious interaction of immune system with the body, especially the myelin—recognizing and loving "self" cells
- Increased suppressor cells

Seeds for Imagery

- A honey-like substance coats the nerves—melting tough scars into viable, powerful myelin material—filling any gaps in or degeneration of the myelin sheath, perfectly protecting and insulating the nerve fiber, allowing it to carry the nerve impulse precisely from the brain to the muscle where it is needed.

- See a substance pouring over the tangled nerves in nerve trunks, like a soothing oil poured over spaghetti, coating the nerve strands so that they untangle and magically fall into relaxed, straight strands.
- See the damaged nerves arcing like frayed electrical wires. See maintenance workers reweave the tattered insulation so the nerves cease short-circuiting each other.
- (Hand- and foot-warming exercises)
- See white clouds in the head (MS scarring as seen in an MRI) being blown away by a powerful wind.
- See the nervous system in an indigo blue color. Where there is damage, the scales and scars are greyish-white. See a swarm of mud-daubers flying to a palette heaped with translucent myelin. Some of the mud-daubers use their stingers to cut away the damaged myelin and scales from the nerves. Others pick up the myelin compound and spread it into the area perfectly. When the repairs dry, they turn dark indigo blue, blending so perfectly that no trace of the repair work remains.
- See a big eraser rubbing out the lesions in the brain.
- Imagine a worker with scrub brushes, pumice, and rouge cloths scouring away the scars and then painting fresh myelin into the area, which turns indigo blue to match the rest of the system.
- See calamine lotion being patted onto areas by the immune system. See the immune system change from being irritable and angry to protective, loving, and friendly. See the whole body experience regeneration.
- "Demand inwardly that your body (and any medication that you are taking) produce all its healing substances. Sense and feel the substances being released . . . sense the suppressor T cells . . . teaching the other white blood cells to distinguish friend (the myelin sheath) from foe (bacteria). Sense and see this happening all along the spinal column, from the bottom to the top and up into the brain, as a ladder of flashing lights sending sparks of electrical energy throughout the body" (Epstein, 1989, pp. 149–150).

Amyotropic Lateral Sclerosis (ALS)

Description

ALS is a disease of the peripheral nervous system, specifically of the nerves that give messages to the muscles. Because of the degeneration of the motor neurons, the muscles innervated by these nerves atrophy, causing a variety of symptoms—depending on which neurons are affected. Presently there is no established specific treatment for ALS.

Immune dysfunction

With ALS, immunologic factors have been suggested by the cytotoxicity of ALS serum to anterior horn cells in tissue culture.

Desired Immune Response

- Immune system recognition of cells as "self"
- Harmonious interaction of immune system with all parts of the body
- Increased suppressor cells, and *selective* suppressor response

Seeds for Imagery

- See new cable being laid in the body from the brain to the muscles.
- See a spark jump the distance of the motor neuron — from the brain to the muscle if necessary.
- See the body loving itself, nurturing itself, regenerating itself. Know that the immune system can love the body, not attack it.
- Hold the intent of regeneration. Realize that conscious intent is the most powerful force in the universe and supersedes any technique.

Chronic Fatigue Immune Dysfunction Syndrome (CFIDS) and Fibromyalgia

Descriptions

CFIDS is a disease process that is professionally controversial. Some see it as a viral infection (e.g., Epstein-Barr) and others see it as an autoimmune disorder. Many believe that CFIDS is a direct result of depression. Others believe it is a physical disease with emotional components. CFIDS is a disease process that is difficult to diagnose and one which exhibits a variety of nonspecific symptoms, including severe fatigue, weakness, malaise, subjective fever, sore throat, painful lymph nodes, decreased memory, confusion, depression, and decreased ability to concentrate on tasks, with a remarkable absence of objective physical or laboratory abnormalities. CFIDS undoubtedly has multiple causes, and is definitely a syndrome rather than a disease.

Fibromyalgia is a condition of widespread pain and profound fatigue. The pain, which is located in connective tissue, tends to be felt as diffuse, aching, or burning. The pain may be of varying intensity and focus, usually more severe in parts of the body used most. The fatigue, which may come on suddenly, may range from simply feeling tired to the exhaustion of flu-like illness, and usually is more evident in the morning after one rises from bed. Depression and the sensations of "crawling skin" are also present in fibromyalgia.

Immune Dysfunction

CFIDS is a disease process of an overactive immune system—actually a failure to down-regulate the immune response. The decreased number of suppressor T cells fails to signal the down-regulation of immune function, and there is a decreased number of natural killer T cells.

Fibromyalgia is also a disease process of the overactive immune system. It appears to be a twin of CFIDS, and may be related to it. In fibromyalgia, the immune system fails to down-regulate, indicating a decrease in the number and effectiveness of suppressor T cells, but with a lack of resistance to other infections, signaling weakness in the killer T cells as well.

Desired Immune Response

- Increased suppressor T cells and increased number and power of natural killer T cells
- Reduced interleukin I
- Increased suppressor T to helper T cell ratio
- Balance restored to the immune system

Seeds for Imagery

- See the body in a bubble of light. This bubble maintains the current energy level and allows only love, positive energy, and healing to enter. It protects against any negative energies that might be around, yet allows all positive energies and love to flow in.
- See yourself breathing in light energy from the universe, from the crown of your head. Feel that light energy going to every cell, every corpuscle, every tissue, bringing love, energy, joy, and feelings of well-being to every part of your being.
- See that light energy perfectly balancing the immune system and restoring perfect function. Remember that the energy is intelligent and has the ability to restore balance without our consciously needing to know what is not functioning properly.
- See the body filled with millions of tiny orange balls, bouncing like ping pong balls. They touch every cell, and every cell receives a charge of energy. The helper T, killer T, and suppressor T cells all line up in parallel files, like little soldiers, with exactly the proper

number in each file. They are enthusiastic and pepped up by the bouncing orange balls. As each file is correctly filled, the soldiers march forward and form a unit with the proper number each of helper, suppressor, and killer cells. Singing, they march off into the body to do their work.

Myasthenia Gravis (MG)

Description

MG is a condition producing progressive weakness and fatigability of the skeletal muscles. The weakness and fatigue are aggravated by exercise and repeated movement. It usually affects the facial, tongue, neck, and throat muscles, but may affect any muscle group. MG causes failure of nerve impulses at the junction of the nerve and the muscle. It is subject to intermittent aggravations and periodic remissions.

Immune Dysfunction

MG is a condition in which the immune system attacks the muscles, causing them to be progressively less responsive to neural stimulation. The body appears to develop an immunity to medications designed to ameliorate symptoms.

Desired Immune Response

- Increased suppressor cells
- Increased ability of the immune system to recognize the body's own tissues
- Balance restored to the immune system

Seeds for Imagery

- See the weakened, flat, flaccid muscles lying in a state of exhaustion. See them flooded with a river of electric-blue water, and the exhausting impurities being flushed away. As the water subsides, a pair of hands made of light begin to massage the muscles, kneading into them light and power. See the muscles increasing in bulk and sustained energy. See the muscles taking the form of an athlete, jumping on a trampoline, laughing as he bounces ever higher and breathes in more oxygen.
- See the weakened muscles laid out like instrument strings. The strings are placed in a harp frame. The harpist's fingers are tipped

with smooth picks (nerves) which pluck the strings and cause them to vibrate. The longer the harpist plays, the finer the tune and power of the harp. The strings are energized by their own music. The harpist plays more rapidly and skillfully. The music becomes rich and fulfilling as scores of happy dancers swirl to its beat. Feel the music of the harp reverberating throughout the body. The mice that had nibbled at the harp strings and weakened them scurry from the room and out of the building.

Immune Hypersensitivity
(Allergic) Disorders

Although there is a large overlap in autoimmune disorders and immune hypersensitivity disorders, we have considered them separately in order to allow a somewhat different conceptualization of several conditions such as myasthenia gravis, lupus, and hepatitis B, which can be thought of allergies to one's own body. It also allows the consideration of allergies under the umbrella, as a hypersensitivity to substances which have entered the system from the outside rather than a reaction to the tissues of the body itself.

Immune hypersensitivity disorders are categorized as Type I (allergic), Type II (antibody-dependent cytotoxicity), Type III (immune complex disease), and Type IV (delayed hypersensitivity disease).

In Type I (allergic), allergens induce production of an immune-globulin which binds to receptors on the surface of the cell. When the cell is re-exposed to the antigen, the allergen binds to the immune-globulin, cross-links with the receptors, and causes a reaction which releases mediator enzymes such as histamine and heparin. The effects of the mediators in the system produce the allergic symptoms such as wheezing, swelling, hives, and runny nose. Allergies can be considered an overzealous immune response during which too much IgE antibody is produced and chemicals are released that cause the classic symptoms of an allergic reaction.

In Type II, the antibody is directed against the cell surface allergens or cell surface receptors, rather than against the cell itself. Tissue damage may be caused by the binding of the antibody and the antigen, which activates an enzyme that ultimately disrupts cellular membranes. Additionally, various phagocytic cells with receptors for immunoglobulin and enzyme fragments may envelop and destroy sensitized targets such as red blood cells, leukocytes, or platelets. Cytotoxic T cells and natural killer cells can also cause tissue damage in Type II hypersensitivity. Myasthenia gravis is an example of this type of sensitivity.

Type III hypersensitivity results when an excess of circulating antigens (allergens) deposits immune enzymes in tissue (usually the kidneys, joints, and blood vessels). These deposits cause a cascade of serum proteins, resulting in local inflammation. Type III hypersensitivity may be associated with hepatitis B and autoimmune disorders such as lupus erythematosus.

Tuberculin reactions and contact hypersensitivity are two examples of Type IV hypersensitivity. In this form, the antigen is processed by the macrophages and presented to the T cells, which release lymphokines that attract lymphocytes, macrophages, leukocytes, etc., and prepare them for attack. Coagulation and enzymatic reaction contribute to tissue damage.

Desired Immune Response

- Increased "sympathetic tone" (epinephrine response)
- Reduced "parasympathetic tone" (acetylcholine response)
- Modulated hypersensitive immune response
- Damaged tissue regenerated

Seeds for Imagery

- See a spring clamp that closes too tightly as it closes on a timber until the spring is fatigued slightly, and the clamp is balanced.
- See a guard at the gate of the body, making decisions about what can pass into the body without harm to the body. He allows all nourishing and pleasurable substances in, but is vigilant in destroying any germs or poisons that would be harmful to the body.
- See a bucket of too-dark paint being modified by the addition of white paint. See the room then being painted the desired color.
- See a crab growing a new claw.
- See a starfish leg growing and becoming a new starfish.
- Place ice in a cauldron of boiling water, cooling it to the temperature of a luxurious, warm bath.
- See a new forest growing back over land scorched by fire.
- See soda water being poured over encrusted battery terminals. See it loosening and washing away the rust and corrosion.

22

Internal Medicine and Endocrine Disorders

Sustained imagery can facilitate either sickness or healing and growth.
—*Michael Murphy*

Imagery is a window on your inner world; a way of viewing you own ideas, feelings, and interpretations. But it is more than a mere window— it is a means of transformation. —*Martin Rossman*

Every five days we have a new lining of the gastrointestinal tract.... Every six weeks each atom in the liver and kidneys is replaced. —*Deepak Chopra*

Internal medicine in this context deals with the gastrointestinal tract and the renal/hepatic systems. Within these systems, the body receives its energy supply and readies it for distribution throughout the system, as well as elimination of unusable residues. The chemical breakdown of food into its component parts, otherwise known as digestion, composes only part of the process. Through this process, however, carbohydrates, proteins, and fats fuel metabolism, provide energy, or build new tissue. Excesses are stored in the liver or the tissues. Waste products are eliminated through the kidneys or intestines.

The endocrine system is responsible for the production of hormones. Hormones, neuropeptides manufactured in the endocrine glands, may be regarded as the body's communication system. Many bodily functions are monitored and controlled by hormones. After stimulation by the hypothalamus, the pituitary disburses a hormone to a target gland, which, in turn, releases a secondary hormone. When hormones reach target cells, through the blood or lymphatic systems, appropriate cellular activity is initiated. The hormones, having completed their work, are either destroyed at the site or returned to the liver to be broken down and eliminated as water soluble compounds. The major endocrine glands are the pituitary, thyroid, parathyroid, pancreas, adrenal glands, and the gonads.

The effect of compromise of these systems results in the compromise of all systems of the body. Homeostasis is destroyed with the loss of the energy providing regulatory and balancing functions of these internal medicine components and the endocrine system.

Gastrointestinal Disorders

The gastrointestinal (GI) tract is a long, hollow tube with glands and accessory organs that breaks down food, through changes in physical and chemical composition, into particles small enough to permeate cell membranes. The cells are thereby provided energy to function. The GI tract is filled with bacteria and other flora, rendering it an unsterile system. When the integrity of the system is impaired or broken, the result can be infection of other systems. Referred pain is a common indication of GI problems.*

Ulcerative Colitis, Crohn's Disease, and Gastric Ulcers

Ulcerative colitis is an inflammation with the formation of ulcers in the mucosa of the colon. It involves diarrhea, nausea, and vomiting, which may bring about malnutrition and dehydration. Other systems may be affected by the colitis, which can cause iron deficiency anemia and coagulation deficiencies of the blood, inflammation of the tissue surrounding the bile ducts and cirrhosis in the liver, arthritis and ankylosing spondylitis, loss of muscle mass, and increased risk of developing colorectal cancer.

Crohn's disease has many similarities to ulcerative colitis but evidences, in addition, fissure ulcers and fistulae. Although primarily disorders of the gut, both are frequently systemic diseases with a wide range of extraintestinal manifestations such as skin lesions, eye lesions, and bone and joint lesions.

The functional causes of gastric ulcers are the breakdown of mucosal resistance, inadequate mucosal blood flow, and defective mucous. Psychogenic factors can cause overproduction of gastric secretions that can erode the stomach, the duodenum and the esophagus. The effects of gastritis and irritants such as aspirin and alcohol are also implicated.

In both ulcerative colitis and Crohn's disease, circulating lymphocytes have been demonstrated to be cytotoxic for epithelial cells in the gut, and it is hypothesized that these immune cells attack, inflame, thicken, and create the lesions in the intestines and other parts of the body. Psychological factors are significant, but not as directly involved as in irritable bowel syndrome (IBS).

---

*The general information on the disorders discussed in this chapter is taken from the *Professional Guide to Diseases, Third Edition.*

Desired Response

- Reduction of production of gastric secretions to appropriate levels
- Increased suppressor cells
- Amelioration of inflammation and removal of deposits in the intestinal wall
- Healing tissue disintegration and the rebuilding of healthy mucosa from the inside of the lesion
- Entire immune system balanced and epithelial cells befriended
- Lining of the gut protected
- Reduction of emotional stress

Seeds for Imagery

- See a magical, healing, thick substance covering and protecting the lining of the gut, see it fill and heal fissures and cracks in the intestinal wall.
- See the gut as a twisted, tortured rope. As a special blue healing spray covers the rope, it begins unwinding, and finally becomes smooth, supple, and relaxed.
- See a delicate powder puff dabbing on soothing pixie dust, calming and healing the lining of the gut, allowing discomfort to disappear magically.
- Image a little fire department quenching the fires with a wonderful, soothing elixir which not only puts out the fires but also removes any charring or scarring and brings an analgesic balm and salve to that burning feeling.
- See yourself wringing out a rough and wrinkled towel that discharges thick, cloudy fluid. Holding the twisted towel under flowing water, watch it become soft and smooth, and see clear water draining from it.
- Imagine a tree, smothered with moss and dying. As you remove the moss, the tree breathes deeply and healthy new growth springs forth.
- A tiger stands over a grass-covered piece of meat, licking the meat, cleaning away the dirt and grass, leaving the meat clean, healthy, and life-giving. He eats the meat, and it gives him energy and power.
- You are walking through a tunnel which gets hotter with each step you take. The walls of the tunnel are pitted from the heat. You find that the tunnel is leading to a furnace which is operating full blast. Donning a fireman's suit, you are able to reach the control lever that lowers the fire in the furnace. Another knob sends a cooling spray through the tunnel. Then you paint the tunnel with a protective

coating that fills all the pits, leaving the tunnel a safer, friendlier passageway.

- See a hose, twisted and curled around itself, held up, then allowed to fall free, unwinding and relaxing.
- Imagine a kitchen sponge filled with food particles, being swished back and forth in mild soapy water until it is washed clean and fresh.
- See yourself painting the barnacle-crusted hull of a ship with a watery glue-softener. The barnacles fall away, leaving the ship's hull smooth and clean.
- Imagine walking through an underground tunnel, bumping into stalactites and stumbling over stalagmites. You illuminate the tunnel with your light, then, from a canister, you spray the walls, ceiling and floor with a soothing mist. The deposits disintegrate to powder, fall to the side of the path, and are carried away by a small stream. The mist coats the walls, which absorb the light from your lamp and begin to glow.
- Imagine the immune system as perfectly balanced and friendly to the whole body. Although it fights off foreign organisms, it cherishes the body and acts as a healing agent.
- Imagine a mermaid with delicate golden hair swimming through your intestinal tract, her lithe, silvery-blue body and tail moving in a gently rhythmic manner. See her touching everywhere you are having problems, with her magical, healing touch, and see the area soothed and healed immediately. See her complete the journey through the tract, healing any other disturbances and checking to see that everything is in order (Epstein, 1989, p. 115).
- A river afire meets a glacier; the river and the glacier exchange their temperatures. The glacier melts and the river cools, flowing peacefully on its way.
- See two children playing on a see-saw. One child holds the other up in the air. The other child moves toward the end of the board, and the board reaches balance.
- Imagine a forest fire, subdued by rains which carry the ash into the earth to enrich it. Rich new growth springs forth to replace that which was destroyed.
- A hole dug in the beach is washed over and refilled by the rhythmic flow of the ocean waves, leaving the beach smooth within minutes.

Gastroesophageal Reflux

Gastroesophageal reflux is a back-flowing of the contents of the stomach or the duodenum, or both, into the esophagus. The back-flow results when the lower esophageal sphincter (LES) is not strong enough to withstand the pressure in the stomach and exudes the contents. Persistent reflux may cause symptoms such as inflammation of the esophageal mucosa, which may be experienced as heartburn or even as chest pain that mimics angina. Hiatal hernia may be one of the underlying causes, as may be the consumption of certain foods and/or agents (fatty and/or highly acidic foods, chocolate, cigarette smoking, anticholinergics). Sitting or lying on one's side may lower LES pressure.

Desired Response

- Increased lower esophageal sphincter (LES) strength
- Decreased abdominal pressure
- Lining of the areas in which there may be reflux

Seeds for Imagery

- See yourself climbing down through a tube. At the bottom, you find yourself standing on a floor inlaid in a starburst pattern. Examine this area carefully for any signs of weakness, splintering, discoloration, or irregularities of texture. Look around to find the tools needed for repair. Ask the floor to tell you what it needs, and do it. Climb the ladder at the side of the tube and find the switch that governs the floor; move the switch up and see the floor opening by extending conically downward. Move the switch down and see the floor draw up flat again, firmly closed.

Renal and Hepatic Dysfunction

Kidney Dysfunction

The kidneys maintain homeostasis by regulating volume, electrolyte concentration, acid/base balance of body fluids, and blood pressure, and by contributing to the production of hemoglobin. They do their work by filtering, purifying, cleaning, and adjusting the blood as it circulates through the maze of microscopic blood vessels and tubes that make up the interior of these organs. The kidneys eliminate waste materials from the system as well. Chronic conditions in other systems, including collagen and endocrine diseases, impact the structure and function of the kidneys. Primary chronic kidney conditions appear to relate to obstruction, stenosis, sclerosis, or lesions caused by infections affecting the nephrons, blood vessels, and arteries of the kidneys. Because of the wide-ranging function of the kidneys, renal failure impacts almost every system of the body. Renal conditions are often asymptomatic until significant damage has occurred.

Desired Response

- Removal of obstructions, whether precipitate (matter), sclerotic (hardening), or stenotic (narrowing)
- Restoration of nephrons, which are the structural and functional unit of the kidney

Seeds for Imagery

- You are standing in the midst of a bombed-out building. Much of the roof is gone; the walls are partially standing; the majestic windows blown out; debris and rubble are in piles around you. But you, and the enthusiastic crowd with you, are determined to restore the building to its previous glory. You have the plans and detailed pictures to do the job perfectly. At your direction the people, talented artisans, go to work cleaning up the rubble, reopening each hallway and room, rebuilding the walls with the finest materials and techniques. You walk through the building supervising and approving each phase of the reconstruction until every part of the structure has been completed and every piece of furniture, carpet, and artwork is in place. You thank each member of the crew, and the joyous celebration spreads through the whole building. Every fixture and implement is functioning perfectly. Take a deep breath and grow, allowing the building to become part of you. Experience a sense of balance and cleansing taking place throughout your body.
- You are standing over a labyrinth with a sandy floor. Some of the walls are thickened with deposits. There may even be rocks strewn around the desolate scene. With a roar, water begins to gush through the structure, swirling into the chambers and cubicles. Deposits start breaking from the walls and fall into the rushing, swirling water. The flood passes through and disappears. The walls become trees; the sand is covered with rich grass and daffodils. The labyrinth has become a beautiful, life-sustaining park.
- "See yourself in an aviary. The birds are flying freely overhead. Then see, sense, and feel yourself as the mighty ostrich, the bird of the earth. Breathe out once. As the ostrich, imagine yourself forming the largest of its eggs. Sense this egg growing until you gently give it forth into the nest. Sit on it until it becomes the perfect egg. Sense the movements of the yolk and the young bird growing within as the

egg grows larger and larger. As it grows, see and know that your kidney(s) is healing" (Epstein, 1989, p. 141).

Liver Dysfunction

The liver is responsible for more than 100 separate functions. The most important of these functions are the formation and secretion of bile, detox-ification of harmful substances; storage of vitamins; and metabolism of carbohydrates, fats, and proteins. The primary conditions of the liver with which we may be concerned are viral hepatitis (A, B, and non-A, non-B, also called C), non-viral hepatitis (toxic or drug-induced), cirrhosis and fibrosis (normal liver cells are destroyed and replaced with fibroid cells, altering structure and function), and steatosis (fatty liver from accumula-tions of triglycerides).

Desired Responses

- Cleansing of virus and cooling of inflammation
- Removal of toxins, irritants, and their residues
- Liquification and removal of fatty deposits

Seeds for Imagery

- A large muddy-looking sponge lies on a flat rock at the bottom of a tall waterfall. The water falls on the sponge and flows through it. The sponge absorbs the water and expands to perfect fullness. The water flowing from the sponge carries sand and silt, which is washed away by the river. As the impurities flow away, the sponge changes to a healthy, vibrant color. The sponge is pliable but soothing to the touch, and it is happy.
- An old house needs renovation. The plumbing is clogged and broken; the plaster, cracked and falling; the woodwork has dry-rot; and the wiring is frayed. But the house is to be preserved. With a master plumber, a master carpenter, and a master electrician, the house is closely inspected and found salvageable. Each master craftsman brings a carefully selected crew. The patient supervises the work, encouraging the workers and celebrating each accomplishment until the project is completed, every clogged pipe and fixture replaced, the wiring redone, the walls replastered from the lath, the woodwork replaced with the finest trim, the painting complete, and the house refurnished to perfection. With the crew, you hold a big party to celebrate the beautiful day.
- The air in a room is filled with feathers. The room is useless filled

with feathers. Open the window and then open the door. A breeze blows through the room, sweeping the feathers out the window. The feathers are blown up into the sky where they cluster to become clouds, then turn to rain, causing the grass to grow, and the flowers to burst into colorful bloom. Smell the freshness of the day, and hear the birds singing. Feel the cool, clean air circulating through your body.

- You create laser rays of light with your fingers, and gently lift your liver from your solar plexis. With consummate sensitivity, you massage it, paying particular attention to any areas which are hard, spongy, or fatty. As you massage, see the blood flowing more quickly, carrying poisons and destructive elements out of the liver and out of the body. See your liver as smooth, resilient, and functioning just perfectly.
- "See your liver as a smooth mirror reflecting your pent-up emotions. Wipe them away to your left with your left hand. Turn the liver over, and on its underside, in the mirror see your newly reconstructed emotions" (Epstein, 1989, p. 145).
- See the building blocks of your liver as brittle, crumbling, or spongy. With your work crew, begin replacing those crumbling, spongy, or worn-out blocks with fine, strong, resilient new ones.

Endocrine Disorders

Diabetes Mellitus

Diabetes is a chronic disease of absolute or relative insulin insufficiency. It occurs in two forms, Type I (insulin dependent) and Type II (non-insulin dependent). Type I usually occurs before age 30, while Type II normally occurs in obese adults after age 40. Some recognized risk factors are genetic, autoimmune, or viral in nature. Also recognized are elements of physiologic or emotional stress which cause prolonged elevation of stress hormone levels and raise blood glucose, thereby placing increased demands on the pancreas. Insulin, like other hormones, is a neuropeptide, which means it is produced at many other sites in the body and brain than the pancreas. Insulin deficiency compromises the body's access to nutrients for fuel and storage.

Desired Response

- Normalized blood glucose levels
- Restored insulin levels, through either pancreatic output or increased access to insulin neuropeptides generated on other areas of the body
- Increased sensitivity of insulin receptors at the cellular level

Seeds for Imagery

- "Your body is a magnificent machine. It really is. We are like all machines; they need fuel to run properly. Now, just having sugar in the blood is not enough. It must enter the cells, all the muscles and tissues. Think of a toaster that is plugged in and not turned on. Or you may to prefer to think of a car with a tank full of gas that is not running ... the toaster is plugged in ... the fuel's in the car, but it is not getting to the right parts to make the machine run. If you are a diabetic, that is how your body is functioning improperly. Picture your body with plenty of fuel rushing into your veins, but the fuel doesn't get to where it is needed, doesn't get into the cells of your muscles and tissues. It stays in your blood stream. Our bodies have a very special way of helping sugar get into the cells of the muscles and tissue.... You have a hormone that you manufacture within your body called insulin ... which helps the cells of your muscles and tissues take in the sugar ... and use it.... Your own insulin is not helping the sugar into the cells.... The insulin that you take in, that your doctor prescribes, acts like the insulin that you manufacture yourself ... imagine for a minute that insulin working in a way that makes sense to you. Imagine your cells with the insulin helping sugar from your blood into the muscles, into the tissue, into the cells. See [your pancreas] manufacturing more insulin ... [and see the insulin] being released into your blood.... See the sugar enter the cell as it leaves the blood stream" (Achterberg & Lawlis, 1984, pp. 207–208).
- You are in a car, driving down an empty highway; you are in the driver's seat, but you may not be steering. The car gathers speed, then pulls to the side and stops. Floating in the air are three-dimensional star-bursts, but some of their spines are broken. See the defective star-bursts being replaced by perfect ones that draw from the atmosphere a balance of energy-giving elements. Within minutes, the car's engine starts again, and you drive down the highway at a moderate, comfortable pace, in total control of your vehicle.
- You are sitting beside an oblong, rounded rock in a beautiful field. You pet the rock, stroking it from one end to the other. As you stroke the rock, you find it becoming warm and soft; it begins to move and wiggle, and turns into a joyful, energetic puppy that leaps lovingly into your lap, then springs into your body and begins lapping up the extra sugar in your system. His tail wags happily, and he is very healthy as he keeps the balance.
- You are watching a multitude of people milling about in a state of confusion near an abundant field. They are all wearing earmuffs

and cannot hear anything; they are bundled up and cannot feel the weather; they are hungry but cannot help themselves. You call for assistance, and from all directions come energetic little helpers, lightly clothed and hatless. They rush among the multitude, removing their earmuffs and telling them to remove the heavy clothes and harvest the field. They in turn help others as they move toward the field. They consume enough to satisfy their hunger and harvest the rest for storage. The people are alert, healthy, happy; the harvest is efficiently stored for future use; and the field is swept clean.

- Fish are darting in and out among water grasses eating morsels of free-floating algae.
- See a warehouse with the floor covered with sugar; the workers vacuum the sugar into boxes which are placed on the proper shelves.
- A furnace fueled by sugar burns with a lively flame, propelling an engine at optimum speed.
- Imagine insulin receptors on every cell in your body. These receptors have been dulled and blunted so that it is hard for them to recognize insulin. See the receptors being cleaned and scoured by sensitizing agents, so that they are again bright and glistening and exquisitely sensitive to even the smallest amount of insulin.
- As you are exercising, see your insulin receptors like the fine antennae of an exquisite communication machine, which may have been sullied and caked with dirt and grime. As you feel the blood flow increase, feel the blood with its cleansing energy chemicals clean those antennae, gently but relentlessly, until their delicate reception is restored. And now see those antennae picking up the tiny insulin keys that unlock the cell and allow it to use the body's abundant sugar energy.
- Imagine the cells of the brain making up any deficit in the pancreas' production of insulin. In the beginning this may be difficult, and the brain produces only a few drops at a time. As the brain's cells learn this new "trick" and practice it time after time, they become expert insulin producers and begin to rival the pancreas. As a matter of fact, the brain and the pancreas begin a friendly competition as to who is the most creative producer of insulin.
- See the immune system becoming aware that it had declared war on the Islets of Langerhans and destroyed a large part of their virgin territory before it realized the islanders were not only friends but actually members of its family. The immune system feels profoundly sorry and sets about making reparations, rebuilding the Islets and their insulin factories and improving the quality of life there until it returns to its original balance and natural beauty.
- "See yourself crossing over a flowing stream. Become an acrobat, tumbling, jumping, and gyrating your way across, a welcome guest in

a new land that awaits you on the other side. Know that your diabetes has subsided when you reach the far shore. Also, give yourself the intention to do something 'sweet' for yourself at least once a day" (Epstein, 1989, p. 93).

- "See yourself in a meadow. Sit in the middle of this meadow communing with nature and with your higher nature. Know and feel the beauty of both. Breathe out once. Know, feel, and sense the sweetness of life from this contact. Know that your insulin flow is being normalized" (Epstein, 1989, pp. 93–94).

- Imagine your insulin factories as being rusty, sluggish, and inefficient. See a wonderful healing mist, like WD-40, blow through the factory, bringing cleansing, lubrication for the machinery, and an electric energy to get the generators moving. See the rust being dissolved by the mist, the moving parts moistened, cleaned, and lubricated, and gentle, but effective, jolts of energy bringing the electric generators up to par. See the production of insulin beginning to increase until it is exactly correct for the body.

- See the cells' insulin receptors as having been so sated by floods of insulin that they never want another bite of insulin or the sugar the insulin transports into the cell for energy. In fact, the receptors are so full that they have gone to sleep. See the receptors waking up, yawning, and realizing that they are really hungry for insulin. They grab it out of the bloodstream as if it were manna from heaven. As they consume the manna, they realize that they have made a pathway for the delicious sugar to come into the cell, nourish it, and give it energy. And there is a sense of deep satisfaction.

Thyroid Problems

Hypothyroidism results from thyroid insufficiency. It may be caused by external conditions such as surgery or irradiation, or it may result from autoimmune inflammation or other inflammatory conditions. As the thyroid seeks to compensate for inadequate output, it may become enlarged, resulting in goiter.

Hyperthyroidism is a metabolic imbalance resulting from overproduction of thyroid hormone, usually a genetic or immunologic condition. The production of autoantibodies in Graves' disease indicates a link with defects of T4 suppressor lymphocytes. Stress appears to be a triggering factor in cases of latent hyperthyroidism.

Desired Response

- Enhanced suppressor cell production and efficiency
- Normalized production of thyroid hormones

Seeds for Imagery

- An intricate control panel which regulates the power source for a complicated city shows all its control levers turned to one side. Move across the panel, adjusting the control levers and knobs to the center point so that all output is at perfect balance. Hear a change in the sound of the machinery as it is appropriately slowed or sped up, until it reaches optimum pitch and rhythm.
- A group of children wearing the uniforms of two schools are playing in a park. The children from one school begin to attack the children from the other school. They fight for a while, then nannies begin to move among the children with treats, encouraging them to sit down and rest. They do so, and begin to make friends and work cooperatively together toward a mutual goal.
- See generalized autoimmune images (Chapter 21).

Adrenal Dysfunction

Adrenal hypofunction (Addison's disease) occurs when 90 percent of the adrenal tissue is destroyed. The primary cause is autoimmune response. Other causes may be tuberculosis, surgery, or other neoplasms or infections. Long-term corticosteroid therapy causes adrenal atrophy. Stress exacerbates the symptoms, probably because the body's response to stress *is* the production of corticosteroids, which it is no longer able to do. Symptoms include weight loss, fatigue, weakness, gastrointestinal disturbance, decreased heart size, and hypotension, among others.

Cushing's syndrome results from excessive levels of adrenalcortical hormones. Symptoms vary according to the adrenalcortical hormones involved, usually a result of excess production of ACTH (adrenocorticotropic hormone). It may stem from pituitary hypersecretion or from ACTH-producing tumors in other parts of the body. Symptoms may also be duplicated by the introduction of corticosteroid therapy (e.g., for Addison's disease or other autoimmune diseases, or in organ transplants).

Pheochromocytoma is a tumor of the adrenal medulla. It causes the secretion of excess epinephrine and norepinephrine, resulting in severe hypertension, increased metabolism, and hyperglycemia. Surgery is treatment of choice. The tumor is usually benign, but may be malignant approximately 10 percent of the time. It occurs primarily between the ages of 30 and 40, and there are indications of genetic predisposition. Symptoms are so dramatic that imagery may serve only an emotionally palliative value.

Desired Response

- Restore normal adrenal function

- Eradication of ACTH-producing tumors
- Normalize the balance of adrenal hormones

Seeds for Imagery

- A dry river bed is followed to its source. A rock slide has sealed the spring so that only the smallest hint of water escapes and is quickly absorbed into the earth. Scraping away the dirt and roots, you reach the rocks and begin gently removing them and setting them aside. A trickle of water appears, and as more stones are removed, the stream becomes heavier. As the water flows into the bed, you can see several streams of different colors. They merge to create a perfectly shaded blue flow of exactly desired power. You watch as the river fills its banks and nourishes the earth around it.
- A thunderous cataract is bearing down on you. It uproots trees and shoves houses off their foundations. You step to the edge of the flood so that only your feet are wet. You will yourself to the source, and find yourself atop a dam where a pump is spewing water from the reservoir into the flood. Forcing the wheel to the left, you begin to close the pulsing flow until a perfect balance is restored between the level of the reservoir and the needs of the river. The river returns to its banks and flows peacefully.
- See your adrenal glands as mountains normally heavily covered with snow and glaciers. Unfortunately, there has been an unusual warm spell, which is quickly melting the snow and glaciers. Vast streams of water are barreling down the mountain, engorging the rivers, flooding everywhere, and threatening to snuff out the life of the community below. In order for the community to be saved, the source of the flooding must be stanched. See the temperature beginning to drop far below zero, and observe the glaciers beginning to refreeze and the snow drifts becoming hard and frozen. The mountain streams slowly begin to return to normal, carrying just enough water from their source to meet the needs of the community. See the proper balance of nature returning.
- To address the autoimmune aspects of these conditions, consult the images in Chapter 21.
- To address the destruction of tumors, consult Chapter 20.

23

Cardiovascular and Pulmonary Disorders

The expression of intentionality is the missing link between the body and the mind. — *Rollo May*

Simply put, the heart is the seat of love.... In every case that I have treated, I have found that using mental imagery has not only yielded insight into the love-heart disease connection, but that it has speeded up the healing process as well. — *Gerald Epstein*

Breathing problems are statements of our experience of many life situations—constriction versus freedom, life versus death, crying versus joy. — *Gerald Epstein*

The cardiovascular and pulmonary systems work as a team for oxygenating the system and cleansing it of carbon dioxide. Environmentally, the cardiovascular system is vulnerable to stress and feelings of isolation; the pulmonary system is at risk from airborne pollutants.

Cardiovascular Disorders

The functions of the cardiovascular system are to carry materials and to regulate temperature. Every cell of the body needs a continuous supply of oxygen and nutrients that furnish energy and raw materials for cellular metabolism. The importance of the cardiovascular system to the survival of the body is illustrated by the fact that it is the first system to develop in the fetus. The cardiovascular system is comprised of the heart, arteries, capillaries and veins. If blood supply is obstructed, cellular death occurs within minutes.

Hypertension

Hypertension is the intermittent or sustained elevation of diastolic and/or systolic blood pressure. It may be the result of dysfunctions within other organs (e.g., kidneys, thyroid, pituitary, parathyroid), neurological disorders, or pregnancy, or it may result from the breakdown of or an inappropriate response to intrinsic regulatory mechanisms. Hypertension may occur when the narrowing of blood vessels from vasoconstriction or plaque buildup creates resistance to bloodflow. Stress, obesity, and high intake of fats and sodium are risk factors.

When threatened, the body responds to stress by shutting down the immune system with a shower of corticosteroids, blood flows more rapidly to feed the muscles more oxygen to meet the perceived threat, the heart beats faster to move the blood, and all "unnecessary" systems shut down to prevent dissipation of energy from its focal point. Because the body does not distinguish between sabre-toothed tigers, forest fires, and angry bosses, the physical response is uniform. Systems in a state of chronic "shut-down" begin to accept that status as the norm, resulting in failure of intrinsic regulatory mechanisms, such as baroreceptors and renin conversion inhibitors, to respond appropriately.

Desired Response

- Pacified stress response
- Normal blood pressure
- Appropriate stimulation of baroreceptors and other regulatory mechanisms

Seeds for Imagery

- A raging river fills its banks. The banks work hard to contain the river. A small child stands on the bank and casts a line into the water. He begins drawing out fish as fast as he can sink his line. As his pile of fish grows higher, the waters begin to drop and calm, until the waters are flowing calmly in the river bed. The child picks up his trove of fish and takes them home to fertilize his garden. The river flows peacefully through the countryside.
- See a pendulum swinging back and forth rapidly and violently. Reach your large and powerful hand up and firmly place the palm on the pivot bolt supporting the pendulum. As you maintain firm and steady pressure, the swing of the pendulum begins to slow and become steadier. You continue to apply the firm, steady pressure until the pendulum swings at a perfect beat. You lift your hand away, and the pendulum continues its steady pace.
- "Imagine yourself going to the refrigerator and taking out three or four ice cubes. Wash your head, skull, face, and neck with the ice and sense and feel the coolness coursing through every pore and

entering into your bloodstream in the brain. See this ice-blue coolness circulating into your trunk, into and through your upper and lower extremities and out to the tips of your fingers and toes. Know that when you see and sense this ice-blue coolness reaching to your fingertips and toes, your blood pressure has returned to normal" (Epstein, 1989, p. 129).

- Take a deep breath, and as you let it out, see the linings of your arteries seep nitric oxide into your blood stream, relaxing and calming your whole body.
- See a team of miners swarming through the coronary and other arteries, deftly chopping away at the plaque, creating larger tunnels which do not restrict the blood flow.
- See a special drain cleaner being poured into your cardiovascular system. This cleanser is quite soothing to healthy tissue; however, it totally dissolves plaque and fat buildup on arteries and other vessels. Follow the progress of the cleaner as it scours the coronary arteries and goes through the other major arteries of the body, leaving those vessels free of buildup and the arterial walls supple and pliant, yet strong and resilient. As the arteries are cleansed and enlarged, the blood flow slows to a normal pace.
- Imagine a river of blood going through the liver to be cleansed of cholesterol and fatty acids. The liver is an immense field of ripe dandelions with each feathery seed eager to soak up as much fat as it can. Watch with pleasure as you see the blood wend through the cleansing dandelion field and leave, clarified and purified of any harmful substances.

Varicosity

Varicosity is a condition in which the veins are dilated and tortuous. This condition may result from congenital weakness of the valves or veins, from diseases of the venous system (e.g., thrombophlebitis), conditions producing venostasis (e.g., pregnancy), or occupations that require standing for extended periods. The weakened, dilated blood vessels allows pooling of the blood which raises the risk of clots.

Desired Response

- Increased venous return
- Increased power of muscle "pumps" returning blood from the extremities
- Increased smooth muscle strength and resilience in veins and other affected area

Seeds for Imagery

- Take a walk through your blood vessels. The round tunnels are empty, and you can examine the walls carefully. Notice any places where the walls are sagging, the plaster is falling, the paint is peeling, and any other signs that maintenance is needed. Clap your hands, and a team of expert craftspeople appear. They are nattily clad in sparkling clean uniforms. They erect scaffolds and commence rapid, skillful repairs, reinforcing weakened areas, tightening loose connections, and scraping away old paint and plaster until the area is perfectly rebuilt. You congratulate the workers on their fine job as they pack away their equipment, and you continue your assessment tour.
- See a lovely young woman sitting in the sun before a beautiful cottage in a peaceful glen. She is swiftly knitting a tube of silken thread. Each stitch is uniform and firm. When it is finished, she slips the silken tube over the area of the weakened vein and crochets the ends into the healthy vein. The silk merges and becomes a firm, healthy part of the vein.
- See workers on the inside of the distended vein painting the walls of the vein with a rubber-based paint. As this incredible paint dries, it evenly shrinks the tissue, leaving the vein tight, but elastic.
- See the valves that aid return of the blood to the heart through the veins as part of a chain of buckets, dipping the blood up and carrying it up through the legs and torso to the heart. Many of the buckets are leaking badly so that the blood pools in the ankles or legs. See a repair team go in and begin to mend the buckets, repairing the binding on the buckets and putting putty into the leaks, until the bucket chain is picking up *all* the pooled blood and dumping it into the vena cava. And this process continues, over and over.

Coronary Artery Disease (CAD)

CAD is that condition which results when oxygen and nutrients fail to reach the heart muscle (myocardium) because of diminished blood flow, causing myocardial ischemia (restriction of blood flow). The diminishment is usually caused by atherosclerosis—narrowing of the channel of the coronary arteries by fatty, fibrous plaque. It has been linked to stress, family history, hypertension, obesity, smoking, diabetes mellitus, sedentary lifestyle, and high serum cholesterol and/or triglyceride levels. Angina is a symptom of CAD, usually described as a burning, squeezing, or crushing tightness in the chest that radiates to the left arm, neck, jaw, or shoulder.

Desired Response

- Elimination of plaque and obstructions of the arteries
- Restoration of normal flow of blood
- Reduced serum low density lipoprotein (LDL) cholesterol and/or triglycerides
- Repair of damage from myocardial ischemia (decreased blood supply to the heart muscle)
- Increased supply of oxygen to the myocardium

Seeds for Imagery

- A glowing sun in the heart lights the way, peeling away scarring and damage. Then the light spreads through all the arteries, veins and capillaries, disintegrating and dissolving all plaque, obstructions, and blockages. Slowly the light becomes a clear green glow, bringing a feeling of deep peace and balance.
- Imagine a tall waterfall in a dense rain forest; the trees are focusing their energy toward the fall. All the oxygen which the vegetation in the rain forest created by the plants' life process is focused toward the falling water. The water embraces and consumes the oxygen. From the base of the falls, the water, its volume increased by the oxygen, flows calmly and with strength. Feel that oxygen is being discharged into the muscles of the heart, and the whole body is filling with laughter and energy.
- See a laser light flooding, not only the coronary arteries, but all the arteries of the body. This laser light totally zaps the ugly, fatty build-up on the vessels—that buildup which has made the arteries so clogged that the nurturant blood finds it difficult to reach the muscle of the heart and the other cells of the body. This intelligent, powerful laser light, however, is quite friendly to healthy tissue and actually massages the walls of the artery, heals any lesions, and leaves the tissue supple and flexible.

Valvular Heart Disease

There are two types of mechanical disruption which lead to valvular heart disease: stenosis (narrowing of the valve opening) and incomplete closure of the valve. The disruptions can result from rheumatic endocarditis, congenital defects, and inflammation, all of which can lead to heart failure.

Desired Response

- Complete and efficient closing of the heart valves
- Renewed flexibility and widening of stenotic valves

Seeds for Imagery

- A series of gates forms locks on a river. Stand astride the river facing the gates and see them opening and closing in a perfect rhythm. See that as each gate closes, its outside dries rapidly, demonstrating there is no seepage. As each gate opens, the river flows into a dry chamber to be passed quickly and in orderly fashion along its way.

- See a large, round portal with a hand crank beside it. The crank is the tool for opening and closing the portal. As you turn the crank clockwise, the canvas covering is drawn toward the center on a fine chain that works as a drawstring. But the crank is rusty, and the chain is tangled in the equipment. The door operates raggedly and refuses to close properly. You clap your hands to summon a repair crew. They appear—well groomed, well trained, and eager to go to work. You work along with them to straighten the chains, and to dismantle and clean the cranking mechanism. The work is done, and as the captain of the crew turns the crank, it works quietly and smoothly to open and close the door completely. You know the door is completely closed, because when it is closed, even the noise from outside the building is completely silenced. Thank the crew, tell the door of your admiration for its fine work. Ask the crew to remain with the door and to call you immediately if needed. Return to the door regularly to praise it for its good work.

- See Eskimo women working over hides, rubbing soothing oil into the stiff, brittle material. The warmth of their hands and the moisturizing quality of the oil causes the hides to become soft and elastic. Now see the women, in their colorful costumes, working inside your heart valves, replacing the stiff, thickened valve with the fresh, soft, warm new valve that opens and closes in a supple manner. The women laugh and clap their hands, proud of their work. You thank them and congratulate them for their fine job.

- See yourself standing in a tunnel. There is a fire and flood safety door which is stuck at half closure, narrowing the width of the tunnel. You have with you a large hot air balloon which you place in the middle of the opening of the half-closed door. You start the burner and the balloon inflates. It pushes against the door, warming the leading edge. The edge softens, and the warmth is radiated through all the folds and fibers of the door. The door becomes warm and flexible, sending forth feelings of contentment. You realize that the door has been feeling unhappy, abused and ignored. The door opens fully, almost disappearing into the walls of the tunnel. Then, it closes completely with a quiet, consistent murmur and opens fully. The tunnel smiles, and you take a deep, energizing breath.

Pulmonary/Respiratory Diseases

The pulmonary system supplies oxygen to the body. The nose, sinuses, throat, and bronchial tubes contain mucous membranes which warm and moisturize incoming air while trapping foreign matter. Hair-like structures called cilia sweep the trapped substances back into the throat or nose to be coughed or sneezed away. The lungs are of nonmuscular tissue; the diaphragm and chest wall muscles, by contracting, draw air into the lungs. Oxygen enables the body to utilize the nutrients in food. Through respiration, the body brings oxygen to the lungs to be absorbed through the alveoli (air sacs) into the blood and transported through the system. Blood returns to the lungs at the end of its cycle carrying carbon dioxide, which is released through the alveoli to be exhaled from the body.

Chronic Obstructive Pulmonary Disease
(COPD)

COPD is a chronic airway obstruction that results from emphysema, chronic bronchitis, asthma, or any combination of those disorders. It does not always cause symptoms, and may cause only minimal disability. However, it tends to worsen with time. Studies (e.g., Polonski, Knapp, Brown, Schwartz, Osband, & Cohen, 1988) indicate that imagery can effect significant physical change with COPD.

Emphysema is an "irreversible" enlargement of air spaces within the lungs due to destruction of the walls of the alveoli. This causes the lungs to lose their elasticity and creates difficulty in absorbing O_2 and expelling CO_2 and other vestigial gases from the lungs.

Chronic bronchitis occurs when excessive mucus production leads to productive cough at least three months a year for two years.

Asthma results with increased bronchial reactivity to a variety of stimuli which produces episodic bronchiospasm and airway obstruction. Childhood-onset asthma is often associated with distinct allergens. Adult-onset asthma is often without distinct allergies.

Desired Response

- Increased cilial activity
- Restructured alvioli and pulmonary elasticity, together with increased lung capacity

Seeds for Imagery

- See a field of sea anemones sweeping food out of the water for the clown fish nestled within their tentacles. As the fish eat the food, see the water becoming crystal clear. As you watch, more and more anemones appear.

- See grass, grown tall, bowing and rippling before the winds of a summer rain storm.
- In an upholstery shop, see many seamstresses gathered around a large pillow filled with air. Their job is to tuft the pillow with thousands of buttons. When they have finished, the pillow is firm, bouncy, and gives uniform support all over.
- You are making bread. The dough has risen and you are kneading it. The more you knead the dough, the stronger and more elastic it becomes. You set it aside to rise again. It takes up more air, and becomes lighter and lighter. Breathe deeply, and smell the fresh bread.
- You are standing in the midst of a pack of excited puppies. They are barking and jumping against you, vying for your attention. You lean down and speak gently to each puppy and stroke it; it sits contentedly at your feet.
- It is a hot and dusty summer day. You can see, smell, and feel the dust in the air. Suddenly the sky clouds over, and rain begins to fall. The rain cleans the dust from the air, washes it from the grass and trees, and dampens the road. When the shower passes, the air smells fresh and clean, the grass and leaves are greener, and colorful flowers burst forth into bloom. Breathe deeply, allowing the clean air to circulate in your body, cleaning all the dust from your lungs.
- You are relaxing in a garden. You look over and see your lungs as a labyrinth, a maze formed by high hedges. As you try to enter the maze, you are unable to get in and out of it because of giant mole holes—and as you look in, you see fierce giant moles militating against your moving around. You now see your therapy as giving you great power—both the power to leap over the mole holes, and also great height so that you can see over the hedges, note the design, and know how to get in and out (Snyder, 1985).
- It is a beautiful dawn and you hungrily breathe in the fine air. This wonderful essence is pulled into your lungs where it begins the healing process in all the tubes, sacs, and tissues of the lungs—cleansing, strengthening, tightening where needed, and relaxing where needed. See total healing take place and all obstructions removed or dissipated.

24

Pain, Neurological Disorders, and Psychological Problems

The spirit is the master, imagination the tool, and the body the plastic material. — *Paracelsus*

Imagination is not the talent of some men, it is the health of every man. — *Ralph Waldo Emerson*

Every atom in the brain and nervous system is replaced every five weeks . . . as is the DNA itself. — *Deepak Chopra*

The common thread of this chapter is that all these challenges involve direct brain function. Pain, whether acute or chronic, is transmitted by way of respective neurons to and through the spinal cord to the brain for recording and processing. The neurological conditions each relate to dysfunction or damage at the site of the brain or central nervous system. The limbic system is the center of emotions, and the cerebral cortex, which comprises the two lobes of the forebrain, is the seat of reason, imagination, and creativity. Persistent stress to the neurological and other systems can engender psychological problems; however, tapping into one's emotions, imagination, and creativity frequently have a healing effect on both mind and body.

Pain

In looking at pain, we need to make the distinction between acute pain and chronic pain. Acute pain serves an identifiable function of protection from further harm. It tells us there is something wrong and something needs to be done about it—an adjustment in our behavior or lifestyle needs to be made. Chronic pain, on the other hand, serves no biological purpose (Morris, 1992). Chronic pain is pain that does not disappear or that reappears over extended periods—even though the original "cause" is gone or the injury has healed. Chronic pain persists even when the nerves to the site of the pain have been surgically cut or the site of the pain has

376

been amputated (phantom limb pain). This leads Morris to suggest that the human brain is able to produce pain in the absence of tissue damage and that "pain comes into existence only at the moment when it makes its way into our consciousness. Without the mind's contribution, there is no pain" (p.15).

According to Morris, it's as if there is "a central generator mechanism responsible for keeping the pain alive" (p. 19); this may involve not only memories of the pain but also deep anxieties about the meaning of the pain in the person's life. "Could it be that our brain alone really spins out a cycle of chronic suffering, like an endlessly replaying tape with no continuing injury needed to keep it going?" he asks. He comes to the conclusion that "Pain, in effect, is not merely a physiological event. It is simultaneously emotional, cognitive, and social . . . anything beyond the most commonplace acute pain is a complex perceptual experience . . . an experience that continues to change as it passes through the complicated zones of interpretation we call culture, history, and individual consciousness" (p. 23).

This "centralist" view of pain (as opposed to the "peripheralist" view that pain emanates from the injury site) has immense implications for imagery and behavioral medicine. The idea that "pain is always in your head" (Morris, p. 9) can be extremely empowering or totally excruciating for participants. Therefore, we strongly suggest that you become familiar with the work of Morris and other centralists before you present these hypotheses to patients suffering from pain.

Generalized Seeds for Imagery for Pain

A stumbling block to imagery may occur in patients who are keeping physical pain under control by dint of mind power. As these patients relax to prepare for imagery, their physical discomfort may increase, interfering with their ability to focus attention on the task at hand. To address this challenge, the facilitator may suggest an image of floating down through colored layers. The first layer may be golden-yellow—there the patient gains insight; the second layer may be emerald green, to establish calm and relieve anxiety; the third layer may be an indigo blue which draws the pain from the body and traps it, so the patient leaves the layer released from impediments to concentration; the next layer may be soft pink, giving a feeling of love and comfort; the final layer may be clear—a synthesis of all the colors of the rainbow and a reminder of the balance we need in our lives.

- See pain as a good friend of yours. It tells you when you're picking up something sharp or something that is red-hot. Pain is your body asking for help. When pain is felt we can say, "Thank you, pain, for

reminding me to send blood flow, white blood cells, and love to that part of the body. Thank you, unconscious, for letting me know that you are scared so that I can comfort you" (Norris, 1992).
- "Scan your body . . . gather any pains, aches, or other symptoms up into a ball. Begin to change its size . . . allow it to get bigger . . . just imagine how big you can make it. Now make it smaller. . . . See how small you can make it. . . . Is it possible to make it the size of a grain of sand? (Change the size several times in both directions). Now allow it to move slowly out of your body, moving further away each time you exhale. . . . Notice the experience with each exhale . . . as the pain moves away" (Dossey, 1988, p. 239).

Headache and Chronic Pain

Headaches are usually symptomatic of underlying disorders. They are often the result of muscular or vascular constriction, or a combination thereof. Those constrictions may be attributable to poor stress response or allergy.

Chronic pain may be experienced as a result of trauma or systemic degeneration. Medications may be inadequate, or concerns over side effects or addictive properties may undermine the patient's willingness to utilize them. At GETTING WELL, we find that patients are often astounded at the power they possess to ameliorate their pain without the use of medications. In addition to using imagery for symptomatic relief of pain, the patient may wish to use transformational fantasy to investigate underlying issues or emotions that he or she needs to address to facilitate more complete physical healing.

Desired Response

- Reduction or disappearance of pain
- Resolution of underlying causes of pain

Seeds for Imagery

- A large indigo blue silk scarf floats from the sky and comes to rest on your hands. You fold it and place it over the painful area. The scarf is absorbed into the body and wraps itself around the pain, trapping the pain in its fibers. Then a pocket appears in the area, and a corner of the scarf peeks through. Gently withdraw the scarf through the pocket, drawing the pain out with it. Drop the scarf into a wastebasket at your feet, and walk away, comfortable, and pain-free.
- See yourself sitting on a bed of luxuriously soft grass beside a beauti-

ful, deep pond. The water is a deep indigo blue. Slip into the cool, soothing waters and swim slowly about the pond. Feel any pain being drawn through your skin into the water, being trapped there, and falling to the bottom of the pond. Swim around until you are completely relaxed and comfortable, then swim back to the edge of the pond and walk out.

- See yourself sitting in a beautiful and peaceful place. Locate the pain and tell it to come out. The pain assumes the form of a small creature with a friendly face. Allow it to say everything, and listen with an open mind. When you understand the lesson the creature has come to teach, thank it and tell it what you have learned. The creature gives a cheery smile and a wave and walks away.

- "Be present with the pain. Let your pain take on a shape . . . any shape that comes to your mind. Become aware of the dimensions of the pain. . . . What is the height . . . width . . . and depth of the pain? Give it color . . . a shape . . . feel the texture. Does it make any sound? Let your hands come together with palms turned upward as if forming a cup. Put your pain object in your hands . . . [how would you change the size, shape, color, texture, etc., of the pain?] And now, let yourself decide what you would like to do with the pain . . . just accept what feels right to you. You can throw the pain away . . . or place it back where you found it . . . or move it somewhere else. Let yourself become aware . . . of how pain can be changed. . . . By focusing with intention the pain changes" (Dossey, 1988, pp. 239–240).

Other Neurological Conditions

Epilepsy

Epilepsy is a condition characterized by seizures resulting from the abnormal electrical discharge of neurons in the brain.

Desired Response

- Balanced electrical discharge of neurons in the brain
- Understanding of the triggering mechanisms of the discharge

Seeds for Imagery

- A damaged, live wire is shorting, arcing, and sending sparks in all directions. With each outburst, the wire jumps. Throw a soft woolen shawl over the wire, covering the wire completely, tucking the shawl's edges under the wire. Take the wire and shawl on your lap, and feel the activity becoming calm. Notice a rhythmic vibration and realize that you are hearing purring. Remove the shawl to find a bright-eyed friendly kitten who snuggles happily against you.

- Take a walk inside your brain. Notice any damaged switches, crossed wires, blocked paths, or any other unusual situations or items. Talk with anyone or anything there to learn what you need to do to correct these problems. Every tool will be supplied in some form. You may even want to ask why the problem was created. When you have corrected as many problems as you wish to work on at this time, return to the here and now and open your eyes. (This seed may also be useful for stroke or dystrophic conditions.)

Cerebrovascular Accident (Stroke)

A cerebrovascular accident (CVA) is the sudden impairment of circulation in one or more of the brain's blood vessels. The resulting interruption or diminishment of oxygen supply often causes serious damage or cell death in the brain tissue. The major causes are thrombosis (blood clot), embolism (air, gas bubble, foreign matter, or bit of tissue that circulated in the blood until becoming trapped in the blood vessel), or hemorrhage.

Desired Response

- Repair of or bypassing of damage caused by CVA
- Prevention of recurrence

Seeds for Imagery

- Imagine a traffic bottleneck at a bridge. A car has stalled, and there is no room for cars to pass. The traffic backup gets larger and larger, until, at last, the stalled car comes to life and safely moves on. See the traffic begin to move, slowly at first, then gradually up to speed.
- See water which has built up behind a dam. Only a little water trickles over that earth barrier, but, as it does, it begins to create a larger and larger furrow in the top of the dam. More and more water is flowing over and through the dam, breaking the dam down into tiny particles which will not disturb the flow of the river ahead or lodge in any bends. Now, see a free flow of water over and through the dam, and see the dam beginning to disappear.
- Look down upon the main street of the city. The street and sidewalk are filled with people, all walking the same direction. They jostle and bump, but continue to move smoothly until the way narrows. People

from the rear throw their parcels over the heads of those in front, beyond the narrowing; they occupy less room so all can move smoothly through the gate. After they pass through, they pick up their bundles and move on to their destination.

- See a frayed old hose being dipped into a vat of liquid rubber. See the hose emerge, looking like new.
- See a grain elevator unloading wheat into a railroad car. There seems to be something wrong with the chute because there is only a trickle of grain. The supervisor checks the chute and finds that the wheat has backed up on itself. It is quite easy to dislodge the wheat and re-establish the powerful flow of the grain from the elevator to the boxcar.
- You are walking through the woods on a beautiful day. The path is comfortable and well used. You come to a place where the path has been destroyed. You look to see the best direction to take to reach your destination. You walk around the obstruction, smoothing the way, and making a new path. On the other side, you find the path again. You move ahead confidently to the end of your errand, knowing the new path is as good or better than the old.

Tic Douloureux

Tic douloureux (trigeminal neuralgia) is a painful disorder of the fifth cranial nerve or its branches, producing spasmodic attacks of excruciating facial pain.

Desired Response

- Cessation of short-circuiting of touch and pain fibers
- Resolution of underlying stress that may be triggering touch/pain fiber interaction

Seeds for Imagery

- You have an electrical cable that produces a shock every time you use it. You open the wrap covering the cable to reveal the wires within. You see that the insulation is missing from some of the wires, and the live wires are touching each other. Pick up your pot of rubber paint and a brush and separate the wires, gently giving each wire a solid coating of rubber paint. The paint dries almost immediately. When each wire is well coated, re-wrap the cable and find that it works perfectly.
- Three rooms of the mind need to be visited: the anger room, the

pain room, and the self-esteem room. Slowly and carefully clean and/
or rearrange each room. Taking your time to choose only perfect
items, furnish the self-esteem room beautifully. Allow yourself to
spend a lot of time there.

Psychological Problems

Consider the hypothesis that nearly all, if not all, psychological problems
seem to come from negative beliefs about self, and the communication of
those messages to the self. Before these messages can be expunged, they
must be recognized. An effective method of attaining such recognition is
to have the individual create a dialogue like the following one with himself
or herself:

> "What is really going on? What that person is saying or doing has nothing to
> do with me, but is only a reflection of how he or she feels about himself or
> herself. What am I saying to myself about myself?"

Then have the patient allow his or her mind to go blank so the question
can drop like a pearl in clear oil. When the pearl reaches the bottom,
words of self-criticism will rise to the surface. Have the patient deal with
each critical comment and balance it against cognitive reality and experience in order to counteract and cancel the destructive message.

Panic Disorder/Agoraphobia

Anxiety disorders, which include panic and phobias, are described as being
a persistent, irrational fear of places or things that compels the patient to
avoid them. Though the patient may recognize the irrationality of the
fear, he or she is unable to control the experience or even explain it. Panic
is overwhelming reaction to an internal threat to a person or to his or her
values (as opposed to fear, which is a reaction to danger from a specific
external source).

If the patient is asked to locate the physical source of his or her symptoms, tightness in the midriff is often noted. Relaxing this area of the
body will dispel the debilitating feelings at least temporarily, so that cognitive work can be done to create a longer-lasting result.

Desired Response

- Reduction of the feelings of anxiety or doom
- Moving into, accepting, relabeling, and embracing feelings of anxiety
  as stimulating and life-enhancing

- Balancing of the emotional and cognitive components of the thought process

Seeds for Imagery

- As you feel the anxiety build up in your body and mind, realize it is a gift of energy. You can use this gift in any way you wish. You are really excited to know you have so much energy and that you can use it in any way you wish.
- See yourself wearing an emerald green cashmere cloak with a deep hood. As the cloak surrounds you, your muscles relax wherever your body is touched, and all feelings of tension fade away.
- See yourself with a protective shield, a tough, semi-permeable membrane around your whole being. This membrane blocks any fear or negativity from coming into your space, yet allows love, confidence, and other positive things to come in and stay in your space. Your semi-permeable-membrane shield protects you from events and people . . . as you wish. You can go anywhere and do anything, knowing that your wonderful bubble protects you from anything you fear.
- Image yourself floating in a pool of emerald green water. All the tension is being drawn through your skin into the water where it sinks below the surface and falls to the bottom of the pool.
- Be in a box or bubble of clear light or glass that moves with you wherever you go, protecting you from any external dangers. See the dangers striking the barrier and bouncing away.
- See yourself fighting a wave of panic. You fight so hard and try to stand so firm, but the wave simply knocks you over. Now see yourself, rather than fighting the wave, riding the wave like a skilled body-surfer. As you relax, the wave carries you up to the crest, then gives you an exciting, but relaxing, ride onto the beach, where the wave dissipates, leaving you a little breathless, but happy and content that you rode the wave to its finish. As you arise and head into the waters again, you are surprised at the strength you have gained, and you actually look forward to catching your next wave.

Depression

Depresson is a syndrome of sad, dysphoric mood, accompanied by feelings of powerlessness, hopelessness, guilt, and self-deprecation, among others. Depression has been defined as "anger turned inward," because the individual attacks himself or herself (consciously or not) for all of his or her deficiencies.

Desired Response

- Self-forgiveness and self-acceptance
- Recognition of self as powerful

Seeds for Imagery

- See yourself in the rain, throwing yourself over and over against a brick wall. There is only one thickness of brick at that point, although the rest of the wall is several layers thick. Finally, you pick up a tool lying on the ground and begin to beat on the wall. Suddenly the bricks give way, and you cross through the opening into a beautiful meadow on a brilliantly clear day.
- You see a tall mound of rags and trash and garbage, and you realize that under all that debris is the real YOU. You begin to remove the layers, piece by piece. Each layer is labeled as a negative belief you hold about yourself. As you remove each layer, you recognize that the belief it represents is a lie. As you throw each layer over your shoulder, it disintegrates into smoke and is blown away. When the last layer is removed, the YOU springs forth as a being of pure, perfect, brilliant light, and embraces you joyfully. You and YOU merge, and the joy fills your body, and the light shines through.
- The confident, upbeat part of you is talking to the unhappy side of you, who sits, head lowered, feeling sad, guilty, hopeless. Hear from the sad you about the mistakes and failures of your life. Put your arms around the sad you and remind yourself that along the way you have always made the best choices you could, considering the circumstances, the knowledge you had, what you believed, and the penalties you thought might result. Discuss these things between your two selves. Understand that the most wonderful person in the world could have made a "mistake" or been a "failure" under the same circumstances. Remind yourself that when new information came to light, you changed your actions, and that nothing more was required. Know that each circumstance was only a lesson, each action you took was only part of your unique texture at the time; that with the learning of each lesson you become perfect in a new way. You are always the perfect YOU. See and feel the sadness leaving the "sad" you as your two selves embrace each other joyfully.

Codependency/Self-Esteem Issues

From the belief that survival depends on the largess and acceptance of others grow issues of co-dependency and low self-esteem. To achieve autonomy, one must believe in his or her ability to meet personal needs.

Only when one realizes that his or her value is innate and that acceptance by others (probably conditional) is only a reflection of how those others feel about *themselves* can these issues be resolved.

Desired Response

- Establishment of individual autonomy
- Weakened dependency bonds to others

Seeds for Imagery

- See yourself as a child of about two, thirsty for love and acceptance, standing before an old-fashioned well. The child lowers the bucket into the well and draws it up—empty. The child thinks that he or she did it wrong, and tries again. Again, the bucket is empty. Lift the child to see into the well. It is dry and dusty, and has been for years. Explain to the child, so that it understands, that the well was dry long before the child was alive, and the child had nothing to do with the fact that the well is dry. See the child searching for ways to fill the well. Explain to the child that no one can fill the well but the well itself, that the child cannot fill the well. Pick up the child and take it to a nearby stream. Sit down on the bank and scoop the water in your hands, then give the child a drink. Cuddle the child and say that *you* will always be there to satisfy its thirst.
- You are holding in your hand a large and beautiful jewel. Other people are walking around holding jewels, too. When they begin to criticize your jewel, see yourself covering it with dirt and mud. Notice that the gems being held by the others look dirty just like yours. Look at your jewel and realize that you can no longer see it at all, that it looks like a lump of dirt, as does everyone else's jewel. Go over to a fountain or some other running water. Hold the lump of mud under and let it flow over the packed, crusted dirt. See the beautiful gem sparkling in your hand, and notice you can now see that everyone else is carrying a sparkling gem as well.
- See yourself in a rich wheat field. The grain has been harvested. You have given your harvest to the people around you, not because you wanted to, but because they demanded it, and you thought you had to comply. Now your field is empty, and you have nothing to sustain you. Go to the neighboring fields and take back your grain, *your* wheat only—nothing that belongs to anyone else. Bring the wheat back to your own barn. The others complain, but they know you are taking back only that which is yours. They are just angry that you ceased to allow them to raid your field. Allow yourself to feel happy that you have protected your own crop and field.

25

Common Trauma and
Generalized/Preventive Imagery

Imagery does not heal. Rather, imagery opens the passageways to the soul to tap the resources we have that do heal. *—Louis Mehl*

Every month our skin is completely replaced—atom for atom. . . . every three months we have a totally new skeleton. *—Deepak Chopra*

Imagery is not only a set of tools for healing, but for preventing illness and living the highest quality daily life. *—Martin Rossman*

The emerging concept of teleological coherence (Booth & Ashbridge, 1993) emphasizes the interconnectedness of the psychosocial, neurological, and immunological systems. The theory proposes that disease-associated changes depend on pathological stimulus, "classical" immune responses to it that are expressions of current dynamics, and intention of the whole psychoneuroimmune-determined self. If these premises continue to be validated, they clarify the power and the vehicle through which thoughts and imagery accept or reject the onset of illness and enhance or delay healing.

In this chapter we go from broken bones to warts to prevention/maintenance, making clear that imagery has a powerful role in every aspect of our lives—body, mind, and spirit.

Surgery, Cuts, Fractures, Burns, and Warts

Although surgery is not a daily experience for most people, the principles, such as controlling blood flow, handling pain, and healing damaged tissues, are applicable to a variety of problems most of us encounter daily. Burns, warts, cuts, scrapes, and bruises occur to the largest organ of the body, the skin and its underlying substrates. Blood flow and the lymphatic system are eminently responsive to imagery.

Seeds of Imagery

- See the surgical area as a desert. The whole area is dry sand. Oases are far beyond the horizon, and there is no moisture at all in this area.
- See yourself in a beautiful, peaceful place. See yourself dancing, leaping, cavorting, in perfect physical condition.
- See yourself standing beside the surgeon as he or she operates. You are telling the surgeon exactly what to do and how to do it. As each step is finished, concentrate on the site and see it healed immediately. By the time the surgeon has finished, even the surgical scar has disappeared.
- See yourself feeling well, but bearing a wound. If it is bleeding, see the blood disappear and the wound become clean and dry. See inside yourself as your body mends rapidly from the inside out. As you watch, even the scar disappears without a trace.
- You or a loving guardian angel is placing broad leaves of healing herbs on the burned area. The leaves send their healing essence into the body. All physical discomfort disappears. The body responds immediately by rebuilding itself with perfect cells. When the healing is complete, you stand. The leaves fall away, revealing you as happy and well.
- See the burn covered by sky-blue foam, which is a self-contained ice pack. Feel the cold of the pack as the heat is drawn from the tissue and the cooking of the flesh ceases. Concentrate on the coolness, which neutralizes any pain. See the tissue rebuilding under the ice pack, shoving the damaged skin out of the way. When the ice pack is removed, see the area as fully healed. (This imagery also works well when a finger has been closed in a car door or a crushing injury is creating swelling or bruising.)
- (Burn graft) "In your mind, go to the area where you have been burned . . . and go to the area of your body where you have received your new graft. In your mind, begin to imagine the healing process . . . imagine that your own skin secretes a kind of glue. This glue is very important, because it will allow your new graft to stick and hold in a healthy way. Your own body now . . . sends nutrients to the graft, and small blood vessels begin to sprout out . . . just like little 'hands' moving out, sending nutrients to every cell in this area for healthy survival . . . the blood vessels from your own body . . . and the blood vessels from your graft actually grow together. . . . You might even imagine this as those blood vessels joining hands . . . just imagine now that this graft is part of your body just like all the other tissues of your body" (Dossey, 1988, pp. 257–258). (Note: this image has

been greatly edited. If you are working with burn patients, be sure to consult the original source.)

- Look inside your body to find a broken bone. See it as it is. Then see sparking lights as the bone fragments locate each other and send out threads to knit themselves together again. See the threads filling in with new bone, and see the broken bone thicker, heavier, and stronger than it was before the break.
- "New cells are gathering very fast at the site of your fracture . . . right now your body is allowing those new cells to multiply rapidly. Your blood cells . . . at the site of your fracture, are arranging themselves in a special healing pattern. In a few days . . . your wise body will begin to create a strong lattice network of new bone. . . . This will allow your bone to become stable, bridging the new bone that is forming . . . natural deposits of calcium will be taken into the place of healing. Allow an image to come to your mind now of beautiful, healed bone" (Dossey, 1988, pp. 255–256).
- See a young tree branch, twisted and broken. Straighten the branch, place a stick to support it, and wrap the break and splint together. Listen to the branch and hear the healing taking place within the wood. When the healing sounds stop, and you hear only the normal growing sounds, unwrap the branch and find it whole again.
- See your warts with roots deep in your flesh, seeking succor from your bloodstream and breathing from pores on their surface. Imagine the surface of the warts covered with a nail polish-like substance which cuts off their ability to breathe. And now see the blood supply withdrawing from the roots of the warts, circumventing the warts. Additionally, you may see a knife cutting off the roots, or you may see the roots withering from lack of nurturance from the blood.

Generalized/Preventive Images

Generalized images are useful with people who have no specific condition, in groups where several diverse conditions are represented, and even in specific imagery sessions. Their focus is on balance, harmony, surveillance of any dangerous elements in the mind/body/spirit, wholeness, and connectedness with the universe. This is certainly not an exhaustive list; rather, it is meant to give one seeds for one's own meaningful imagery. Healthy people need to image, too (remember the several hundred cancer cells we each produce daily!).

- Breathe from a funnel of light energy from the crown of your head. This is a healing, healthy-cell-friendly laser light. It destroys cells that don't belong, like an electric bug-killing device. It goes through blood vessels and destroys unhealthy tissue and scarring, embracing and enhancing healthy tissue. The light is able to go into a healthy cell containing a hidden virus, destroy the virus, and leave the cell intact. It is very intelligent and knows exactly what to do.

- See a healing light going into the control centers of your brain, restoring balance and harmony to any specific system and to your whole being.
- Feel yourself where you are sitting becoming heavier and heavier, beginning to go down like a root into the earth, stabilizing, grounding, bringing nurturance and love from the earth source throughout your whole being. Your body, mind, and spirit are feeling totally loved, totally nourished, totally protected. Feel the earth energy surging through your being, connecting you with the incredible force of the universe, the incredible force of love, the incredible healing that is ours when we don't struggle against the universe, but float with it.
- See yourself lying on a beach with the healing waters of the sea lapping at your feet. As a wave comes in, it sweeps through your being, healing, cleansing with its primeval power—gently healing, soothing and protecting. As the wave recedes, it carries with it any disease, any discomfort, any debris—leaving your body whole, clean, energetic, and completely healthy.
- Visualize endorphins being released—flooding your body. Imagine them in various forms coming in, making you feel good, healing your body—in their own particular forms.
- Hear the doorbell ring. Open the door and see a delivery person holding a package. Tell the person that the package is not for you. See the package being taken away. Close the door.
- You are standing in the rain wearing a raincoat, boots, and a hat. You are holding a large umbrella over your head. The rain is falling heavily, but you are dry and cozy under your umbrella and in your rain gear.
- "Imagine a mountain scene. See yourself walking on a path toward the mountain. You hear the sound of your shoes on the path . . . smell the pine trees and feel the cool breeze as you approach your campsite. You have reached the foothills of the mountain. You are now higher up the mountain . . . resting in your campsite. Look around at the beauty of the place" (Dossey, 1988, p. 239).
- Float on a cloud of your healing color, breathing this beautifully colored healing energy into your left arm, seeing your arm change color as the energy goes into every cell, every tissue, and deep into the bone—bringing peace, tranquility, and healing into each part of the area. As you breathe out, breathe out any discomfort, any disease, any negativity, any blockage to healing. (Repeat using left leg, right

leg, right arm, pelvis, solar plexus, chest and shoulders, head and brain.) At the end, breathe in several breaths that keep this healing energy surging through your body, with the final suggestion that each breath you take, 24 hours a day, seven days a week, will regenerate this wonderful healing energy.

Expanding Seeds for Imagery

Using the previous seed for imagery, we will illustrate how one can plant and fertilize the seed and allow it to develop into an image in full bloom. This is an opportunity to allow your creativity to flourish. We present "Color Imagery" as an example of how this might be done:

Color Imagery

Let yourself relax as completely as you can, letting feelings of relaxation fill your whole body and mind. Now take in a deep breath, deep into your solar plexus, feel it radiate in ripples throughout your body . . . feelings of peace . . . and love . . . and healing . . . in every part of your body. . . . As you exhale, breathe out any negativity, any distress, any disease, and let yourself relax even further. And take another deep breath into the center of your body . . . where it cascades out to every cell, every corpuscle, every tissue . . . bringing peace and love and relaxation and healing . . . and breathing out any problems . . . any discouragements . . . anything in your body that does not belong, and let your body be at peace, at one. . . .

In your mind's eye imagine one of those sublime mornings . . . dew is glistening on the ground . . . the air is cool. . . . You are standing by a body of water facing east . . . and it feels so good . . . just filled with the transcendent power of that early morning glow and mist. As the sun begins to rise, you notice the clouds in the sky taking on rainbow hues from the rays of the sun . . . and you look at that glowing sunrise resplendent with colors . . . a majestic sight . . . and you see every color of the rainbow . . . the depth of every color . . . the subtlety of every color that is known. And there's such a remarkable feeling . . . an enthralling, delicious feeling . . . being there with all that majesty and magnificence. . . . And you feel as if you're radiant and glowing as you look up into that splendorous sky.

You find that you're mysteriously attracted to one of those clouds . . . one of those colors . . . your body is attracted to it . . . and you get your eye on that cloud and look at the transcendent splendor . . . that cloud is just for you, and you know that's true. You're going to fly up to that cloud. In order to fly, all you need to do is take three steps . . . and then up and flying. . . . One . . . two . . . three . . . and up. You feel yourself go through that wonderful morning air . . . the misty air . . . toward the sunrise . . . toward the cloud your body has chosen.

You see yourself flying higher . . . and higher . . . until the earth begins to fade from your sight. You let yourself shrug your shoulders and just let any fears or any problems, any worries, any discomforts, simply drop from your shoulders. You're flying high . . . soaring among the gulls and eagles and other birds. You know the perfect freedom of unobstructed flying, high up in the sky . . . feeling so free . . . and so relaxed as you aim toward that perfect cloud . . . that cloud of healing color . . . that cloud of healing energy.

And soon you become involved with it . . . and you allow yourself to enter it and settle down into that cloud . . . and amazingly, it is very soft, but it supports you in every way you need to be supported . . . and it feels so good . . . enveloped in that healing color, in that healing energy . . . that cloud the color your body has chosen. You feel so much at peace. Breathe deeply of the cloud . . . and feel that healing color . . . that healing energy . . . going to every part of your body. And when you breathe out, see any discomfort or worries or difficulties leaving your body. And as you breathe in again, see your healing color go to every cell, every corpuscle, every tissue, and every organ . . . bringing peace and healing. And as you breathe out, see all tension, all dis-ease, all discomfort leave . . . and feel the peace that envelopes your mind and spirit just as your healing cloud envelopes your body.

As you lie there quietly, breathe into various parts of your body, and feel that healing energy go very specifically to each part of your body. First breathe deeply into your left arm . . . feel that healing energy of that color going into every cell, the veins and the arteries, the nerves, every tissue, every muscle, every tendon, every capillary . . . and you feel your arm become heavy . . . and warm. You see that healing color both inside and outside of your arm . . . and see that energy going to any place that needs attention, or love or healing . . . and see the color intensify there.

As you breathe out, breathe out any negativity, any disease, any blockages to healing . . . and you feel so much at peace . . . at one. And now breathe in deeply to your left leg . . . and feel the warmth and heaviness of that energy going into your leg . . . into every muscle . . . every corpuscle . . . all lymph nodes . . . into the skin . . . into the bone tissue . . . and deep into the bone marrow where it awakens all the bone marrow factories . . . seeing them hard at work producing healthy lymphocytes . . . producing cells for the blood and cardiovascular system . . . and seeing that color intensify in any place that needs extra attention or healing. And as you breathe out, breathe out any negativity . . . any problems or difficulties . . . any dis-ease or any discomfort . . . and feel totally at peace . . . totally relaxed. (*Continue similarly, breathing in the color into the right leg, the right arm, the pelvis and base of the spine, the solar plexus and the organs therein, the chest and the organs found there, the shoulders, neck, throat.*)

And now see this healing color filling your head and brain . . . with peace . . . positive ideas . . . and self-affirming messages. See the color go deep into your mind and spirit . . . and breathe out guilt . . . resentment . . . lack of forgiveness . . . disease . . . or discomfort. Take another deep breath and let this breath go to any part of your body which needs more healing . . . see the color intensify . . . and see the blockage being dissolved . . . and as you breathe out let anything that is left of the blockage leave with your breath. And now take another deep breath and let it fill your body inside and out . . . feel that energy throughout your body . . . radiating gentle but powerful waves throughout your body . . . starting at your solar plexus . . . radiating ripples of energy and peace . . . feeling that healing force throughout your body . . . throughout your cardiovascular system . . . your nervous system . . . throughout your bones and bone marrow . . . feeling that gentle relentless energy of the healing power within you . . . and letting that energy be activated by every breath you take . . . feeling the love and the peace that it brings with every breath you take.

And now let your mind wander back to your cloud, your beautiful cloud of healing color energy . . . seeing your body, mind, and spirit at one with this healing energy . . . and feeling its force surging powerfully through you . . . totally at peace . . . all your goals met . . . and it feels so good . . . so comfortable. And now let yourself drift down on your cloud . . . feeling the energy of the universe coursing through your body . . . and when you feel ready float back to where you started . . . your cloud gently settling down to earth . . . and as you slowly climb out of the cloud, allow that color to continue to course through your being . . . as you return from this transcendent journey. At peace with yourself — mind, body and spirit . . . and so refreshed, relaxed, and at one with yourself.

SECTION IV

Practical Considerations

Change may still be possible: It's just a matter first of finding the door through which beneficial improvement can enter, and then simply learning how to open it. —*Herbert Benson*

There are a lot of things that work for everyone; everything works for someone; and not everything works for everybody. —*Jeanne Achterberg*

The only way to pass any test is to take the test. It is inevitable. —*Chief Regal Black Swan*

26
Administrative Issues, Professional Training, and Cost-Effectiveness

A cardinal aphorism of traditional medicine has always been that "care of the patient requires caring for the patient." This aphorism needs to be more actively kept in mind by health professionals. — *Jon Kabat-Zinn*

When the inner and outer physicians are working together, you get the best results. — *Lawrence LeShan*

Health care systems are more and more becoming cost conscious. Accordingly, the argument for behavioral medicine interventions must increasingly be made on the basis of cost containment. Well designed, carefully targeted, clinical behavioral medicine interventions can not only improve health outcomes, but can save money. — *David Sobel*

L et me share my thinking on some of the administrative and philosophical issues I have encountered in my years of directing the GETTING WELL program. I tend to eschew the role of administrator for that of clinician and designer; however, in reality those roles are no more separable than the mind and the body. My thoughts come from my own experience with specific institutions and participants rather than from broad knowledge about "the way things are."

Inpatient vs. Outpatient

GETTING WELL has experienced a variety of settings: inpatient general hospital; inpatient private psychiatric hospital; and free-standing, not-for-profit outpatient with only minimal connections to a hospital. Certainly, each situation has its advantages, disadvantages, and idiosyncrasies, so it may be unsafe to generalize about other institutions, even those of the same type.

In both hospital settings, the program was autonomous, an "independent contractor" with its own billing and payroll, using hospital space for offices and group rooms. The participants were inpatients of the hospitals. Although we were not hospital employees, we thought of ourselves as part of the hospital team and were treated as such. In many ways this arrangement was mutually advantageous; it also allowed us to maintain clinical autonomy and to preserve the soundness of the program. Virtually all the problems we experienced with hospitals and physicians threatened GETTING WELL's clinical and ethical integrity, which makes me believe that the program would have been greatly changed and far less effective by now if it had not remained separate from hospital administrations.

Although we had our problems, I am deeply grateful to the hospitals for sticking their necks out and taking a chance on us. Without the opportunities they gave us, GETTING WELL would not exist—and certainly would not be the powerful healing entity it is today. And I am grateful for what I learned from the impediments the hospitals provided, as well.

General Hospital Setting

At the general hospital where we were housed for over four years, patients were admitted with a psychiatric diagnosis (usually major depression or anxiety disorder) and stayed in "med-psych" beds. Almost to a person, patients hated the idea of a psych diagnosis, although the procedure had been explained to them thoroughly before admission *and* they easily met the DSM-III criteria for these disorders—frequent tears, hopelessness, helplessness ("I feel so low at times that I feel like stopping treatment and just letting the cancer kill me," etc.).

The hope GW engendered in these patients caused almost immediate upward emotional swings; consequently, insurance companies or in-house utilization review nurses questioned the need to be hospitalized. However, we kept good records and never had problems defending the diagnosis rationale for inpatient hospitalization when an insurance company reviewed. Once, a patient left the program feeling terrific after just a few days, only to have his deep despair return quickly. After this experience, we established a 10-day minimum stay in the program.

Patient housing was a major problem in the general hospital. Participants fought being on the psychiatric floor ("I have cancer, I'm not crazy"), and they hated being on a medical floor ("It really brings me down, seeing people so sick"). Fortunately, our group rooms and offices were located elsewhere in the hospital, so we were usually able to keep patients off the medical floors except when they were sleeping.

Although having medical treatment handy was an advantage, dealing with the physicians was a major drawback. With few exceptions, GETTING WELL participants were not in the hospital for medical treatment, usually having chosen a hiatus in their medical regimens to join the program. For the most part, participants were medically stable and objected to being put through repetitive tests, especially when they had brought their records with them. They also did not like having problems uncovered that were not germane to their treatment or to our program. Although we did have legitimately ill individuals who wanted medical treatment, there continued to be problems for those who were medically stable and in the hospital only for our program.

The best solution to this occurred when our medical director was also the chief of medical education and let medical residents do initial physicals and any follow-ups. Because many residents had been in GETTING WELL as part of their psychiatric rotation, they were open to the interface between mind and medicine and had a good feel for what we were trying to accomplish. Unfortunately, this situation ended when some older physicians objected to loss of revenues.

I believe it is necessary to have a physician intimately connected with any hospital-based program—but he or she must be totally commited philosophically to the goals of the program. Although we have several wonderful physicians we can count on now, they were not in our circle at that time.

Another surprise was learning that people admitted to the hospital for medical reasons rarely were good candidates for GETTING WELL. Although we regularly saw patients who had undergone cancer surgery or been hospitalized for an ongoing condition, less than a handful came into GETTING WELL from that population. I believe these poor candidates were in shock or denial; most seemed to feel that medical treatment was their only answer, and if that didn't work, it was God's time to take them.

We also found that someone hospitalized for a medical condition has little time for formal groups. In such cases there needs to be a shift in the consciousness and conversation of physicians, nurses, and other hospital caregivers vis-à-vis the patient—a shift to hope and self-empowerment. Ideally, a complementary in-house program would include laughter rooms, personal or video imagery training, counselors on the unit, and healing video and audiotapes. Support groups begun during hospitalization could continue on an outpatient basis. With this foundation in place, it would be a natural progression for some to choose an intensive, specialized program like GETTING WELL. I want to emphasize that GETTING WELL does *not* take the place of a good psychosocial program intertwined with patients' hospital treatment and providing outpatient support—all patients need that support. However, only 15 to 20 percent of patients (in both Bernie Siegel's and my experience) are candidates for a more intensive, committed program, given the present level of public awareness.

Private Psychiatric Hospital

The private psychiatric facility had the advantage of beautiful grounds, a swimming pool and gym, attractive meeting rooms, and a gourmet dining room. Unfortunately, the house rules were so rigid (set for the other patients) that GETTING WELL participants were rarely able to use the facilities or even to get outside to exercise by themselves. We were quite clear in our initial negotiations about the difficulties a psych hospital presented for "our kind of patient" and the special needs our participants had for choice, trust, and freedom—perhaps quite different from those of the typical psychiatric patient. Nevertheless, the realities of a psychiatric hospital were daunting to participants. Such realities included a mountain of paperwork; the ubiquitous locked doors; luggage, room, and personal searches; confiscation of car keys; and limited privileges.

Many of the psych nurses saw having us there as an opportunity to learn powerful new strategies for dealing with psych patients and gave us wonderful support. Unfortunately, because training for psychiatric nurses is nearly counter to the behavioral medicine philosophy, the late-shift nurses, with whom we had no contact, were in constant power skirmishes with our patients over medications, participants listening to tape players after hours, etc. This situation had an ill effect on GETTING WELL patients and the administration's opinion of them. (All of this points up the real need to have all nurses specially trained in bodymind medicine and philosophy!)

Luckily, we *were* held in high regard by a number of the psychiatrists at the hospital, who found that we could work psychological miracles with some of their more difficult inpatients. They frequently referred these patients to GETTING WELL. (This, I am sure further endeared us to the administrator!) Several psychiatrists and psychologists even wanted to start a program philosophically in line with GETTING WELL for higher functioning psychiatric patients in the hospital; however, that was vetoed by the administrator.

Another problem with being in a private facility concerns the vast amount of money the institution needs to generate to keep its shareholders happy. This strongly impacted our scholarship program (where participants stayed at a motel outside the hospital and attended the program during the day), our family program, and our follow-up program. Administration finally limited us to three support (non-paying) individuals at *any* given time, which further demoralized our participants and therapists.

One of the bright spots at the psych hospital was having as our medical director a psychiatrist who validated and supported what we were doing, was actively using cognitive therapy in his private practice, and thought GETTING WELL was the most powerful program he had ever seen. Our experiences would have been very different at both the medical facility and the psychiatric hospital if most of the physicians, nurses, and administrators had the mindset of Charles (Ed) Bailey, M.D. (who continues to be our psychiatric consultant and is on our board of directors). Although traditionally there are limits on medical treatment in psych settings (and one must consider protection of and from suicidal and psychotic patients), I believe that a program like GW could work well if everyone had the same goal. In addition, there is no question in my mind but that behavioral medicine strategies are the wave of the future for psychiatric programs.

Free-Standing, Outpatient, Not-For-Profit

I am glad for many reasons that we did not start in the outpatient, not-for-profit arena, although I feel strongly this is where GETTING WELL truly belongs. Experience in the hospital settings taught us what works best, at what point a patient is too ill or ennervated to gain from the program, what sort of time/emotional commitment we need to demand, etc. The strengths, the weaknesses, the limits, the resources, and the potential of GETTING WELL have stood the test of fire. We have a good sense of ourselves now. The program has survived incredible adversities, and the individuals involved have become stronger, more resilient, and more open to the lessons of love, forgiveness, and letting go.

Indeed, although we have traded the hospital problems for a new set of issues, these new ones seem "right" and the answers within our power. Raising money, writing grants, asking managed care organizations to become preferred providers, marketing, raising the consciousness of the lay and medical community, designing clinical strategies to facilitate breakthroughs for participants, and providing medical attention for people in need of it are only a few of our constant problems. However, in a certain sense, these are stimulating problems, not the soul-strangling issues of the hospitals. We leased a comfortable old house in an area with hospitals close by. We have an arrangement with Visiting Nurse Association (VNA) to work with participants' hometown physicians to provide chemotherapy or other nursing services if they are needed at our site. And out-of-town participants stay at nearby motels or at the homes of local program graduates.

I had feared that our house's comfortable atmosphere might engender a casual attitude toward attendance or a decrease in the program's intensity. However, the intensity has increased, if anything. Since the clinical staff all have their offices in the house, we have a sense of "what's happening in group" most of the time, and can gear our own sessions around that. Attendance generally has not been a problem, probably because we state so unreservedly the necessity of prompt, regular attendance, and insist on a 14-day minimum. Even though participants are sleeping off the premises, they still experience the 24-hour-a-day, seven-days-a-week focus on their issues, values, and purpose—which I believe to be the key to the spectacular changes participants make in their lives at GETTING WELL.

When we first moved to an outpatient setting, we closed down on weekends since some people wanted time off to recoup. That proved to be disastrous, however, because participants who began deep work during the week frequently had crises on weekends. It was also not fair to leave out-of-towners adrift over the weekend. So we instituted a compromise whereby local people could choose to come their first four weeks Monday through Friday and come on weekends for the next four weeks. Now we have sessions seven days a week, people who come here from a distance can have the program in 28 contiguous days, and area commuters or local people can have an extended program, which may be more physically manageable for them.

Training of Clinicians

Since the inception of the program we have had interns from a number of graduate clinical psychology and counseling programs, and at the hospital we were the site for psych rotations for medical residents and nursing students. Now we find ourselves becoming a training site for physicians, nurses, and other allied health professionals. One of the requirements for working at GW, whether as volunteer, receptionist, or clinician, is to have gone through the program.

Rather than providing separate "training programs," we have trainees participate in the program, since such participation is the best way for them to learn the didactic material and to become enlightened. Nurses, physicians, and counselors often fight this concept initially, probably because our training as "helpers" has proscriptions about being in the role of the "helpee." However, hearing a "trainer" tell how a certain intervention worked on a given patient does not hold a candle to actually seeing it make an impact on a participant—particularly if that participant is oneself!

Indeed, attending American Association for the Study of Mental Imagery (AASMI) or National Institute for the Clinical Application of Behavioral Medicine (NICABM) conferences, attending professional training sessions, or even reading and digesting this book are important parts of training; however, they *do not take the place of the experience!* Since the people we are training are also working on their own issues, they are usually able to use the outpatient psych/counseling benefits of their insurance, making the experience quite affordable.

Although GETTING WELL does not in any way take the place of behavioral medicine psychosocial programs in hospitals or specialized treatment centers, it is excellent training for those who wish to implement such a program as a complement to an oncology center, an endocrine unit, or a cardiovascular treatment center. One current training focus is educating nurses and social workers from a "Life and Living" (as opposed to "Death and Dying") program of the Visiting Nurse Association. It is sometimes hard to get across to them that these "lessons" are not just another thing to accomplish during a visit. Their medical intervention will probably be exactly the same; however, our training allows them to bring a different consciousness — an attitude of hope and purpose — to the task. ("Before enlightment: chop wood, carry water; after enlightment: chop wood, carry water.")

It is our plan to have several of VNA's key trainers complete the GET-TING WELL program and use their new perspective to design more special-ized training for VNA home-care nurses and social workers. I feel quite strongly that anyone doing training in this field first needs to go through intensive inner training, beyond just reading books or attending a few experiential workshops. At the present time this training is not widely available; however, The Simonton Center in Pacific Palisades, California, Commonweal in Bolinas, California, Wainwright House in Rye, New York, ECaP in New Haven, Connecticut, the University of Louisville's Arts in Medicine program, and of course, GETTING WELL in Orlando, Florida, do provide training or are resources for it. (If the reader is aware of other intensive training sites, I would appreciate information about them.)

Cost-Effectiveness

With the spiraling cost of health care, health-care systems are becoming extremely cost-conscious. David Sobel (1992) feels that, accordingly, the argument for behavioral medicine interventions must increasingly be made on the basis of cost-effectiveness and cost containment. Decisions by managed-care institutions are not made so much on the basis of human-ity, reduced suffering, or even improved health outcomes as on the basis of how much money a given intervention can save their company. If well-designed, behavioral medicine programs like GETTING WELL are to survive, we need to meet the needs of those who hold the purse strings in such institutions.

GETTING WELL has been involved in several research projects, all of which indicated that we can improve health outcomes and possibly in-crease length of life. Insurance companies are not impressed by these results, however. In fact, studies show that increased length of life goes against the true intent of health insurance. I learned this several years ago while treating a young woman (who, ironically, was an insurance adjustor) with metastatic breast cancer and concomitant deep depression. Her insurance representative told us: "We're not going to pay for treatment for her depression, because she's going to die soon anyway." We made certain the company *did* pay for her depression treatment; however, that negative comment continues to haunt me. Certainly, our clinical goals of better health and increased quality of life will remain primary, but we obviously must also focus on cost-effectiveness research if we are to survive.

Heidi is an excellent (although not unusual) example of the cost-effectiveness that almost automatically follows therapeutic effectiveness at GETTING WELL. At 29, Heidi had struggled with systemic lupus literally since the day of her wedding nine years previously to a "wonderful" man whom her parents loved—but *she* didn't. These years were filled with frequent flare-ups, visits to doctors several times a month, and continual lost workdays. When she joined GETTING WELL, her job as a travel agent was threatened and she was discouraged by constantly being sick. Heidi eagerly embraced the idea of the mind-body connection, and when physical symptoms occurred, she began to look at the parallel emotional turmoil present at the same time. She found power in being able to alleviate physical symptoms by attending to her psychological needs. Of course, this led Heidi to a core issue—her "perfect," but loveless, marriage. Despite pressures from her church and other "support systems," she made the difficult decision to end her marriage.

Heidi was in the midst of a major exacerbation when she made this resolution. Within hours the inflammation disappeared, and a subsequent annual exam at the Mayo Clinic showed amazing changes in her blood work. Her lupus had gone into remission for the first time in nine years. Several years later, notwithstanding major changes in her life, she wrote, "Despite all that has happened to us, I have never been happier or felt better. To think that for nine years I was in doctors' offices constantly for one thing or another. For the last three years I have not been once, except for annual checkups. I can really thank my GETTING WELL experience for that."

In his "Mind Matters & Money Matters" presentation to the 1992 NICABM conference, David Sobel, stated,

> The predominant approach in medicine is to treat people as though they were mindless machines and to seek physical and chemical treatments to fix the disordered machine. Yet, nearly a third of patients visiting a doctor develop bodily symptoms as an expression of psychological distress. Another third have medical conditions which result from behavioral choices such as smoking, alcohol and drug abuse, poor diets, etc. And even in the remaining patients with medical disease such as arthritis, heart failure or pneumonia,

the course of their illness is often strongly influenced by their mood, coping skills, and social support. This critical mismatch between the real health needs of people and the usual medical response leads to frustration, ineffectiveness, and a gross waste of vital health care resources. This approach ignores the striking fact that what goes on in our heads — our thoughts, feelings, and moods — can have a dramatic effect on the onset of some diseases, the course of many, and the management of nearly all. Psychological and behavioral interventions can be developed to help patients more directly address their distress and, in the process, help them become less dependent upon medical care.

Dr. Sobel cites a number of studies which give scientific credence to behavioral interventions. He has graciously given me permission to use his striking distillation of two studies (Figure 7) involving medical and surgical procedures, which have been most useful to me in approaching managed-care companies.

Cost-effectiveness research in behavioral medicine programs such as GETTING WELL is long overdue. A few months ago I prepared a statement

Figure 7. Effects of Psychoeducational Interventions for Surgical Patients

---

Study Design: Meta-analysis of 191 studies (70% randomized, 70% unpub. theses) involving adult surgical patients. Interventions included one or more of provision of relevant information to prepare patient for surgery, skills teaching (e.g., coughing, breathing, relaxation), and psychosocial support. Interventions ranged from 7 to 90 minutes (median 30 min.) with RN, + AV or written materials. Wide range of minor and major surgery.

OUTCOMES (80% of studies indicated beneficial effects)
  ↑ Recovery (fewer complications, better respir. function)
  ↓ Postsurgical pain
  ↓ Psychological distress
  ↓ Hospital length of stay an average of 1.5 days (12%)

Later studies (1985–1989) showed similar effect sizes to earlier studies. More domains of intervention, greater effects. Consistent findings with 3 previous meta-analyses.

Data source: Devine, 1992.

PSYCHIATRIC CONSULTATION WITH ELDERLY HIP FRACTURE PATIENTS

Design: 452 elderly patients admitted for surgical repair of fractured hips in two hospitals received screening for psychiatric consultation. Compared to nonintervention baseline.

OUTCOMES
  ↑ Psychiatric consultations (from 5% to 70%)
  60% Patients with psychiatric diagnoses
  ↓ Hospital length of stay 1.7–2.2 days
  ↓ Costs $270,000 (cost of intervention $40,000)

Data source: Strain, 1991.
With permission from David S. Sobel, M.D., M.P.H.

on cost-effectiveness we have observed at GW. Although anecdotal in origin, it does reflect our observations of several hundred patients over a six-year period. Although the statement may not be a research document in itself, I hope it will provide seeds for the gathering of data and future research projects in the PNI field:

GETTING WELL, a nonprofit, outpatient, intensive, cost-effective behavioral medicine program, deals with psychological, emotional, and relationship issues which may significantly interfere with medical treatment for cancer, heart disease, lupus, chronic pain, MS, HIV, and other life-challenging conditions. Although we believe in the efficacy of brief therapy in a large percentage of situations, GETTING WELL addresses the issues of the small minority for whom "returning to normal" may actually negatively affect the course of the disease, inhibit the effectiveness of standard treatment, and significantly affect job performance. In six years of operation we have consistently observed that this 14- to 28-day program pays for itself more rapidly (in lowered medical costs, quicker recovery, and return to productivity) than do interventions including only medical treatment and brief psychosocial support.

Examples:

- Surgery itself takes significantly less time than was predicted by participants' surgeons, and patients typically leave the hospital several days earlier than anticipated. It is not unusual for participants to save the cost of our program for their insurance carriers in just one surgery through reduced hospital time, shorter surgery time, fewer complications, and less pain after surgery.
- Graduates of GETTING WELL consistently are able to return to work more quickly after surgery. Typically they are back on the job at some level in three to four weeks, whereas the usual expected return time is six weeks.
- Intensive training in imagery and attitude restructuring ensures that GETTING WELL participants will have optimal response to their medical treatment with substantially fewer side effects from chemotherapy, radiation, and other procedures. (In clinical trials at NIH, GW participants have consistently been in the top 10 percent response to experimental treatment, which the project scientists attribute to their use of imagery.) Such a response to treatment means a reduction in medical visits for dealing with side effects and a shortened course of treatment, resulting in significantly lower medical costs.
- In a number of cases patients were so fearful of surgery, chemotherapy, or radiation that they refused treatment, which, due to their terror and panic, would almost certainly have engendered poor results. After attitude and imagery restructuring, these same patients chose to proceed with life-saving interventions—and did so with excellent results and virtually no side effects.
- Chronic pain patients begin to take responsibility for their own pain managment and tend to release the search for a medical solution, especially when one does not exist. When these unproductive searches are abandoned in favor of techniques patients themselves can use, medical costs

drop dramatically. In addition, dealing with the patient's depression often significantly reduces his or her perceived pain. Patients can further reduce medical focus and costs by learning to meet secondary gains in healthy ways rather than relying on the pain or the disease to do so. A number of our chronic pain patients have been able to go off disability and return to productive work.

- GETTING WELL's intense psychological program is for many an excellent alternative to inpatient psychiatric hospitalization. It is extremely effective in uncovering and dealing with deep psychological issues, which are frequently major factors in cancer, HIV, heart disease, and other life-challenging conditions. As a result, patients receive responsible treatment at an immense savings and become more effective, productive employees.

- Completing our full program entitles an individual to weekly group follow-up for one year without further charge. For most of our graduates, life issues can be resolved effectively within these sessions. The momentum of the program continues until the individual completely internalizes strategies for coping, creating peace of mind, and taking responsibility for his or her life.

- GETTING WELL is an excellent preventive program. Participants feel it is responsible for their experiencing fewer exacerbations of their chronic diseases, and many believe it to be a deterrent to recurrences and metastases. This is consistent with our observations over the years, both in terms of quality of life *and* cost containment. Additionally, allowing family members to attend the program with the participant at no extra cost ensures a more health-enhancing family situation.

- At GETTING WELL we embrace the concept that death is not a failure. When it becomes time for a participant to turn that corner, the end seems to come within days or weeks, rather than months and without the long, drawn-out suffering or lengthy hospitalizations usually characterized by diseases such as cancer or AIDS. When the time comes, we find that individuals and their families are able to "let go" and make the transition with peace and without the emotionally and financially high cost of "maintaining life without meaning."

27

Seeds for Research and Evaluation

Skepticism is the chastity of the intellect. —*George Santyana*

When I discuss survivors, I'm interested in how they embrace life, not how they avoid death. —*Bernie Siegel*

Absence of evidence is not evidence of absence. —*Nicholas Hall*

Nick Hall keeps me grounded. This astute researcher at the University of South Florida, with whom GETTING WELL has collaborated on a feasibility study on the effects of imagery on women with breast cancer, warns me to be very careful about the assumptions made from a single research study or selected groups of data. For example, he recently showed me a meta-analysis of the research done on grieving and the subsequent impairment of the immune system.

"The data are quite selective," he stated in his charming British accent. "Yes, these guys born before World War II die off quickly after their wives pass on. *But,* is it because they are mourning or because their wives were responsible for cooking—and now they're eating only Twinkies? And they're not dying of cancer, they're dying of heart disease—probably from an OD of Twinkies."

In other words, even though we may intuitively sense that loss and mourning are going to affect the immune system and that it certainly needs to be a part of any psychosocial program, we can't prove it from the research. This is a major dilemma facing clinicians as well as researchers. Dr. Hall feels there is no way we can measure important parameters such as synergy, epiphanies, miracles—the very lifeblood of a program such as GETTING WELL—with the Euclidian techniques of the scientific method. "I know that what you tell me is happening at GETTING WELL *is* happening," he said. "Yet, we cannot prove it. And certainly, we cannot relinquish those strategies that we have seen to be successful in individuals' lives because they cannot be proven without a doubt through research."

In the winter 1993 issue of the *ISSSEEM Newsletter*, Elmer Green states, "When we know something is a fact, there is a tendency to be impatient with scientific requirements, but in my view it is compliance with these normal rational scientific requirements that makes it possible for the public to develop confidence both in us, as scientists, and in their own potential to transcend limitations and be more than they thought they were" (p. 11). Carol Schneider (editor of the *ISSSEEM Newsletter*) comments in the same issue, "We must learn, and use, evaluation methods, applicable to our healing methods, or they will never be accepted as efficacious beyond an inside believer group" (p. 13). Dr. Green urges us to be scientific in the best sense of the word by finding that fine balance between intuition and intellect.

In consonance with Green and Schneider, Nicholas Hall feels that a whole new set of research strategies needs to be put into place, and although he does not know the shape these strategies will take, he does believe they "will probably take the form of looking at those to whom miracles have occurred, studying in detail their lives, and examining the factors which may have contributed to the miracle."

As a result of my graduate studies, I have developed a consummate respect for scientific research and have become a pretty decent evaluator of research studies. However, in the years with GETTING WELL I have realized how inadequate research methods are for measuring the salient effects of a program of this sort. Research, as we know it, is analytic, reductionistic, and focused on isolating a causal effect. However, the meaningful changes at GETTING WELL involve synergy of elements and effects. Thus, the truly consequential thrust of the research, say in imagery, rests in the knowledge that our images can actually change parameters of physical function. The stickiness of neutophils or the number of T lymphocytes one changes probably is not as important as the belief that one *can* change what is happening in one's body or in one's life. I believe that the feeling of personal power is probably more contributory to "miracles" than any specific change in the system through imagery.

Carolyn Peterson, who has written eight books and received a national lifetime achievement award in her field of library science, decided in midlife to pursue her second master's degree, in the areas of psychology, counseling, and PNI. We were fortunate that she chose GETTING WELL, not only as her internship site, but also as the subject for her master's thesis, *The Mind-Body Partnership in the Treatment of Cancer Patients* (1993). Her original idea was to evaluate both the long-term efficacy and cost-effectiveness of the program, but she decided instead to do a preliminary study as a prototype for a more extensive study to be done at GETTING WELL in the future.

The five subjects (two white males and three white females) were chosen by Carolyn from a list of 15 graduates who were likely to be willing participants and healthy enough to participate. The subjects ranged in age from 30 to 63 years of age, had the same diagnosis (cancer), and had enrolled in the program one month to four years prior to the study. Carolyn devised a series of 30 interview questions designed both to evaluate the GW program and to compare responses of GW graduates with those in previously published studies, in order to determine the long-term effectiveness of mind-body interventions.

That these individuals were still alive, in some cases several years after their diagnoses, speaks for one aspect of "success"; however, perhaps an even more important aspect is the quality of their lives. Peterson is cautious about the implications of her "results," but I think they assume a certain importance in view of Hall's suggestion regarding the factors that go into "success." Carolyn is also frank in admitting that her study demands revision of the evaluation instrument. "People had so obviously incorporated GETTING WELL into their lives that the second set of questions (about how the program had changed their lives) seemed rather stupid to them," she said. Although the study is skewed due to the researcher's beliefs and the means of subject selection, it provides a basis for developing a more pointed and succinct set of evaluation questions and creating an instrument that can give a clearer picture of the results a behavioral medicine program can elicit.

Wayne Hill, a professor in the College of Human Sciences at Florida State University, is helping us design a more far-reaching study, using Carolyn's evaluation instrument and instruments he has used in qualitative research projects (Hill & Bailie, 1993; Mullen & Hill, 1990; Mullen, Smith, & Hill, in press) to hone questions that will target the participant's experience in the healing process. Hill combines his training in science and theology to bring to the behavioral medicine field a rare quality of excitement, joy, excellence, and meaning. He is, certainly, a superb example of the philosopher-scientist, and we are honored that he is a member of our team.

Carolyn Peterson has generously given me permission to present the results and discussion sections of her thesis. In addition to being a fine analysis of participants' experience in the program, it also gives a perspective on GETTING WELL presented from a different angle.

The Mind-Body Partnership in the
Treatment of Cancer Patients
by *Carolyn S. Peterson, M.S., M.A.*

Results

Each of the five subjects selected for this study was a willing, eager participant; each expressed pleasure at the opportunity to discuss the GETTING WELL experience. All five reported that the PNI-based intervention was an effective treatment. When asked what, if any, impact GETTING WELL had on their lives, they answered as follows: (1) "It's the best thing that ever happened to me." (2) "It taught me to enjoy life and gave me back control." (3) "It opened my mind. Taking control of my life is really beneficial." (4) "It was a catalyst for change for the good. It helped me to let go of old behaviors and begin anew." (5) "The whole philosophy—changing things so that I can get well and stay well; doing things for myself. I wouldn't trade that time in my life for anything. I would rather have the cancer than go through life as I was living it before going to GETTING WELL."

When asked what led to their decision to enroll at GETTING WELL, four of the five subjects indicated that they were open to the concept of mind-body healing. Three had already read books by Bernie Siegel, one had called the Louise Hay Center, and two were actively seeking mind-body programs. One went to GETTING WELL after seeing an advertisement in *Reader's Digest*. Two persons were brought to the program by others: one's spouse heard about GETTING WELL on the radio; the other was introduced to it by a friend. Three subjects said that they came to GETTING WELL because they were looking for a place to be with others with similar problems. The remaining two were more passive: one said, "I came because I had nothing to lose," and another stated, "I came by default—I was too weak to keep running."

To describe themselves prior to their cancer diagnoses, the subjects used some of the following adjectives: caring (mentioned by three), helpful, sensitive, trusting, positive, kind, loving, overworked, frustrated, optimistic, competitive, impatient, and introverted. All of the five described their lives at the time of diagnosis in negative terms. Four said they were depressed, three were unhappy with their jobs, two said they felt a general anxiety, two said they were not very content, and one reported feeling that "there was nothing in my life." When asked how throughout their lives they had responded to unpleasant incidents, two said they ran away. Other responses included anxiety, avoidance, confrontation, procrastination, passive-aggressive behavior, depression, isolation, disappointment, feeling let down, feeling it can be fixed, and fear disguised as anger.

Each of the subjects felt himself or herself to be at a very low ebb at the time of receiving the cancer diagnosis. All five used the word "shock" to describe their reactions to their diagnoses, and then described themselves as devastated. One said, "I was totally devastated—after open heart surgery 15 years before, I had had myself on a fitness regimen." Another stated, "I felt as though the room was spinning; I was devastated." Still another reported, "I didn't know how to respond. I became hyper to avoid facing it. I was in terror. I couldn't share how I was feeling, which I think is why I got cancer." The fourth said, "I was shocked, devastated, in denial, fear, lots of anxiety—that's pretty much it." The fifth subject reported being "shocked and down" but did not have a really bad reaction because "the cancer was discovered during surgery and the surgeon was sure that he had gotten it all." Although all five were experiencing very negative feelings and all had described themselves as responding passively to negative life events, all were willing to take action to help themselves.

The subjects described themselves at the present time as being more thoughtful, more patient, more open-minded, more sensitive, less rigid, more caring, more helpful, more forgiving of self, less needy, having more friends, and having a better sense of humor. The changes came about, they reported, because of the following reasons: "A lot of working on myself," "Being open," "Knowing I can make choices," "Facing my own mortality," and "Meeting others with life-threatening diseases." Three gave credit to their cancer: "Cancer made me more aware of what was in my life," "Cancer let me know who I am," and "Cancer and GETTING WELL gave me back control of my life."

When asked about the social support systems in their lives at the time of diagnosis, responses varied. One married subject felt that there was no support system other than one friend who was always there; the spouse had assumed an attitude of avoidance ("If we don't talk about it, it will go away") and the parents were more concerned with themselves ("What am I going to do?"). The remaining three married subjects felt that they had supportive spouses. Four of the five reported support from other family members, three from friends, one from the church, and one from Alcoholics Anonymous. All reported that they now have a wider support base, but three commented that support is becoming less intense with time because "now you are supposed to be well." When asked if their physicians were supportive, two reported theirs as being compassionate and concerned while the remaining three said theirs were cold and dispassionate. One reported first hearing the diagnosis when the oncologist announced to a group of medical residents in her presence that she had cancer and would require disfiguring surgery. When she asked him who he was talking about, he informed her that she was raising her voice and that the consultation was closed. Another reported that the doctor gave the diagnosis by phone, adding that there was nothing he could do because the cancer was untreatable.

All five subjects turned to God for support, although one reported "not as much as I thought I would." One stated, "As a result of cancer I got a revelation that God is there and I could talk to Him and that everything will be okay. Lots of things were confirmed. Cancer was the catalyst. It helped pull me through rough times." Another said, "I knew right off that God hadn't given me cancer." Still another stated, "Sure I turned to God— I'm an elder in the church." The fifth said, "Yes, I turned to God, but I didn't much hear Him then—it was a very confusing time. After GETTING WELL and putting into practice what I had learned, I became closer to God. Putting things away in a loving way instead of an angry way—to me that is God."

During the time span of one to two years prior to diagnosis, all had experienced loss: two were in unwanted divorces, two moved to new locations, three experienced job disillusionment, one changed jobs, one's last child left home, one experienced the failure of fertility drugs, and one had problems with a stepchild. None were happy with their lives at the time of diagnosis. One reported feeling very frustrated by foiled attempts to change life circumstances and that "we were buckling down and getting on with it."

The most useful part of the GETTING WELL program, according to all five subjects, was group interaction, which is not surprising since three were actively seeking a program offering social support. Three persons said imagery was important, two said meditation, and two said all of it. Other specific parts of the program mentioned as helpful included dealing with forgotten issues, e. g., childhood abuse, adolescent despair, emotional abandonment; sharing humor; building self-esteem; relaxation; the structure of the day; and inner child work. All subjects had difficulty in identifying a least useful part of the program. Some of the segments listed included play, the handouts, therapeutic touch, lectures on vitamins, and no private time to digest information.

To determine which, if any, tools presented at GETTING WELL had lasting value, the subjects were asked which tools they had incorporated into their daily lives. Three persons reported that they are using imaging and meditation; two commented that they had more control of their lives. Other tools mentioned were the use of positive affirmations, humor, assertiveness, self-esteem builders, journal writing, and verbal reminders of self-worth. Four of the five subjects reported little or no pain as a result of their cancer. One of the four uses prayer to manage what pain is present. The fifth subject reported having much pain but managing it with visualization and imagery with little or no medication. All five subjects noted that they have changed the way they express feelings after participating in the GETTING WELL program. They attribute this to learning to talk more about problems, putting things into proper perspective, having more courage, being more assertive, being at peace, and living for oneself instead of others. When asked what coping strategies they used to deal with their cancer, the subjects offered the following: verbalizing feelings, using white light, taking care of self, keeping a journal, attending a support group, talking to other survivors, relaxation, meditation, self-talk, watching funny movies and comedians, imaging, positive affirmations, setting goals for oneself, and reclaiming power.

In describing life at the present time, the subjects reported variously: (1) "I have a lot of sadness, fear, and depression, but I'm doing things I've never done before, like white water rafting. It's good but painful." (2) "Overall, great; I'm working too hard, but I know I can make choices. I meditate daily." (3) "Evolving; I still have some trepidation about my cancer. It is definitely a wake-up call for me as I have lots of things I need to change to make my life healthier." (4) "Good. I'm doing lots of things for fun. I'm enjoying my spouse and my new grandchild. We are going to plays, concerts, and so forth." (5) "Both my spouse and I have grown so much. We communicate better. I've always lived for others; now I'm living for myself."

Although initially none of the subjects had suggestions for changes in the GETTING WELL program, when pressed they suggested the following. (1) Have a specific beginning date or a cycle for new patients. (2) Add a structured weekly program for graduates so that they review the program every six months to a year. (3) Have fewer but longer sessions to avoid rushing. (4) Have more information on nutrition and preparing healthy meals. (5) Provide a specific time to discuss books on the reading list. (6) Have an exit session to prepare patients to return home. (7) Provide sponsors for each patient to maintain a connection.

When asked if they had anything to add to the interview questions, four of the five subjects commented on GETTING WELL staff members, describing them in terms such as "concerned," "genuine," "generous with time," "motivated by a desire to help," and "loving." Three of the five subjects volunteer, and a fourth has plans to volunteer, with cancer patients; all indicated that they try to pass on techniques that they learned at GETTING WELL.

Discussion

The results of this study indicate that an intensive intervention program based on the principles of psychoneuroimmunology is effective for a small group of self-selected cancer patients. All five subjects interviewed believe that their participation in GETTING WELL was life-changing. All reported feeling as though they had more control over their lives. All felt that some aspects of their lives had improved as an outcome of dealing with their cancers. Biologically, they may have created stronger immune systems because, according to Seligman (1991), developing an optimistic outlook is likely to result in increased natural killer cell activity.

Within a two year span prior to the diagnosis of cancer, all of the subjects had experienced loss. The work of Kiecolt-Glaser and Glaser (1991) shows that persons undergoing recent major negative life changes may be at greater risk for a variety of illnesses. Two of the individuals interviewed had experienced unwanted divorces. Both LeShan (1977) and Sabbioni (1991) found that, among women, those who are divorced have the second highest cancer mortality rate, preceded by widowed women, and followed by married women and finally single women. On the Holmes-Rahe Social Readjustment Scale, divorce is ranked second only to the death of a spouse as a stress-producing life event; in fact, divorced persons have an illness rate twelve times higher than married persons in the year following divorce (Benson, 1975). Four of the subjects had experienced a loss of positive feelings related to their jobs; however, three have remained with the same employer and are attempting to change their attitudes regarding their work. The fourth, who made a job change, said that it is important to know that one's work is not oneself. Acknowledging the stress that is related to an unpleasant work environment, the Holmes-Rahe Scale includes "Change in responsibilities at work" and "Trouble with boss" on its 43-item list (Benson, 1975).

All five subjects indicated that they had experienced feelings of depression following their diagnoses. Constant depression, which Seligman (1975) equates with pessimism, is known to upset the endocrine balance by elevating the immunosuppressant hormone cortisol. Sheridan and Radmacher (1991) include the presence of depression on their list of biopsychosocial "precursors" of cancer. Depression, according to Eysenck (1991), produces hormonal reactions such as increased production of cortisol and natural opiates, which cause an immune deficiency, which in turn permits "budding" cancers to develop.

Each of the five subjects reported that, prior to participating in the GETTING WELL program, he or she had difficulty expressing emotions. Their statements support the findings of Eysenck (1991), Kissen (1966), and Temoshok and Dreher (1992), which show a relationship between poor emotional outlet and cancer. One of the participants stated, "In the past I would have stayed in a bad situation and been miserable." Another said, "I probably would not have expressed any emotions, as I always avoided confrontation." Still another reported, "I held in my anger until I exploded." The fourth said, "I would be angry for days because I had no outlet—no one would let me talk." The fifth stated, "I would have simply run away from the problem." According to Temoshok's findings, repression of emotions increases the beta-endorphins, which numb the emotions and suppress the immune system. All five subjects described a life-span pattern of not expressing emotions, and thus suppressing the immune system; all developed cancer. This sample of cancer patients is too small to yield significant findings; it does, however, support those of Temoshok.

In discussing how they express emotions at the present time, specifically in regard to a recent incident in their lives, four of the subjects reported being able to express anger in healthier ways and one is learning to do so. One became angry and lost control, then was able to stop, take stock, and apologize. One talked out a problem with a spouse. Another wrote down angry feelings in a letter which was not delivered. Still another mulled over the problem, faced the fear and depression accompanying it, and then took action for change. All of the five felt that techniques they learned in GETTING WELL were responsible for the change in the ways that they expressed emotion.

A number of studies have been conducted that point to the beneficial effects of social support for persons with cancer (Bloom, Kang, & Romano, 1991; Feder, 1966; Sheridan & Radmacher, 1991; Spiegel et al., 1989). This study tends to confirm previous ones. Three subjects reported having strong support from spouses and families. One felt there was no support from spouse or family, but strong support from one friend. Three subjects said that they were seeking a program where they could be with others who had cancer because "people who don't have it just cannot understand." All five interviewees reported that the group interaction was the most valuable part of GETTING WELL. Feder (1966) states that cancer patients must share their experiences and they are often not sure they will find someone with whom to do it. Lack of social support from physicians was reported by three subjects. In their assessment of psychosocial problems of cancer patients, Mathieson and Stam (1991) found that patients had difficulty in making themselves heard by health-care professionals.

Four of the subjects in this study have found that their support systems have broadened since their diagnoses, although three lamented that friends tend to pull away after a period of time. The fifth subject seems to have had a smaller support system both at the time of diagnosis and at the present time; this individual was also less positive in describing life currently. A large amount of data, as noted by Hall and O'Grady (1991), indicate that interpersonal relationships have the capacity to protect the patient from the potential morbidity associated with stressful events. According to Bloom, Kang, and Romano (1991), social support may prompt emotionally induced effects on neuroendocrine or immune system functioning and thus influence physical health outcomes. The work of Spiegel et al. (1989) suggests that psychological support may increase the activity of natural killer cells. Sheridan and Radmacher (1991) recommend social support to help cancer patients in reducing emotional distress and in increasing self-esteem.

A number of researchers have hypothesized about a Type C personality or behavior pattern (Eysenck, 1991; LeShan, 1977; Temoshok & Dreher, 1992). Four of the subjects interviewed used descriptive adjectives that matched those which have been associated with Type C. Included were such terms as helpful, caring, sensitive, trusting, kind, pessimistic, and passive. The fifth subject used descriptors such as optimistic, frustrated, smiling, and positive; throughout the interview, however, this individual described behavior that appeared to be passive and non-assertive and indicated difficulty in expressing emotion. It would, therefore, indicate that all five subjects reflected the "nice guy" Type C behavior pattern as suggested by other researchers. Blumberg, for example, as cited by Locke and Colligan (1986) found that persons with the fastest-growing tumors tended to be "consistently serious, over-cooperative, over-nice, over-anxious, painfully sensitive, passive, apologetic personalities" and had been all their lives (p. 160).

There appeared to be a subtle difference in each interview as a whole, based on the chronological age of the participants; due to the small population in this study, however, differences could also be attributed to personality traits. The difference is only apparent in self-reports of subjects' lives prior to diagnosis; following the diagnosis, responses were very similar. The youngest subject appeared to have a different attitude before diagnosis. This individual, although unhappy with life situations, was actively, though unsuccessfully, trying to change them. As one attempt after another was thwarted, it appears that stoic acceptance gradually replaced frustrated optimism. The oldest member in the study seemed bewildered by unhappy changes in life situations and appeared willing to stand by and wait passively for the inevitable outcome. The three subjects in the middle age range seemed to describe feelings of unidentifiable restlessness and dissatisfaction with their life situations. None appeared able to see hope for change.

Male and female responses to all questions were virtually interchangeable, with no noticeable differences based on gender. Both men and women reported feeling a general sense of anxiety in their lives prior to diagnosis, both described themselves as passive-aggressive, and both said they had difficulty expressing feelings. Support systems, reactions to their diagnoses, and responses to GETTING WELL were all similar.

Responses seem to indicate that techniques learned at GETTING WELL may have long-lasting effects on the subjects. The individual who completed the program four years ago reported active daily use of GETTING WELL's tools, as did the persons who completed the program two years ago, one year ago, and eight months ago. The person most recently out of the program appears to be having a more difficult time incorporating techniques into daily activity; this person, however, indicated an intention to return to GETTING WELL for further work.

It is noteworthy that four of the five subjects volunteered their belief that their cancer is a gift; the fifth implied the same. The following statements were unsolicited. "My illness makes me look at things differently." "I have self-selected important people to include in my life and have dropped those who affect me negatively. I discovered God as a result of my cancer." "Cancer made me more aware of what was going on in my life; it's beginning to let me know who I am and that's a blessing." "I'd rather have cancer than to continue living my life as I lived it before." "I'm more laid back and don't take my job or my life so seriously."

All subjects attributed major positive changes in their lives to their stay at GETTING WELL. Their statements included the following.

- "GETTING WELL taught me that life was passing me by."
- "It gave me back my sense of humor."
- "It gave me the ability to take control of my life."
- "It taught me about accepting personal responsibility."
- "It improved my relationship with my spouse."
- "I now make choices."
- "It helped me to let go of old behaviors and start anew."
- "It helped me to get out of the victim role."
- "GETTING WELL is the best thing that ever happened in my life."

While the participants were lavish in praise for the GETTING WELL program, they did offer some suggestions for making minor changes; all were related to specific activities rather than to philosophy.

All five subjects reported that the group interaction was the most valuable part of their stay at GETTING WELL. Also mentioned by all five as being useful were a number of hypnotherapeutic methods, including imaging, meditation, and relaxation. This correlates with studies by Rossi (1986) and Hall and O'Grady (1991). Rossi (1986) reports that these techniques have been found to enhance immunocompetence in cancer patients. Hall and O'Grady (1991) found that patients with metastatic cancers who were taught relaxation and imaging showed increased internal control, adequate coping skills, no undue stress or anxiety, a positive attitude, and a good morale when psychometric testing was administered twelve months later. They also found in another study that while high stress correlates with low phagocytic capability, phagocytic potential can be augmented following relaxation training. Although only one of the subjects mentioned any aspect of cognitive therapy on his or her list of useful techniques learned at GETTING WELL, all talked about using tools such as assertiveness, self-talk, self-esteem builders, positive affirmations, and journal writing. Seligman (1991) reports that he, Rodin, and Levy used cognitive therapy with cancer patients and found two years later that their NK cell activity was up sharply compared to the control group.

Although the five individuals in this study all indicated evidence of passive, Type C behavior patterns, all took action in seeking out a PNI-based program. In asking what was different about these five cancer patients who chose to seek psychotherapeutic treatment to supplement conventional protocols, this writer feels that there is evidence of what some researchers refer to as "the fighting spirit" (Temoshok & Dreher, 1992). Temoshok and Dreher quote Steven Greer in defining fighting spirit: "The patient fully accepts the diagnosis of cancer, adopts an optimistic attitude, seeks information about cancer and is determined to fight the disease" (p. 125). Three of the five subjects actively sought a program where they could be with persons with similar problems. The other two responded willingly when a member of their support system offered GET-TING WELL as an option.

A question that continues to surface is this: What motivates cancer patients who self-select a PNI-based program? What distinguishes the persons in this study from cancer patients who do not seek adjunctive treatment? If there is a "fighting spirit," how can it be instilled in those who are overwhelmed with feelings of helplessness? It seems imperative that in future study researchers attempt two things: (1) to isolate the "fighting spirit" and analyze its characteristics, and (2) to develop techniques for teaching it to cancer patients who experience helplessness/hopelessness. Since this study supports results obtained from previous research, this writer feels that there is strong evidence that psychoneuroimmunology-based interventions may affect cancer patients positively. If this should prove true, it is vital to discover ways to instill the fighting spirit into those who have difficulty in overcoming their feelings of helplessness. Seligman's (1991) theories on learned optimism come to mind. But to utilize his relatively simple techniques, ways must be discovered to alert individuals to their own pessimistic lifestyles and to motivate them to make changes before, not after, they are struck by life-threatening illnesses. Stress has been strongly implicated in the promotion of cancer. It would, therefore, appear that one avenue for future research might be the development of a stress management curriculum for elementary and secondary school students. Future studies correlating the effects of such a program with cancer incidence could offer insights necessary for cancer prevention. All subjects in this study stated that they wished they had acquired early in life the training and tools that they received in GETTING WELL. While psychoneuroimmunology-based interventions appear to be valuable in the treatment of cancer patients, perhaps they can be of even greater value in the arena of prevention.

References

Achterberg, J. (1985). *Imagery and healing.* Boston: New Science.

Achterberg, J. (1991). Enhancing the immune system. Keynote address, Fourth World Conference on Imagery, Minneapolis.

Achterberg, J., & Lawlis, G.F. (1980). *Bridges of the bodymind.* Champaign: IPAT.

Achterberg, J., & Lawlis, G.F. (1984). *Imagery and disease.* Champaign: IPAT.

Achterberg, J., & Lawlis, G.F. (1992). Human research and studying psychosocial interventions for cancer. *Advances,* 5(4):2-4.

Acierno, L.J. (1985). Comprehensive cardiac rehabilitation and prevention: A model program. New York: Immergut & Siolek.

Adams, K. (1990). *Journal to the self.* New York: Warner.

Ader, R. (1980). Psychosomatic and psychoimmunologic research. *Psychosomatic Medicine,* 42(3):307-321.

Ader, R. (Ed.) (1981). *Psychoneuroimmunology.* New York: Academic Press.

Ader, R., & Cohen, N. (1984). Behavior and the immune system. In W.D. Gentry (Ed.), *Handbook of behavioral medicine.* New York: Guilford.

Ader, R., Felten, D.L., & Cohen, N. (Eds.) (1991). *Psychoneuroimmunology* (2nd ed.). Orlando: Academic Press.

Alexander, F. (1950). *Psychosomatic medicine.* New York: Norton.

Alberti, R.E., & Emmons, M.L. (1970). *Your perfect right.* San Luis Obispo: Impact.

Anderson, G. (1988). *The cancer conquerer.* New York: Andrews & McMeel.

Anderson, W. (1992). The great memory. *Noetic Sciences Review,* 21:21-28.

Andrews, L.M. (1989). *To thine own self be true.* New York: Doubleday.

Angell, M. (1985). Disease as a reflection of the psyche. *New England Journal of Medicine,* 312(24):1570-1572.

Ardell, D. (1979). *High level wellness.* New York: Bantam.

Armstrong, B., & Doll, R. (1975). Dietary factors and cancer. *International Journal of Cancer,* 15:617-631.

Assagioli, R. (1976). *Psychosynthesis.* New York: Penguin.

Bailey, C. (1977). *Fit or fat.* New York: Houghton Mifflin.

Bandler, R., & Grinder, J. (1975). *The structure of magic I.* Palo Alto: Science and Behavior Books.

Bankier, S. (1986). Imagery techniques in the work of Jean Houston. In A. Sheikh (Ed.), *Anthology of imagery.* Milwaukee: American Institute of Imagery.

Beck, A. (1979). *Cognitive therapy and emotional disorders.* New York: New American Library.

Benson, H. (1975). *The relaxation response.* New York: Avon.

Berk, L. (1989). Neuroendocrine and stress hormone changes during mirthful laughter. *American Journal of the Medical Sciences*, 298(6):390.

Block, J., Mott, J.R., Swanson, J., & Wallace, C. (1992). *The healing "I"*. Gainesville, FL: The Write Solutions.

Bloom, J.K., Kang, S.H., & Romano, P. (1991). Cancer and stress. In C.L. Cooper & M. Watson (Eds.), *Cancer and stress* (pp. 95–124). New York: Wiley.

Bohm, D. (1980). *Wholeness and the implicate order*. London: Routledge & Kegan Paul.

Booth, R.J., & Ashbridge, K.R. (1993). A fresh look at the relationship between the psyche and immune system: Teleological coherence and harmony of purpose. *Advances*, 9(2):4–23.

Borland, C., & Landrith, G. (1973). Improved quality of city life through the Transcendental Meditation program. *Scientific research of the Transcendental Meditation and TM-Siddhi program: Collected papers*. Livingston Manor, NY: Maharishi International University Press.

Borysenko, J. (1988). *Minding the body, mending the mind*. New York: Bantam.

Borysenko, J. (1990). *Guilt is the teacher, love is the lesson*. New York: Warner Books.

Borysenko, J. (1990a). Keynote address. Psychology of Health Immunity and Disease conference, Orlando, FL.

Bradshaw, J. (1988). *Healing the shame that binds you*. Deerfield Beach, FL: Health Communications, Inc.

Brennan, B.A. (1988). *Hands of light*. New York: Bantam.

Brigham, D. (1988). *Lifestyles, mindstyles and cancer*. Master's thesis, University of Central Florida, Orlando.

Brigham, D. (1990). Designing imagery for specific conditions. NICABM Conference, Orlando.

Brigham, D., & Toal, P. (1990). The use of imagery in a multimodal psychoneuroimmunology program for cancer and other chronic diseases. In R.G. Kunzendorf (Ed.), *Mental imagery* (pp. 193–198). New York: Plenum Press.

Brody, J. (1985). *Jane Brody's good food book*. New York: Norton.

Brody, J. (1982). *Jane Brody's nutrition book*. New York: Bantam.

Bruun, R.D., & Bruun, B. (1982). *The human body: Your body and how it works*. New York: Random House.

Buffone, G.W. (1984). Running and depression. *Running as therapy*. Lincoln: Univ. of Nebraska (pp. 6–12).

Burns, D. (1980). *Feeling good*. New York: William Morrow.

Buzan, T. (1974). *Use both sides of your brain*. New York: Dutton.

Buzby, G. (1980). Host tumor interaction and nutrient supply. *Cancer*, 45:2940.

Byrd, R.C. (1988). Positive therapeutic effects of intercessory prayer in a coronary care unit population. *Southern Medical Journal*, 81(7):826–829.

Campbell, D. (1991). Sound imagery: The vital role of music in therapy and education. Fourth World Conference on Imagery, Minneapolis.

Cannon, J.G., Evans, W.J., Hughes, V.A., Meredith, C.N., & Dinarello, C.A. (1986). Physiological mechanisms contributing to increased interleukin-1 secretion. *Journal of Applied Physiology*, 61(5):1869–1874.

Capacchione, L. (1979). *The creative journal*. Athens: Ohio University Press.

Casarjian, R. (1992). *Forgiveness*. New York: Bantam.

Cassidy, J. (1978). *Juggling for the complete klutz*. New York: Klutz Press.

Cassileth, B.R., Lusk, E.J., Miller, D.S., Brown, L.L., & Miller, C. (1985). Psychosocial correlates of survival in advanced malignant disease. *New England Journal of Medicine*, 312(24):1551–1555.

Chiappone, J. (1989). *The light touch*. Lake Mary, FL: Holistic Reflections.

Chopra, D. (1989). *Quantum healing*. New York: Bantam.

Chopra, D. (1990). *Perfect health: The complete mind-body guide*. New York: Harmony.

Chopra, D. (1991). *Unconditional life*. New York: Bantam.

Chopra, D. (1991a). Keynote address, National Institute for the Clinical Application of Behavioral Medicine conference, Orlando, FL.

Clark, J.O. (Ed.) (1989). *The human body*. New York: Arch Cape Press.

Clausen, J.P. (1977). Effect of physical training on cardiovascular adjustments to exercise in man. *Physiological Review*, 57:779.

Coem, M.G., & McNamara, P. (1980). Effect of dietary vitamin E on dimethylhydrazine-induced colonic tumors in mice. *Cancer Research*, 4:1329–1331.

Cogan, R., Cogan, D., Waltz, W., & McCue, M. (1987). Effects of laughter and relaxation on discomfort thresholds. *Journal of Behavioral Medicine*, 10:139–144.

Cordain, L. (1986). Exercise and bowel transit. *Journal of Sports Medicine*, 42:34–38.

Cornell, J. (1990). *Drawing the light from within*. New York: Prentice Hall.

Cotter, S.B., & Guerra, J.T. (1976). *Assertion training*. Champaign: Research Press.

Course in miracles. (1975). Farmingdale, NY: Foundation for Inner Peace.

Cousins, N. (1979). *Anatomy of an illness*. New York: W.W. Norton.

Cousins, N. (1989). *Head first: The biology of hope*. New York: Dutton.

Cousins, N. (1989a). Personal communication.

Cunningham, A. (1989). *Helping yourself: A workbook for people living with cancer*. Toronto: Ontario Cancer Institute.

Cunningham, A., Edmonds, C., Hampson, A., Hanson, H., Hovanic, M., Jenkins, G., & Tocco, E. (1991). A group psychoeducational program to help patients cope with and combat their disease. *Advances*, 7(3):41–46.

Dacher, E. (1991). *The new mind/body healing program*. New York: Paragon.

Davidson, P.O., & Davidson, S.M. (1980). *Behavioral medicine: Changing health lifestyles*. New York: Brunner/Mazel.

Dawber, T.R. (1980). *The Framingham study: The epidemiology of artherosclerotic disease*. Cambridge: Harvard University Press.

Devine, E.C. (1992). Effects of psychoeducational care for adult surgical patients: A meta-analysis of 191 studies. *Patient Education and Counseling*, 19:129–142.

deVries, H.A. (1982). On exercise for relieving anxiety and tension. *Executive Health*, 18(12):1–6.

Diaz, A. (1992). *Freeing the creative spirit*. San Francisco: Harper.

Dienstfrey, H. (1986). Candace Pert at the Symposium on Consciousness and Survival. *Advances*, 3:3,15.

Dienstfrey, H. (1991). Neal Miller, the dumb autonomic nervous system, and biofeedback. *Advances*, 7(4):33–44.

Dinarello, C.A. (1985). An update on human interleukin 1: From molecular biology to clinical relevance. *Journal of Clinical Immunology*, 5:1–11.

Doll, R., Muir, C., & Waterhouse, J. (1970). Cancer incidence in five continents. Vol. II. *International Union Against Cancer*.

Donigan, J., & Malnati, R. (1987). *Critical incidents in group therapy*. Pacific Grove, CA: Brooks/Cole.

Dossey, B.M. (1988). Imagery: Awakening the inner healer. In B.M. Dossey, L. Keegan, C.E. Guzzetta & L.G. Kolkmeier (Eds.), *Holistic nursing*. Rockville, MD: Aspen.

Dossey, L. (1982). *Space, time, and medicine*. Boston: Shambala.

Dossey, L. (1989). *Recovering the soul*. New York: Bantam.

Dossey, L. (1990). Keynote address, NICABM Conference, Orlando, FL.

Dossey, L. (1993). How to have a miracle, IONS Conference, Washington, DC.

Dunbar, F. (1954). *Emotions and bodily changes: A survey of literature-psycho-somatic interrelationships 1910-1953* (4th ed.). New York: Columbia University Press.

Dyer, W. (1989). *You'll see it when you believe it*. New York: Morrow.

Edwards, B. (1979). *Drawing on the right side of the brain*. Los Angeles: Tarcher.

Edwards, B. (1986). *Drawing on the artist within*. New York: Simon & Schuster.

Eichner, R. (1988). The race against cancer. *Runner's World,* April: 68-70.

Eisenberg, D. (1985). *Encounters with Qi*. New York: Penguin.

Eliot, R., & Breo, D. (1987). *Is it worth dying for?* New York: Bantam.

Elliott, J. (1976). *Reproducible handouts*. Explorations Institute, PO Box 1254, Berkeley, CA 94701.

Epstein, G. (1989). *Healing visualizations*. New York: Bantam.

Estes, C.P. (1992). *Women who run with the wolves*. New York: Ballantine.

Eysenck, H.J. (1991). Cancer and personality. In C.L. Cooper & M. Watson (Eds.), *Cancer and stress* (pp. 73-94). New York: Wiley.

Fabry, J. (1988). *Guideposts to meaning*. Oakland: New Harbinger.

Fadiman, J. (1991). Being in the right mind at the right time. Fourth World Conference on Imagery, Minneapolis.

Feder, S.L. (1966). Psychological considerations in the care of patients with cancer. *Annals of the New York Academy of Sciences,* 125, 1020-1027.

Fehmi, L. (1975). Open focus training. Paper presented at the Council Grove Conference on Voluntary Control of Internal States, The Menninger Foundation.

Fehmi, L., & Fritz, G. (1980). Open focus: The attentional foundation of health and well-being. *Somatics,* Spring, pp. 24-30.

Fensterheim, H., & Baer, J. (1975). *Don't say yes when you want to say no*. New York: Dell.

Fezler, W. (1990). *Imagery for healing, knowledge, and power*. New York: Simon & Schuster.

Fox, B.H. (1978). Premorbid psychological factors as related to cancer incidence. *Journal of Behavioral Medicine,* 1(1):45-118.

Fox, M. (1983). *Original blessing*. Santa Fe: Bear & Co.

Frank, A.W. (1992). Honoring the ill person's story. Presentation at the Psychology of Health, Immunity, and Disease Conference, Hilton Head, South Carolina.

Frankl, V. (1959). *Man's search for meaning*. New York: Pocket Books.

Friedlander, M.P., & Phillips, T.M. (1986). *Winning the war within*. Emmaus, PA: Rodale.

Friedman, M., & Rosenman, R.H. (1974). *Type A behavior and your heart*. New York: Ballantine.

Friedman, P.H. (1989). *Creating well-being*. Plymouth Meeting, PA: Foundation for Well-Being.

Frisch, R. (1985). Incidence of breast cancer in former college athletes. *British Journal of Cancer,* 62:186-187.

Fry, W.F. (1979). Using humor to save lives. Address given at the Annual Convention of the American Orthopsychiatric Association, Washington, DC.

Fry, W.F. (1980). Humor and healing. Address given at the Healing Brain Symposium, San Francisco, CA.

Fry, W.F., & Salameh, W.A. Eds. (1987). *Handbook of humor and psychotherapy*. Sarasota: Professional Resource Exchange.

Furth, G.M. (1988). *The secret world of drawings*. Boston: Sigo.

Gendlin, E. (1981). *Focusing*. New York: Bantam.

Gentry, W.D. (Ed.) (1984). *Handbook of behavioral medicine*. New York: Guilford.

Gershon, D., & Straub, G. (1989). *Empowerment*. New York: Delta.

Gilman, S.C., Schwartz, J.M., Milner, R.J., Bloom, F.E., & Feldman, J.D. (1982). Beta-endorphin enhances lymphocyte proliferative responses. *Proceedings of the National Academy of Science USA*, 79:4226–4230.

Gimenez, M., Mohan-Kumar, T., Humbert, J.C., De Talance, N., Teboul, M., & Belenguer, F.J. (1987). Training and leucocyte, lymphocyte and platelet response to dynamic exercise. *Journal of Sports Medicine*, 27:172–177.

Godin, G., & Shephard, R.J. (1985). Psycho-social predictors of exercise intentions among spouses. *Canadian Journal of Applied Sports Science*, 10:36.

Goldbeck, N., & Goldbeck, D. (1983). *American wholefoods cuisine*. New York: Plume.

Goodman, D.S. (1984). Vitamin A and retinoids in health and disease. *New England Journal of Medicine*, 310:1023–1031.

Gottman, J., Notarius, C., Gorso, J., & Markman, H. (1976). *A couples guide to communication*. Champaign: Research Press.

Green, E.E. (1993). "New science" and the role of the researcher. *ISSSEEM Newsletter*, 3,4:11–12.

Green, E.E., & Green, A.M. (1977). *Beyond biofeedback*. New York: Delacorte.

Green, E.E., & Green, A.M. (1986). Biofeedback and states of consciousness. In B. Wolman & L. Ullmann (Eds.), *Handbook of states of consciousness*. New York: Van Nostrand Reinhold.

Green, E.E., Green, A.M., & Walters, E.D. (1969). Feedback techniques for deep relaxation. *Psychophysiology*, 6: 371–377.

Grof, S. (1988). *The adventure of self-discovery*. Albany: SUNY Press.

Hall, H.R. (1983). Hypnosis and the immune system. *American Journal of Clinical Hypnosis*, 25, 92–103.

Hall, H.R. (1990). Imagery, PNI, and the psychology of healing. In R. Kunzendorf & A. Sheikh (Eds.), *The psychobiology of mental imagery*. Amityville, NY: Baywood.

Hall, H.R. (1990a). Voluntary immunomodulation. *The Challenge*, 12:4, 18–20.

Hall, N.R.S. (1988). The virology of AIDS. *American Psychologist*, 43:11, 907–913.

Hall, N.R.S. (1990). The immune system: Minding the body and embodying the mind. Cortext Symposium presented in Gainesville, Florida.

Hall, N.R.S. (1992). Personal communication.

Hall, N.R.S. (1993). Personal communication.

Hall, N.R.S. (1993a). Stress and disease. Presentation for Institute for Cortext, Orlando, Florida.

Hall, N.R.S., & Goldstein, A.L. (1986). Thinking well. *The Sciences*, March: 33–41.

Hall, N.R.S., & Kuarnes, R. (1988). Behavioral intervention and disease: Possible mechanisms. *Proceedings of the International Biological Society Meeting*, Hawaii.

Hall, N.R.S., & O'Grady, M.P. (1991). Psychosocial interventions and immune function. In R. Ader, D.L. Felten, & N. Cohen (Eds.), *Psychoneuroimmunology* (2nd ed.) (pp. 1067–1080). Orlando: Academic.

Halpern, S. (1985). *Sound health*. New York: Harper & Row.

Hansen, J. (1982). Can science allow miracles. *New Scientist*, p. 51.

Harman, W.W. (1991). Reconciling science and metaphysics. *Noetic Sciences Review*, 17:4–10.

Hart, L. (1989). *Learning from conflict*. Amherst, MA: Organization for Design and Development.

Hatfield, B.D., Goldfarb, A.H., Sforzo, G.A., & Flynn, M.G. (1987). Serum beta-endorphin and affective responses to graded exercise in young and elderly men. *Journal of Gerontology*, 42(4):429–431.

Hay, L. (1984). *You can heal your life*. Santa Monica: Hay House.

Henderson, B. (1987). Risk of breast cancer cut by exercise. *Medical World News*, August: 34–35.

Hill, W., & Bailie, S. (1993). Coping with the stress of pastoral counseling. *Journal of Religion and Health*, 32(2):121–130.

Hirshberg, C. (1993). Spontaneous remission research implications. Paper presented at the IONS second annual conference, Washington, DC.

Hoffman-Goetz, L., Keir, R., Thorne, R., Houston, M.E., & Young, C. (1986). Chronic exercise stress in mice depresses splenic T lymphocyte mitogenesis in vitro. *Clinical and Experimental Immunology*, 66:551–57.

Holloszy, J. (1985). Reduction of tumors in rats with exercise. *Journal of Applied Physiology*, 42:22–25.

Holmes, T.H., & Rahe, R. (1967). The social readjustment rating scale. *Journal of Psychosomatic Research*, 11:213–218.

Hookham, V. (1991). Imagery in conjunction with art therapy. In R. Kunzendorf (Ed.), *Mental imagery*. New York: Plenum.

Hookham, V. (1992). Personal communication.

Horvath, P.M., & Ip, C. (1983). Synergistic effect of vitamin E and selenium in the chemoprevention of mammary carcinogenesis in rats. *Cancer Research*, 43: 5335–5341.

House, J.S., Robbins, C., & Melzner, H.L. (1982). The association of social relationships with mortality: Prospective evidence from the Tecumseh community health study. *American Journal of Epidemiology*, 116(1):123–140.

Houston, J. (1982). *The possible human*. Los Angeles: Tarcher.

Howe, C.M. (1993). *Homeward to an open door*. Altamonte Springs, FL: Browning Press.

Hurley, T.J. (1985). Inner faces of multiplicity. *Investigations*, 13(4): 4.

Jacobson, E. (1938). *Progressive relaxation*. Chicago: University of Chicago Press.

Jahn, R.G., & Dunne, B.J. (1987). *Margins of reality*. New York: Harcourt Brace Jovanovich.

Jampolsky, G. (1979). *Love is letting go of fear*. Berkeley: Celestial Arts.

Jampolsky, G. (1986). *Goodbye to guilt*. New York: Bantam.

Jensen, M.R. (1987). Psychobiological factors predicting the course of breast cancer. *Journal of Personality*, 55:317–42.

Jevne, R. (1991). *It all begins with hope*. San Diego: LuraMedia.

Johnson, R.A. (1986). *Inner work: Using dreams and active imagination for personal growth*. San Francisco: Harper & Row.

Jones, A. (1992). The Chartres labyrinth. *Noetic Sciences Review*, 22:25.

Joy, W.B. (1979). *Joy's way*. Boston: Houghton Mifflin.

Kabat-Zinn, J. (1990). *Full catastrophe living*. New York: Bantam.

Kalamegham, G. (1984). Reversal of mammary tumorogenesis. *Nutrition and Cancer*, 6:22–31.

Kalff, D.M. (1980). *Sandplay*. Boston: Sigo.

Keeling, W., & Martin, B. (1987). *Journal of Applied Physiology*, 44:320–323.

Keen, S., & Valley-Fox, A. (1989). *Your mythic journey*. Los Angeles: Tarcher.

Kennedy, B.J., Tellegen, A., Kennedy, S., & Havernick, N. (1972). Psychological response of patients cured of advanced cancer. *Cancer*, 38, 2184–2191.

Keyes, K. (1987). *The hundredth monkey*. Coos Bay, OR: Vision Books.

Keyes, K., & Keyes, P. (1987). *Gathering power through insight and love*. Coos Bay, OR: Living Love Publications.

Keyes, L. E. (1973). *Toning: The creative power of the voice*. Marino del Rey: DeVorss.

Khan, P.V.I. (1986). Imagery-related meditations. In A. Sheikh (Ed.), *Anthology of imagery techniques*. Milwaukee: American Imagery Institute.

Kiecolt-Glaser, J.K., Garner, W., Speicher, C., Penn, G.M., Holliday, J., & Glaser, R. (1984). Psychosocial modifiers of immunocompetence in medical students. *Psychosomatic Medicine*, 46(1):7–16.

Kiecolt-Glaser, J.K., & Glaser, R. (1987). Psychosocial moderators of immune function. *Annals of Behavioral Medicine*, 9(2):16–20.

Kiecolt-Glaser, J.K., & Glaser, R. (1991). Stress and immune function in humans. In R. Ader, D. Felten, & N. Cohen (Eds.), *Psychoneuroimmunology* (2nd ed.) (pp. 849–868). Orlando: Academic Press.

Kiecolt-Glaser, J.K., Richer, D., George, J., Messeck, G., Speicher, C.E., Garner, W., & Glaser, R. (1984). Urinary cortisol levels, cellular immunocompetency and loneliness in psychiatric inpatients. *Psychosomatic Medicine*, 46(1):15–23.

Kissen, D.M. (1966). The significance of personality in lung cancer in men. *Annals of the New York Academy of the Sciences*, 125, 820–826.

Klopfer, B. (1957). Psychological variables in human cancer. *Journal of Projective Techniques*, 31:331–340.

Kohn, A. (1986). *No contest: The case against competition*. New York: Houghton Mifflin.

Kohn, A. (1990). The case against competition. *Noetic Sciences Review*, 14:12–19.

Krieger, D. (1979). *Therapeutic touch*. Englewood Cliffs: Prentice Hall.

Krieger, D. (1987). *Living the therapeutic touch*. New York: Dodd Mead.

Kübler-Ross, E. (1969). *On death and dying*. New York: Macmillan.

Kuhn, C. (1993). Personal communication.

Kunzendorf, R. (1990). The causal efficacy of consciousness in general, imagery in particular: A materialistic perspective. In R. Kunzendorf (Ed.), *Mental imagery*. New York: Plenum.

Lange, A. J., & Jakubowski, P. (1976). *Responsible assertive behavior*. Champaign: Research Press.

Langer, E.J. (1989). *Mindfulness*. New York: Addison-Wesley.

Lappe, F.M. (1971). *Diet for a small planet*. New York: Ballantine.

Larsen, S. (1990). *The mythic imagination*. New York: Bantam.

Lashley, K. (1950). In search of the engram. In *Psychological mechanisms in animal behavior* (pp. 454–482). New York: Academic Press.

Leff, H. L. (1984). *Playful perception*. Burlington, VT: Waterfront Books.

Lerner, H. G. (1985). *The dance of anger*. New York: Harper & Row.

LeShan, L. (1959). Psychological states as factors in the development of malignant disease: A critical review. *Journal of the National Cancer Institute*, 22(1):1–18.

LeShan, L. (1977). *You can fight for your life*. New York: Evans.

LeShan, L. (1989). *Cancer as a turning point*. New York: Dutton.

LeShan, L. (1992). Cancer as a turning point. Keynote Presentation, Psychology of Health, Immunity, and Disease Conference, Hilton Head, South Carolina.

LeShan, L., & Margenau, H. (1982). *Einstein's space and Van Gogh's sky*. New York: Macmillan.

Levine, S. (1987). *Healing into life and death*. Garden City: Anchor.

Levitan, A. (1991). Hypnotic death rehearsal. Fourth World Conference on Imagery, Minneapolis.

Levy, S.M., Herberman, R.B., & Whiteside, L. (1990). Perceived social support and tumor estrogen/progesterone receptor status as predictors of natural killer cell activity in breast cancer patients. *Psychosomatic Medicine*, 52:73–85.

Levy, S.M., Lee, J., Bagley, C., & Lippman, R. (1988). Survival hazards analysis in recurrent breast cancer patients: Seven year followup. *Psychosomatic Medicine*, 50(5):520–528.

Lewis, B.L. (1989). Including the family: A systems approach to cancer treatment. Presentation at the Conference on Psychology of Health, Immunity, and Disease, Boston.

Lingerman, H. (1983). *The healing energies of music*. Wheaton, IL: Theosophical Publishing House.

Linn, B.S., Linn, M.W., & Jensen, J. (1981). Anxiety and immune responsiveness. *Psychological Reports*, 49:969–970.

Locke, S., & Colligan, D. (1986). *The healer within*. New York: New American Library.

Locke, S.E., Kraus, L., Leserman, J., Hurst, M.W., Heisel, J.S., & Williams, R.M. (1984). Life change stress, psychiatric symptoms, and natural killer cell activity. *Psychosomatic Medicine*, 46(5):441–453.

London, P. (1964). *The modes and morals of psychotherapy*. New York: Holt.

London, P. (1989). *No more secondhand art*. Boston: Shambala.

London, R.S., Murphy, L., & Kitowski, K.E. (1985). Hypothesis: Breast cancer prevention by supplemental vitamin E. *Journal of the American College of Nutrition*, 4:559–564.

Lusebrink, V.B. (1990). Levels of imagery and visual expression. In R. Kunzendorf (Ed.), *Mental imagery*. New York: Plenum.

Mariechild, D. (1987). *The inner dance*. Freedom, CA: Crossing Press.

Masuhara, M., Kami, K., Umebayasi, K., & Tatsumi, N. (1987). Influences of exercise on leukocyte count and size. *Journal of Sports Medicine*, 27:285–290.

Mathieson, C.M., & Stam, H.J. (1991). What good is psychotherapy when I am ill? In C.L. Cooper & M. Watson (Eds.), *Cancer and stress* (pp. 71–196). New York: Wiley.

Mathur, D.N., Toriola, A.L., & Dada, O.A. (1986). Serum cortisol and testosterone levels in conditioned male distance runners and nonathletes after maximal exercise. *Journal of Sports Medicine*, 26:245–250.

May, R. (1969). *Love and will*. New York: Norton.

McArdle, W.D., Katch, F.I., & Katch, V.L. (1981). *Exercise physiology: Energy, nutrition, and human performance*. Philadelphia: Lea & Febiger.

McKay, M., Davis, M., & Fanning, P. (1981). *Thoughts and feelings*. Richmond, CA: New Harbinger.

McKay, M., Davis, M., & Fanning, P. (1983). *Messages: The communication book*. Oakland: New Harbinger.

McKay, M., & Fanning, P. (1987). *Self-esteem*. Oakland: New Harbinger.

McClelland, D.C. (1988). The effect of motivational arousal through films on salivary immunoglobulin A. *Psychology and Health*, 2:31–52.

Medina, J. (1993). Cloning down memory lane. *Psychiatric Times*, May: 17.

Mehl, L. (1990). Storytelling as healer. Workshop at AASMI Conference, Lowell, MA.

Meichenbaum, D. (1977). *Cognitive behavior modification*. New York: Plenum.

Menkes, J.R. (1986). Beta carotene, vitamins E and A, selenium, and lung cancer. *New England Journal of Medicine*, 315:1250–54.

Merritt, S. (1990). *Mind, music, and imagery*. New York: Plume.

Miller, N.E. (1969). Learning of visceral and glandular responses. *Science*, 163: 434–435.

Miller, R. (1992). The future of the body: A conversation with Michael Murphy. *Noetic Sciences Review*, 22:6–14.

Mitchell, E.D. (1992). Consciousness research and planetary change. *Noetic Sciences Review*, 21:30.

Morgan, M. (1991). *Mutant message downunder*. Lees Summit, MO: M.M. Company.

Morgan, W.P. (1985). Affective beneficence of vigorous physical activity. *Medicine and Science in Sports and Exercise*, 17(1):94–100.

Morowitz, H.J. (1987). *Cosmic joy and local pain*. New York: Charles Scribner's Sons.

Morris, D.B. (1992). The place of pain. *Advances*, 8(2):3–23.

Mowrer, O.H. (1977). Mental imagery: An indispensable psychological concept. *Journal of Mental Imagery*, 1:303–325.

Mullen, P., & Hill, W. (1990). Family stress theory: A perspective on pastoral counseling. *Journal of Religion and Health*, 29(1):29–39.

Mullen, P., Smith, S., & Hill, W. (In press). Sense of coherence as a mediator of stress for cancer patients and spouses. *Journal of Psychosocial Oncology*.

Murphy, M. (1992). *The future of the body*. Los Angeles: Tarcher.

Newberne, P., & Suphakarn, C. (1983). Nutrition and cancer: A review with emphasis on the role of vitamins C and E and selenium. *Nutrition and Cancer*, 5: 107–118.

Norris, P.A. (1988). Clinical psychoneuroimmunology. In J.V. Basmajian (Ed.), *Biofeedback: Principles and practice for clinicians*. Baltimore: Williams & Wilkins.

Norris, P.A. (1992). Creating the inner physician. Fourth Annual Conference on Health, Immunity, and Disease, Hilton Head, SC.

Norris, P.A., & Porter, G. (1985). *Why me?* Walpole, NH: Stillpoint.

O'Connell, W.E. (1987). Natural high theory and practice: The humorist's game of games. In W.F. Fry & W.A. Salameh (Eds.), *Handbook of humor and psychotherapy*. Sarasota: Professional Resource Exchange.

O'Regan, B. (1986). Healing, remission, and miracle cures. *Noetic Sciences Collection*, 44–54.

O'Regan, B. (1989). Barriers to novelty II. *Noetic Sciences Review*, 13:10–16.

Ornish, D. (1984). *Stress, diet & your heart*. New York: Holt, Rinehart, and Winston.

Ornish, D. (1990). *Dr. Dean Ornish's program for reversing heart disease*. New York: Ballantine.

Ornish, D., Brown, S.E., & Scherwitz, L.W. (1990). Can lifestyle changes reverse coronary heart disease? *The Lancet*, 2:888–891.

Ornstein, R., & Sobel, D. (1987). *The healing brain*. New York: Simon & Schuster.

Pachuta, D. (1989). Inner peace. Talk at the Third World Conference on Imagery, Washington, DC.

Paffenbarger, R.S., Hyde, R.T., Wing, A.L., & Hsieh, C. (1986). Physical activity, all-cause mortality, and longevity of college alumni. *New England Journal of Medicine*, 314:605–613.

Paffenbarger, R.S., Hyde, R.T., & Wing, A.L. (1987). Physical activity and incidence of cancer in diverse populations: A preliminary report. *American Journal of Clinical Nutrition*, 45:312–317.

Pearsall, P. (1991). *Making miracles*. New York: Prentice Hall.

Pennebaker, J. W. (1990). *Opening up: The healing power of confidence in others*. New York: Avon.

Pennebaker, J.W., Kiecolt-Glaser, J.K., & Glaser, R. (1988). Disclosure of traumas and immune function. *Journal of Counsulting and Clinical Psychology*, 56:239–245.

Pert, C.B. (1985). Keynote address at the Symposium on Consciousness and Survival, San Francisco, CA.

Pert, C.B. (1986). The wisdom of the receptors: Neuropeptides, the emotions and bodymind. *Advances*, 3(3):8–16.

Peter, L.J., & Dana, B. (1982). *The laughter prescription*. New York: Ballantine.

Peterson, C.S. (1993). *The mind-body partnership in the treatment of cancer patients*. Orlando: Moonlight Press.

Phelps, S., & Austin, N. (1975). *The assertive woman*. San Luis Obispo: Impact.

Pion, R.J. (1981). Prescription for wellness. In R. Ryan & J.W. Travis (Eds.), *Wellness workbook*. Berkeley: Ten Speed Press.

Polonski, W.H., Knapp, P.H., Brown, E.L., Schwartz, G.E., Osband, M.E., & Cohen, E. (1988). Psychological factors, immunologic function, and bronchial asthma. I. Mental imagery and immunologic change. II. Emotional defensiveness and immune function. Dept. of Psychiatry, Boston University. Typescript.

Ponder, C. (1966). *The prospering power of love*. Unity Village, MO: Unity Books.

Pribram, K. (1969). The neurophysiology of remembering. *Scientific American*, 220:75.

Pritikin, N. (1979). *The Pritikin program for diet and exercise*. New York: Bantam.

Professional guide to diseases, Third Edition. (1989). Springhouse, PA: Springhouse Corporation.

Reddy, B.S., Cohen, L.A., McCoy, G.D., Hill, P., Weiburger, J.H., & Wyder, E.L. (1980). Nutrition and its relation to cancer. *Advances in Cancer Research*, 32: 237–331.

Remen, R.N. (1993). Panel at IONS Heart of Healing conference, Washington, DC.

Rico, G.L. (1983). *Writing the natural way*. Los Angeles: Tarcher.

Riley, V. (1981). Psychoneuroimmunologic influences on immunocompetence and neoplasia. *Science*, 212:1100.

Robertson, L., Flinders, C., & Godfrey, B. (1976). *Laurel's kitchen*. New York: Bantam.

Rodegast, P., & Stanton, J. (Eds.) (1985). *Emmanuel's book*. New York: Bantam.

Rodin, J. (1986). Handling stress. *Bodywatch*. PBS television series.

Rogers, M.P., Deibey, D., & Reich, P. (1979). The influence of the psyche and the brain on immunity and disease susceptibility. *Psychosomatic Medicine*, 41(2): 147–164.

Rose, R. (1956). *Living magic: The realities underlying the psychical practices and beliefs of Australian Aborigines*. New York: Rand McNally.

Ross, H.S., & Mico, P. (1980). *Theory and practice in health education*. Palo Alto: Mayfield.

Rossi, E.L. (1986). *The psychobiology of mind-body healing*. New York: Norton.

Rossi, E.L. (1990). From mind to molecule: More than a metaphor. In J.K. Zeig & S. Gilligan (Eds.), *Brief therapy: Myths, methods, and metaphors*. New York: Brunner/Mazel.

Rossi, E.L. (1993). *The psychobiology of mind-body healing*. Revised edition. New York: Norton.

Rossi, E.L., & Cheek, D.B. (1988). *Mind-body therapy*. New York: Norton.

Rossman, M.L. (1989). *Healing yourself*. New York: Pocket Books.

Rossman, M.L. (1992). Imagery and visualization: An overview. NICABM Conference, Hilton Head.

Roud, P.C. (1990). *Making miracles*. New York: Warner.

Ryan, R., & Travis, J.W. (1981). *Wellness workbook*. Berkeley: Ten Speed Press.

Ryce-Menuhin, J. (1992). *Jungian sandplay.* New York: Routledge.

Sabbioni, M.E.E. (1991). Cancer and stress: A possible role for psychoneuroimmunology in cancer research? In C.L. Cooper & M. Watson (Eds.), *Cancer and stress* (pp. 3–26). New York: Wiley.

Samuels, M., & Samuels, N. (1975). *Seeing with the mind's eye.* New York: Random House.

Sandich, K. (1993). The art of survival. *Orlando Sentinel,* 2/21:10.

Sapse, A.T. (1984). Stress, cortisol, interferon, and "stress" diseases. *Medical Hypotheses,* 13:31–44.

Schneider, J. (1989). Imagery and immune function. Paper presented at the 11th annual conference of the American Association for the Study of Mental Imagery, Washington, D.C.

Schneider, J. (1989a). The transformative power of grief. *Noetic Sciences Review,* 12, 26–31.

Schneider, J., Smith, C.W., Minning, C., Whitcher, S., & Hermanson, J. (1990). Guided imagery and immune system function in normal subjects: A summary of research findings. In R. Kunzendorf (Ed.), *Mental imagery.* New York: Plenum.

Schneider, J., Smith, C.W., & Whitcher, S. (1984). The relationship of mental imagery to white blood cell function. Paper presented at 36th annual convention of the Society for Clinical and Experimental Hypnosis, San Antonio, Texas.

Schwartz, G. E. (1990). Psychobiology of repression and health: A systems approach. In J.L. Singer (Ed.), *Repression and dissociation: Implications for personality theory, psychopathology, and health.* Chicago: University of Chicago Press.

Seligman, M.E.R. (1975). *Helplessness: On depression, development and death.* New York: W.H. Freeman.

Seligman, M.E.R. (1991). *Learned optimism.* New York: Knopf.

Selye, H. (1956). *The stress of life.* New York: McGraw-Hill.

Shaffer, J.T.A. (1986). Transformational fantasy. In A.A. Sheikh (Ed.), *Anthology of imagery techniques.* Milwaukee: American Imagery Institute.

Shaffer, J.T.A. (1989). *Be your own healer.* St. Louis: J.T.A. Shaffer, 3460 Jamieson Ave., St. Louis, MO 63139.

Shaffer, J.T.A. (undated). *Psyche-feedback: The use of induced guided fantasy as a creative therapeutic process.* Unpublished manuscript.

Shedler, J. (1992). Hidden psychological problems and heart disease. Presentation at the American Psychological Association Convention, Washington, DC.

Sheehy, G. (1981). *Pathfinders.* New York: Morrow.

Sheikh, A.A. (1978). Eidetic psychotherapy. In J.L. Singer & K.S. Pope (Eds.), *The power of human imagination.* New York: Plenum.

Sheikh, A.A. (Ed.) (1986). *Anthology of imagery techniques.* Milwaukee: American Imagery Institute.

Sheldrake, R. (1989). Cause and effect in science: A fresh look. *Noetic Sciences Review,* 11:8–17.

Sheridan, C.L., & Radmacher, S.A. (1991). *Health psychology.* New York: Wiley.

Shuman, S.G. (1989). *Source imagery.* New York: Doubleday.

Siebert, A. (1985). The human of the future. Presented to the Western Psychology Association Convention, San Jose, CA.

Siebert, A. (1993). *The survivor personality.* Portland, OR: Practical Psychology Press.

Siegel, B. (1986). *Love, medicine, and miracles.* New York: Harper & Row.

Siegel, B. (1989). *Peace, love, and healing.* New York: Harper & Row.

Siiteri, P. (1987). Endocrine sources and cancer. *American Journal of Clinical Nutrition*, 45(1):277.

Simon, S.B. (1990). *Forgiveness*. New York: Doubleday.

Simonton, O.C. (1987). *Getting well*. Audio Renaissance Tapes.

Simonton, O.C., & Henson, R. (1992). *The healing journey*. New York: Bantam.

Simonton, O.C., Matthews-Simonton, S., & Creighton, J. (1978). *Getting well again*. Los Angeles: Tarcher.

Sivin, C. (1986). *Maskmaking*. New York: Harper.

Skekele, R.B., Raynor, W.J., Ostfield, A.M., & Garron, D.C. (1981). Psychological depression and 17-year risk of death from cancer. *Psychosomatic Medicine*, 43(2): 117-125.

Sklar, L.S., & Anisman, H. (1979). Stress and coping factors influence tumor growth. *Science*, 205(3):513-515.

Sklar, L.S., & Anisman, H. (1981). Stress and cancer. *Psychological Bulletin*, 89: 369-406.

Snyder, M. (1985). *Independent nursing interventions*. New York: Wiley.

Sobel, D. (1992). Mind matters and money matters. Proceedings of the Fourth Annual NICABM Conference, Hilton Head, SC.

Solomon, G. (1985). The emerging field of PNI with a special note on AIDS. *Advances*, 2:6-19.

Solomon, G.F., Temoshok, L., O'Leary, A., & Zick, J. (1987). An intensive psychoneuroimmunological study of long surviving persons with AIDS. *Annals of the New York Academy of Science*, 496:647-655.

Sotile, W.M. (1992). *Heart illness and intimacy*. Baltimore: Johns Hopkins Press.

Spiegel, D., Bloom, J., Kraemer, H., & Gottheil, E. (1989). Effect of psychosocial treatment on survival of patients with metastatic breast cancer. *The Lancet*, 2: 888-891.

Spiegel, D. (1991). A psychosocial intervention and survival time of patients with metastatic breast cancer. *Advances*, 7(3):10-19.

Sporn, M.B., & Roberts, A.B. (1983). Role of retinoids in differentiation and carcinogenesis. *Cancer Research*, 43:3034-3040.

Strain, J.J., Lyons, J.S., Hammer, J.S., et al. (1991). Cost offset from a psychiatric-liaison intervention with elderly hip fracture patients. *American Journal of Psychiatry*, 148:420-421.

Switzer, E. (1987). Blaming the victim. *Vogue*, September: 182-219.

Symynkywicz, J.B. (1991). Vaclav Havel and the politics of hope. *Noetic Sciences Review*, 18:21-25.

Talbot, M. (1991). *The holographic universe*. New York: HarperCollins.

Tart, C. (1987). *Waking up*. Boston: Shambala.

Telch, C.F., & Telch, M.J. (1986). Group coping skills instruction and supportive group therapy for cancer patients. *Journal of Consulting and Clinical Psychology*, 54(6):802-808.

Temoshok, L. (1983). Emotion, adaptation, and disease. In L. Temoshok, C. Van Dyke, L.S. Zegans (Eds.). *Emotions in health and illness* (pp. 207-233). New York: Grune & Stratton.

Temoshok, L. (1991). Malignant melanoma, AIDS, and the complex search for psychosocial mechanisms. *Advances*, 7(3):20-28.

Temoshok, L., & Dreher, H. (1992). *The Type C connection*. New York: Random House.

Thomas, C.B., & Duszynski, K.R. (1974). Closeness to parents and the family constellation in a prospective study of five disease states: Suicide, mental illness, malignant tumor, hypertension, and coronary heart disease. *Johns Hopkins Medical Journal*, 134:251–270.

Thomas, C.B., Duszynski, K.R., & Shaffer, J.W. (1979). Family attitudes reported in youth as potential predictors of cancer. *Psychosomatic Medicine*, 41:287–302.

Tubesing, N.L., & Tubesing, D.A. (1983). *Structured exercises in stress management*. Duluth: Whole Person Press.

Tubesing, N.L., & Tubesing, D.A. (1983). *Structured exercises in wellness promotion*. Duluth: Whole Person Press.

Vaillant, G.E. (1979). Natural history of male psychologic health: Effects of mental health on physical health. *New England Journal of Medicine*, 301:1249–1254.

Vasquez, S. (1992). Mind body medicine for healing AIDS. Fourth International Conference of Health Immunity and Disease, Hilton Head.

Vaughan, F.E. (1979). *Awakening intuition*. New York: Anchor Books.

Vaughan, F.E. (1985). *The inward arc*. Boston: Shambala.

Weinstein, M., & Goodman, J. (1980). *Playfair*. San Luis Obispo: Impact.

Weinstock, C. (1977). Recent progress in cancer psychology and psychiatry. *Journal of the American Psychosomatic Dentistry and Medicine*, 24(1):4–14.

Weisburger, T. (1986). Role of fat, fiber, nitrate and food additives in carcinogenesis. *Nutrition and Cancer*, 8:47–62.

White, B. (1990). Why normal isn't always healthy. NICABM Conference, Orlando, FL.

Whitfield, C.L. (1987). *Healing the child within*. Deerfield Beach, FL: Health Communications.

Whitman, W. (1983). *Leaves of grass: The 1892 edition*. New York: Bantam.

Whitney, E.N., & Hamilton, E. (1984). *Understanding nutrition* (3rd ed.). St. Paul: West Publishing.

Williams, R. (1989). *The trusting heart*. New York: Times Books.

Williamson, M. (1992). *A return to love*. New York: Harper.

Wisneski, L.A. (1988). Biopsychology: Overlapping systems of mind-body-environment. *Noetic Sciences Review*, 9:12–16.

Wolpe, J. (1969). *The practice of behavior therapy*. New York: Penguin.

Wurtman, J.J. (1986). *Managing your mind and mood through food*. New York: Rawson.

Yalom, I.D. (1985). *The theory and practice of group psychotherapy* (3rd ed.). New York: Basic Books.

Zdenek, M. (1983). *The right-brain experience*. New York: McGraw Hill.

Zinker, J. (1978). *Creative process in Gestalt therapy*. New York: Vintage.

Zukav, G. (1979). *The dancing Wu Li masters*. New York: Morrow.

Videotape Resource Guide

The Art of Being Fully Human, Leo Buscaglia, Nightingale Conant.

The Art of Healing, Bill Moyers, Mystic Fire Videos, 58 minutes (29.95).

Awakening Your Body's Energies, George Leonard, Inner Work Videotape, 90 minutes.

Bradshaw: Homecoming, PBS Series.

Candid Candid Camera, Allen Funt, Live Home Video.

Classical Images: A Concert in Nature, Kulture, 45 minutes (39.95).

Conscious Living, Conscious Dying, Stephen Levine, Inner Work Videotape, 90 minutes.

Fight For Your Life, Bernie Siegel, Fight For Your Life Company, 146 minutes
Gallagher: The Bookkeeper, Paramount Home Videos.
Gallagher: The Maddest, Paramount Home Videos.
Gallagher: Over Your Head, Paramount Home Videos.
Gallagher: Stuck in the 60s, Paramount Home Videos.
The Healing Force, Norman Cousins, Media Home Entertainment, 76 minutes (14.95).
Healing Yourself With Mental Imagery, Martin Rossman, Inner Work, 90 minutes
Health and Your Whole Being, Kenneth Pelletier, Inner Work, 90 minutes.
Health Imaging, Institute of Human Development, 20 minutes.
Healing from Within, Bill Moyers, Mystic Fire Videos, 58 minutes (29.95).
Healing and the Unconscious, Brugh Joy, Inner Work, 90 minutes.
Hope and a Prayer, Bernie Siegel, Placebo Production.
The Hundredth Monkey, Hartley Film Foundation, 29 minutes.
Inner Vision, Hartley Film Foundation, Cat Rock Road, Cos Cob, CT 06807, 40
    minutes.
Inner Workout, Shirley McLaine, Vestron Video, 70 minutes (24.95).
Let the Living Begin, GETTING WELL, Inc. (407) 426–8662.
Life After Death, Hartley Film Foundation, 33 minutes.
Life and Depth, Joe Kogel, 502 N. 100th, Seattle, WA 98133.
The Light Touch, Judie Chiappone, Holistic Reflections, 13836 Laurel Rock Ct.,
    Clifton, VA 22024.
Love, Medicine, and Miracles, Bernie Siegel, Mystic Fire Video (29.99).
The Mind Body Connection, Bill Moyers, Mystic Fire Video, 58 minutes (29.95).
Mindwalk, Fritjof Capra, available at video stores.
The Mystery of Chi, Bill Moyers, Mystic Fire Video, 58 minutes (29.95).
Ocean Symphony, MCA Home Video, 47 minutes.
Perspectives on Healing, with Jeffrey Mishlove, Thinking Alowed, 120 minutes
    (69.95).
The Power of Myth, Joseph Campbell/Bill Moyers, Mystic Fire Videos, six tapes
    (124.95).
A *Question of Faith* (formerly A *Leap of Faith*), a made-for-television movie now
    available at video stores.
Round Trip: The Near Death Experience, Tim O'Reilly Productions, 15-03 79th
    Ave., Flushing, N.Y. 11367.
Therapeutic Touch, Hartley Film Foundation, 32 minutes.
Transformation and the Body, with Jeffrey Mishlove, Thinking Alowed, 90 minutes.
Wounded Healers, Bill Moyers, Mystic Fire Video, 58 minutes (29.95)
You Can Heal Your Life, Louise Hay, Hay House, 120 minutes.

Audiotape/Compact Disc Resource Guide

Effortless Effort, Nadia Colby, four relaxation cassettes, 5400 Glenwood Ave.,
    Minneapolis, MN 55422.
Getting Well, O. Carl Simonton, 1987, two cassettes, Audio Renaissance.
Heal Yourself with Your Own Voice, Don Campbell, Sounds True.
The Journal Tape, Kathleen Adams, 1989, Sounds True.
Learned Optimism, Martin Seligman, Simon & Schuster Audiotapes.
Many Blessings, On Wings of Song, 1980, Spring Hill Music.
Open Focus Training, Lester Fehmi, Ph.D., Princeton Biofeedback, 317 Mt. Lucas
    Rd., Princeton, NJ 08540.

The Right-Brain Experience, Marilee Zdenek, two cassettes, Audio Renaissance.
Skeleton Woman, Flesh & Bone, 1993, Silver Wave Records (CD).
Writing the Natural Way, Gabriele Rico, 1987, Audio Renaissance.

To order Adelaide Davis' audiotapes mentioned in the text, please send $10.00 per tape, plus $1.00 per tape shipping and handling, to GETTING WELL, PO Box 2628, Orlando, FL 32802.

Tape 1:	Indigo Blue Scarf (for pain)
	Emerald Green Cloak (for anxiety)
Tape 2:	Building Healing Imagery
	Cleansing Ocean
Tape 3:	Handling Anger and Self-Validation
	Balancing Power Centers
Tape 4:	The Daisy Field (Child within)
	Visit with the Inner Guide
Tape 5:	Beams of light
	Dusty Roads
Tape 6:	Rabbits and Urchins (HIV)
	Envelopes of Light (HIV)

Tapes geared to other specific conditions are also available. Please call 1-800-426-8662 for further information on specialized tapes or on the GETTING WELL program.

Index

Name Index

435

Subject Index